The Beacon Handbook

and Desk Reference

FIFTH EDITION

Robert Perrin
Indiana State University

Houghton Mifflin Company   Boston   New York

PE
1408
.P41395
2000
c.1

Senior Sponsoring Editor: Dean Johnson
Editorial Associate: Bruce Cantley
Project Editor: Rebecca Bennett
Senior Production/Design Coordinator: Jill Haber
Senior Manufacturing Coordinator: Marie Barnes
Senior Marketing Manager: Nancy Lyman

Contents

Diction   197

Grammar   217

Appendixes   465

Desk Reference   555

Preface

The primary goal of *The Beacon Handbook and Desk Reference* is to offer students clear, succinct explanations of the basic issues of grammar, usage, punctuation, and mechanics within the larger context of writing to communicate meaning.

Recognizing that a handbook must be complete, accurate, and easy to use, *The Beacon Handbook and Desk Reference* includes many features designed to enhance both accessibility and content.

Accessibility

"QUICK REFERENCE." A "Quick Reference," placed near the beginning of each chapter, presents succinctly the most important information in that chapter. "Quick References" preview chapters and provide quick answers to students' pressing questions.

CLEAR EXPLANATIONS. Grammatical terms and principles are defined and explained in everyday language, with sample sentences to illustrate discussions.

TABLES AND OTHER GRAPHIC DISPLAYS. Numerous tables, charts, lists, and checklists present information clearly and concisely.

THEMATIC EXERCISES. Each exercise treats a single topic, allowing students to apply newly learned information and skills within a coherent context.

Content

THE WRITING PROCESS. *The Beacon Handbook and Desk Reference* emphasizes the writing process—the discovery of meaning, expression, and form through planning, drafting, and revising—providing thorough grounding in writing the essay and the research paper, two formats typical in college writing.

CRITICAL THINKING AND WRITING.   Chapter 5, "Critical Thinking and Writing," leads students through some of the basic concepts underlying critical thinking and writing skills, emphasizing the importance to communication—whether spoken, read, or written—of logical sequences of ideas, clearly and correctly articulated assertions, and apt and adequate supporting evidence.

PROFESSIONAL SAMPLES.   Paragraph-length samples from respected writers such as Henry David Thoreau, as well as samples from recent writers, provide students with interesting reading and effective models.

SAMPLES OF FULL-LENGTH PAPERS.   *The Beacon Handbook and Desk Reference* includes a full-length model of each of the four types of papers discussed in detail: the essay, the argument, the research paper, and the literary paper. "The Composing Process" follows Adam Solari through the planning, drafting, and revising stages of a paper on film viewing. "Critical Thinking and Writing" contains Michael Denne's "Learning the Hard Way,"[1] annotated to show the use of logical strategies. The research process and final paper of Angela Rios illustrates "Research"; this paper, on preventing Internet plagiarism, is annotated to show Angela's rhetorical, stylistic, and technical choices. Christin Scott's paper on developing characterization in *The Great Gatsby* provides a sample of a literary paper.

THE RESEARCH PAPER.   *The Beacon Handbook and Desk Reference* describes and illustrates the entire research process, beginning with the selection and evaluation of potential topics and sources and ending with preparation of the final paper. Through the model of one student's research and paper, students see the relation among all stages and the bearing of each on the final paper. Coverage of proper documentation forms includes both the Modern Language Association of America[2] style and, in an appendix, the American Psychological Association[3] style.

INTERNET SOURCES.   Acknowledging the increasing use of Internet sources in research, *The Beacon Handbook and Desk Refer-*

ence gives special attention to the critical evaluation of these sources and provides clear and current descriptions of documentation patterns.

WORD PROCESSING AND MANUSCRIPT DESIGN. Appendix A describes the technical preparation of papers, providing practical discussions of the benefits of word processing, advice on manuscript features such as font selection and the use of graphics, and formatting guidelines for final manuscripts.

DESK REFERENCE. A new feature with the fifth edition, the Desk Reference is a compendium of useful information related to a variety of disciplines. Divided into six thematic clusters—Science, Mathematics, and Technology; Language, Literature, and the Arts; Business and Economics; U.S. History and Government; Geography and the Environment; and General Reference—the Desk Reference provides historical time lines, glossaries of terms, tabular material, and lists of relevant information. When appropriate, related Internet sites are provided.

The Desk Reference may be used as a way to explore topics about which to write; further, it is a convenient, accessible resource for checking factual information as students explore ideas and develop papers.

Instructional Supplements

DIAGNOSTIC TESTS. These tests are available on disk.

BEACON EDITING EXERCISES. Sixty-four thematic exercises available in computerized form as ASCII files, also free to adopters.

---

1. Michael Denne, "Learning the Hard Way," *Newsweek* 23 Nov. 1998: 14.
2. Joseph Gibaldi, *MLA Handbook for Writers of Research Papers,* 5th ed. (New York: MLA, 1999).
3. *Publication Manual of the American Psychological Association,* 4th ed. (Washington: APA, 1994).

Acknowledgments

My work on the fifth edition of *The Beacon Handbook and Desk Reference* has been made infinitely easier and more productive because of the excellent staff at Houghton Mifflin. I particularly appreciate Bruce Cantley's enthusiastic and informed assistance with the Desk Reference and Becky Bennett's smooth handling of production work. I am also grateful for the advice from a number of teachers who reviewed the previous editions in preparation for this edition:

Ronald L. Ballard, Hagerstown Junior College (MD)
Peggy Brent, Hinds Community College (MS)
Patricia H. Graves, Georgia State University
Christine Jensen Hogan, University of Notre Dame (IN)
Francis A. Hubbard, Marquette University (WI)
Ruth Y. Jenkins, California State University–Fresno
Colin K. Keeney, University of Wyoming
Alleen Pace Nilsen, Arizona State University
Jane H. Keller, Pitt Community College (NC)
Lyle W. Morgan, Pittsburg State University (KS)
Charles C. Nash, Cottey College (MO)
Carol Pemberton, Normandale Community College (MN)
Michael J. Rossi, Merrimack College (MA)
Lisa R. Schneider, Columbus State Community College (OH)
Tom Smith, Pennsylvania State University–Abington
Mitchell E. Summerlin, Calhoun College (AL)
John W. Taylor, South Dakota State University
Amy Ulmer, Pasadena City College (CA)
John O. White, California State University–Fullerton
Pamela L. White, Central Carolina Community College (NC)
Jane R. Zunkel, Portland Community College (OR)

In addition, I would like to thank a number of people at Indiana State University: Scott Davis, Librarian and Head of Information Services, Cummingham Memorial Library, for his technical advice; Laura Bates, Instructor, Department of English, for her thoughtful review of the manuscript; the students in my writing classes for their comments about the effectiveness of the explanations, samples, and exercises; and the instructors, lecturers, and teaching assistants in the Department of English for their suggestions and recommendations.

As always, I wish to thank Judy, Chris, and Jenny for their patience and encouragement.

R. P.

To the Student

The Beacon Handbook and Desk Reference is organized so that you can easily find the information you need. And after you have found what you are looking for, *The Beacon Handbook and Desk Reference*'s features also help you to understand clearly and apply effectively the principles of good writing.

Finding Information

ORGANIZATION. The seven parts of *The Beacon Handbook and Desk Reference* are divided into thirty-five chapters, each treating a specific aspect of composition or English grammar and usage. Each chapter is divided into precepts (rules to guide your work), coded with the chapter number and a letter of the alphabet; up to three levels of headings may subdivide precept sections. Look, for example, at Chapter 15, "Fragments": the first precept, coded 15a, is labeled "Without Subjects or Verbs." Two headings, "Lacking Subjects" and "Lacking Verbs," subdivide the discussion. For an example of subdivisions at more than one level, see precept 22d.

Precept numbers appear in the top outside corner of each page. These work like the guide words at the tops of dictionary pages; the precept number at the top of the left page indicates the first precept on that page, and the precept number at the top of the right page indicates the last precept on that page.

GUIDES TO THE ORGANIZATION. The insides of the front and back covers contain a brief outline of the book and a list of correction symbols, respectively, with cross-references to relevant text sections.

The table of contents provides a complete outline of the text. See pages v–xii.

A general index (see pages 637–73), provides detailed, alphabetical listings of the text's contents.

"Quick Reference." A "Quick Reference," located near the beginning of each chapter, lists in a clear, brief, accessible format the most crucial information in the chapter. See page 2.

Appendixes and Glossaries. Five appendixes are included: Appendix A, on preparing computer and typed manuscripts (see pages 467–76); Appendix B, on the basic features of the American Psychological Association documentary style (see pages 477–94); Appendix C, on writing essay examinations (see pages 495–501); Appendix D, on the basic forms of business letters and résumés (see pages 503–10); and Appendix E, on writing about literature (see pages 511–23).

Two glossaries are included: the Glossary of Usage explains troublesome or often-confused words and provides examples of correct usage (see pages 525–38); and the Glossary of Grammatical Terms defines grammatical terms used in the book and provides an example of each (see pages 539–53).

Desk Reference. The eighty-page Desk Reference is a compact, easily accessible collection of information in six disciplinary clusters. Leaf through its pages (555–634) to get a general sense of what is included; then review a section that relates either to your major or to an area of special interest. Familiarizing yourself with the kinds of information that the Desk Reference contains will save you time later, when you wish to locate a pertinent piece of information.

Using Information

Examples, Tables, and Special Notes. Throughout the text, examples, tables, and special notes augment definitions and explanations.

Examples, set off with extra space and distinguished by typeface and labels, illustrate the principle under discussion. Explanation of examples may follow in square brackets, when needed, to discuss specific choices. See page 20 for a sample.

Tables, charts, and lists present crucial information succinctly in an easily located, readable format. See pages 132 and 133.

WORD PROCESSING AND MANUSCRIPT DESIGN.   In this edition of *The Beacon Handbook and Desk Reference,* all information on word processing has been collected in Appendix A. With the assumption that most current students are moderately fluent computer users, the appendix highlights the advantages of computer use but incorporates discussions of the technical and more sophisticated issues of manuscript design.

In addition, Appendix A discusses the requirements for preparing a manuscript according to the guidelines of the Modern Language Association (fifth edition).

COMPUTERIZED EXERCISES.   You will notice that some of the exercises in *The Beacon Handbook and Desk Reference* are followed by the note "available on disk." These exercises are collected on a disk entitled *Beacon Editing Exercises* and may be available from your instructor or in your writing lab. If so, you can complete the exercises using your word-processing program, which will enable you to correct, rewrite, and revise freely, without retyping.

Whether you are using *The Beacon Handbook and Desk Reference* as a text, with chapters assigned by your instructor, or as a reference, using it as necessary when you are writing for courses or for personal reasons, a preliminary review of its principles will give you increasing control of your writing.

The Composing Process

1 Planning

Before sitting down at a desk or computer to write, you need to make plans. Whether these plans are formulated in your mind or on paper, begin to focus on particular subjects and make choices about ways to explore them, responding to the individual requirements and challenges of each project.

QUICK REFERENCE

Use the following approaches to explore your subject:

▶ Be open-minded about potential subjects.

▶ Consider the general subject from a variety of perspectives.

▶ Develop topics that interest you.

▶ Clearly state your main idea in a working thesis statement.

1a A General Subject

Because the most effective writing develops from an interest in or commitment to a subject, select a general subject that you find appealing. Keep an open mind and consider various general subjects, such as the following:

Regular activities. Think of your routine activities: working, studying, listening to music, shopping, watching television, eating, exercising, reading. Any of these routines can yield interesting topics if thoughtfully explored.

Note: The exercises in Chapters 1, 2, and 3 will take you from idea to final paper. Keep the work from each exercise to use in later exercises.

General reading. Thoughts about, associations with, and responses to your general (non-course-related) reading in books, magazines, and newspapers can lead to interesting subjects.

Special interests. Your special interests—whether they are foreign films, baseball, computers, or ecology—make good subjects because the more you know about a subject, the more you will have to write about it.

People you know. The appearance, personality, behavior, and beliefs of the people you know can provide interesting subjects. Consider anyone you know—a newspaper vendor, your landlord, a professor—not just close friends and family.

Places you have visited. Both familiar and unfamiliar places—a relative's farm, a local gym, Montreal, the Grand Canyon—make interesting subjects if explored in detail and without preconceptions.

Unusual experiences. If you have had experiences that most others have not had—foreign study, extended medical care, specialized work—you have the beginning of a good subject.

Problems people face. Personal, social, economic, and political problems—divorce, relocation, bankruptcy, protest—to which you have given or would like to give serious thought can be provocative subjects.

Changes in your life. Exploring your feelings and thoughts about significant changes in your life—going to college, getting a job, adjusting to the aging or death of a parent—may provide a rewarding subject.

Likes and dislikes. Think about things that you find appealing or unappealing—the network news, mystery novels, reunions, jazz—especially considering the underlying attitudes and values that your preferences may reveal.

Social, political, and cultural events. Local, national, and international issues and events can be fascinating to write about, whether the topic is the politics of the Olympics, the collapse of a local bridge, or the latest Broadway musical hit.

Academic courses.   The information, insights, and associations that you have absorbed in academic courses make productive subjects to explore in writing, whether the topic is birth order, genetic research, or federal support for the arts.

■ EXERCISE 1.1   General subjects

For each of the eleven general subjects previously presented, list at least two potential subjects for a paper, for a total of twenty-two.

1b   Ideas and Planning

Rather than moving directly from selecting a general subject to writing a paper, first take time to explore your general subject. Select and develop a manageably narrow topic by focusing on one aspect of the subject, consider your knowledge and opinion of the topic, and explore alternative ways to develop ideas.

Consider using the following strategies to decide how to narrow your topic. Try several.

Planning Strategies

Freewriting	Looping
Journal writing	Clustering
Journalists' questions	Brainstorming

■ Freewriting

Freewriting—writing spontaneously for brief, sustained periods—can be *unfocused* if you are searching for a subject, or it can be *focused* if you know the subject but are deciding how to approach it. Because freewriting generally uses sentences but does not impose any other formal constraints, it gives you an opportunity to relax and explore ideas that might not otherwise have occurred to you.

To begin, think briefly about your subject and then start writing about it. Write quickly, without worrying about grammar or mechanics, neatness or form. Avoid the urge to revise sentences or to worry about logical connections among ideas. Write until you can think of nothing else to say.

Consider this freewriting sample, which helped Adam, a student writer, to identify a general subject for a paper assigned in his English class:

```
It was Thursday night, and my girlfriend Jenna
and I were trying to decide what to do over the
weekend. She said she'd gone to enough basketball
games to last a lifetime, so there went that
plan. I suggested that we go see a movie, and the
routine began. Where would we go? What movie
would we see? Would we go out to eat first?
Afterward? Would we want anyone else to go along
with us? You know, double-date. I like early
movies the best, but she gets hungry. But if we
go someplace to eat, and they take too long, we
miss the previews and sometimes even the begin-
ning of the movie. And I love previews—and even
those corny ads for keeping the theater clean and
buying stuff at the concession stand. So we
agreed to check the papers to see what
was on when. I sat the phone down and trotted
down the hall to the lounge to find a newspaper.
It was rather amazing: between the cineplex
```

```
(eight theaters) and the four other theaters in
town, there wasn't anything we really wanted to
see . . . at least not enough to spend that much
money. So we started talking about just going by
Blockbuster to rent a movie to watch at home--
meaning, of course, my room or her suite. Just
when we started to talk about what movie we might
rent, I got a call-waiting beep. It was some guy
who needed to talk to my roommate. So Jenna and I
agreed to finish making plans the next day.
```

Notice that Adam's word choices are sometimes colloquial and vague, his sentences sometimes informal, and his ideas only loosely linked. But his ideas are flowing, and he is getting them down on paper.

■ Journal Writing

Journal writing—recording thoughts and observations for your own use, usually in a notebook reserved for that purpose—gives you a chance to record ideas for later evaluation. Reflective by definition, journal writing offers you the chance to explore privately and in detail your thoughts and feelings about people, actions, events, ideas—in short, anyone or anything that interests or concerns you.

Try to write in your journal every day. Carry your notebook with you, writing whenever a thought occurs to you or an event or comment interests you. Or write in your journal by appointment, choosing a convenient time. Whenever and wherever you write in your journal, give the activity a long trial, perhaps a month. Journal writing may seem awkward at first, but it will become easy and pleasurable as you find your own best method of working.

Adam wrote systematically in his journal about one aspect of his freewriting:

I've always enjoyed going to the movie theater.
There's something about <u>going</u> that makes the
film more intense than the ones I see <u>staying</u> at
home to watch on videocassette. Maybe it's
because I have to go to more trouble, which
makes it somewhat special. Maybe it's that my
reactions are heightened because of the other
people in the audience. Maybe it's the size of
the screen and the quality of the sound. Maybe
they put something in the popcorn!

Adam's journal entry, though not fully focused or developed,
draws connections more clearly than did his freewriting as he
explores the facets of film viewing that interest him most.

■ Journalists' Questions

The **journalists' questions**—*who, what, when, where, how,* and
why—focus explorations of subjects, prompting writers to provide specific, detailed information. Use these questions or refine
them to suit your needs.

Adam specifically modified the journalists' questions to
extend his exploration of his subject, producing these notes:

FILMS AND VIEWING EXPERIENCES

<u>Who watches films?</u> Almost everyone: students, of
course, but many others, too; my parents; most
of my friends; film buffs; people who go for
social reasons; students who go because of class
assignments; kids.

<u>What kinds of films?</u> Drama, comedy, action-
adventure, romance, musical, science fiction,

```
mystery, historical, suspense, children's ani-
mated, foreign; new releases, old releases;
classics, cult films.
```

```
When do people see films? As soon as they are
released; after they hear about them; weekends,
weeknights, matinees, late showings; as kids,
teens, young adults, adults.
```

```
Where do people see films? At movie theaters
(big or small, old or new, interesting or bor-
ing), at home (family rooms, bedrooms, media
rooms), at school (auditoriums, classrooms).
```

```
How do people watch films? Alone, with groups of
people, on dates, as part of classes, in a
social environment, in a private setting, on big
screens vs. on small screens, with enhanced
sound vs. regular sound.
```

```
Why do people see films? Relaxation, entertain-
ment, study (information or aesthetics), popular
references, to follow favorite performers, to
avoid boredom, social event, friend's recommen-
dation.
```

Some of Adam's questions yield more ideas than others. *When, where,* and *how* provide particularly specific and useful responses. The questions most useful for a given subject will vary, though any might provide useful details or lead to an interesting, focused topic.

■ Looping

Looping—a series of progressively more specific pieces of freewriting—helps you to move from a general subject to a narrow topic. First, freewrite. Then circle one element or detail, focus on it, and freewrite again. Repeat the process as often as necessary until you decide on a specific, restricted topic.

Adam's looping produced this series of brief paragraphs:

Freewriting

The reasons people have for going to see films vary. It's always interesting that this activity we all seem to share--going to the movies--we really approach in (contrary ways). Some people see films as a social event, while others see films for personal reasons. Some people like to rush to films the first day they open, while others wait to hear what their friends think about them.

Loop 1

Seeing films is an experience in contraries--and maybe of complaints. Almost everyone I know has commented at the theater that they wish movies weren't so expensive and crowded. On the other hand, people at home watching films on videocassettes comment that the sound and picture are worse (of course!) and that the popcorn isn't as good either. Many of us like seeing films at theaters _and_ at home--but for (different reasons).

```
This may be why theaters are booming, as are
video rentals.
```

Loop 2

```
Film viewing in a theater is an audience exper-
ience--including you and lots of other people
reacting together. Film viewing at home is a
private or personal experience--maybe involving
just you and a few other people. The different
settings alter the film-viewing experience in
some interesting ways.
```

Notice the pattern in Adam's looping: he writes first on a general subject, then on a specific element of the subject, and finally on smaller details. Looping frequently, though not always, follows this sequence, allowing you to explore a subject and perhaps to select a topic and method of development.

■ Clustering

Clustering—a flexible, nonlinear planning strategy that emphasizes associations of ideas—combines verbal and visual prompts.

Begin a cluster with a circled key word or phrase. Then, add lines radiating from the central idea leading to additional circled words or phrases that describe, define, or explain it. These ideas in turn will prompt further associations that branch out from them. Evaluate your finished cluster, looking for self-contained satellite clusters that move beyond the original idea. Consider whether portions of your cluster correspond to portions of the paper you are planning, thus indicating an organization.

Adam, for example, began his clustering with the phrase *film viewing,* which he had used repeatedly in his other planning exercises, and produced the cluster shown on page 11. Analyzing his cluster, Adam concluded that the branches "home" and "theater," by producing contrasting examples, illuminated *film viewing* and each other intriguingly.

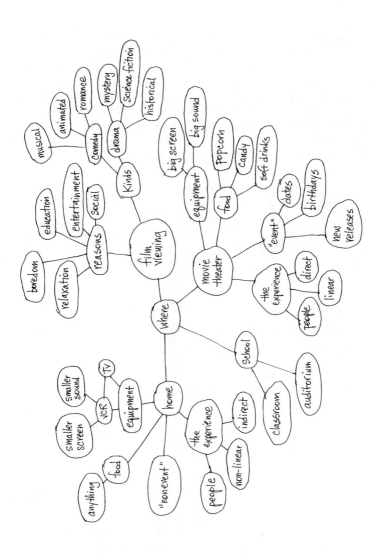

■ Brainstorming

Brainstorming—a list of freely associated ideas expressed in words and phrases—can help you to think broadly and creatively about your subject.

To begin brainstorming, think briefly about your subject; then write without pausing, using single words or short phrases, until you run out of ideas. Brainstorming should be done rapidly and spontaneously, so do not pause to evaluate, analyze, or arrange ideas.

Adam's brainstorming produced this list:

```
FILM-VIEWING EXPERIENCES
    kinds of films          pauses
    social experiences      different rhythms
    sound systems           privacy
    screen size             public
    cineplex                new releases
    "grand" theaters        convenience
    numbers of people       Blockbuster Video
    food                    Old Towne Video
    popcorn                 "event" movies
    drinks                  Star Wars
    candy                   Titanic
    Raisinets               Jurassic Park
    Milk Duds               dates
    Twizzlers               family time
    closeness to screen     responding to film
    darkened theater        quiet
    lighting at home        different theaters
    stopping and starting   group responses
```

interruptions	shared reactions
telephone	The Rocky Horror Picture Show

Adam's long and varied list shows that he looked at his subject from many angles. The list reveals some connections among ideas but shows no formal arrangement.

After brainstorming, arrange items from the list in groups unified by a common idea or theme. Do not let your original list limit your thinking while grouping ideas: drop items that do not fit, repeat items in several groups if appropriate, and add new items when they are necessary.

Grouping Ideas

Classify by topics.

Identify examples.

Arrange elements chronologically.

Compare or contrast.

Classify by Topics

Items from your list will frequently suggest logical ways to subdivide your subject. Group items from your list into the appropriate categories. Sometimes an item from your list will be a comprehensive category that in turn will suggest additional items. At this point in planning, categories need not be logically related.

Items from Adam's list suggested many categories, two of which are shown here:

FOOD	"EVENT" MOVIES
popcorn	Star Wars
soft drinks	Titanic
candy	Jurassic Park
Raisinets	Armageddon

```
Milk Duds          Saving Private Ryan
Twizzlers          Gone with the Wind
Junior Mints       The Sound of Music
Jujubees           Ben Hur
nachos
ice cream
Klondike bars
```

Identify Examples

When appropriate, use examples from your brainstorming list to focus your topic, adding further details.

Adam mentions several specific films in his brainstorming list. Discussing one could unify his ideas or stimulate new ones. Here is a sample:

```
STAR WARS SERIES
secrecy about plots
previews for months
web sites
toy promotions
reserved tickets
lines for tickets
television coverage
newest technology
```

Arrange Elements Chronologically

Many subjects suggest a chronological (or historical or narrative) pattern in which a series of events or the stages of a single event are recounted in sequence.

Adam's subject, for example, could be further developed chronologically:

```
THE THEATER EXPERIENCE

getting to the theater

standing in line to buy tickets

buying refreshments

selecting seats

waiting

watching promotions/previews

seeing the film

leaving the theater

getting home
```

Compare or Contrast

Similarities or differences among items on your brainstorming list may suggest logical groupings. Compare similar items or contrast dissimilar ones. Parallel lists, as shown in the following example, may be used to explore these relations.

```
THEATER                   HOME

large screen              smaller screen

"movie" food              any food

linear experience         fragmented experience

pricey                    cheap

focused experience        unfocused experience

public                    private/personal
```

■ EXERCISE 1.2   Planning strategies

Using several of the general subjects you listed in Exercise 1.1, try each of the planning strategies: freewriting, journal writing, journalists' questions, looping, clustering, and brainstorming.

1c   A Specific Topic

To begin identifying a specific, narrowed topic, review your planning materials, using these questions to help you to select an effective topic:

- Which topic seems most original?
- Which topic interests you most?
- About which topic are you most informed?
- Which topic is the most useful?
- Which topic can you best cover in the length allowed for your paper?

Finally, state your chosen topic in a sentence.

Reviewing his planning materials using the questions listed above, Adam discovered several distinct patterns. His focus on movie theaters and home—which appeared in several planning strategies—suggested that the place *where* he viewed a film was highly important. Interestingly, Adam's opinion on which setting was better seems unclear. On the basis of these discoveries, Adam chose to compare and contrast the two contexts for viewing films. Perhaps during the writing process, he reasoned, he would clarify his preference while using his experience, knowledge, and ideas to write a focused paper.

■ EXERCISE 1.3   A specific topic

Review your planning materials and select a specific topic. Then write a brief paragraph describing how you arrived at your selection. Describe your review of the planning materials, comment on how you selected some ideas and rejected others, and end the paragraph by stating your topic in one sentence.

1d Your Role, Readers, and Purpose

Because writing always occurs in a unique context, consider your role, readers, and purpose.

■ Your Role as a Writer

Consider your individual perspective on the topic: are you writing as an authority, an unbiased observer, or a probing nonspecialist? Considering each perspective will help you to make choices of content and presentation.

Adam has obviously considered the relative merits of seeing films at the theater and at home and can write about them without bias. His film-viewing experiences are varied, so he can write open-mindedly and with a broad perspective.

■ Your Readers

Consider the expectations, concerns, and knowledge of your audience. To begin, answer these questions:

- What are the probable age, educational level, and experience of your audience?
- What information, concerns, and interests do your readers probably share?
- What choices of language and tone will help you to communicate best with your audience?

For example, twenty-year-olds and forty-year-olds have different experiences and concerns, so they are likely to be familiar with and interested in different examples. Adam might discuss social dates at the theater for a younger audience and anniversary dates for an older audience—or vary the examples of films, depending on the audience. Similarly, appropriate language and tone can vary with audience; one audience might understand and enjoy reading current slang, while another might be confused by it. Differences in education and general knowledge require differences in the amount of detail offered in explanations.

Adam decided that the audience for his paper—his teacher and college classmates—ranged in age from seventeen to forty-five, though most fell between seventeen and twenty-two. Going to the movie theater and watching films at home are common experiences for all age groups. To avoid lengthy descriptions and clarifications, Adam realized that he would have to refer to films that appealed to many age groups. Concluding that he had a useful point to make on a popular topic, he decided that his readers would expect informal language.

■ Your Purpose

Most writing for college has one of five general purposes: expressive, literary, referential, persuasive, or argumentative. **Expressive writing** explores the writer's perspective by sharing experiences, opinions, perceptions, and feelings. **Literary writing** shares perceptions and insights using artistic forms such as the short story, poem, novel, or play. **Referential writing** emphasizes the topic and specialists' views, gathered through systematic research, and is carefully documented. (For a discussion of documentation, see Chapters 33–35.) **Persuasive writing** relies on evidence to convince readers to rethink a topic and to alter their views or perceptions. **Argumentative writing** presents writers' opinions on topics that have many possible viewpoints and supports their positions by using ideas, information, experience, and insights.

In most writing contexts, the general purposes overlap. For example, most persuasive writing is also expressive, and referential writing is often persuasive. As you develop a paper and make choices about structure, content, and style, you will discover how purposes blend naturally.

Adam, for example, decided that his paper would be primarily expressive because it would be based on his experiences, perceptions, and observations. However, the paper would also have a central element of persuasion.

■ **EXERCISE 1.4   Your role, readers, and purposes**

Make a list that characterizes your role, readers, and purpose for the paper you have been planning. Consider how the results of this analysis will influence further planning and drafting.

1e   A Working Thesis Statement

A **working thesis statement**—a brief statement of your topic and your opinion on it—provides focus during the drafting of a paper. Later in the writing process, you will revise the working thesis statement into a **final thesis statement**—generally a single sentence near the end of the introduction that makes your topic and opinion clear to readers.

An effective thesis statement provides three kinds of essential information and may have three optional characteristics:

Essential

Identify a specific, narrow topic.

Present a clear opinion on, not merely facts about, the topic.

Establish a tone appropriate to the topic, purpose, and audience.

Optional

Qualify the topic as necessary, pointing out significant opposing opinions.

Clarify important points, indicating the organizational pattern.

Acknowledge your readers' probable awareness of the topic.

A carefully planned and written working thesis statement will help suggest the focus for your thinking and a structure for your writing. In the final paper, a well-expressed thesis statement will prevent confusion by clarifying for readers the paper's central idea. Ineffective thesis statements like these are not helpful:

Attics are places to store belongings.
[**This topic lacks an opinion; it merely states a fact.**]

Cats make weird pets.
[**This narrowed topic contains an opinion, but it is imprecise, is stated too informally, and fails to qualify its criticism for readers who like cats.**]

Liquor advertisements glamorize the drinking that leads to thousands of highway deaths each year.
[**The topic and opinion are clear, but this thesis statement ignores the variables in a controversial issue.**]

First drafts of thesis statements are often as vague and incomplete as these. However, weak thesis statements can be revised to produce improved versions:

Attics are great places to store useless belongings.
[**The inclusion of *great* and *useless* defines the writer's opinion and establishes a humorous tone.**]

Cats make unusually independent pets.
[***Independent* is more precise and therefore clearer than *weird*. The change in wording creates a tone appropriate to a college paper.**]

Although some advertisements now include warnings not to drink and drive, most continue to glamorize the drinking that leads to thousands of highway deaths each year.
[**This thesis statement still expresses a strongly held opinion, but the introductory qualification and the inclusion of *most* help make it more judicious than the original version.**]

Here are Adam's attempts to write an effective thesis statement:

First attempt

```
Watching a film on a videocassette at home is
different from going to the theater to see a
film.
```

[**The point is vague, and the sentence presents a fact, not an opinion.**]

Second attempt

```
Seeing a film at the theater is better than
seeing one at home on videocassette.
```

[The topic is clearer and an opinion is stated, but the thesis statement is still imprecise and ineffectively worded.]

Third attempt

```
Although seeing film at home on a videocassette
has its charms, nothing can match the experience
of seeing a film at the theater.
```

[The topic is more explicit, and placing the qualification first creates emphasis at the end.]

Before writing a working thesis statement, review your planning materials, concentrating on recurrent or fully developed ideas. Analyze your role, readers, and purpose to discover the general approach you want to take. Then try writing a draft version of your thesis statement, remembering that it may take several attempts.

■ **EXERCISE 1.5   Thesis statements**

Evaluate each of the following thesis statements, noting the strengths and weaknesses of each. Revise any ineffective thesis statements by narrowing and focusing the topic, changing the tone, or adding an opinion or any necessary qualifications.

1. Companies gain access to computer records and collect information that once was considered private.
2. The 1996 Summer Olympics were held in Atlanta.
3. Even though a lot of people will disagree, I think that prayer is okay in public schools.
4. We taxpayers should not have to bear the burden of rising medical costs without federal assistance.
5. The United States government should retaliate quickly against terrorism.

6. Some critics say professional athletes make too much money, while others say the wages are justified.

7. Achieving competency in a foreign language is among the highest rewards of education.

8. Women should not always be awarded custody of children in divorce settlements.

■ **EXERCISE 1.6   Thesis statements**

Write a thesis statement about your topic. Revise it, if necessary, to achieve a clear statement of the topic, your opinion on it, and any necessary qualifications. Consider carefully your role, readers, and purpose, and establish an appropriate tone.

Writing a rough draft is a rehearsal, an opportunity to explore possibilities for the arrangement and expression of ideas. In the drafting stage, you can organize ideas from your planning materials and experiment with ways to express them in sentences, paragraphs, and ultimately a complete, though not yet final, paper.

QUICK REFERENCE

Drafting is an opportunity to experiment with ways to express ideas, knowing that you can revise the work later. Keep these principles in mind:

▶ Use the broad organizational pattern that emerges most naturally from your planning.

▶ Use outlining to help you achieve a logical structure for your ideas.

▶ Use drafting to get ideas on paper in a reasonably coherent form without pausing too much over the exact expression or striving for technical correctness.

▶ Experiment with various techniques for introducing and concluding the paper.

2a Organization

Review your planning materials, looking for important or useful information and emerging patterns among ideas. Planning materials will generally suggest a natural pattern for organizing the paper, probably following the common patterns of chronological, spatial, and topical arrangement.

■ Chronological

Chronological arrangement presents information in sequence, explaining what happened first, second, third, and so on. Personal narratives such as a description of your first day at a new job and narratives of events such as a political debate make good use of a chronological arrangement.

■ Spatial

Spatial arrangement recreates the physical features of a subject. For instance, a writer might describe a town by "leading" readers from a residential area in the north to a commercial or industrial area in the south. When physical features are important, spatial arrangement can convey insights more effectively than other methods.

■ Topical

Topical arrangement organizes supporting ideas to present the thesis with the greatest possible emphasis. Topical arrangement can follow a number of patterns according to your purpose—from most important point to least important, for instance, or from simplest to most complex. Sometimes a mixed pattern works best. For example, present the second-most important point first, interesting readers with strong material, and then sandwich in lesser points to fill out the discussion; use the most important point last, thus closing with especially convincing evidence. Topical arrangement is common for persuasive and argumentative papers.

■ Other Methods

The organizational patterns used to arrange ideas within paragraphs can also be used to organize full-length papers. Your planning materials, for example, may suggest one of these common patterns: analogy, cause and effect, process, classification, and definition. The principles discussed in Chapter 4, "Paragraphs," can be expanded for use in a complete paper.

■ **EXERCISE 2.1   Organizing materials**

Review your thesis and planning materials from Chapter 1 and experiment with each of the organizational patterns just described. (For more information on alternative patterns, see section 4d.) Choose one pattern and then organize your planning materials accordingly.

2b   An Outline

An **outline** is a structural plan using headings and subdivisions to clarify the main features of the paper and the interrelationships among them. Loosely structured, informal outlines provide simplicity and freedom, while highly systematic, formal outlines emphasize clarity and completeness.

In the earliest stages of drafting—when you are deciding what should come first, second, third, and so on—informal outlines work well. At later stages of writing—when you need to analyze your work for consistency, completeness, and logic—formal outlining is helpful. Importantly, informal and formal outlines are plans, not descriptions of what you must do. If your plan does not work, decide why and make the necessary changes.

■ An Informal Outline

An **informal outline** is intended for your use only. Consequently, it may follow a pattern that is uniquely yours, as long as it is consistent. Consider writing lists marked with numbers, arrows, dots, dashes, or any other convenient symbol to indicate relative importance among ideas.

This is Adam's brief, informal outline:

```
Viewing Equipment

→ Home: screen and sound

→ Theater: screen and sound
```

Food

→ Home: anything available

→ Theater: special junk food

Viewing Process

→ Home: interrupted and nonlinear

→ Theater: uninterrupted and linear

■ **EXERCISE 2.2   Informal outlining**

Compose an informal outline that arranges the large elements from your planning materials. Add missing details and examples as you draft your paper.

■ A Formal Outline

A **formal outline** is intended for readers. For this reason, it must adhere to the following labeling conventions of formal outlines:

- Indicate *major topics* with uppercase roman numerals (*I, II, III*).
- Indicate *subdivisions* of topics with uppercase letters (*A, B, C*).
- Indicate *clarifications* of subdivisions (examples, supporting facts, and so on) with arabic numbers (*1, 2, 3*).
- Indicate *details* with lowercase letters (*a, b, c*).

In addition, a formal outline must adhere to the following structural conventions:

Use parallel forms throughout. Use phrases and words in a **topic outline** and full sentences in a **sentence outline.** An outline may use topic sentences for major topics and phrases in subdivisions of topics (a **mixed outline**) but should do so consistently.

Include only one idea in each entry. Subdivide entries that contain more than one idea.

Include at least two entries at each sublevel.

Indicate the inclusion of introductions and conclusions, but do not outline their content.

Align headings of the same level at the same margin.

The formal outline presented next organizes Adam's materials. It is a mixed outline, using sentences at the roman numeral (paragraph) level and phrases for the topics within paragraphs.

```
INTRODUCTION

Thesis Statement: Although seeing a film at home
has its charms, nothing can match the experience
of seeing a film at the theater.

    I. The projection equipment at home simply can-
       not compare to that at a theater.

       A. Home

          1. Screen size

          2. Sound quality

       B. Theater

          1. Screen size

          2. Sound quality

   II. The food available at home simply doesn't
       have the weird appeal of theater food.

       A. Home

          1. Everyday food and drink

          2. Reasonably priced

       B. Theater

          1. Odd food and drink

          2. Outrageously priced
```

III. The process of viewing a film at home cannot recreate that at a theater.

    A. Home

        1. Frequent interruptions

        2. Nonlinear pacing

    B. Theater

        1. Few interruptions

        2. Linear pacing

CONCLUSION

■ **EXERCISE 2.3   Formal outlining**

Using your informal outline from Exercise 2.2 as a starting point, complete a formal outline, providing necessary elaboration. Create either a mixed outline or a sentence outline, labeling it appropriately. Double-check your work against the guidelines for outlining given on pages 26–27.

2c   A Rough Draft

A **rough draft** is the first full-length, written form of a paper. It is usually messy and unfocused because some parts develop clearly and smoothly from planning materials, while others develop only after several tries. Uneven development and difficulties with expression are typical in rough drafts because drafting is a shifting process that requires thinking, planning, writing, rethinking, replanning, and rewriting.

The following general strategies will prove helpful as you compose the draft of your paper:

Gather all your materials together.   Your work can proceed efficiently if your planning materials and writing supplies are nearby.

Have your working thesis statement in mind. The topic and opinion presented in your working thesis statement should guide your work, so have the written version in front of you.

Work from your outline. Write one paragraph at a time, in any order, postponing work on troublesome sections until you have gained momentum.

Remember the purpose of your paper. Arrange and develop only the ideas presented in your outline—or closely related ideas that occur to you.

Use only ideas and details that support your thesis statement. Resist any tendency to drift from your point or to provide interesting but extraneous details.

Remember your readers' needs. Include the information and explanations that readers will need to understand the discussion.

Do not worry about technical matters. Concentrate on getting ideas down on paper. You can attend to punctuation, mechanics, spelling, and neatness later.

Rethink and modify troublesome sections. If the organization of the paper is not working, if an example seems weak, or if the order of the paragraphs no longer seems logical, change it.

Reread sections. As you write, review earlier sections so that you can maintain a reasonably consistent tone throughout the paper.

Write alternative versions of troublesome sections. If a section is problematic, write multiple versions of it and then choose the one that works best.

Give yourself a periodic break from writing. Get away from your writing occasionally; time away from writing will help you to maintain a fresh perspective and attain objectivity.

■ EXERCISE 2.4   Rough draft

Write a rough draft of your paper, using the guidelines given previously. Work from your outline to ensure that each idea is supported by adequate detail.

2d   A Title and Introductory and Concluding Paragraphs

Titles and introductory and concluding paragraphs deserve special attention because they create the first and final impressions of your paper. These elements can be developed at any time during planning, drafting, or revising.

■ A Title

A good **title** should be descriptive, letting readers know what the paper is about, and imaginative, sparking readers' interest. To achieve these ends, try one or more of these strategies:

Use words or phrases that explicitly identify the topic.   Search your draft for expressions that are clear and brief.

> Charles A. O'Neill's "The Language of Advertising"
>
> Judith Ortiz Cofer's "The Myth of the Latin Woman"

Play with language.   Consider variations of well-known expressions. Use **alliteration** (repetition of initial sounds) or **assonance** (repetition of vowel sounds).

> Margaret Carlson's "The Boredom of Proof"
>
> Shelby Steele's "Affirmative Action: The Price of Preference"

Consider two-part titles.   The first part is often inventive, the second descriptive. Separate the two parts with a colon.

> Holly Brubach's "Heroine Worship: The Age of the Female Icon"
>
> Susan Douglas's "Remote Control: How to Raise a Media Skeptic"

Match the tone of the title to the tone of the paper.   Use serious titles for serious papers, ironic titles for ironic papers, and so on.

Philip Wheelwright's "The Meaning of Ethics"

Benjamin Demott's "Sure, We're All Just One Big Happy Family"

Write several alternative titles and select the one that best clarifies the topic for readers and piques their interest.

Adam began his search for an effective title by describing his topic in a phrase: "Viewing films at home and at the theater." Although the phrase labeled the paper clearly, it would not create any special interest among readers. He tried experimenting with language and considered "Out There in the Dark" (a partial quote from the end of *Sunset Boulevard*); he considered "Home Theater—A Contradiction in Terms" (a play with the language used to describe new television systems). Adam eventually tried combining two approaches—creating "Out There in the Dark: The Film-Viewing Experience"—but decided it was too long and not very interesting. He finally selected "Home Theater—A Contradiction in Terms" because it was both ironic and clear.

■ Introductory Paragraphs

The **introduction** to a paper creates interest and clarifies the subject and opinion for readers. Depending on the length of the paper, an introduction may be one or several paragraphs long.

As you prepare drafts of alternate introductions, keep these general goals in mind:

Adjust the length of the introduction to the length of the writing. A brief paper needs a proportionately brief introduction; a long paper requires a long introduction.

Match the tone of the introduction to the tone of the paper. A casual, personal paper needs an informal introduction, whereas a serious, academic paper requires a formal introduction.

Use the introduction to draw readers into the discussion. The introduction should create interest, suggest the direction the paper will take, and indicate the paper's development.

Most introductions use one or more of the following general strategies to create interest and, at the end, present a specific thesis statement.

These ten introductory strategies—described and illustrated with examples—are most common.

■ Allusion

Refer to a work of art, music, literature, film, and so on, or to a mythical, religious, or historical person or event.

> Pity-and-terror, the classically prescribed emotional response to tragic representation, was narrowly restricted to drama by the ancient authorities. In my view, tragedy has a wider reference by far, and pity-and-terror is aroused in me by works of art immeasurably less grand than those which unfold the cosmic undoings of Oedipus and Agamemnon, Antigone, Medea, and the women of Troy. The standard Civil War memorial, for example, is artistically banal by almost any criterion, and yet I am subject to pity-and-terror whenever I reflect upon the dense ironies it embodies.   —Arthur C. Danto, "Gettysburg"

■ Analogy

Make a comparison that is interesting, helpful, and relevant to the topic.

> Visiting Catalina Island is like stepping into a postcard of southern California in the 1930s: there are palm trees, sparkling

seas, and Spanish-style buildings that gleam as white as a
movie idol's smile.

> Couples once sailed here on white steamships to dance in
> a vast ballroom overlooking the harbor lights of Avalon, the
> island's only town. Yachtsmen, families, beach buffs, and sports
> fishermen still flock to Avalon, which parties all summer but is
> pleasantly sleepy in the off-season. Many of Catalina's 2,900
> residents came for the weekend—and simply never left.
> —Merry Vaughn Dunn, "The Island of Romance"

◼ Anecdote

Begin with a short description of a relevant incident.

> My husband and I just got back from a week's vacation in
> West Virginia. Of course, we couldn't wait to get there, so we took
> the Pennsylvania Turnpike and a couple of interstates. "Look at
> those gorgeous farms!" my husband exclaimed as pastoral
> scenery slid by us at 55 mph. "Did you see those cows?" But at 55
> mph, it's difficult to see anything; the gorgeous farms look like
> moving green checkerboards, and the herd of cows is reduced to
> a sprinkling of dots in the rear-view mirror. For four hours, our
> only real amusement consisted of counting exit signs and won-
> dering what it would be like to hold still again. Getting there cer-
> tainly didn't seem like half the fun; in fact, getting there wasn't any
> fun at all.   —Janet Mendell Goldstein, "The Quick Fix Society"

◼ Definition

Define a term that is central to your topic. Avoid defining terms
already understood unless such a definition serves a special
purpose.

> One of the most interesting and characteristic features of
> democracy is, of course, the difficulty of defining it. And this
> difficulty has been compounded in the United States, where we

have been giving new meanings to almost everything. It is, therefore, especially easy for anyone to say that democracy in America has failed.

"Democracy," according to political scientists, usually describes a form of government by the people, either directly or through their elected representatives. But I prefer to describe a democratic society as one which is governed by a spirit of equality and dominated by the desire to equalize, to give everything to everybody. In the United States the characteristic wealth and skills and know-how and optimism of our country have dominated this quest.   —Daniel J. Boorstin, "Technology and Democracy"

■ Description

Use a description of a scene, person, or event to establish context or mood for your topic.

I'm in my kitchen, browsing through Puerto Rican cookbooks, when it hits me. These books are in English, written for people who don't know a *sofrito* from a *sombrero*. Then I remember the afternoon I returned to Puerto Rico for the summer after 15 years of living in the United States. The family gathered for dinner in my mother's house. The men settled in a corner of the living room, while Mami and my sisters chopped, washed, seasoned. I stood on the other side of the kitchen island, enjoying their Dance of the Stove with Pots and Pans— the flat metal sounds, the thud of the refrigerator door opening and closing, the swish of running water—a percussive accompaniment enhancing the fragrant sizzle of garlic and onions in hot oil.

"Do you cook Puerto Rican?" Norma asked as she cored a red pepper.

"No," I answered, "I never got the hang of it."

"How can you be Puerto Rican without your rice and beans?" joked Alicia.

"Easy," said Mami, "She's no longer Puerto Rican."

If she had stabbed me with the chicken-gutting knife in her hand it would have hurt less. I swallowed the pain. "Si, Mami," I said, "I have become *Americana*."   —Esmeralda Santiago, "A Puerto Rican Stew"

■ Facts and Figures

Begin with specific, interesting, useful information or statistics.

The Crystal Palace, designed in 1850 by the English architect Joseph Paxton to house showpieces of Victorian technology, was 1,848 feet long and 408 feet wide. It supported 293,655 panes of glass, and over the 140 days of its original use, it sheltered 6,063,986 people, or roughly one-third the total population of the United Kingdom at the time. In his diary, the historian and statesman Thomas Babington Macaulay called the Crystal Palace "a most gorgeous site; vast; graceful; beyond the dreams of the Arabian romances." A detail that Macaulay failed to remark upon was that the great dome, or transept, of the Crystal Palace was framed in wood painted to look like steel merely to allay public fear that so vast and important an edifice could be held aloft by so "flimsy" a material as wood. Yet in relation to its density, wood is stiffer and stronger, both in bending and twisting, than concrete, cast iron, aluminum alloy, or steel.   —Karl J. Niklas, "How to Build a Tree"

■ New Discussion of an Old Subject

Explain why a topic that may be "old hat" is worth examining again.

As recently as 1960 infertility in couples was, to put the matter delicately, not a top priority for the medical establishment: it was a women's problem. Demographers routinely attributed the reproductive success of a couple to the woman if the fertility of the individuals was unknown. In other words, if a couple tried and failed to have children, the presumption was that the woman was barren, not that the man was sterile. In general, an infertile couple was regarded as exceptional.

These days infertility is not so casually dismissed. For one thing, the man falls under suspicion as well. The evidence of the past twenty years shows what, with hindsight, may always have been the case: that the male is a contributing factor in a couple's infertility 50 percent of the time—sexual equality with a vengeance.   —Diana Lutz, "No Conception"

■ Question

Use a question or a series of questions to prompt readers to think about your subject.

When did terra firma firm up? And what happened to it once it did?

These are among the great unanswered questions in earth science. Prevailing wisdom holds that the bulk of Earth's continental crust didn't form until at least 2.5 billion years after Earth's birth. And like scum floating on the surface of a bubbling broth, this early crust was too buoyant to founder into Earth's interior, melt and be recycled into the raw material for new crust. According to this view, most, if not all, of the continental crust ever formed is still present on the surface in one form or another, as it has never been recycled in the mantle. —Roslyn M. Dupré, "Earth's Early Evolution"

■ Quotation

Use what someone else has said or written in a poem, short story, book, article, or interview.

Thoreau once wrote, "For my part, I could easily do without the post office. I never received more than one or two letters in my life . . . that were worth the postage."

Well, that was long before the mail became electronic and postage became almost obsolete, but once again, the cabin-dwelling ascetic raises an interesting question. With all of these words rushing up and down, to and fro, back and forth, with thousands of messages crossing the Net on a daily basis, is any of it worth reading?   —Dinty W. Moore, *The Emperor's Virtual Clothes: The Naked Truth about the Internet*

■ Startling Statement

Use an arresting statement to get readers' attention and arouse their interest.

The prevalence of malnutrition in children is staggering. Globally, nearly 195 million children younger than five years are undernourished. Malnutrition is most obvious in the developing countries, where the condition often takes severe forms; images of emaciated bodies in famine-struck or war-torn regions are tragically familiar. Yet milder forms are more common, especially in developed nations. Indeed, in 1992 an estimated 12 million American children consumed diets that were significantly below the recommended allowances of nutrients established by the National Academy of Sciences.

Undernutrition triggers an array of health problems in children, many of which can become chronic. It can lead to extreme weight loss, stunted growth, weakened resistance to infection and, in the worst cases, early death. The effects can be particularly devastating in the first few years of life, when the body is growing rapidly and the need for calories and nutrients is greatest.   —Larry J. Brown and Ernesto Pollitt, "Malnutrition, Poverty and Intellectual Development"

Adam considered a number of introductions for his paper, trying to find one that would interest his readers as well as clarify his topic:

```
FACTS AND FIGURES

Present the total domestic profits from the top
ten movies of 1998 ($1,565,700,000), as well as
the sales of the top ten videos ($716,900,000).

DESCRIPTION

Use an extended description of standing in line
to see a movie.

ANECDOTE

Tell about looking for a big-screen television
at the local electronics store or selecting a
film at the neighborhood video store.
```

Adam considered the anecdote but decided that it directed too much attention to the video format; similarly, the description of waiting in line to see a movie, though potentially interesting, would direct too much attention to the theater experience. Through a process of elimination, Adam chose to use facts to stress the popularity of films and to create a useful, involving transition into his paper.

■ EXERCISE 2.5 Title and introductory paragraphs

Write several titles for your paper and select the most effective one. Then write two draft versions of the introduction, using the previous guidelines. Make sure that the strategies both create interest and clearly and appropriately introduce your topic.

■ Concluding Paragraphs

A **conclusion** reemphasizes the point of the paper and allows you to create a final impression. Most conclusions incorporate a brief but specific summary and then use a concluding strategy to present a general observation.

specific thesis statement

general strategy

Some introductory strategies—such as allusion, analogy, anecdote, description, and quotation—can also be useful concluding strategies. The following strategies are particularly appropriate for conclusions.

■ Challenge

Ask readers to reconsider and change their behavior or ideas.

> I wouldn't dream of arguing that we Americans have found the Holy Grail of cultural diversity when in fact we're still searching for it. We have to think hard about our growing pluralism. It's useful, I believe, to dissect in the open our thinking about it, to see whether the lessons we are trying to learn might stimulate some useful thinking elsewhere. We do not yet quite know how to create "wholeness incorporating diversity," but we owe it to the world, as well as to ourselves, to keep trying.
> —Harlan Cleveland, "The Limits of Cultural Diversity"

■ Framing Pattern

When appropriate, repeat the introductory strategy as the concluding strategy, but be sure that it reflects the progress of thought in the paper. (The corresponding introduction appears on pages 34–35.)

> I've learned to insist on my peculiar brand of Puerto Rican identity. One not bound by geographical, linguistic or behavioral boundaries, but rather, by a deep identification with a place, a people and a culture which, in spite of appearances, define my behavior and determine the rhythms of my days. An identify in which I've forgiven myself for having to look up a recipe for *arroz con pollo* in a Puerto Rican cookbook meant for people who don't know a *sombrero* from a *sofrito*.
> —Esmeralda Santiago, "A Puerto Rican Stew"

■ Summary

Summarize, restate, or evaluate the major points in your paper.

> The mysterious nature and economic cost of back pain are driving a growing interest in research, and the coming years may reveal the fundamental aspects of this problem in more detail. In the meantime, for most back-pain patients the stereotypical physican advisory to "take two aspirin and call me in the morning" comes to mind. A richer and better course of action might be to take pain relievers as needed, stay in good overall physical condition, keep active through an acute attack if at all possible and monitor the condition for changes over a few days or a week. Back pain's power to inflict misery is great, but that power is usually transient. In most cases, time and perseverance will carry a patient through to recovery.   —Richard A. Deyo, "Low-Back Pain"

■ Visualization of the Future

Predict what the nature or condition of your topic will be like in the near or distant future.

> Will politicians respond? The science is solid but not 100 percent certain, and it will be a lot more expensive to contain carbon dioxide than it has been to limit CFCs. So the politicians probably won't respond, at least for now. Maybe the Nobel committee will someday give a prize to the scientists who conducted pioneering studies of global warming. Maybe the Republicans, if they're still in power, will take action. Or maybe it will be too late. —Michael D. Lemonick, "When Politics Twists Science"

Adam though aware that his plans might change as he wrote his paper, considered several conclusion strategies:

```
Challenge readers to consider their preferences
    and select their entertainment more sensibly.

Allude to several specific films, drawing atten-
    tion to the fact that they are better when seen
    at the theater.

Imagine the future when visual and sound quality
    will improve home viewing.
```

Adam ultimately decided to combine the challenge and allusion strategies to encourage thought and close the paper effectively.

■ EXERCISE 2.6   Concluding paragraphs

Write two draft versions of your conclusion. Make sure that the strategies are closely connected to the tone and topic of your paper.

3 | Revising

Revision, which means "to see again," provides an opportunity for you to rethink, reorganize, rephrase, refine, and redirect your work.

QUICK REFERENCE

Use revision to refine, clarify, and, if necessary, reconceive the entire paper—from its small to its large features.

▶ Evaluate your content critically and delete or replace anything that does not effectively support your main idea.

▶ Improve the style of your paper by reworking elements of your sentences.

▶ Eliminate the technical errors that interfere with easy reading and draw attention away from your ideas.

▶ Use peer review to get responses to your specific questions and an assessment of the strengths and weaknesses of the paper as a whole.

▶ Prepare the final copy of your paper, making necessary changes and following accepted guidelines for manuscript preparation.

Global revision—a multiperspective reworking of your writing—involves rereading your paper and making changes in content, sentence structure, word choice, punctuation, and mechanics all at once. As an alternative, consider revising your paper by concentrating on separate features of writing in discrete stages: **content revision, style revision,** and **technical revision.**

A Revision Sequence

- Set aside the rough draft.
- Reread the draft.
- Revise the content.
- Revise the style.
- Correct technical errors.
- Consult a peer editor.
- Make final changes.
- Prepare a final copy to submit.

3a Setting Aside the Rough Draft

Take a break from writing after finishing your draft. By interrupting your work to relax briefly, you will gain (or regain) objectivity before you begin revising.

Set aside your rough draft for as long as possible. Several days would be best, but at least stop working on the paper for several hours. Do anything that will rest and refresh your mind and allow you to return to your work with detachment.

3b Content Revision

Examine the content of your draft for clarity, coherence, and completeness. Consider the following questions:

- Are the title and the introductory strategy interesting, clear, and appropriate in tone?
- Does the thesis statement clearly present the topic and your opinion about it?
- Do the topics of the paragraphs support the thesis statement?
- Are the topics presented in a clear, emphatic order?

- Are the paragraphs adequately developed? Is there enough detail? Are there enough examples? Does the information in each paragraph relate to the thesis statement?
- Are the summary and concluding strategy effective?

When you have many content revisions, do more than one revised draft.

Figure 1 shows the content revisions that Adam made in the rough draft of his first body paragraph: (1) he added some clarifying words, (2) he deleted several extraneous sentences, and (3) he added useful details.

Figure 1

One of the important differences between
   film-viewing
the experiences is that the projection equipment
      ^
at home simply cannot compare to that at a the-

ater. ~~Home equipment is limited by conventional~~
~~television screen size.~~ The largest traditional

television screen available is about 36 inches,

with the biggest projection screen at around

80 inches. While those are much larger then was
                        in Star Wars
once available, the Death Star will still only
                        ^   Traditional
be about the size of the kitchen table. Stereo
                                        ^
televisions have only two speakers; projection

systems also come with two speakers, although
                        A T Rex in
you can, if you want, purchase more. Jurassic
                              not
Park will be loud, but will it reverberate and

make you quake? ~~I don't think so.~~

■ **EXERCISE 3.1**   **Content revision**

Reread your draft and respond to the questions on pages 43–44. Unless you can answer each question with an unequivocal yes, revise the draft until the content is clear, coherent, and complete.

3c   Style Revision

Examine your draft to see whether you can refine its style. Consider the following questions:

- Are the sentences varied in both length and type?
- Do sentences clearly and concisely express their meaning?
- Are word choices vivid, accurate, and appropriate?
- Are most sentences in the active voice?
- Do transitions adequately connect ideas?

To get a sense of how your paper flows, read it aloud—with or without an audience—noting awkward word choices or confusing phrases. Your hesitations while reading will indicate areas that require reworking.

After revising the content of his paper, Adam considered the effectiveness of its style. He decided to make a number of major and minor changes: (1) he further clarified his word choices, (2) he added some helpful transitions, (3) he adjusted the word order, and (4) he clarified his point of view. Adam's style revisions are shown in Figure 2.

Figure 2

> One of the ~~important~~ *most critical* differences between
>
> the film-viewing experiences is that the projec-
>
> tion equipment at home simply cannot compare
>
> to that at a theater. The largest traditional
>
> television screen available is about 36 inches,

~~with~~ the biggest projection screen ~~at~~ around

these models are   *what*

80 inches. While ~~those a~~ much larger then was

on one of them the image of

once available, The Death Star in Star Wars

a

will still (only be) about the size of ~~the~~ kitchen

top, which is pretty unimpressive.

table. ~~T~~raditional stereo televisions have only

Similarly

two speakers; projection systems also come with

owners

two speakers, although ~~you~~ can, ~~if you want,~~

additional ones. The roar of in

purchase ~~more.~~ X T Rex Jurassic Park will be loud,

of course,   *viewers*

but it will not reverberate and make ~~you~~ quake.

■ **EXERCISE 3.2   Style revision**

Revise the style of your paper by answering the questions on page 45.

3d   Technical Revision

Technical revision focuses on grammar, punctuation, mechanics, spelling, and manuscript form—the features of writing that will make the paper correct and precise.

Ask yourself the following general questions, watching especially for technical errors that you make frequently:

- Are all sentences complete? (See "Sentences," starting on page 140.)
- Do nouns and pronouns and subjects and verbs all agree in number and gender? (See "Agreement," starting on page 226.)

- Are all pronoun antecedents clear? (See "Pronoun Reference," starting on page 187.)
- Are all modifiers clearly positioned? (See "Positioning Modifiers," starting on page 192.)
- Are all words spelled correctly? (See "Spelling," starting on page 334.)
- Is the punctuation accurate? (See "Punctuation," starting on page 265.)
- Are elements of mechanics properly used? (See "Mechanics," starting on page 313.)

Make technical revisions slowly and carefully, paying particular attention to the kinds of errors you typically make. If you are uncertain about whether you have made an error, look up the applicable rule.

After making his content and style revisions, Adam made his technical revisions: (1) he corrected his presentation of numbers, (2) he inserted necessary italics, (3) he added necessary punctuation, and (4) he corrected a spelling error that had not been caught through spellchecking. Adam's technical revisions are shown in Figure 3.

Figure 3

One of the most critical differences ~~in~~ between the

film-viewing experiences is that the projection

equipment at home simply cannot compare to that

at a theater. The largest traditional television

screen available is about ~~36~~ thirty-six inches, the biggest

projection screen at ~~80~~ eighty inches. While these mod-

els are much larger then a what was once available,

on one of them the image of <u>The Death Star</u> in

<u>Star Wars</u> will still be only about the size of a kitchen tabletop, which is pretty unimpressive. Similarly traditional stereo televisions have only two speakers; projection systems also come with two speakers, although owners can purchase additional ones. The roar of a T Rex in <u>Jurassic Park</u> will be loud, of course, but it will not reverberate and make viewers quake.

■ **EXERCISE 3.3   Technical revision**

Return to your paper and examine it for technical errors, revising to eliminate them as you work. Work slowly and carefully, using Chapters 15–31 to review rules of grammar, punctuation, and mechanics.

3e   Peer Editing

During peer editing, another writer, often another student in the course for which you are writing, reads your paper and evaluates its content, style, and technical correctness. A peer editor should read and respond to your paper—not to rework it for you but to point out anything incomplete, unclear, inconsistent, or incorrect.

Consider these basic approaches to peer editing:

Find a peer editor with writing experience and standards similar to yours.   A peer editor from your class is ideal because you will share similar expectations about the audience, purpose, and requirements for the paper.

Ask a peer editor specific questions, focusing on issues of importance to you.   In addition to having a peer editor respond generally to your paper, ask him or her to respond to specific matters that concern you: the thesis, transitions, use of examples, and so on. Expect criticism as well as praise.

Ask the peer editor to identify problems but to refrain from altering your paper. A peer editor should note ineffective elements of your paper and, perhaps, make recommendations for improvement. The student should not rewrite your paper.

Consider the comments and queries of a peer editor but trust your own judgment. Notes about confusing, incomplete, or incorrect passages will always require attention. But on matters of judgment or personal taste—specific word choices, titles, and so on—consider the editor's notations carefully but remember that the paper is *yours*. Make no subjective changes that do not seem right and necessary.

Peer editing should be seen as a useful supplement to your own thorough evaluation and revision of your paper. Although it will not eliminate all problems, it will elicit useful responses to your work before you prepare the final copy.

■ EXERCISE 3.4 Peer editing

Prepare for peer editing by listing four to six features of your paper that you would like an editor to check. They may relate to any aspect of content, style, or technical correctness. Using your list of specific concerns and the following list of editing questions, ask a peer editor to evaluate your revised paper.

Introduction

Are the title and introductory strategy appropriate and interesting?

Is the thesis statement correctly positioned? Does it express a clear topic and opinion? Does it include necessary qualifications and clarifications?

Body paragraphs

Is the order of the paragraphs effective? Would another arrangement work better?

Does the topic of each paragraph relate clearly to the thesis statement? Are topics developed sufficiently?

Are transitions smoothly made between sentences, within paragraphs, and between paragraphs?

Conclusion

Does the conclusion effectively summarize the key points of the paper?

Is the concluding strategy appropriate?

Style

Are the sentences varied, coherent, forceful, and smooth?

Are the word choices vivid, accurate, and appropriate?

Technical matters

Are the sentences grammatical?

Is the usage standard?

Are the punctuation and mechanics correct?

3f   The Final Draft

Most papers should be laser or inkjet printed or typewritten, following the manuscript guidelines that appear in Appendix A, "Word Processing and Manuscript Form." Your instructor will explain any specific requirements for preparing a final manuscript.

■ **EXERCISE 3.5   The final draft**

Prepare the final draft of your paper. Work carefully, proofreading each page. Submit the paper—on time.

3g   A Sample Paper

Adam Solari

Dr. Robert Perrin

English 107

March 22, 1999

Home Theater--A Contradiction in Terms

$1,565,700,000. $716,900,000. No, these are not the gross national products of two small, underdeveloped countries. No, these are not the amounts paid for this year's Superbowl tickets, although they may be close. Instead, these dollar amounts, according to Entertainment Weekly (February 5, 1999), represent the amount of money Americans spent in 1998 seeing the top ten films at theaters and buying the top ten videocassettes for home viewing. These figures suggest that we Americans are fascinated by both kinds of film-viewing experiences, even though they are distinctly different. Although seeing a film at home has its charms, nothing can match the experience of seeing a film at the theater.

One of the most critical differences between the film-viewing experiences is that the projection equipment at home simply cannot compare to

that at a theater. The largest traditional television screen measures about thirty-six inches,
the biggest projection screen around eighty
inches. While these models are much larger than
what was once available, on one of them the image
of <u>The Death Star</u> in <u>Star Wars</u> will still be
only about the size of a kitchen tabletop, which
is pretty unimpressive. Similarly, traditional
stereo televisions have only two speakers;
projection systems also come with two speakers,
although owners can purchase additional ones.
The roar of a T. Rex in <u>Jurassic Park</u> will be
loud, of course, but it will not reverberate and
make viewers quake.

In contrast, the screens at even the smallest cineplex theaters measure in yards, sometimes
making them the size of people's yards. The image
of Dr. Frank N. Furter's lips at the opening of
<u>The Rocky Horror Picture Show</u> is impressive when
it is the size of a school bus, rather than the
size of a footlocker. And the multispeaker, surround-sound provided by the advanced THX systems
installed in today's theaters provides knock-
your-socks-off quality, turning the explosions
that level the White House in <u>Independence Day</u>
into powerful sensory experiences.

Solari 3

Another critical difference in the viewing experiences centers on refreshments. Food at home may be cheaper and healthier than what people can buy at the theater, but it simply doesn't have the weird charm of theater food. For example, at home people tend to eat what they've already purchased--potato chips, lunch meat, microwave popcorn, cookies, chopped vegetables, cheese and crackers, or pretzels--washed down with the family's beverage of choice. But where's the fun in eating broccoli and carrot sticks while laughing along with Dumb and Dumber or of drinking iced tea while screaming through Scream?

At the theater, however, people buy and eat "special event" food, a kooky and outrageously expensive assortment of edibles. Where else would most people eat Jujyfruits, Twizzlers, Klondike Bars, or Milk Duds--slurped down with a thermos-jug-sized soft drink. A film as "out there" as Armageddon or as off-kilter as Something about Mary deserves some seriously out-there, off-kilter food as well.

But probably the most important difference between home and theater viewing is what can best be called the "viewing process." No matter how much people try, viewing a film at home simply cannot match viewing a film at the theater. Home is just too, well, homey. People slouch. People go to sleep. People pause the film to answer the phone. People leave some lights on. People walk in and out. People do the wash. And in the process of doing all these things, they destroy the impact of a film's linear development. Just when Rhett is about to leave Scarlett, the phone rings, and though they may not "give a damn" who's calling, most people will answer the phone anyway--and the emotional moment is lost.

The circumstances of the theater-viewing experience help to keep people where they need to be to react most fully to a film. Viewers sit in a totally darkened space, the seats keep people sitting straight and generally awake, and no one intrudes (except a few stray mumblers). Because it is tactically difficult, few people choose to drift in and out, and so they give their attention to the film. That's partly why people laugh louder at Dr. Dolittle at the theater and cry more intensely when the Titanic sinks. Theater viewers are, consequently, in a circumstance that enables them to have a complete, intense "movie experience."

Solari 5

So the next time you're trying to decide whether to rent a video to watch at home or whether to head to a theater to see a film, remember how different the experiences will be. If you want your <u>Ten Commandments</u> to be more than ten inches tall, pick the cineplex; if you want a barrel of popcorn with extra butter with your <u>Antz</u> experience, choose the local movie house; if you want to feel the complete impact of <u>The Truman Show</u>'s world, select the theater nearest to you. After all, <u>home theater</u> will remain a contradiction in terms as long as the viewing experiences are so different.

4 Paragraphs

Paragraphs are groups of sentences that describe or explain one idea; as part of a series of paragraphs in a paper, a single paragraph develops one aspect of the paper's thesis. Paragraph length varies with the purpose of the paragraph, the nature of the material in the paragraph, and the function of the paragraph. To present ideas effectively, however, all paragraphs—short or long—should be unified, coherent, and complete.

QUICK REFERENCE

Paragraphs, the building blocks of papers, must be focused, structured, and developed.

▶ Write paragraphs that elaborate single ideas, using topic sentences, when appropriate, to clarify your focus.

▶ Use the stylistic techniques of transition and repetition to link ideas within and between paragraphs.

▶ Use varied methods of paragraph development, selecting patterns appropriate to your ideas.

4a Unified Paragraphs

A **unified paragraph** includes information pertinent to the main idea and excludes unrelated information. Often a topic sentence states the main idea explicitly and indicates by its phrasing the pattern of development that the paragraph follows.

Note: Many of the exercises in this chapter will take you through the steps of writing paragraphs. Keep the work from each exercise to use in later exercises.

■ One Topic

A unified paragraph develops one main idea only; it does not include loosely related information or an additional main idea. The following paragraph is not unified because it describes two museums (two topics) without establishing a connection between them.

> The Metropolitan Museum of Art in New York City is an impressive example of nineteenth-century architecture. Made of stone with massive columns and elaborately carved scroll-work, it is institutional architecture of the sort we expect in public buildings. Farther up Fifth Avenue, the Guggenheim Museum of Modern Art is built of reinforced concrete. This museum forms a spatial helix, a continuous spiral that expands as it rises; each level is marked by a narrow band of windows. Its design is severe and unusual.

Without suggesting an association between the museums, the paragraph shifts topics in a confusing way. A topic sentence explaining the relationship between the Metropolitan Museum of Art and the Guggenheim would create focus, or each museum could be discussed in a separate, single-topic paragraph:

> The Metropolitan Museum of Art in New York City is a typical example of nineteenth-century public architecture. Made of stone, with massive columns, tall casement windows, and an elaborately carved entablature, it is institutional architecture that conveys the dignity we expect in great public museum buildings. It is reminiscent of the Louvre in Paris, the British Museum in London, and the National Gallery in Washington. Familiar yet impressive, it suggests a grand purpose.
>
> Farther up Fifth Avenue, the Guggenheim Museum of Modern Art offers a contrasting, twentieth-century view of museum architecture. Built of reinforced concrete in the form

of a spatial helix, a continuous spiral that expands as it rises, it is adorned only by a band of simple windows. In 1937, when it was designed by Frank Lloyd Wright, the building's severity made it seem very modern, very alien, and austere rather than august. Yet it changed the way Americans perceived institutional architecture, and we now find similar designs in a range of public buildings from libraries to high schools.

■ Relevant Details

Including marginally related or irrelevant details, no matter how interesting, takes a paragraph in too many directions and destroys unity, as in this paragraph:

> **(1)** Hurricanes are cyclones that develop in the tropical waters of the Atlantic Ocean. **(2)** Forming large circles or ovals, they have winds of 75 miles per hour or more and can measure 500 miles across. **(3)** Years ago, hurricanes were named after women—Irene, Sarah, and Becky, for example—but now they are also named after men. **(4)** They usually form hundreds of miles from land and then move slowly to the northwest at about 10 miles per hour. **(5)** For reasons unknown, they pick up speed rapidly when they reach the twenty-fifth parallel. **(6)** That means, in very practical terms, that they reach peak speed and destructive power by the time they hit North American coastlines. **(7)** Hurricanes that form in the Pacific Ocean are commonly called typhoons.

In this paragraph, all material relates to hurricanes, but some of it only loosely. Sentences 1, 2, 4, 5, and 6 are factual descriptions of how the storms form and move. Sentences 3 and 7 include interesting but only marginally connected information. The unity of the paragraph would be improved by omitting the unrelated material, which might fit into another paragraph.

■ Topic Sentences

A **topic sentence**—a succinct statement of an idea and its intended development—unifies a paragraph. In long papers, the topic sentences of all body paragraphs, taken together, constitute the ideas and major illustrations that support the paper's thesis.

A topic sentence at the beginning of a paragraph works like a map, guiding readers through the ideas in the paragraph. A topic sentence at the end of a paragraph summarizes its ideas. Sometimes, especially in descriptive paragraphs, a topic sentence is unnecessary; readers will be able to infer the point from the paragraph as a whole.

Topic sentence at the beginning.

   More recently, diamond has proved to be the ideal material for a number of industrial uses. The mineral, an incredibly pure composition of more than 99 percent carbon, is the hardest substance known. It is capable of scratching almost anything, making it suitable for use in abrasives and in cutting, grinding and polishing tools. Diamond also has high thermal conductivity—more than three times that of copper—and is thus optimal for spreading and dissipating heat in electronic devices such as semiconductor lasers. Because most of these applications can be accomplished with tiny crystals, both scientific and technological interest has begun to focus on microdiamonds, samples that measure less than half a millimeter in any dimension.   —Rachael Trautman, Brendan J. Griffin, and David Scharf, "Microdiamonds"

Topic sentence at the end

   Advertisers use weasel words to appear to be making a claim for a product when in fact they are making no claim at all. Weasel words get their name from the way weasels eat the eggs they find in the nests of other animals. A weasel will make a small hole in the egg, suck out the insides, then place the egg back in the nest. Only when the egg is examined closely is it found to be hollow.

That's the way it is with weasel words in advertising: Examine weasel words closely and you'll find that they're as hollow as any egg sucked by a weasel. **Weasel words appear to say one thing when in fact they say the opposite, or nothing at all.**
—William Lutz, "With These Words I Can Sell You Anything"

No topic sentence

In the 19th century and for the first few decades of [the 20th] century, carnivals criss-crossed the United States, providing entertainment to people in small towns. Carnivals catered to the dark side of man's need for spectacle by allowing people to escape temporarily from their dull everyday lives into a world that was dark, sleazy, and seemingly dangerous. Of course, the danger wasn't real, and the ultimate lure of the carnival was that you could safely return from its world to your everyday life.
—Charles Oliver, "TV Talk Shows: Freak Parades"

■ **EXERCISE 4.1   Topic sentences**

The following paragraph lacks unity because it has a poor topic sentence. Revise the topic sentence to give the paragraph a clearer focus and then strike out any irrelevant material. (Available on disk.)

In the early days of MTV, the network showed only videos. For twenty-four hours a day, programmers rotated samples of the new musical form. Some music videos were simply taped versions of live performances. However, some performers like Rod Stewart, Jefferson Starship, Blondie, and Duran Duran produced other, more innovative videos that took advantage of the new format. Peter Gabriel was particularly innovative, and his video for "Sledgehammer" remains one of the best, with its heavy use of stop-action photography. These days, MTV presents more than just music videos; there are biographical programs, news shows, talk shows, and game shows. *Road Rules* and *Real World* are two of the oddest and most interesting programs because they feature "real" people who are simultaneously annoying and fascinating. I wonder what the original hosts think of today's programming?

■ EXERCISE 4.2 Topic sentences

Using four of the subjects listed next, write topic sentences. Make sure that your topic sentences clearly identify the subject and indicate how you will discuss it. (Available on disk.)

Example

Subject:	lawyers
Topic sentence:	Lawyers sometimes act more as legal interpreters than as advocates.

1. Censorship on the Internet
2. Sibling rivalry
3. Nonsmoking policies
4. The Superbowl
5. Credit-card debt
6. Standardized achievement tests
7. Drug abuse
8. Dating
9. Holiday celebrations
10. Computers in the classroom

4b Coherent Paragraphs

Effective paragraphs are clear and thorough and explain ideas and the connections among ideas. Using transitions and repetition will help you to write coherent paragraphs.

■ Transitions

A **transition** is a word or phrase that signals and facilitates the movement from one facet of a subject to another. The English language is rich in such words and phrases. Coordinating conjunctions (*and, but,* and others), subordinating conjunctions (*although, since,* and others), and correlative conjunctions (*either . . . or, not only . . . but also,* and others) are the most commonly used transitional words and phrases. However, many other words and phrases help to establish important relationships.

Addition

also	furthermore
and	in addition
besides	moreover
equally	next
further	too

Similarity

also	moreover
likewise	similarly

Difference

but	on the contrary
however	on the other hand
in contrast	yet
nevertheless	

Examples

for example	specifically
for instance	to illustrate
in fact	

Restatements or summaries

finally	in summary
in brief	on the whole
in conclusion	that is

in other words	therefore
in short	to sum up

Result

accordingly	so
as a result	therefore
consequently	thereupon
for this reason	thus

Chronology

after	meanwhile
afterward	next
before	second
during	simultaneously
earlier	soon
finally	still
first	then
immediately	third
in the meantime	when
later	while

Location

above	opposite
below	there
beyond	to the left
farther	to the right
here	under
nearby	

The following paragraph makes use of a number of transitional words and phrases, each marked with italics, to emphasize the relationships among ideas.

In recent years, some doctors have begun diagnosing allergies by combining blood droplets with different allergens to determine a sensitivity. [Allergy specialist] Lieberman warns, *however,* that this method is less accurate, is more expensive, and takes longer to get answers than skin testing. *Generally,* doctors recommend the blood test when it might be dangerous to use the allergen directly on the skin—as might be the case in someone hypersensitive to bee venom, *for example*—or if a skin disease *such as* eczema makes it difficult to see the results of a skin test.   —Cynthia Green, "Sneezy and Grumpy? See Doc"

■ Selective Repetition

Selective repetition can make writing unified and effective. Use variations of key words or phrases, synonyms (words with the same meaning), and pronouns to create variety as you create unity. The following paragraph uses all three.

Laughter is surely one of humanity's greatest gifts, for the ability to *laugh*—to appreciate the pleasure or *absurdity* in daily activities—allows people, young and old alike, to keep problems in perspective. Children are natural *laughers.* In situations, both appropriate and inappropriate, the *chuckles, giggles,* and outright *peals of laughter* of children can emphasize their innocence, their joyful ignorance of the problems of the world. *Levity* among adults is, unfortunately, far less common, but *it* is equally welcome. How fortunate are the adults who can react to potentially frustrating situations—a collapsed tent, a split seam in a pair of pants, a surprise guest—and see the sheer *laughability* of their attempts to maintain absolute control. *Laughter* expresses pleasure, eases tension, and lifts the spirit. *It* is a gift we should all share more often.

Repeating sentence structures also creates unity within a paragraph by presenting similar ideas in similar ways. If you strive for variety in most sentences, then patterns of repetition will stand out. The following paragraph uses repeated sentence structures to focus attention on similar ideas.

It is not the critic that counts; not the man who points out how the strong man stumbles, or where the doer of deeds could have done them better. The credit belongs to the man who is actually in the arena, whose face is marred by dust and sweat and blood; who strives valiantly; who errs, and comes short again and again, because there is not effort without error and shortcoming; but who does actually strive to do the deeds; who knows the great enthusiasms, the great devotions; who spends himself in a worthy cause, who at the best knows in the end the triumphs of high achievement and who at the worst, if he fails, at least fails while daring greatly so that his place shall never be with those cold and timid souls who know neither victory nor defeat.   —Theodore Roosevelt, Sorbonne, Paris; April 23, 1910

■ **EXERCISE 4.3   Transitions and repeated sentence elements**

Notice the use of transitional words and phrases and repetition in the following paragraphs, and comment on the purpose and effectiveness of each use.

One great difficulty in getting straightforward answers is that so many of the diseases in question have unpredictable courses, and some of them have a substantial tendency toward spontaneous remission. In rheumatoid arthritis, for instance, when such widely disparate therapeutic measures as copper bracelets, a move to Arizona, diets low in sugar or salt or meat or whatever, and even an inspirational book have been accepted by patients as useful, the trouble in evaluation is that approximately 35 percent of patients with this diagnosis are bound to recover no matter what they do. But if you actually have rheumatoid arthritis or, for that matter, schizophrenia, and then get over it, or if you are a doctor and observe this happen, it is hard to be persuaded that it wasn't *something* you did that was responsible. Hence, you need very large numbers of patients and lots of time, and a cool head.

Magic is back again, and in full force. Laetrile cures cancer, acupuncture is useful for deafness and low-back pain, vitamins are good for anything, and meditation, yoga, dancing, biofeedback, and shouting one another down in crowded rooms over weekends are specifics for the human condition. Running, a good thing to be doing for its own sake, has acquired the medicinal value formerly attributed to rare herbs from Indonesia.   —Lewis Thomas, "On Magic in Medicine"

■ **EXERCISE 4.4   Transitions and repeated sentence elements**

Revise one of your paragraphs to make effective use of transitional words and phrases and repeated words, phrases, and sentence structures.

4c   Paragraph Length

Paragraphs vary in length, depending on their purposes and patterns of development. Short paragraphs create emphasis by presenting simple ideas in brief, uncluttered forms, but too many in succession may seem choppy and leave ideas undeveloped. Long paragraphs present complex ideas in comprehensive, detailed form, but too many in a row may become tiring and may make ideas difficult to follow. The best general rule about paragraph length is to make paragraphs long enough to explain ideas fully and to serve their purpose in a paper—and no longer. Look at the following series of paragraphs, noting how the author uses paragraphs of different lengths to serve different purposes.

Here in the Someday Café, I sit at a rickety wooden table on which are laid: a newspaper, Sunday-fat; and a tall glass tumbler filled with steaming coffee.

The Someday Café sports two large plate-glass windows, which look out upon a busy, twisty intersection; and a small, not-quite-square interior, which manages, just, to accommodate six tables, fourteen mismatched chairs, a slip of bookshelf, and the coffee bar. The furniture looks as though it might have been picked up at a fraternity-house yard sale, late in the day. The café is full this morning, as it often is on Sunday mornings. Its clientele appears homologous in a motley sort of way: holey jeans abound, as do thick sandals and thick socks, cracked leather jackets, plaid flannel shirts, and heavy, earth-colored sweaters.

It is late winter and the plate-glass windows, the pastry case, and the eyeglasses on people's faces are all slightly fogged, glazed with a fine moisture signifying warmth and close bodies and the pressurized pulling of espresso shots. Jazz meanders from large mounted speakers. There are hanging plants, and a collection of vivid, juicy-looking oil paintings on the walls. Some of the paintings have objects glued to them: for example, a pair of mittens and a tiny plastic shopping cart. There are almond biscotti and German chocolate brownies and something called Stroopwaffles in the pastry case, and a gumball machine in the corner that dispenses chocolate-covered espresso beans into your palm when fed a quarter. Some wilting orange snapdragons stick out of a thermos on the counter; beside them, taped to the back of the cash register, is a printed card advising, "COFFEE KILLS." Six feet overhead, a tiny cardboard carton labeled "Suggestion Box" has been masking-taped upside down to the ceiling.   —Leah Hager Cohen, *Glass, Paper, Beans: Revelations on the Nature and Value of Ordinary Things*

A complete paragraph presents information and ideas clearly, along with enough supporting detail to satisfy readers.

■ EXERCISE 4.5   Paragraph length

Select one topic sentence from Exercise 4.2; then write three paragraphs—one brief, one moderate, and one long.

■ EXERCISE 4.6   Paragraph completeness

Use the topic sentence that follows and the accompanying examples (or others of your choosing) to construct a paragraph that is complete enough to satisfy a reader's expectations. (Available on disk.)

Topic sentences

In recent decades, presidents' wives have drawn attention to important national issues.

Examples

Eleanor Roosevelt: minority and women's rights and international cooperation

Jacqueline Kennedy: historical preservation and the fine arts

Lady Bird Johnson: environmental protection, forestation, and parks preservation

Betty Ford: substance-abuse programs and the arts

Nancy Reagan: substance-abuse programs and foster-child programs

Barbara Bush: substance-abuse programs and literacy programs

Hillary Rodham Clinton: health care reform and education

4d   Organization and Development

■ Alternative Organization

Deductive Structure

A **deductive paragraph** begins with a topic sentence and continues with supporting descriptions, examples, and facts. This paragraph has a deductive structure:

> The rain forest ecosystem, the oldest on Earth, is extremely complex and delicate. In spite of all the greenery one sees there, it is a myth that rain forest soil is rich. It is actually quite poor, leached of all nutrients save the most insoluble (such as iron oxides, which give lateritic soil—the most common soil type found there—its red color). Rather the ecosystem of the rain forest is a "closed" one, in which nutrients are to be found in the biomass, that is, in the living canopy of plants and in the thin layer of humus on the ground that is formed from the matter shed by the canopy. Hence the shallow-rootedness of most tropical forest plant species. Since the soil itself cannot replenish nutrients, nutrient recycling is what keeps the system going.   —Joseph K. Skinner, "Big Mac and the Tropical Forests"

Inductive Structure

An **inductive paragraph** begins with descriptions, examples, and facts and ends with the topic sentence. This structure builds suspense, heightens interest, and emphasizes details over generalization. This paragraph has an inductive structure:

> On that particular day [4 September 1893] Beatrix Potter decided to write a letter, which was to become famous. It was to five-year-old Noel Moore, the youngest son of her ex-

governess Annie Moore, a delicate boy who was often ill and who found great comfort in the generously illustrated letters that arrived regularly from "Yours affectionately, Beatrix Potter." This particular letter began: "My dear Noel, I don't know what to write to you, so I shall tell you a story about four little rabbits whose names were Flopsy, Mopsy, Cottontail and Peter. They lived with their mother in a sand bank under the root of a big fir tree. . . ." The letter continued with the whole of the now famous story of Peter Rabbit.   —Judy Taylor, "The Tale of Beatrix Potter"

■ **EXERCISE 4.7   Deductive and inductive structure**

Using two of the topic sentences you wrote for Exercise 4.2, write one deductive and one inductive paragraph. Underline the topic sentence in each and number the details in the margin of the paper. Be ready to explain why you chose the paragraph structure you did for developing each topic sentence.

■ Paragraph Development

Purpose

Although it is possible first to select an appropriate pattern of development and then to fit information to the pattern, the result is often awkward or mechanical. A better strategy is to complete some planning activities, decide on a general purpose and thesis for the whole paper, outline the information, and then write the first draft, letting the patterns of the paragraphs develop naturally. In this way, each paragraph extends and strengthens the paper's purpose.

Descriptions

Use apt and vivid details to evoke the five senses. Search for words to describe your subject's sights (*dove gray* sky, *glistening* chrome), sounds (*faint* tapping, *shrill* laughter), textures (*corrugated* tin, *leathery* skin), tastes (*salty* tears, *tart* berries), and smells (*fishy* odor, *lilac* scent). Be specific and try for both originality and accuracy.

> To new arrivals in London, it seemed pitch black out of doors, too, but not, by 1943, to Londoners. People had become conscious again of the phases of the moon, the light from the stars. They had regained their country eyes. The darkness was full of noises, the echo of footsteps, of people talking, the cries for taxis. Sound itself seemed amplified and dependable in the half-blindness of the street. The smell was of dust, of damp plaster in the air, and of the formaldehyde scent of the smoke from the dirty coal that lodged in the yellow fog. The stained sandbags, the rust, the dull, peeling paint, damp that made great dark lines down the walls, made London seem like a long-neglected, leaky attic.   —Mary Lee Settle, "London—1944"

Examples

Use specific, appropriate, developed examples to show readers how you reached your conclusion. Be precise: instead of "a dramatic program," write *"ER"*; instead of "a school in the Midwest," write "University of Chicago." Use examples that are representative, not exceptional. Also consider presenting a single extended example that will answer journalists' questions (*who, what, when, where, how,* and *why*) to ensure that you have provided readers with the information that they need.

> Still, plastic's legendary endurance has provided us with a few unforeseen benefits. In January 1992, a freak ocean squall washed a container of cargo off a freighter crossing the international date line. The container broke up in mid ocean, releasing twenty-nine thousand plastic bathtub toys being shipped from Hong Kong to Tacoma, Washington. Months later, hundreds of

blue turtles, red beavers, yellow ducks, and green frogs were sighted washing up on the shores of Sitka, Alaska. For the next year, thousands more washed up along a five-hundred-mile stretch of the Gulf of Alaska coast, giving oceanographers "the greatest boon for research on North Pacific patterns and currents since 61,000 Nike athletic shoes had been spilled in the same area two years before," according to Reuters. What became known to the marine research community as "the quack heard round the world" enabled scientists to adjust their computer models of the northern Pacific tides to account for the effects of the wind.　—Stephen Fenichell, *Plastic: The Making of a Synthetic Century*

Facts

Use facts and technical and statistical information to demonstrate how and why you reached your conclusion. Be as specific as possible: rather than write that a car costs "a lot," write "$64,000"; rather than write that tuition has "increased dramatically" in the last decade, write "26 percent." Simply incorporate facts that you have gathered yourself, but fully document those gathered from research (see pages 426–42 for guidelines).

Avalanches are triggered most frequently in the periods during and immediately following heavy snowstorms. The slopes most likely to avalanche will be the lee slopes, where wind-deposited snow compacts into slabs that precariously balance on the unstable snow underneath. Other variables in the avalanche equation include temperature changes, as well as the steepness and shape of the slope. Convex slopes tend to be more dangerous than concave slopes; those that fall from a 30- to 50-degree angle pose the greatest risk. Steep drops of 60 degrees or more avalanche almost constantly, so the snow seldom builds up to dangerous depths. Cornices, which are windswept waves of hard-packed snow that form on the lee side of exposed ridgelines, should be strictly avoided.   —Keith McCafferty, "Avalanche!"

Comparison and Contrast

Use comparison and contrast to analyze the similarities and differences of two subjects or to explain the unfamiliar in terms of the familiar. Comparison and contrast paragraphs can be structured in two ways: whole-to-whole and part-to-part.

Whole-to-whole development (or **divided development**) fully discusses first one subject and then the other. The topic sentence of a paragraph with this pattern generally emphasizes the two subjects' subordinating features or qualities.

> The paradox is that we get two sets of messages coming at us every day. One is the "permissive" message, saying, "Buy, spend, get it now, indulge yourself," because your wants are also your needs—and you have plenty of needs that you don't even know about because our consumer culture hasn't told you about them yet! The other we would call, for lack of a better word, a "puritanical" message, which says, "Work hard, save, defer gratification, curb your impulses." What are the psychological and social consequences of getting such totally contradictory messages all the time? I think this is what you would call "cognitive dissonance," and the psychological consequence is a pervasive anxiety, upon which the political right has been very adept at mobilizing and building.   —Barbara Ehrenreich, "Spend and Save"

Part-to-part development (or **alternating development**) provides a point-by-point, alternating comparison between two subjects. The topic sentences generally emphasize qualities, features, or consequences following from the topic.

> In 1973 I stayed in the four-story Erawan Hotel, then one of the tallest buildings around. Small lizards skittered over the

moist walls like leaf shadows. Today the new Erawan stands
22 floors high and has a disco and a gym. In a huge glass lobby
filled with trees, Thais, Americans, Japanese, and Germans
make deals to the clink of spoons on china cups. The sidewalks
outside are filled with young workers striding to their offices.
Thailand's economic success is most obvious in the cities,
but it filters into the countryside as well. Where families once
tended small paddies just outside Bangkok, large tractors now
groom the sweeping fields of commercial farms. Many farms
have given way to golf courses in the past decade. On quiet
side roads where I once slowed for water buffalo, I now dodge
motorcycles piloted by young Thai men in love with speed.
—Noel Grove, "The Many Faces of Thailand"

Analogy

Use analogy, an extended comparison, to point to an unexpected connection between dissimilar things.

The garment industry is like a pyramid, with retailers—
department stores like Bloomingdale's, Macy's, Sears, and others—at the top. They buy their fashions from companies like
Liz Claiborne and Guess?, who are known as manufacturers
although they rarely make their own clothes. The majority farm
out their work to thousands of factory owners—the contractors
whose factories are often sweatshops. Contractors are the small
fry in the pyramid; they are often undercapitalized entrepre-
neurs who may be former garment workers themselves, taking
in a small profit per garment. At the bottom of the pyramid is
the worker, generally a woman—and sometimes her child—
who is paid $0.50 or $1 for a dress that costs $120 at retail. As a
general rule, prices within the pyramid follow a doubling effect
at each tier. The contractors double their labor costs and overhead when quoting a price to the garment companies, which,
in turn, calculate their overhead and double that to arrive at a

price to charge the retailer. The retailer then doubles this price, and sometimes adds still more, to assure a profit even after two or three markdowns.   —Helen Zia, "Made in the U.S.A"

Cause and Effect

Use cause and effect to analyze an event or condition in order to understand how something came to be or what its results are. Remember that a single cause may have multiple effects, and a single effect multiple causes. Remember, too, that a cause-and-effect relationship is not established by mere association.

> On a direct level, lower interest rates make it cheaper for firms to borrow money with which to buy new plants and equipment. They also have some indirect effects. Lower interest rates mean that a firm earns less interest on its own uninvested funds, so that it has more incentive to use them for something productive. Lower interest rates also encourage people to buy stocks instead of earning interest, thus making it easier for firms to raise money for investment by selling stock. Rising stock prices make it worthwhile for entrepreneurs to offer stock to the public in order to launch new ventures, which typically use the money to purchase new plants and equipment. In all these ways, lower interest rates encourage private investment.   —James L. Medoff, *Indebted Society: Anatomy of an Ongoing Disaster*

Process Analysis

Use process analysis to describe accurately and completely how something is done or made or how something happens. A paragraph describing a process presents a chronologically arranged series of steps.

> To fabricate dark chocolate, the roasted cocoa nibs are ground into liquor, and the sugar pulverized; these two are then brought together in a *mélangeur* or mixer, which is a rotating pan, generally with a granite bed on which granite rollers

rotate; heat is applied by steam or hot water, essentially making this an up-to-date version of the old heated *metate* or *mano.* Next, the mixed mass is worked by multiple-roller refiners to ensure smoothness. Conching [heating and mixing] is the last step, imparting the final flavor to the chocolate mass; in good-quality dark chocolate, this might take from 72 to 96 hours.
—Sophie D. Coe and Michael D. Coe, *The True History of Chocolate*

Classification

Use classification to divide a large subject into its parts or sub-groups. Establish meaningful, consistent criteria for division, supplying readers with the information they need to distinguish among the classes. Subgroups should not overlap.

For present purposes, it will be useful to distinguish four degrees of poverty: *destitution,* which is lack of income sufficient to assure physical survival and to prevent suffering from hunger, exposure, or remediable or preventable illness; *want,* which is a lack of enough income to support "essential welfare" (as distinguished from comfort and convenience); *hardship,* which is lack of enough to prevent acute, persistent discomfort or inconvenience; and *relative deprivation,* which is lack of enough to prevent one from feeling poor by comparison with others.   —Edward C. Banfield, "Several Kinds of Poverty"

Definition

Use definition to explain terms and concepts. A **formal definition,** such as those in dictionaries, places the subject in a class and then distinguishes it from other items in the same class.

The goal of the measurement is easy to understand. According to Isaac Newton, any two material objects in the universe attract each other with a force that is proportional to the mass of the objects and that diminishes with their distance from each other. To quantify this phenomenon, physicists define as G the magnitude of the attraction that two one-kilogram masses, exactly one meter apart, exert on each other. Strictly speaking, G is an odd quantity with no intuitive meaning, so for this reason physicists take the liberty of referring to it in more familiar terms as a force.   —Hans Christian Von Baeyer, "Big G"

An **informal** (or extended) **definition** describes the subject, provides examples of it, or compares or contrasts it with some other thing.

Gardeners have long squabbled over what wildflowers are. Purists insist that they are native plants that grew before the arrival of the Europeans. Others include naturalized plants in the classification—those introduced from other parts of the world that reproduce freely in their nonnative habitat. Opinion these days favors the definition that includes both native and naturalized plants. Weeds, incidentally, are just wildflowers that grow when they are not wanted. Noxious weeds are plants that the authorities have determined threaten human health or agricultural practices. Some common attractive weeds are Queen Anne's lace *(Daucus carota)*, chicory *(Cichorium intybus)* and even oxeye daisy *(Chrysanthemum leucanthemum)*. —Eva Hoepfner, "Wildflower Meadows"

■ **EXERCISE 4.8   Paragraph development**

Write a paragraph using one of the following methods of development. Use one of the topics provided or select one of your own.

Descriptions: an incident of prejudice, a scene showing family support, a depiction of a badly run business

Examples: the importance of energy conservation, the practical value of hobbies, the increasing dependence on computers

Facts: the high costs of education, everyday uses of mathematics, the basic equipment necessary for cooking

Comparison and contrast: shopping at a store and on the Internet, celebrations in different cultures, the language patterns you use with close friends and with parents

Analogy: political ads and soft-drink ads, a college campus and a city, marriage and a corporate merger

Cause and effect: a death in the family, a major industry closing in your city, personal financial difficulties

Process analysis: preparing a speech, buying a stereo, applying for college admission

Classification: kinds of cartoon strips, types of radio stations, kinds of football fans

Definition: interactive videos, a good parent-child relationship, luck

All purposeful verbal communication—whether speaking, listening, reading, or writing—requires critical thinking, that is, an active, focused engagement with the topic. When people speak or write, they first synthesize ideas and experiences and then communicate their insights or observations to others. Conversely, when people listen or read, they actively seek to comprehend the insights and observations of others, thus responding to the speaker's or writer's intended communication.

The systematic study and practice of critical thinking and writing improves all forms of communication by fostering substantive, precise, and thorough analysis, expression, and response.

QUICK REFERENCE

Think critically when you read and write to improve your understanding of others' writing and their understanding of yours.

▶ Focus on the topic and its development.

▶ Support different kinds of assertions with the appropriate kinds of evidence.

▶ Evaluate discussions to determine whether the supporting evidence is adequate.

▶ Recognize patterns of fallacious reasoning.

5a   A Topic and Its Development

Critical thinking involves systematic and rigorous scrutiny and evaluation of ideas—in both what you read and what you write. When you read a paper, article, report, or book that argues a position, think about it critically, actively examining and evaluating its purpose, assumptions, evidence, and development. Ultimately, you must decide whether it has succeeded in establishing the validity of its position.

To work as a writer, you must use your critical thinking skills to clarify and support your own purposes, assumptions, evidence, and development. Your general goal in thinking critically when you write is to ensure that you demonstrate the validity of your position.

Critical thinking, then, can be used as you read, to deconstruct someone's thought processes, and as you write, to construct a presentation that will effectively convey your ideas.

Three basic patterns of reasoning—induction, deduction, and warrant-based reasoning—organize ideas and evidence in different ways, reflecting differences in thinking patterns. Be aware of these patterns as you read and write.

■ Inductive Reasoning

Induction builds from specific evidence (observations, experiences, examples, facts, statistics, testimony) and then, through interpretation, derives a **claim** (described as a conclusion or a generalization). The soundness of inductive reasoning depends on careful evaluation and description of evidence, reasonable interpretation, and clear expression of the claim.

Consider this evidence regarding Maxwell Elementary School:

- Children at MES have an absence rate higher than the school district average.

- Children at MES have the second-lowest standardized test scores in the school district.

- More children at MES receive suspensions because of fighting than do children at other elementary schools in the district.

- Fewer children at MES go on to graduate from high school than the district average.

You could make several different claims based on a review of this evidence: (1) Maxwell Elementary School students face greater obstacles to success than do children at other elementary schools in the district, (2) MES students experience a disproportionately high amount of educational interference, and (3) MES students are less likely to succeed than are students at other schools.

While reading and writing, analyze the cumulative evidence that leads to a claim or claims. As this example shows, slightly different interpretations of the same evidence can result in different, though related, claims.

■ Deductive Reasoning

Deduction begins with a general claim (or premise) and then clarifies or illustrates the original claim with supporting information. The effectiveness of deductive reasoning depends on a reasonable claim, thorough description of related evidence, and sound use of logic in reaching a conclusion.

For example, consider this general claim, which many people believe: Children learn from the examples set by the adults around them. Interestingly, the support for a general claim like this varies as much as the types of writers who support it. The supporting evidence could be presented positively through examples related to work, education, human relations, good health, fiscal responsibility, and so on. Conversely, the same generalization could be supported negatively through examples related to drug and alcohol abuse, physical violence, crime, compulsive behavior, and so on.

While reading and writing, analyze the original claim and the evidence used to support it. As the previous example shows, different kinds of evidence can illustrate the same claim.

■ Warrant-Based Reasoning

Warrant-based reasoning begins with an idea expressed as a claim (or conclusion); it is presented in conjunction with related evidence. The **warrant** is the underlying assumption, often unstated, that establishes a relationship between the claim and the evidence in the same way in which a warranty (from the same root word) makes a claim ("this product will work for at least one year") based on evidence ("this product has been tested and has worked for at least one year").

Claim

Hospice care is the most beneficial medical care for the elderly.

Evidence

Hospice care provides homelike settings with familiar living arrangements.

Warrant

Homelike settings, with more familiar living arrangements, are beneficial.

Carefully evaluate warrants, especially unstated ones. An invalid warrant, even an implicit one, leads to unreasonable claims.

Because college admissions tests are administered nationwide, they are an effective measure of student potential.
[**The implicit warrant is that widely used tests are effective. Because this notion is questionable, the conclusion is questionable as well.**]

■ EXERCISE 5.1   Patterns of critical thinking

To practice applying the principles of critical thinking, complete the following arguments. Compare your responses with those of your classmates to see the variations that occur when people interpret the same evidence.

Inductive Argument

Evidence

Tuition costs have increased, on the average, 5–15 percent yearly.
Books often cost $75–$125 per course.
Student fees average $200 per year.
School supplies can cost well over $200 a year.

Room and board now averages between \$5,000 and \$7,000.

Claim

_____

_____

Deductive Argument

Claim

We have become a society of complainers.

Evidence

_____

_____

_____

_____

Warrant-Based Argument

Claim

Computers have improved people's lives.

Evidence

People keep records efficiently, conduct business quickly, and communicate easily.

Warrant

_____

_____

_____

■ **EXERCISE 5.2   Claims, evidence, and warrants**

Identify the claims, evidence, and warrants (both implicit and explicit) in the following paragraph.

It is not known whether any single vertebrate species is more or less immune to pain than another. A neat line cannot be drawn across the evolutionary scale dividing the sensitive from the insensitive. Yet the suffering of laboratory rats and mice is regarded as trivial by scientists and the public alike. These rodents have the dubious honor of being our No. 1 experimental animals, composing possibly 75 percent of America's total lab-animal population. As Russell Baker once wrote, "This is no time to be a mouse."

—Patricia Curtis, "The Argument against Animal Experimentation"

5b   Purpose, Audience, and Content

To read and write effectively, you must analyze the roles of purpose, audience, and content in ensuring effective communication. See section 1d for related information on audience and purpose.

■ Purpose

To think critically about a written work—one that you are reading or one that you are writing—you must evaluate its general purpose. Although writing can serve a variety of purposes simultaneously, five types apply to both spoken and written communication.

Purposes of Writing

Expressive writing   shares perceptions and experiences gathered from an individual's observations. Personal essays and letters, poetry, and fiction are examples of expressive writing.

Literary writing   shares perceptions and insights using artistic forms. Short stories, poems, plays, and novels are examples of literary writing.

Referential writing shares information and ideas gathered through systematic research. Reports, research papers, memoranda, and informational articles in newspapers and magazines are examples of referential writing.

Persuasive writing presents information and observations with the specific intent of convincing readers to alter their perceptions or to take action. Letters to editors, requests, petitions, arguments in court, and advertisements are examples of persuasive writing.

Argumentative writing presents ideas, information, experiences, and insights to articulate an opinion about an debatable topic. Argumentative writing articulates an opinion and illuminates the topic. Debates, political speeches and articles, editorials, and essays of criticism and analysis are examples of argumentative writing.

Recognizing the different purposes that expressive, literary, referential, persuasive, and argumentative writing serve—and recognizing when their goals overlap—will help you to test the validity of a paper's assumptions and presentation. For instance, a single apt, well-written example may effectively illustrate a point in an expressive paper but be inadequate support in a persuasive paper on the same topic. The different reasons for writing establish different expectations for development.

■ Audience

To improve your work as a critical reader and writer, evaluate the needs, demands, and challenges of your audience and assess how to meet their needs.

Questions About Readers

• How much will they already know about the topic?
• How skeptical might they be about your claims?

- What preconceptions or misconceptions might they have?
- What kinds of evidence will they require?
- What kinds of objections might they raise?
- What needs will they bring to the reading?

To write a balanced, informed paper that clearly acknowledges the needs of varied readers, consider how the opposition might refute your claims. Similarly, how might you refute theirs? How might you reconcile these opposing views? Keep these opposing views in mind when writing, conceding points when necessary and countering objections when appropriate. You cannot accommodate all readers, but you should anticipate the needs, expectations, and objections of critical readers.

■ Summaries

A **summary** is a brief restatement, in your own words, of the central idea presented in a short written work or in a portion of a longer work. For brief texts of only a few paragraphs, a summary may be a single sentence; for longer texts, a complete summary may require several sentences or a whole paragraph.

Strategies for Writing Summaries

- Read the text carefully and then put it aside. Do not look at the text while writing your summary.
- Identify the writer's thesis statement or topic sentence. It presents the most direct, comprehensive statement of the central idea.
- Select and restate the central idea(s) only.
- Omit details, explanations, examples, and clarifications.
- Express the text's main idea(s) in your own words, not in the writer's.
- Name the author or source explicitly in the summary and provide a page citation.

Expect to revise a summary several times to make it brief, accurate, and complete.

To demonstrate how summaries work, first read the following passage from a chapter on waste disposal in Jacqueline Vaugn Switzer's *Environmental Politics: Domestic and Global Dimensions.*

> The effectiveness of recycling in the United States appears to be largely dependent on the way in which the programs are implemented. A national survey of 450 municipal recycling programs found several characteristics common of successful recycling efforts. The most successful voluntary efforts were in cities with clear, challenging goals for recycling a specific proportion of their waste stream, curbside pickup, free bins, private collection services, and compost programs. Mandatory recycling programs were most successful when they included the ability to issue sanctions or warnings for improper separation. In both types of programs, the highest participation was in cities that employed experienced recycling coordinators. What this means is that there are still a number of obstacles to be overcome before recycling—despite its inherent attractiveness—can be considered more than a supplemental answer to the solid waste dilemma.
> —"Dilemmas of Waste and Cleanup: Super Mess and Superfund"

A clear, concise, and complete summary of Switzer's paragraph requires several drafts:

First attempt

Recycling works best under certain circumstances.
[**Though concise, this summary is too simplistic.**]

Second attempt

Recycling works best when cities organize their efforts and institute specific programs.
[**Although this summary is clearer than the first, it presents only part of Switzer's point. It needs further elaboration.**]

Third attempt

Recycling works best when cities hire coordinators who can organize their efforts to target materials for recycling and to make the process convenient, as well as fine people who don't recycle properly.
[**This summary presents the major points of Switzer's paragraph.**]

Fourth attempt

Jacqueline Vaughn Switzer, in *Environmental Politics: Domestic and Global Dimensions,* asserts that recycling works best when cities hire coordinators who can organize their efforts to target materials for recycling and to make the process convenient, as well as fine people who don't recycle properly (97).
[**Citing the author, title, and page number completes the summary.**]

■ EXERCISE 5.3   Summaries

Write a summary of each of the following paragraphs.

1. The mother-child relationship is the foundation from which the child's developing mind and personality is based. As such, it has a profound effect on the process of establishing a self-identity, a process which cannot be completed overnight. It involves various factors, such as the potential of the genes with which the child has been biologically endowed as well as the child's family and cultural environment. All of these factors go through the "channel" of the mother-child relationship and become the construction blocks from which the developing child can build an identity and personality. Once various life experiences combine with the child's biologically determined potential, the child's initial unformed mental world can begin to organize itself step-by-step. Then the child gradually becomes able to differentiate between the various aspects of himself— e.g., his pleasurable self, painful self, angry self, etc. He must integrate these different nuclei in order to achieve a cohesive

sense of self. In normal development, after initial confusion, the infant progresses from viewing the world as black or white, either "bad" (unpleasant and dangerous) or "good" (pleasurable and safe)—to seeing greys (achieving integration where "good" and "bad" images intertwine realistically).　—Vamik D. Volkan, Norman Itzkowitz, and Andrew W. Dod, *Richard Nixon: A Psychobiography*

2. Both candidates worked hard studying up for the first debate, which was telecast from Chicago on September 26. The topic, unfortunately for Nixon, was domestic rather than foreign affairs and the cameras were kinder to Kennedy than to Nixon. During the debate Kennedy looked pleasant, relaxed, and self-assured, while Nixon (who had barely recovered from his illness) looked pale, tired, and emaciated, with his customary five o'clock shadow making him look a bit sinister. Kennedy was on the offensive throughout; he listed the shortcomings of the Eisenhower administration and impressed viewers with his factual mastery of a mass of material. Nixon was perforce on the defensive; he concentrated on Kennedy's criticisms and tried to score points by effectively rebutting them one by one. While Nixon, in short, addressed himself mainly to Kennedy, the latter directed his remarks to the television audience and on the whole came off better. Radio listeners had the impression that Nixon did as well as, if not better than, Kennedy in the confrontation; but televiewers, including Nixon's own fans, generally agreed that Kennedy came out ahead in the first debate.
—Paul F. Boller, *Presidential Campaigns*

5c　Evidence

Evidence is the illustrative material used to support a claim. As a critical reader, analyze what kinds of evidence authors use and how well they use it. As a writer, select and present evidence with care because critical readers will examine the evidence to decide whether it substantiates your claims.

Evidence can be classified as facts and statistics, examples, and expert testimony.

Facts and Statistics

Facts are verifiable pieces of information (58,135 American soldiers died in the Vietnam War); **statistics** are mathematical data (approximately 65 percent of soldiers killed in Vietnam were in the U.S. Army). Well-chosen facts and statistics clarify and, consequently, support many of the claims made in writing. However, be skeptical about the use of factual and statistical information because authors with special interests may manipulate information to support their claims.

Examples

Examples are individual cases that illustrate claims (the Watergate cover-up as an example of the abuse of executive power). Examples from personal experience are considered primary evidence, while examples from other people's experiences are considered secondary evidence. To be effective, examples must be relevant, representative, and complete.

Relevant

Relevant examples illustrate a claim in a timely way and present single cases that correspond effectively to the larger issue presented in the claim. Relevance is also determined by how well the example correlates with the claim. To illustrate the claim that Jimmy Carter was an ineffectual president, a relevant example might be the mishandling of the hostage crisis in Iran; such an example corresponds to the seriousness of the claim and illustrates it in an important way. However, an example about the embarrassments caused by President Carter's brother Billy ignores the important values presented in the claim and does not address President Carter's effectiveness as a leader.

Representative

Representative examples are neither extremely positive nor extremely negative. Extreme examples are ineffective because careful readers will see them as exceptions and will not find them convincing. In a paper on the negative effects of state lotteries on family finances, for instance, a $6-million winner would not be representative, nor would a person who spent the family food money on lottery tickets. Neither extreme example would support the assertion convincingly.

Complete

Complete examples provide sufficient information to allow readers to see how the examples work as evidence. Incorporating responses to the journalists' questions (*who, what, when, where, how,* and *why*) is one useful way to guarantee completeness. Adding a summary can further clarify important connections.

◼ Expert Testimony

Expert testimony in written work, like expert testimony in court trials, is a statement of opinion or a judgment made by an expert or authority in a field. For example, a specialist in labor practices or a statistician working with government hiring data could speak authoritatively to support a claim about sexual discrimination in government hiring. A feminist critic of literature would not necessarily have expertise with regard to hiring practices, even though he or she might have an informed opinion on discriminatory hiring practices.

◼ Appeals

Appeals to readers stress the logic of claims, emphasize the ethical nature of positions, and focus on the emotional nature of discussions. Most writing blends these appeals to emphasize multiple perspectives.

Logical Appeals

Appeals to logic emphasize evidence, providing facts or statistics to support a claim. The following paragraph uses technical information—thereby appealing to logic—to emphasize why one product—olestra—required unique testing procedures.

> Olestra is probably the most studied of all food additives, and its market approval process was one of the costliest and the longest in history. But the case of olestra is also remarkably different from that of other food additives because the decision process also took twists and turns equally different from the path of other food additives. For one thing, olestra may replace a major portion of fat in the diet, a "macroingredient" that typically furnishes about 35 percent of calories in the diets of American consumers. This is not a coloring agent or sweetener that substitutes for minor ingredients in food. Because olestra would be replacing such a large proportion of the fat in the diets of some people, the [Food and Drug Administration] recommended that [Proctor & Gamble] examine olestra's nutritional and gastrointestinal effects, not just toxicity. —Laura S. Sims, *The Politics of Fat*

Ethical Appeals

Appeals to ethics stress the writer's trustworthiness, honesty, fairness, clarity, and directness. The following paragraph establishes the writer's role as a patriot and citizen, as well as his understanding of prejudice; by providing a balanced description that even includes humor, he establishes an ethical perspective.

> After I was honorably discharged from the U.S. Air Force in 1975, the FBI opened a file on me. It began with the ominous suggestion that I might be involved in "suspected" terrorist organizations, but the investigation concluded two years and 23 pages later that I was concerned only about improving my community.

The investigation seemed based on the assumption that because I was an Arab, I must be a potential terrorist. Most of the juicy text was blocked out with heavy, black Magic Markered lines, so it's hard to know for sure.   —Ray Hanania, "One of the Bad Guys?"

Emotional Appeals

Appeals to emotion emphasize the needs, desires, hopes, and expectations of readers, particularly sympathy and self-interest. The following paragraph, emphasizing the personal and emotional dimensions of health care, appeals to readers' sympathy.

> Obviously the decisions that must be made when an elderly patient faces a medical crisis are difficult ones for everyone—patient, loved ones, doctors, hospitals and health-care personnel alike. When a satisfying, although perhaps restricted, life is possible if treatment is successful, the decisions are easy: You do everything you can. But when someone has had a medical crisis and is in failing health with little hope of recovery; when all the painful, costly, possibly degrading though heroic measures may gain no more than a few extra days or weeks or, maybe, months for a patient who is probably miserable and often unconscious, the decisions are more difficult and individuals may vary widely in their preferences—if, indeed, they are given a choice.   —Roy Hoopes, "Turning Out the Light"

■ EXERCISE 5.4   Evidence

Identify the kinds of evidence used in the following paragraphs. Discuss with class members whether or not this evidence is effective and consider alternative ways to support the claims in the paragraphs.

The economist and legal scholar Michael K. Block, who believes that American sentencing policies are still not harsh enough, offers a straightforward explanation for why the United States has lately incarcerated so many people: "There are too many criminals committing crimes." Indeed, the nation's prisons now hold about

150,000 armed robbers, 125,000 murderers, and 100,000 sex offenders—enough violent criminals to populate a medium-sized city such as Cincinnati. Few would dispute the need to remove these people from society.

The level of violent crime in the United States, despite recent declines, still dwarfs that in Western Europe. But the proportion of offenders being sent to prison each year for violent crimes has actually fallen during the prison boom. In 1980 about half the people entering state prison were violent offenders; in 1995 less than a third [were] convicted of a violent crime. The enormous increase in America's inmate population can be explained in large part by the sentences given to people who have committed nonviolent offenses. Crimes that in other countries would usually lead to community service, fines, or drug treatment—or would not be considered crimes at all—in the United States now lead to a prison term, by far the most expensive form of punishment. "No matter what the question has been in American criminal justice over the last generation," says Franklin E. Zimring, the director of the Earl Warren Legal Institute, "prison has been the answer."   —Eric Schlosser, "The Prison-Industrial Complex"

5d   Logical Fallacies

Logical fallacies are errors in thinking and writing that result from faulty logic.

■ Hasty Generalization

A **hasty generalization** is a conclusion based on too little evidence, suggesting a superficial investigation of an issue.

The recent increase in the numbers of tornadoes, hurricanes, heavy rains, and intense snow indicates that we are currently experiencing the effects of global warming.
[Although recent weather has been severe, it is illogical to assume that weather is solely related to global warming. In

addition, the statement ignores the fact that weather patterns have always occurred in cycles.]

■ Oversimplification

Oversimplification ignores the complexities, variations, and exceptions relevant to an issue.

> Violence on television leads to violence in society.
> [Television violence *may* contribute to societal violence, but it is a single factor among many. The statement ignores the complex and multiple causes of violence.]

■ Either/Or

The **either/or fallacy** suggests that only two choices exist when, in fact, there are more. This type of thinking is not only illogical (because multiple alternatives are almost always available) but also unfair (because ignoring complexities and choices distorts a discussion).

> For the sake of learning, we must maintain the firmest kind of discipline, including corporal punishment, in our public schools, or we can expect chaos, disorder, and the disintegration of education as we know it.
> [The two alternatives presented are extremes: firm discipline resulting in order versus relaxed discipline resulting in chaos. The statement both ignores moderate methods of maintaining discipline and asserts that without firm discipline the worst will happen. It is highly manipulative.]

■ Begging the Question

Begging the question distorts a claim by including a secondary idea that requires proof, though none is given.

> Since wealthy doctors control health-care services, Americans can only expect the costs of medical treatment to escalate.
> [The writer has provided no evidence that doctors control health-care services. Further, the use of the word *wealthy*

implies that doctors' salaries directly determine treatment costs. Both of these issues muddy the logic of the argument.]

Sometimes begging the question is done very subtly through word choice.

The antiwar demonstrators of the 1970s should be remembered as the cowards that they were.
[**The writer uses the word** *cowards* **to define the group without making any attempt to prove the implicit warrant that protesting is cowardly.**]

■ Association

Fallacies of association suggest that ideas or actions are acceptable or unacceptable because of the people who are associated with them. Such a fallacy ignores that ideas or actions should be evaluated on their own merits.

Arab terrorists have repeatedly threatened peace around the world; is it any wonder that people from the Middle East are viewed with suspicion.
[**This assertion links all people in the region with a small group of terrorists. Such reasoning ignores the fact that terrorists often act alone or as part of small, fanatical groups that do not represent the larger population.**]

■ Non Sequitur

Non sequitur, a Latin phrase meaning "it does not follow," presents a conclusion that is not the logical result of a claim or of evidence that precedes it.

Japanese children spend 40 percent more time in the classroom than, and perform better than, American children. American parents should take more interest in their children's schooling.
[**Both statements may be true, but the writer does not establish any logical connection between them.**]

▇ Bandwagon

The **bandwagon fallacy** suggests that if a majority of people express a belief or take an action, everyone else should think or do the same. Such arguments give the weight of truth or inevitability to the judgments of the majority, which may not be justified.

> Over 70 percent of Americans favor tariffs on imports from China, and you should, too.
> [**The argument falsely implies that the force of public opinion alone should sway undecided opinion. Such arguments are often bolstered by statistics from studies or surveys, but the use of numbers alone does not sufficiently support the writer's position. The advisability of tariffs should be decided on the basis of their effect on national and international interests, not on possibly uninformed or self-interested and emotional opinions.**]

▇ Red Herring

A **red herring** is an irrelevant issue introduced into an discussion to draw attention from the central issue.

> State boards of education should not vote to spend money for art and music programs when so many of our children fail to read at their grade levels.
> [**Deplorable as the children's poor preparation in reading may be, it has no bearing on the quality, or benefit to students, of arts education programs.**]

▇ Post Hoc, Ergo Propter Hoc

Post hoc, ergo propter hoc—a Latin phrase meaning "after this, therefore because of this"—suggests a cause-and-effect relationship between two actions, even though one action simply preceded the other.

Since the artificial sweetener aspartame was introduced in 1981, the cancer rates have risen in the United States.
[**Although cancer rates increased following the introduction of aspartame, there is not necessarily a verifiable link between the two.**]

Ad Hominem

Ad hominem, a Latin phrase meaning "to the man," is an attack on the people involved with an issue, rather than on the issue itself. By shifting focus from ideas to individuals, writers fail to address the real issues.

Freedom of speech statutes should be restricted. After all, current law supports Larry Flynt, enabling him to publish *Hustler,* an offensive, degrading magazine.
[**The issue of free speech statutes should be addressed on its own merits. The mention of Flynt, a visible and controversial publisher, sidetracks the discussion and fails to make any case against the statutes themselves.**]

False Analogy

A **false analogy** is a comparison that is not based on relevant points of similarity. For an analogy to be logical, the subjects must be similar in several important, not superficial, ways.

Today's stock market, just like the stock market in the 1920s, seems headed for trouble.
[**Although the stock market follows some similar procedures, today's market has many more checks and balances and regulations that make this analogy strained.**]

EXERCISE 5.5   Logical fallacies

Identify and explain the logical fallacies in the following sentences. (Available on disk.)

1. Jean Genet's plays should not be regarded so highly. After all, he was a thief and served time in prison.

2. Many Nobel Prize winners in science used animals in their experiments, so using animals in research must be acceptable.

3. I saw a man on a road crew sitting in the back of a truck reading a magazine and drinking a Coke. Obviously, road-crew jobs are extremely easy.

4. If the federal government stopped paying child support, fewer unmarried women would have children.

5. If business people can deduct the cost of their lunches, then factory workers should have the same right.

6. To reduce the deficit, all we have to do is increase taxes.

7. Unless we outlaw all corporate donations to candidates, all our politicians will become pawns of business.

8. New York has exceptional museums, beautiful parks, varied entertainment, and fabulous restaurants. It is a great place to raise a family.

9. Any student who tries hard enough is sure to make an *A* in the introductory speech class.

10. Since smoking marijuana is immoral, we should punish anyone caught using it.

5e   A Sample Argument

The following article appeared in the "My Turn" section of *Newsweek* magazine, 23 November 1998. Notations identify important features and strategies.

Learning the Hard Way
by Michael Denne

Denne begins his expressive-per-suasive essay with a personal anecdote.

It was after midnight when the police came for me. I was standing in the kitchen, stunned, not sure what had just happened or what to do about it. But it all became surrealistically clear as I was led from my own house in handcuffs, bathed in flashing colored lights. Having gone only a few hundred yards on our way to the station, we came upon more flashing lights at the scene of an accident. "See that," the cop snapped at me. "You did that."

The brief quotation creates immediacy and intensity, drawing readers into the essay.

Several warrants are embedded here: (1) society disapproves of drunk drivers, (2) society thinks they should be punished, and (3) prison is a suitable punishment for drunk drivers who injure others.

It's not easy being a menace to society, especially when you always thought you were one of the good guys. But that same society takes a particularly dim view of those of us who drink to excess, crash our cars and send innocent people to the emergency room with life-threatening injuries. So dim a view, in fact, that they send us to prison.

He uses *you* to personalize his writing; he acknowledges his "selfish stu-pidity"; he emphasizes in some detail that the teenagers are recovering.

Before you despise me too much, though, I'd like to report that no one was crippled or killed as a result of my selfish stupidity. Two teenagers did, however, spend a few weeks in the hospital and sev-eral months recovering, as they both suffered head trauma from my Chevy Blazer's broadsiding their Mazda RX-7. Nine months after the crash, at my sen-tencing hearing, the victims appeared as two walk-ing, talking, healthy-looking young adults. Their injuries lingered, though, in the form of a loss of hearing in one ear (for the girl), which may or may not come back, and memory loss (for the boy, who also broke his jaw and was semicomatose for a few weeks). Not quite as good as new, but awfully close and improving, considering their condition that first night in intensive care.

Denne's admissions ("no excuse" and "height of irresponsibility") demonstrate his candor, which establishes for him an ethical position from which to write.

I offer no excuse because there isn't one. What I did was the height of irresponsibility. Like everyone else, I've seen hit-and-run accidents on television and in the newspapers and wondered how the drivers could leave the victims behind. Well, I did, and I still don't know. It's called hit and run, but I didn't run anywhere. I wasn't wearing a seat belt and I'd slammed my head into the windshield. I was shocked, and so close to home I thought that if I could just get to that sanctuary, I'd know what to do and everything would be all right. But somewhere in my beer-soaked brain must have been the fear that generated more concern for myself than for anyone I might have hurt. And I have to live with that.

To underscore the personal costs of his drinking and driving, Denne provides some factual information (presented in dollar amounts), as well as some general details.

I've been locked up for more than a year now and have had plenty of time to think. It seems to me that there's a price exacted for every lesson we learn in life, and the cost is rarely proportional to the relative simplicity or complexity of the idea. Consequently, what should have been a no-brainer is quite often the most expensive education we're ever likely to receive. What it cost me to ignore the most ubiquitous warning in the world (the one not to drink and drive) was merely everything: my license, my car,

$30,000 in legal fees, a $50,000-a-year job I'd had for 10 years and my freedom are all casualties—with my house not far behind.

Denne emphasizes that the teenagers are recovering and that they have received substantial cash settlements. These elements attempt to do two things: (1) establish his ethicalness, since he did at least have good insurance coverage, and (2) demonstrate that there are, at least in some respects, positive outcomes of the accident.

For far too many people this subject will forever be anathema, because the lives of their loved ones have been ruined or ended by some recreational inebriate just like me. To them and countless others I got exactly what I deserve, even though an excellent recovery and $530,000 of liability insurance appear to have left the victims in pretty good shape. I'll not portray myself as some drunken Robin Hood, because these people truly suffered, but they are not from wealthy families and now may well have opportunities they otherwise would never have had. And that's good; they deserve [them].

I refuse to vilify the "demon" alcohol, because that's not what this is about. It's about responsibility. A few years ago, Miller Brewing [Company] promoted an awareness campaign with the slogan "Think when you drink." That's good, but it doesn't go far enough, because we can't think when we drink. It's got to be "Think before you drink"— because as any substance-abuse professional will tell you, judgment is the first faculty that goes.

Denne has several warrants in this paragraph: (1) people are, by nature, drawn to intoxication of one kind or another,

In his book of essays *Fates Worse Than Death,* Kurt Vonnegut wrote, "Life without moments of intoxication is not worth a pitcher of spit." Included therein is intoxication from love or joy or the mystery of life itself, but so [are], surely, a few belts at the corner

(2) harming oneself is, perhaps, acceptable, and (3) harming others is unacceptable.

bar. I'm no social scientist, but like anyone who's ever taken a college anthropology class, I learned that the society without a way to alter its perception is the exception to the rule. It is not aberrant behavior to celebrate, to alter one's consciousness, and to think that people will or should stop it is naive. But when it has a profoundly negative impact on the lives of others, it is totally unacceptable. In fact, it can be downright criminal.

In this very simple paragraph, Denne develops his argument by using one clearly expressed warrant after another.

My negligence was exactly that, though I am innocent of malice, of intent ever to hurt anyone. But it doesn't matter what you mean to do—it matters what you do. And few people know that better than I do.

The probation report said I'd led a respectable life but I should get six years in prison, anyway. The district attorney said I was a decent man and he felt sorry for me, but six years wasn't enough—I should do eight instead. And the judge agreed, but in his benevolence ruled that the extra two years could be served concurrently. There isn't space here to debate the deterrent value of a state prison sentence as opposed to alternative sentences, like making restitution to the injured through a work-furlough program or explaining the consequences of drinking and driving to high-school students, punishments that contain real value for the victims and the community.

Denne's introduction of alternative sentencing includes several implicit warrants: (1) prison sentences aren't always the best forms of restitution,

(2) alternatives are available, (3) some (like community service) may benefit the community, and (4) restitution that benefits the community is best.

As he moves to the closing of his essay, Denne makes a strong emotional appeal, hoping, we assume, both to share his feelings of remorse and to evoke understanding in his readers.

That I deserve to be punished is clearer to me than it ever could be to anyone who hasn't lived it. Until you wake up in a jail cell, not knowing whether the people now in the hospital will be permanently disfigured (or will cease to be altogether) as a result of your recklessness, you can't imagine how it feels. The weight of it is oppressive.

I'm ashamed to have to lend my name to some of the most loathsome behavior known, but not so much so that I won't put forth a face and a fair warning to those who still choose to drink and drive: thinking it could never happen to you is your first mistake—and it only gets worse from there. For everyone.

Effective Sentences

Sentences consist of words used in specific ways according to their parts of speech. Words combined into phrases, clauses, and sentences create meaning.

QUICK REFERENCE

Learning about the parts of speech is a means to an end: Technical knowledge of sentence elements allows you to analyze and improve your sentences.

▶ Use the most specific nouns that suit your meaning.

▶ Use only pronouns that have clear antecedents.

▶ Use verb tenses to create time distinctions.

▶ Use coordinating conjunctions to join equivalent elements; use subordinating conjunctions to join subordinate and independent clauses; use correlative conjunctions in pairs.

English has eight parts of speech: nouns, pronouns, verbs, adjectives, adverbs, conjunctions, prepositions, and interjections. Learning how words work together in sentences will allow you to analyze your writing and to build sentences that convey your exact meaning.

When analyzing the parts of speech in a sentence, note carefully how the words function. Remember that the same word can function as different parts of speech. For example, the word *stone* appears as a noun, a verb, and an adjective in the following sentences.

Noun

Stone—limestone, marble, and granite—is a common material for statuary.

Verb

In ancient times, it was common to *stone* criminals.

Adjective

Many campus buildings constructed in the 1930s and 1940s have *stone* façades.

6a   Nouns

Nouns name people, places, things, ideas, quantities, or conditions and can be proper, common, collective, abstract, or concrete.

Proper Nouns

Proper nouns name specific people, places, and things: *Virginia Woolf, Singapore, Corvette.* They are always capitalized.

> *Phillipe* went to the *Holocaust Museum* when he visited *Washington, DC.*

Common Nouns

Common nouns name people, places, and things by general type: *novelist, city, sports car.* They are not capitalized.

> My *cousin* went to a historical *museum* when he visited the *capital.*

Collective Nouns

Collective nouns name groups of people or things; although each group includes two or more members, it is usually considered *one* group: *team, class, group, audience.*

> At most colleges, the *faculty* has primary authority over curricular matters.

■ Abstract Nouns

Abstract nouns name ideas, qualities, and conditions: *freedom, honesty, shyness.*

■ Concrete Nouns

Concrete nouns name things or qualities perceptible by the senses: *table, pepper, warmth, noise.*

6b Pronouns

Pronouns substitute for nouns. Generally, a pronoun refers to a previously stated noun which is called an **antecedent.**

> Mahatma Gandhi led the struggle for India's independence from Britain. *His* primary means of opposition was passive resistance, *which* was subsequently employed by Martin Luther King, Jr. [*His* and *which* are the pronouns; *Mahatma Gandhi* and *passive resistance* are the antecedents]

Pronouns are classified as personal, possessive, reflexive, interrogative, demonstrative, indefinite, and relative, depending on their function in a sentence.

■ Personal Pronouns

Personal pronouns substitute for nouns that name people or things. The form of the pronoun depends on the gender and number of the antecedent and whether the pronoun is a subject or an object (see pages 232–37 and 238–46).

Subject		Object	
Singular	*Plural*	*Singular*	*Plural*
I	we	me	us
you	you	you	you
he		him	
she	they	her	them
it		it	

After Margaret Mead studied adolescents in Samoa, *she* observed that *they* did not experience stress as did teens in western cultures.

[*She* and *they* are the pronouns; *Margaret Mead* and *adolescents* are the antecedents.]

Possessive Pronouns

Possessive pronouns show ownership.

Singular	Plural
my, mine	our, ours
your, yours	your, yours
his, his	
her, hers	their, theirs
its, its	

For each pair, use the first form, often called a **pronoun-adjective,** with a noun; use the second form if the pronoun stands alone in place of a noun.

Thomas, *your* solution is more practical than *mine*.
[*Your*, a pronoun-adjective, modifies the noun *solution; mine*
stands alone but also implies reference to the same antecedent,
solution.]

■ Reflexive Pronouns

Reflexive pronouns show that someone or something in the
sentence is acting for or on itself; if used to show emphasis, they
are sometimes called **intensive pronouns.**

Singular	Plural
myself	ourselves
yourself	yourselves
himself	
herself	themselves
itself	

Self-related action

Misanthropes hate humankind, but they usually like *themselves*
well enough.
[*Themselves* clarifies a self-related action.]

Emphasis

A true misanthrope shuns social interaction, preferring to stay by
him- or *herself.*
[*Him-* or herself stresses that a misanthrope wants no
company.]

Reflexive pronouns require antecedents within the same
sentence and, as a result, should not be used as subjects.

Laura and ~~myself~~ collaborated on the article.
[*Myself* cannot function as the subject of the sentence.]

■ Interrogative Pronouns

Interrogative pronouns are used to ask questions.

Subject	Object
who	whom
whoever	whomever
Other Interrogative Pronouns	
what	whose
which	

Who won the Nobel Peace Prize this year?

To *whom* should I send the application?

Which musical had the longer Broadway run, <u>Les Misérables</u> or <u>Phantom of the Opera</u>?

■ Demonstrative Pronouns

Demonstrative pronouns are used alone to substitute for specific nouns.

Singular	Plural
this	these
that	those

When used with nouns, these four words function as **demonstrative adjectives.** If the antecedent of the demonstrative pronoun is unclear, use the demonstrative adjective with the noun.

Godfrey hesitated before speaking. That~pause~ helped him to control his emotions.
[Does *that* refer to hesitating or speaking or both?]

■ Indefinite Pronouns

Indefinite pronouns, pronouns without specific antecedents, serve as general subjects or objects in sentences. Because indefinite pronouns can be singular or plural, choose the verbs that agree with the indefinite pronouns.

Common Indefinite Pronouns		
Singular		
another	either	no one
any	everybody	nothing
anybody	everyone	one
anyone	everything	somebody
anything	neither	someone
each	nobody	something
Plural		
all	few	several
both	many	some

When used alone, these words are pronouns. Some of these words can also modify nouns and thus serve as pronoun-adjectives: *any* passport, *another* guess, *several* women.

Someone is sure to discover that the dates on the schedule are inaccurate.
[**The singular pronoun is the subject of the sentence.**]

Both archaeologists agree that their earlier finds were misleading.
[**The pronoun-adjective modifies *archaeologists*.**]

■ Relative Pronouns

Relative pronouns substitute for nouns already mentioned in the sentence and are used to introduce adjective or noun clauses.

To Refer to People	
who	whoever
whom	whomever

To Refer to Things	
that	which
what	whichever
whatever	

To Refer to People or Things	
that (generally for things)	
whose (generally for people)	

Musicians *who* achieve notoriety quickly often fade from view just as quickly.

Anger *that* is not expressed is often the most damaging.

Sometimes the relative pronoun *that* can be left out (understood) when the noun-clause relationship is clear without it. As a general rule, use *that* to introduce essential information but use *which* to introduce information that can be omitted.

An object *that is more than one hundred years old* is considered an antique.
[**The clause is essential to the meaning of the sentence.**]

The steamer trunk, *which we found in Aunt Natalia's attic,* belonged to my great grandfather.
[**The clause can be omitted without altering the meaning of the sentence.**]

■ EXERCISE 6.1   Nouns and pronouns

Underline the nouns and pronouns in each of the following sentences and label each according to type.

1. Acupuncture, a medical treatment, developed centuries ago in China.

2. The acupuncturist uses extremely thin gold needles to pierce a patient's skin.

3. Patients frequently receive sedation before the treatment begins and the needles are implanted.

4. The areas where the needles are inserted do not necessarily correspond to the areas of discomfort or pain.

5. Those who have been helped by acupuncture strongly advocate the treatment.

6. Why should those of us who have not tried acupuncture question their satisfaction?

7. Teams of Western scientists have studied acupuncture and found no physiological explanations for its success.

8. Nevertheless, success rates for patients who have faith in the procedure suggest that we can learn more than we already know about the psychological effects of medical treatments.

9. Ironically, while acupuncture has been attracting attention in Europe and the United States in recent years, its use in China has declined.

10. Some say acupuncture is merely a medical hoax, but others continue to search for scientific explanations for its apparent success.

■ **EXERCISE 6.2   Nouns and pronouns**

Revise the following paragraph, replacing some nouns with pronouns to achieve a smoother style. (Available on disk.)

Theodore Roosevelt, the twenty-sixth president of the United States, was an individualist. Nonetheless, Roosevelt served the public well. Roosevelt's individualistic tendencies were illustrated first by Roosevelt's attempts at boxing, an uncommon activity for an upperclass gentleman at Harvard. After Roosevelt's graduation, Roosevelt made a trip west, where Roosevelt experimented briefly with ranching and cowboy life. Roosevelt returned to the East to serve in the government, but in 1898 Roosevelt resigned Roosevelt's post as secretary of the navy to organize the Rough Riders, a regiment formed to fight in the Spanish-American War. The Rough Riders found Roosevelt to be an able leader, and though the Rough Riders did not follow Roosevelt up San Juan Hill as legend has it, the Rough Riders did fight with Roosevelt in Cuba. Roosevelt returned to the United States a hero; Roosevelt's notoriety helped Roosevelt to win the mayoral race of New York. Two years later, Roosevelt was elected vice president in spite of opposition from political bosses and industrial leaders. Political bosses and industrial leaders must have found Roosevelt's freewheeling individualism unsettling and certainly unpredictable. The political bosses and industrial leaders fought Roosevelt in Roosevelt's antitrust actions when Roosevelt became president after McKinley's assassination. Throughout Roosevelt's presidency and the rest of Roosevelt's life, Roosevelt continued to act as an individual but with the public good in mind.

6c Verbs

A **verb** expresses an action (*organize, sing*) or a state of being (*seem, was*). Grammatically complete sentences contain at least one verb.

■ Types of Verbs

The three types of verbs are action, linking, and auxiliary.

Action Verbs

Action verbs express both physical and mental activities.

action verb
Will Rogers slyly lampooned American politics.

action verb
He thought politicians took themselves too seriously.

Action verbs are either intransitive or transitive. **Intransitive verbs** do not need direct objects (a person or thing that receives the action of the verb, like *politics* in the previous first example) to complete their meaning.

subj.　intrans. verb
The negative ad campaign backfired.
[**Without a direct object, the sentence is still clear.**]

Transitive verbs require direct objects to complete their meaning.

subj.　trans. verb　d.o.　　d.o.
Acid rain threatens forests and wildlife.
[**Without the direct objects** *forests* **and** *wildlife,* **the sentence's meaning would be unclear.**]

Some verbs can be either intransitive or transitive, depending on the meaning of the sentence.

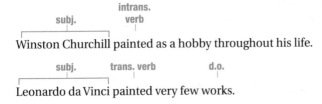

Winston Churchill painted as a hobby throughout his life.

Leonardo da Vinci painted very few works.

Linking Verbs

Linking verbs express either a state of being or a condition.

Common Linking Verbs				
Forms of **to be**				
am	be	being		was
are	been	is		were
Other linking verbs				
appear	feel	look	seem	sound
become	grow	make	smell	taste

Forms of *to be* join the subject of a sentence or a clause with a complement (either a predicate noun or a predicate adjective), creating a parallel relationship.

With predicate nouns

linking verb

Houdini is the best-known escape artist of the twentieth century. [*Houdini* (subject) = *artist* (predicate noun). The predicate noun further identifies Houdini.]

With predicate adjectives

linking verb

Woodrow Wilson was enthusiastic about the League of Nations.
[*Woodrow Wilson* (subject) = *enthusiastic* (predicate adjective).
The predicate adjective describes Wilson.]

Auxiliary Verbs

Auxiliary verbs (or **helping verbs**) work with other verbs to create verb tenses or to form questions.

Common Auxiliary Verbs				
Forms of **to be**				
am	been	is	were	
are	being	was		
Other auxiliary verbs				
can	do	has	might	should
could	does	have	must	will
did	had	may	ought to	would

aux.
verb   verb

The protesters will attract news teams.

aux.
verb   verb

Greenpeace must oppose chemical dumping in our waterways.

When modifiers are used, they often separate the auxiliary verb from the main verb. In forming questions, the auxiliary usually precedes the subject. Auxiliary verbs always precede main verbs.

aux.
verb   mod.   verb

The protesters *will* undoubtedly *attract* news teams.

aux. verb   verb

Must Greenpeace *oppose* chemical dumping in our waterways?

■ EXERCISE 6.3   Verbs

Underline and label the verbs in the following sentences.

1. Founded in the mid-1960s, the National Organization of Women (NOW) is a well-known feminist organization.

2. From its beginning, NOW has opposed gender-based discrimination in the workplace.

3. Through lobbying efforts, NOW has promoted legislation to guarantee women equal pay and employment opportunities.

4. To ensure that their message is heard, representatives of NOW often appear on talk shows and news shows.

5. As society changes, NOW will continually redefine its role in American political and social life.

■ Forms of Verbs

In English, verbs have three principal parts or forms: the infinitive, the past tense, and the past participle. The **infinitive** is a verb's primary form (*work, cope*); it is often used with *to*. For regular verbs, the **past tense** and **past participle** are formed by adding *-ed* or *-d* to the infinitive (*worked, coped*).

Principal Parts of Regular Verbs		
Infinitive	*Past tense*	*Past participle*
select	selected	selected
inform	informed	informed
open	opened	opened

Many common English verbs are irregular and form the past tense and past participles in a variety of ways. Become familiar with the principal parts of common irregular verbs.

Principal Parts of Common Irregular Verbs		
Infinitive	*Past tense*	*Past participle*
arise	arose	arisen
awake	awoke, awakened	awakened
be	was/were	been
beat	beat	beaten, beat
begin	began	begun
bend	bent	bent
bite	bit	bitten
blow	blew	blown
break	broke	broken
bring	brought	brought
build	built	built
burst	burst	burst
catch	caught	caught
choose	chose	chosen
come	came	come
cost	cost	cost
creep	crept	crept
deal	dealt	dealt
dig	dug	dug
dive	dived, dove	dived
do	did	done
drag	dragged	dragged
draw	drew	drawn

Infinitive	Past tense	Past participle
dream	dreamed, dreamt	dreamed, dreamt
drink	drank	drunk
drive	drove	driven
eat	ate	eaten
fall	fell	fallen
fight	fought	fought
find	found	found
fly	flew	flown
forbid	forbade, forbad	forbidden
forget	forgot	forgotten, forgot
freeze	froze	frozen
get	got	got, gotten
give	gave	given
go	went	gone
grow	grew	grown
hang (to suspend)	hung	hung
hang (to execute)	hanged	hanged
have	had	had
hear	heard	heard
hurt	hurt	hurt
keep	kept	kept
know	knew	known
lay (to put)	laid	laid
lead	led	led
lend	lent	lent
let	let	let
lie (to recline)	lay	lain
lie (to tell an untruth)	lied	lied

Infinitive	*Past tense*	*Past participle*
lose	lost	lost
make	made	made
read	read	read
ride	rode	ridden
ring	rang	rung
rise	rose	risen
run	ran	run
say	said	said
see	saw	seen
send	sent	sent
set (to put)	set	set
shake	shook	shaken
shine	shone, shined	shone, shined
shoot	shot	shot
shrink	shrank, shrunk	shrunk, shrunken
sing	sang	sung
sink	sank	sunk
sit (to take a seat)	sat	sat
slay	slew	slain
sleep	slept	slept
speak	spoke	spoken
spin	spun	spun
spring	sprang	sprung
stand	stood	stood
steal	stole	stolen
sting	stung	stung
strike	struck	struck, stricken
strive	strove, strived	striven
swear	swore	sworn

Infinitive	Past tense	Past participle
swim	swam	swum
swing	swung	swung
take	took	taken
teach	taught	taught
tear	tore	torn
throw	threw	thrown
wake (to wake up)	woke, waked	woken, waked
waken (to rouse)	wakened	wakened
wear	wore	worn
wring	wrung	wrung
write	wrote	written

■ Verb Tenses

English has three simple tenses (present, past, and future), three perfect tenses (present perfect, past perfect, and future perfect), and six progressive tenses, one corresponding to each simple and each perfect tense.

Present Tense

The **present tense** indicates an existing condition or state, something occurring at the present time, or a habitual action.

Owls *keep* rodent populations under control.
[**existing condition**]

Federal legislation *protects* a number of endangered birds.
[**occurring at the present time**]

Many North American birds *migrate* to Central America for the winter.
[**habitual action**]

Past Tense

The **past tense** indicates that something has already occurred and is in the past.

Cesar Chávez *founded* the United Farm Workers, an organization of California food harvesters.

Future Tense

The **future tense** indicates that something will happen in the future. Form the future tense by adding the auxiliary verb *will* to the infinitive. (*Shall,* an alternative auxiliary, is rarely used in current American writing.)

Film producers, it seems, *will copy* any previously successful format if profits are likely.

Present Perfect Tense

The **present perfect tense** indicates that something began in the past and continues into the present or that it occurred at an unspecified time in the past. Form the present perfect tense by using the auxiliary verb *has* or *have* plus the past participle of the verb.

Global warming *has contributed* to today's erratic weather patterns.
[beginning in the past, continuing into the present]

Inclement weather *has* always *created* problems for farmers.
[unspecified time]

Past Perfect Tense

The **past perfect tense** indicates that an action was completed before some time in the past. Form the past perfect tense by adding the auxiliary verb *had* to the past participle.

Great cities *had flourished* in the Western Hemisphere long before Spanish explorers reached North and South America.

Future Perfect Tense

The **future perfect tense** indicates that an action will be completed before a certain time in the future. Form the future perfect tense by adding the auxiliary verbs *will have* to the past participle.

> In fifty years, we *will have depleted* many of the earth's natural resources.

Progressive Tenses

For every basic tense, an equivalent **progressive tense** exists to indicate continuing action. Form the progressive tenses by using a form of the verb *to be* (*am, are, is, was, were, will be, has been, have been, had been,* or *will have been*) and the present participle (*-ing*) of the verb.

Progressive Tenses	
Present progressive	*is playing*
Past progressive	*was playing*
Future progressive	*will be playing*
Present perfect progressive	*has been playing*
Past perfect progressive	*had been playing*
Future perfect progressive	*will have been playing*

■ **EXERCISE 6.4 Verb tenses**

Underline the verbs in the following sentences and label each verb with its tense.

1. In 1947, Kenneth Arnold, a pilot, described saucer-shaped objects that traveled at great speeds.

2. Since then, thousands of people around the world have reported similar "unidentified flying objects" (UFOs).

3. During the 1950s and 1960s, Project Bluebook, a division of the U.S. Air Force, attempted to explain these sightings and found that most were misinterpretations of natural phenomena.

4. By the late 1960s, Project Bluebook had served its purpose—it reassured military and civilian populations that the earth was not being watched or attacked—and was consequently disbanded.

5. Today some people still claim to see bright, formless objects in our skies—and no doubt such claims will continue.

■ **EXERCISE 6.5 Verbs**

The following passage from Benjamin Franklin's letter describing how to reproduce his electrical experiments is written primarily in the present tense. Reconstruct the passage as though Franklin had written a narrative of his procedure. Make appropriate changes in the verb forms. (Hint: Many verbs will be in the past tense.) (Available on disk.)

Make a small cross of two light strips of cedar, the arms so long as to reach to the four corners of a large thin silk handkerchief when extended; tie the corners of the handkerchief to the extremities of the cross, so you have the body of a kite; which being properly accommodated with a tail, loop, and string, will rise into the air, like those made of paper; but this being silk, is fitter to bear the wet and wind of a thunder-gust. To the top of the upright stick of the cross is to be fixed a very sharp-pointed wire, rising a foot or more above the wood. To the end of the twine, next the hand, is to be tied a silk ribbon, and where the silk and the tie join, a key may be fastened. This kite is to be raised when a thunder-gust appears to be coming on, and the person who holds the string must stand within a door or window, or under some cover, so that the silk ribbon may not be

wet; and care must be taken that the twine does not touch the frame
of the door or window. . . . And when the rain has wet the kite and
twine, so that it can conduct the electrical fire freely, you will find it
stream out plentifully from the key on the approach of your knuckle.
—Benjamin Franklin, "Letter to Peter Collinson"

6d   Adjectives

An **adjective** modifies or limits a noun or pronoun.

Questions Adjectives Answer	
What kind?	*copper* skillet
Which one?	the *fourth* presentation
How many?	*ten* tribes
Whose?	*Jeffrey's* assessment

■ Forms of Adjectives

Adjectives come in three forms: positive, comparative, and
superlative.

Positive Adjectives

A **positive adjective** modifies a noun or pronoun without suggesting any comparisons.

This computer is *fast.*

Comparative Adjectives

A **comparative adjective** compares two people, places, things, ideas, qualities, conditions, or actions.

Darius's computer is *faster* than mine.

Superlative Adjectives

A **superlative adjective** compares three or more items.

This is the *fastest* computer on the market.

■ Kinds of Adjectives

Regular Adjectives

A **regular adjective** precedes the word it modifies. Several adjectives can modify the same word.

                           adj.   adj.   noun

Grant Wood's *American Gothic* shows a grim, thin farmer holding a pitchfork and standing next to a plain, dour woman.

When adjectives in a series function together as one modifier—that is, when each word alone cannot modify the noun or pronoun—hyphenate the series of words.

<u>American Gothic</u> has been parodied in numerous *laughter-inducing* advertisements.
[not *laughter* advertisements or *inducing* advertisements but *laughter-inducing* advertisements]

Predicate Adjectives

A **predicate adjective** follows a linking verb but modifies the subject of the sentence or clause.

                        pred. adj.   pred. adj.

Vincent Van Gogh's paintings are both *colorful* and heavily *textured.*

When adjectives in a series work as a unit but are in the predicate-adjective position, do not hyphenate them.

Paul Rubens's images of saints are often *larger than life.*

■ Articles and Demonstrative Adjectives

The **articles**—*a, an,* and *the*—and the demonstrative pronouns—*this, that, these,* and *those*—also function as **demonstrative adjectives.**

The shortest distance between two points is *a* straight line.

Those documents go in *this* folder.

6e Adverbs

Adverbs modify verbs, adjectives, other adverbs, phrases, clauses, or entire sentences. Although many adverbs end in *-ly,* many do not, and many words ending in *-ly* are not adverbs. Consequently, identify adverbs by their function in sentences.

The lonely widower was treated well by his neighbors.
[*Lonely* is an adjective; *well* is an adverb.]

Questions Adverbs Answer	
How?	*slowly* approached
When?	laughed *first*
Where?	searched *everywhere*
How often?	praised *repeatedly*
To what extent?	*thoroughly* disliked

■ Forms of Adverbs

Adverbs come in three forms: positive, comparative, and superlative.

Positive Adverbs

A **positive adverb** modifies a verb, an adjective, another adverb, a phrase, a clause, or an entire sentence but does not suggest a comparison.

> Passengers on early trains traveled *quickly* to their destinations.
> [**modifies the verb** *traveled*]

Comparative Adverbs

A **comparative adverb** compares two actions or conditions.

> Diesel trains traveled *more quickly* than earlier steam engines.
> [**modifies** *traveled,* **comparing the two traveling speeds**]

Superlative Adverbs

A **superlative adverb** compares three or more actions or conditions.

> Of passengers choosing ground transportation, those riding today's electric "bullet trains" travel *most quickly.*
> [**modifies** *travel,* **comparing the speeds among forms of ground transportation**]

■ EXERCISE 6.6   Adjectives and adverbs

Underline the adjectives and adverbs in the following sentences and draw arrows to show the word or group of words that each modifies.

1. American folklore has created a number of important national heroes, among them Abraham Lincoln.

2. Lincoln, the sixteenth president of the United States, was a man destined to become a legend.

3. His solemn, idiosyncratic appearance made him an easily recognizable figure, and his pivotal role during the Civil War clearly made him an important historical character.

4. Yet the reverential anecdotes and the blatant fabrications about him must surely seem questionable.

5. Lincoln's early life, though austere, was not backward, yet the rail-splitting Abe of the rustic log cabin in New Salem far overshadows the sophisticated lawyer that Lincoln clearly was in Springfield.

6. Lincoln belonged to no Christian church, yet he was often depicted in Christ-like terms as an always suffering, always kind, and always patient man.

7. Folklore has undoubtedly skewed the biographical facts of Lincoln's life, but it has created a fascinating—albeit false—vision of a man.

■ **EXERCISE 6.7 Adjectives and adverbs**

Underline the adjectives and adverbs in the following paragraph and indicate with an arrow the word or group of words that each modifies.

My favorite spot at Aunt Ruth and Uncle Dan's house is the small, secluded patio just outside their bedroom. Every time I quietly open the sliding doors and step outside, I know I will feel more peaceful. The 10-by-10-foot patio is brick, meticulously set in a herringbone design. A comfortable, well-padded lounge chair provides a place to sit, and a small redwood table is a convenient spot to place my usual drink, a tall glass of Aunt Ruth's lightly spiced tea. Once comfortably seated, I always enjoy the various flowers, my favorite feature. Close to the front edge of the patio are pink, plum, red, and yellow moss roses, gently trailing their waxy green stems onto the dull red bricks. Slightly back, radiating away from the patio, are miniature yellow and orange marigolds, with their dense, round flowers set against dark green, sharp-edged leaves. Close behind those are Aunt Ruth and Uncle Dan's prize roses—white, pink, red, and yellow tea roses that are carefully pruned. The small buds, usually a darker color, contrast noticeably with the large open blossoms that always remind me of fine damask. I always love to escape from the cheerful but noisy family activities to this secluded spot where the flowers are so beautiful. Inevitably, a visit to this floral oasis makes me feel more tranquil than before.

6f   Conjunctions

Conjunctions link words, phrases, or clauses. They show relationships of equivalence, contrast, alternatives, chronology, and cause and effect. Conjunctions may be coordinating, subordinating, or correlative.

■ Coordinating Conjunctions

Coordinating conjunctions link equivalent sentence parts and are the most commonly used conjunctions.

Coordinating Conjunctions			
and	for	or	yet
but	nor	so	

A form of musical drama, the opera is acted *and* sung.
[**joining verbs**]

A comic form of opera, the operetta is acted *and* sung, *but* it also includes spoken dialogue.
[**joining nouns and clauses**]

■ Subordinating Conjunctions

Subordinating conjunctions introduce subordinate clauses (those that cannot stand alone as sentences) and link them to independent clauses (those that can stand alone as sentences).

Common Subordinating Conjunctions			
after	because	so that	whenever
although	before	that	where
as	even if	though	whereas
as if	even though	unless	wherever
as long as	if	until	whether
as though	since	when	while

subordinate clause

Although its initial purpose was to serve Congress, the Library of Congress is now open to all Americans.

subordinate clause

The collection is relatively accessible, *even though* it is the largest library in America.

■ Correlative Conjunctions

Correlative conjunctions always work in pairs and provide additional emphasis. The words, phrases, or clauses joined by these correlative constructions must be written in parallel form.

Correlative Conjunctions	
both . . . and	neither . . . nor
either . . . or	not only . . . but also

Both Mobil *and* Atlantic Richfield underwrite programs for the Public Broadcasting Service.

Many programs are seen *not only* on PBS *but also* on the BBC, England's public television network.

■ Conjunctive Adverbs

Conjunctive adverbs connect ideas in independent clauses or sentences. Like other adverbs, conjunctive adverbs can appear in any position in a sentence. (See sections 22c and 22d for information on punctuating conjunctive adverbs.)

Common Conjunctive Adverbs		
accordingly	however	next
also	incidentally	nonetheless
besides	indeed	otherwise
consequently	instead	similarly
finally	likewise	still
further	meanwhile	then
furthermore	moreover	therefore
hence	nevertheless	thus

Conjunctive adverbs show relationships similar to those shown by conjunctions. For example, the coordinating conjunctions *but* and *yet* signal a simple contrast between balanced clauses; the subordinating conjunctions *although, even though,* and *though* also signal contrast but emphasize one clause over the other; the conjunctive adverb *however* signals contrast but keeps the clauses separate.

Coordinating conjunction

Children learn to use computers with ease, *but* most adults learn with some difficulty.

Subordinating conjunction

Although children learn to use computers with ease, most adults learn with some difficulty.

Conjunctive adverb

Children learn to use computers with ease. Most adults, *however,* learn with some difficulty.

Since they are punctuated differently (see section 22c), it is important to distinguish between short conjunctive adverbs and other short conjunctions. A simple method is to count the letters in the word: all conjunctive adverbs contain at least four letters, while coordinating conjunctions contain either two or three letters.

■ **EXERCISE 6.8   Conjunctions**

Use conjunctions to combine the following sets of sentences. Some rewording will be necessary. (Available on disk.)

1. Nicolas-Joseph Cugnot built a steam-powered, three-wheeled vehicle in 1769. It was difficult to build. It was too troublesome to maintain.

2. Carl Benz and Gottlieb Daimler began producing gasoline-powered cars in Germany in the 1880s. Ranson Olds and James Packard began production at the same time in the United States.

3. By 1908, 241 companies in the United States made cars. Henry Ford introduced the assembly-line-produced Model T that same year.

4. By 1930, cars were extremely common throughout the world. Over the next four decades, American cars got progressively bigger. European cars were comparatively small.

5. Following the international oil crisis of the 1970s, even American cars became smaller and more fuel efficient. By the 1990s, however, fuel prices dropped again. American cars once more became larger and less fuel efficient.

6g Prepositions

Prepositions link words in sentences. **Prepositional phrases** consist of a preposition, a noun or pronoun (the object of the preposition), and frequently modifiers.

                          prep.   obj.

We seem to be losing the fight *against crime.*

             pron.
    prep. adj. adj.   obj.

Because of his heretical views, Galileo was excommunicated.

Prepositional phrases modify specific words or phrases, functioning sometimes as adverbs (answering questions like *when, where,* or *how often*) and sometimes as adjectives (answering questions like *what kind* or *whose*).

                   prep.   obj.

Anne Frank's diary was found *in a secret garret apartment* and
         prep.   obj.

published *after World War II.*
[Adverbial functions: Where was it found? When was it published?]

         prep.   obj.   prep.   obj.

Her descriptions *of family life* include episodes *of wry humor*
  prep.   obj.

and *of intense despair.*
[Adjective functions: What kinds of descriptions? What kinds of episodes?]

Common Prepositions		
Single-word prepositions		
about	by	outside
above	concerning	over
across	despite	past
after	down	since
against	during	through
along	except	throughout
among	for	till
around	from	to
at	in	toward
before	inside	under
behind	into	underneath
below	like	until
beneath	near	up
beside	of	upon
besides	off	with
between	on	within
beyond	onto	without
but	out	

Multiple-word prepositions		
according to	in addition to	in spite of
ahead of	in case of	inside of
as well as	in front of	instead of
because of	in place of	rather than

■ **EXERCISE 6.9** **Prepositions**

Underline the prepositional phrases in the following paragraph and label the preposition and its object in each phrase.

The dog has got more fun out of Man than Man has got out of the dog, for the clearly demonstrable reason that Man is the more laughable of the two animals. The dog has long been bemused by the singular activities and the curious practices of men, cocking his head inquiringly to one side, intently watching and listening to the strangest goings-on in the world. He has seen men sing together and fight one another in the same evening. He has watched them go to bed when it is time to get up, and get up when it is time to go to bed. He has observed them destroying the soil in vast areas, and nurturing it in small patches. He has stood by while men built strong and solid houses for rest and quiet, and then filled them with lights and bells and machinery. His sensitive nose, which can detect what's cooking in the next township, has caught at one and the same time the bewildering smells of the hospital and the munitions factory. He has seen men raise up great cities to heaven and then blow them to hell.
—James Thurber, "A Dog's Eye View of Man"

6h Interjections

Interjections express surprise or other emotion or provide transitions in sentences.

Okay, I'll print your paper for you.

Oh no! The printer can't be broken again!

Strong interjections may be followed by a period or an exclamation point; milder interjections are joined to a sentence with a comma. Because most interjections are conversational, use them sparingly in formal writing.

■ EXERCISE 6.10   Parts of speech

Indicate the part of speech of the numbered and italicized words and phrases in the following paragraphs. For verbs, name the specific tense.

In the (1) *old* days, when I (2) *was writing* a great deal of (3) *fiction,* there would come, once in a while, moments when I was (4) *stymied.* (5) *Suddenly,* I would find I (6) *had written* (7) *myself* (8) *into* a hole and could see no way out. To take care of that, (9) *I* developed a (10) *technique* which (11) *invariably* worked.

It was simply this—I (12) *went* (13) *to* the movies. Not just any movie. I had to pick a movie which was loaded with action (14) *but* (15) *which* made no demands on the (16) *intellect.* (17) *As* I watched, I did my best to avoid any (18) *conscious* thinking concerning my (19) *problem,* and (20) *when* I came out of the movie I knew exactly what I would have to do to put the story back on track.

It never failed.   —Isaac Asimov, "The Eureka Phenomenon"

7 Sentences

Sentences contain at least a subject and a verb and express a complete thought. Although sentences do not depend on groups of words outside of themselves to make their meanings clear, they may contain words, phrases, and clauses—in addition to the essential subject and verb—that enhance their internal clarity.

QUICK REFERENCE

Learn about parts and kinds of sentences so that you can analyze and revise your writing.

▶ Sentences must include a subject and a predicate.

▶ Phrases cannot stand alone but must be parts of sentences.

▶ Subordinate clauses cannot stand alone but must be joined to independent clauses.

▶ Use subjects, predicates, phrases, and clauses to create simple, compound, complex, and compound-complex sentences.

7a Parts of Sentences

A **sentence** consists of at least a subject and verb. As the simplest complete expression of meaning, it is the basic unit of written communication.

■ Subjects

The **subject** of a sentence is the person, place, thing, idea, quality, or condition that acts or is acted upon or that is described or identified in the sentence.

subj.

Gauguin fled to the South Pacific in search of unspoiled beauty and primitive innocence.

The subject consists of one or more nouns or pronouns, together with related modifiers. The subject generally appears near the beginning of a sentence, but it can appear in other positions as well.

Subjects of sentences can never be part of prepositional phrases because the nouns and pronouns in prepositional phrases serve as objects of the preposition and therefore cannot also be subjects.

Subjects can be simple, compound, or complete.

Simple Subjects

A **simple subject** consists of a single word.

simple subj.

Machiavelli changed the way rulers thought about governing. [*Machiavelli* performed the action, *changed*.]

Sometimes the subject *you* is unstated but understood in an imperative sentence (a request or command).

[You] Read *The Prince* if you want to understand Machiavelli's ideas.

Compound Subjects

A **compound subject** consists of two or more simple subjects joined by a conjunction.

compound subject

simple subj.   simple subj.

Locke and Descartes had different views on knowledge.

Complete Subjects

A **complete subject** contains the simple subject plus any words modifying it: adjectives, adverbs modifying adjectives, and prepositional phrases.

complete subject

simple subj.

Modern students of both education and philosophy read both philosophers' works.

■ EXERCISE 7.1   Subjects

Underline the complete subjects in the following sentences. Bracket and label simple subjects; bracket compound subjects and draw an arrow joining the simple subjects within them.

1. The musical, a combination of drama and music, developed as a distinctly American art form.

2. Emerging from vaudeville traditions, productions like George M. Cohan's *Little Johnny Jones* offered engaging tunes like "Yankee Doodle Boy" and "Give My Regards to Broadway" in very predictable plots.

3. However, in 1927, Jerome Kern and Oscar Hammerstein presented *Show Boat,* the first major musical based on a respected novel, and changed musicals forever.

4. *South Pacific, My Fair Lady, West Side Story,* and *Oklahoma!* remain the most lasting contributions of the 1940s and 1950s, the golden years of the American musical.

5. In recent decades, British musicals have enjoyed both critical and popular success on Broadway while American productions have often seemed uninspired by comparison.

■ Predicates

The **predicate** of a sentence expresses the action or state of being of the subject. It states what the subject does, what it is, or what has been done to it.

predicate

simple pred.

As a child prodigy, Mozart was paraded through the aristocratic houses of Europe.

A predicate consists of one or more verbs, together with any modifiers or complements. (Complements are discussed on pages 145–47.) Like subjects, predicates can be simple, compound, or complete. In questions, the parts of the predicate are usually separated by the subject.

Simple Predicates

A **simple predicate** consists of the main verb and any auxiliaries.

simple predicate

Vinyl records dominated the recording industry for nearly four decades.

Compound Predicates

A **compound predicate** consists of two or more verbs joined by a conjunction.

compound predicate

simple pred.

Compact discs have revolutionized the recording industry and,

simple pred.

for the most part, have replaced vinyl records as the most popular recording form.

Complete Predicates

A **complete predicate** consists of the simple or compound predicate plus all related modifiers: adjectives, adverbs, prepositional phrases, and any complements.

complete predicate

simple pred.

CDs provide crisp, clear, consistent sound .

■ EXERCISE 7.2 Predicates

Underline the complete predicates in the following sentences. Bracket and label simple predicates; bracket compound predicates and draw an arrow joining the simple predicates within them.

1. Professional ice hockey associations were first formed in Canada near the beginning of the twentieth century.
2. The first major league, the National Hockey Association, was founded in 1910 and included only teams from eastern Canada.
3. The following year, the Pacific Coast League organized teams from western Canadian cities, cities of the American northwest, and later other American cities.
4. In 1917, the National Hockey Association was reorganized to form the National Hockey League.
5. Since then, teams from both Canada and the United States have competed throughout the regular season and have vied for the Stanley Cup, the symbol of the League championship.

■ EXERCISE 7.3 Subjects and predicates

Underline and label the simple and compound subjects and predicates in each of the following sentences.

Most tarantulas live in the tropics, but several species occur in the temperate zone and a few are common in the southern U.S. Some varieties are large and have powerful fangs with which they can inflict a deep wound. These formidable looking spiders do not, however, attack man; you can hold one in your hand, if you are gentle, without being bitten. Their bite is dangerous only to insects and small mammals such as mice; for man it is no worse than a hornet's sting.

Tarantulas customarily live in deep cylindrical burrows, from which they emerge at dusk and into which they retire at dawn. Mature males wander about after dark in search of females and occasionally stray into houses. After mating, the male dies in a few weeks, but a female lives much longer and can mate several years in succession. In a Paris museum is a tropical specimen which is said to have been living in captivity for 25 years.   —Alexander Petrunkevitch, "The Spider and the Wasp"

■ Complements

A **complement** completes the meaning of a transitive verb. Complements follow the verb and are part of the complete predicate. They can be simple or compound.

Direct Objects

Direct objects complete the action of a transitive verb by answering the questions *what* or *whom.*

Agnes DeMille choreographed the *dances* in Oklahoma!
[*What* **did she choreograph?**]

Indirect Objects

Indirect objects indicate to whom or for whom the action of the transitive verb is intended. Indirect objects follow transitive verbs but always precede direct objects.

DeMille gave *dancers* interesting and challenging roles.
[*To whom* **did she give these roles?**]

Predicate Nouns

Predicate nouns follow linking verbs and restate or identify the subject of a sentence. For a discussion of pronouns used as predicate nouns, see pages 238–40.

DeMille was a skillful and innovative *choreographer.*
[*Choreographer* **restates the subject, *DeMille.***]

Predicate Adjectives

Predicate adjectives follow linking verbs and modify the subject of a sentence.

> DeMille's choreography was sometimes *playful,* frequently *surprising,* and often *austere.*
> [*Playful, surprising,* and *austere* describe the subject, *choreography.*]

■ EXERCISE 7.4   Complements

Underline the complements in the following sentences and label them as direct objects, indirect objects, predicate nouns, or predicate adjectives. Draw an arrow between the parts of compound complements.

1. The year 1896 was not only a tribute to humanity's best but also a reflection of humanity's worst characteristics.

2. At the Democratic Convention, William Jennings Bryan gave his "Cross of Gold" speech and sparked interest in an uneventful campaign.

3. The British Patent Office granted Guglielmo Marconi a patent for the wireless telegraph.

4. When the United States Supreme Court handed down its *Plessy* v. *Ferguson* decision, it established a "separate but equal" standard that institutionalized racism.

5. Athens, Greece, was the site of the first modern Olympiad.

6. Alfred Nobel was the benefactor of an endowment that began by awarding yearly prizes in peace, science, and literature.

■ EXERCISE 7.5   Complements

Underline and label the complements in the following paragraph.

Henry Reed was class valedictorian. He was a small, very black boy with hooded eyes, a long, broad nose and an oddly shaped head. I had admired him for years because each term he and I vied for the best grades in our class. Most often he bested me, but instead of being disappointed I was pleased that we shared top places between us. Like many Southern Black children, he lived with his grandmother, who was as strict as Momma and as kind as she knew how to be. He was courteous, respectful and soft-spoken to elders, but on the playground he chose to play the roughest games. I admired him. Anyone, I reckoned, sufficiently afraid or sufficiently dull could be polite. But to be able to operate at a top level with both adults and children was admirable.   —Maya Angelou, "Graduation"

■ Phrases

Phrases are groups of related words that cannot function as independent sentences because they lack subjects or predicates or both; phrases must be part of a sentence. The three most common are prepositional phrases, verbal phrases, and appositive phrases; they function as nouns, adjectives, or adverbs. Absolute phrases, a fourth kind, modify whole sentences.

Prepositional Phrases

A **prepositional phrase** consists of a preposition, its object or objects (a noun or pronoun), and any modifiers; it functions most often as an adjective or adverb.

prep. phrase		prep. phrase	
prep.	obj.	prep.	obj.

Libya is located on the southern shore of the Mediterranean Sea.
[**Both phrases work as adverbs, answering the question** "*Where is Libya located?*"]

prep. phrase	prep. phrase
prep. obj.	prep. obj.

Libya's role as a haven for terrorists limits its international relations.
[**Both phrases work as adjectives:** "*Which* **role?** *What kind* **of haven?**"]

■ EXERCISE 7.6 Prepositional phrases

Insert parentheses around the prepositional phrases in the following sentences and then underline the word or words that each phrase modifies.

1. The once inexact study of weather has become a highly complex science during the last few decades.

2. The National Weather Service currently uses computers to synthesize data it receives from satellites, balloons, ground stations, and airplanes.

3. Once computers at the National Meteorological Center compile this information, it is relayed by a variety of electronic means to regional weather stations where teams evaluate the results.

4. The findings of the National Severe Storms Forecast Center (NSSFC) in Kansas City, Missouri, are particularly useful because its team channels information about potentially dangerous storms to affected areas.

5. Using data from the NSSFC, local meteorologists issue a wide range of watches and warnings, notably for tornadoes, severe thunderstorms, blizzards, and hurricanes.

6. By providing systematically gathered and carefully organized information, weather forecasters can warn people of danger— protecting millions of dollars' worth of property and saving thousands of lives.

Verbal Phrases

Verbal phrases combine **verbals** (verb forms used as nouns, adjectives, and adverbs) with complements or modifiers. There are three types of verbals: gerunds, participles, and infinitives. Like verbals, verbal phrases function in sentences as nouns, adjectives, or adverbs.

GERUND PHRASES **Gerunds** are *-ing* forms of verbs that function as nouns.

Reading is my favorite winter sport.

Gerund phrases combine a gerund and its complements and modifiers; the entire phrase works as a noun.

gerund phrase

gerund   obj.

Studying chimpanzees in the wild was Jane Goodall's lifelong ambition.
[The gerund phrase is the subject of the sentence.]

gerund phrase

gerund   obj.

She enjoyed watching the chimpanzees at play.
[The gerund phrase is the direct object of *enjoyed*.]

■ **EXERCISE 7.7   Gerund phrases**

Underline the gerund phrases in the following sentences. Bracket the objects and modifiers.

1. Learning a second language is a complicated task, but it is a rewarding one.

2. The benefits can be as simple as reading a menu in a foreign restaurant, a book in a used-book store, an untranslated quotation in a scholarly work, or a magazine in a library.

3. Working for international corporations is one career option open to people trained in a second language.

4. Traveling outside the United States is especially enjoyable when reading and speaking a country's language are possible.

5. Through studying other languages, people become sensitive to language itself, and that sensitivity can increase their effectiveness as thinkers, readers, writers, speakers, and listeners.

PARTICIPIAL PHRASES   **Participles** appear in two forms: the **present participle** (*climbing, going*) and the **past participle** (*climbed, gone*). See the discussion of participles and the list of irregular verbs on pages 119–23.

Scowling, the president responded to the prosecutor's allegations.
[*Scowling* **is a present participle modifying** *president.*]

Overwhelmed, the secretary refused to answer reporters' questions.
[*Overwhelmed* **is a past participle modifying** *secretary.*]

Participial phrases combine a participle and its modifiers;
the phrases work as adjectives. Like other adjectives, participial
phrases must be placed near the nouns and pronouns they
modify.

part. phrase

part.

Fascinated by the proceedings, the American people watched the
news coverage with a mix of shock and disgust.
[**The participial phrase modifies** *American people.*]

■ EXERCISE 7.8 Participial phrases

*Insert parentheses around the participial phrases in the following
sentences and label the participles as present or past. Then underline
the word that each phrase modifies.*

1. Developed to appeal to specialized audiences, unique cable
   television channels have emerged and prospered.

2. Headline News, building on people's seemingly insatiable interest in what's happening around the world, broadcasts a news
   digest every thirty minutes.

3. The Weather Channel provides forecasts, reports, and informational programming around the clock, surprising everyone with
   its popularity.

4. Comedy Central, created from a wild assortment of reruns from
   other networks and newly developed programs, delights young
   and old audiences alike.

5. Offering programs from around the world, Home and Garden
   Television features ways in which to improve lifestyles and living spaces.

6. The Biography Channel, developed first as a single program on the A&E Network, presents the life stories of both famous and infamous people, entertaining and informing audiences at the same time.

INFINITIVE PHRASES **Infinitives** combine the word *to* with a verb's primary form; they are used as nouns, adjectives, or adverbs.

To win four medals was Jesse Owens's goal at the 1936 Olympic games.
[*To win* **works as a noun—the subject of the sentence.**]

After he won four gold medals, he was an easy athlete to *recognize*.
[*To recognize* **works as an adjective, modifying *athlete*.**]

Owens's individual medal record has been too daunting *to match*.
[*To match* **works as an adverb, modifying *daunting*.**]

Infinitive phrases combine an infinitive and its complements and modifiers; these phrases function as nouns, adjectives, or adverbs. When infinitive phrases are used as adjectives, they should be placed near the nouns they modify. When they work as adverbs, however, they can appear in a variety of positions, as can other adverbs.

inf. phrase

inf.

Alex Haley decided to research his family's history and

inf. phrase

inf.

subsequently chose to share its stories in the novel *Roots*.
[**Both infinitive phrases work as nouns, specifically as direct objects answering the question *what*.**]

inf. phrase

inf.

To encompass its many episodes, *Roots* was presented in the miniseries format.
[**The infinitive phrase, working as an adjective, modifies *Roots*.**]

The entertainment establishment found that the miniseries format

inf. phrase

inf.

was too successful *to ignore* completely.
[**The infinitive phrase, working as an adverb, modifies the predicate adjective *successful*.**]

■ EXERCISE 7.9   Infinitive phrases

Underline the complete infinitive phrases in the following sentences and label each phrase as a noun, adjective, or adverb.

1. It is hard to believe how much wood and how many wood products Americans use without being aware of them.

2. To begin our mornings, many of us eat cereals packaged in cardboard boxes while reading newspapers made from wood pulp.

3. To go about our daily routines, we move between rooms built with two-by-fours, walk on hardwood floors, and open wooden doors, often oblivious to the structural uses to which wood is put.

4. We talk on the telephone—to convey messages or simply to converse—without thinking that wood resins are used in the plastic casing for the phone, let alone that millions of wooden telephone poles help to make such communication possible.

5. Many of us use pencils to write with, paper to write on, and desks or tables to write at—all products of forest-related industries.

6. To conceive of how many trees are necessary to support the activities of even one person is virtually impossible.

Appositive Phrases

Appositives explain, describe, define, identify, or restate a noun. They provide either necessary explanation or nonessential information. In the latter case, the appositive must be separated from the rest of the sentence by commas.

The painting *Whistler's Mother* has been amusingly used in many advertisements.
[**Because *Whistler's Mother*, the appositive, is necessary to the meaning of the sentence, no commas are used.**]

Whistler, better known for seascapes than for portraits, is a fascinating American artist.
[**Because the appositive provides nonessential information, it is set off with commas.**]

■ EXERCISE 7.10 Appositives

Combine the following pairs of sentences to form single sentences containing appositives. Be sure to use commas where they are needed. (Available on disk.)

Example

The American Kennel Club recognizes more than one hundred breeds of purebred dogs. The American Kennel Club is the primary organization of dog breeders.

The American Kennel Club, the primary organization of dog breeders, recognizes more than one hundred breeds of purebred dogs.

1. Sporting dogs hunt by smelling the air to locate game. Pointers, setters, retrievers, and spaniels are typical sporting dogs.
2. Working dogs serve or once served as herders, sled dogs, and guards. The group called working dogs comprises twenty-eight separate breeds.
3. Terriers hunt by digging. Their digging is an activity for which their strong front legs are natural.

4. Nonsporting dogs include nine breeds most usually kept as pets. Many nonsporting dogs are descended from breeds in other classifications.

5. Most toy dogs have been bred down from larger breeds of dogs. Toy dogs are almost always kept only as pets.

Absolute Phrases

Absolute phrases consist of nouns and participles, usually with modifiers, and modify whole sentences rather than individual words. They can be positioned anywhere in a sentence but must be separated from the rest of the sentence by commas.

> *Their salaries growing ever larger,* professional athletes have become a distinct class of millionaires.

> Professional athletes, *their salaries growing ever larger,* have become a distinct class of millionaires.

■ EXERCISE 7.11   Phrases

Underline and label the prepositional, gerund, participial, infinitive, appositive, and absolute phrases in the following sentences.

1. Intrigued by the history of Great Britain, many Anglophiles are Americans obsessed by England and English things.

2. To learn about their "adopted" country, Anglophiles often subscribe to magazines like *British Heritage.*

3. They also read materials in books and newspapers that offer insight into the English way of life.

4. Many Anglophiles, their daily schedules rearranged, watched the satellite broadcasts of the royal weddings of Charles and Diana and of Andrew and Sarah.

5. Anglophiles, often people who feel displaced in the rush of American activities, find pleasure in learning about "that sceptered isle."

6. Visiting England is the lifelong dream of most Anglophiles, but spending time there often spoils illusions that have developed through years of active fantasizing.

■ EXERCISE 7.12   Phrases

Place in parentheses and label the prepositional, appositive, and absolute phrases in the following paragraph. Then underline the gerund, participial, and infinitive phrases and label each one.

When in the winter of 1845–6, a comet called *Biela* became oddly pear-shaped and then divided into two distinct comets, one of the astronomers who observed them, James Challis of Cambridge, averted his gaze. A week later he took another peep and *Biela* was still flaunting its rude duality. He had never heard of such a thing and for several more days the cautious Challis hesitated before he announced it to his astronomical colleagues. Meanwhile American astronomers in Washington D.C. and New Haven, equally surprised but possibly more confident in their own sobriety, had already staked their claim to the discovery. Challis excused his slowness in reporting the event by saying that he was busy looking for the new planet beyond Uranus. When later in the same year he was needlessly beaten to the discovery of that planet (Neptune) by German astronomers, Challis explained that he had been preoccupied with his work on comets.   —Nigel Calder, "Heads and Tails"

■ Clauses

A **clause** contains both a subject and a predicate and can be either independent or subordinate.

Independent Clauses

An **independent clause** (sometimes called a **main clause**) is grammatically complete and can be used alone as a simple sentence or combined with other clauses to form other sentence types (see pages 159–60).

subj.   pred.

Eleanor Roosevelt withdrew her membership from the Daughters

of the American Revolution (DAR).

Subordinate Clauses

A **subordinate clause** (sometimes called a **dependent clause**) contains a subject and a predicate but is grammatically incomplete and must be joined to an independent clause to express a complete idea. Subordinating conjunctions and relative pronouns establish this dependent relationship.

conj. subj.   pred.

because she objected to the DAR's discriminatory practices

To make a subordinate clause grammatically complete, join it to an independent clause or revise it into a simple sentence by eliminating the subordinating conjunction or relative pronoun.

Eleanor Roosevelt withdrew her membership from the Daughters of the American Revolution (DAR) *because she objected* to the DAR's discriminatory practices.
[**complex sentence**]

Eleanor Roosevelt withdrew her membership from the Daughters of the American Revolution (DAR). *She objected* to the DAR's discriminatory practices.
[**two simple sentences**]

Subordinate clauses function in sentences as nouns, adjectives, or adverbs, depending on what information they provide.

Noun clause

clause

subj.   pred.

Whoever examined her schedule discovered how tirelessly she worked on other people's behalf.
[**clause used as the subject of the sentence**]

clause

subj.   pred.

Even her detractors knew that Eleanor Roosevelt   was a person

to be reckoned with.
[**clause used as the direct object of** *knew*]

Adjective clause

clause

subj.   pred.

The causes that she supported were widely varied.
[**modifying** *causes.*]

Adverb clause

clause

subj.   pred.

Roosevelt was more politically active than her husband   wanted

her to be.
[**modifying** *active.*]

■ **EXERCISE 7.13   Clauses**

*Underline the subordinate clauses in the following sentences and
indicate whether they are used as nouns, adjectives, or adverbs.*

1. Wherever I hang my hat is home.
2. Don't count your chickens before they hatch.
3. Absence makes the heart grow fonder.
4. All that glitters is not gold.
5. Fools rush in where angels fear to tread.

■ **EXERCISE 7.14**   **Clauses**

The following paragraph contains a number of subordinate clauses. Underline them and indicate whether they are used as nouns, adjectives, or adverbs.

When the credits run at the end of a film, audience members who stay to read them discover the names of people whose contributions are sometimes as important to the film as the actors' are. For instance, producers control and organize the entire film production, finding people who will finance the project and finding creative people who will actually make the film. That directors are in charge of the filming is well known, but many people do not realize that directors also choose and coach actors, find locations, and select technicians. When the filming is finally completed, editors begin their work. They take thousands of feet of film, select the best shots, and piece together the version of the film that audiences eventually see. Besides the producers, directors, and editors, hundreds of other people are involved in the making of a film. Learning who they are and what they do makes audience members more appreciative of the combined efforts involved in film making.

7b   Kinds of Sentences

The four basic sentence types are simple, compound, complex, and compound-complex.

■ **Classifying by Structure**

Simple Sentences

A **simple sentence** is an independent clause that contains at least one subject and one predicate. However, simple sentences may have compound subjects, compound predicates, and compound complements, as well as multiple modifiers and phrases.

subj. pred.

People sing.
[**simple subject, simple predicate**]

compound pred.

subj. pred. d.o. pred.

People sing "The Star Spangled Banner" and recite the

d.o.

Pledge of Allegiance at many school functions.
[**compound predicate, each part having its own direct object**]

Compound Sentences

Compound sentences contain at least two independent clauses, each with its own subject and predicate. The clauses are usually joined by a comma and a coordinating conjunction, but they can also be joined by a semicolon, with no coordinating conjunction.

subj. pred. conj. subj.

Charles Dickens's novels addressed social ills, but they

pred.

were nevertheless extremely popular.

subj. pred.

Dickens assailed the workhouses in *Oliver Twist;* in *Bleak House*

subj. pred.

he took on the Courts of Chancery.

Complex Sentences

Complex sentences contain one independent clause and one or more subordinate clauses. The clauses are joined by either subordinating conjunctions or relative pronouns.

Subordinate clauses may be positioned at the beginning, middle, or end of the sentence. Each position conveys a different emphasis. Note the placement of commas in the examples.

sub. clause

conj. subj. pred.

Although he is best know for designing the Eiffel Tower in Paris,

ind. clause

subj. pred.

Gustave Eiffel also designed the frame for New York's *Statue of*

Liberty.

ind. clause

subj. pred.

Gustave Eiffel designed the frame for New York's *Statue of Liberty*

sub. clause

conj. subj. pred.

although he is best known for designing the Eiffel Tower in Paris.

Compound-Complex Sentences

Compound-complex sentences contain at least two independent clauses and one subordinate clause.

sub. clause   ind. clause

conj. subj. pred.   subj. pred.

After he ran away from home at eleven, W. C. Fields worked

ind. clause

conj. subj.

as a juggler in vaudeville, but his first professional success

pred.

came in the *Ziegfeld Follies.*

■ EXERCISE 7.15   Sentence structures

Combine the following groups of simple sentences to form compound, complex, or compound-complex sentences. Create at least one sentence of each type. Label your revised sentences. (Available on disk.)

Example

Hoover Dam supplies water and electricity to Los Angeles and surrounding areas. The dam was originally built to control the flow of the Colorado River.

Although Hoover Dam currently supplies water and electricity to Los Angeles and surrounding areas, it was originally built to control the flow of the Colorado River. (complex)

1. In the early 1900s, the Palo Verde and Imperial Valleys seemed ideal for development. At times floods washed away crops. At other times crops withered.

2. In 1918, the Bureau of Reclamation submitted a report. The report suggested building a dam. The dam would improve water control.

3. Water control was the primary goal of the project. Generating electricity was a secondary goal.

4. The Bureau of Reclamation designed the dam. Six companies worked on the project. It was a joint venture that involved an average of 3,500 workers a day.

5. The finished dam is 726 feet high. It is 1,244 feet long. It contains 4,400,000 cubic yards of concrete. That is enough to pave a one-lane road from New York to San Francisco.

■ **EXERCISE 7.16**   **Sentence structures**

Label each sentence in the following paragraph as simple, compound, complex, or compound-complex.

    Rodeo, like baseball, is an American sport and has been around almost as long. While Henry Chadwick was writing his first book of rules for the fledgling ball clubs in 1858, ranch hands were paying $25 a dare to a kid who would ride five outlaw horses from the rough string in a makeshift arena of wagons and cars. The first commercial rodeo in Wyoming was held in Lander in 1895, just nineteen years after the National League was formed. Baseball was just as popular as bucking and roping contests in the West, but no one in

Cooperstown, New York, was riding broncs. And that's been part of the problem. After 124 years, rodeo is still misunderstood. Unlike baseball, it's a regional sport (although they do have rodeos in New Jersey, Florida, and other eastern states); it's derived from and stands for the western way of life and the western spirit. It doesn't have the universal appeal of a sport contrived solely for the competition and winning; there is no ball bandied about between opposing players.   —Gretel Ehrlich, "Rules of the Game: Rodeo"

■ Classifying by Purpose

In addition to classifying sentences by grammatical structure, writers classify sentences by their purposes.

Declarative Sentences

A **declarative sentence** expresses a statement.

"God does not play dice."   —Albert Einstein

Exclamatory Sentences

An **exclamatory sentence** expresses an emphatic statement.

"Give me liberty or give me death!"   —Patrick Henry

Imperative Sentences

An **imperative sentence** expresses a command.

"Ask not what your country can do for you—ask what you can do for your country."   —John F. Kennedy

Interrogative Sentences

An **interrogative sentence** asks a question.

"What *is* the answer? . . . In that case, what is the question?" . . .
—Gertrude Stein

■ **EXERCISE 7.17   Sentence purposes**

Label each of the following sentences as declarative, exclamatory, imperative, or interrogative. Then experiment, rewriting each sentence in each of the three remaining forms.

1. "Tell me what you eat, and I will tell you what you are." —Anthelme Brillat-Savarin.

2. "Education is what survives when what has been learnt has been forgotten."   —B. F. Skinner

3. "One only dies once, and it's for such a long time!"   —Molière

4. "How can we know the dancer from the dance?"   —W. B. Yeats

To achieve sentence variety, experiment with alternative methods of constructing sentences.

▶ Use a mix of long, short, and medium-length sentences.

▶ Use loose, periodic, and balanced sentences to vary rhythm and emphasis.

▶ Experiment with new ways to begin sentences.

▶ Coordinate and subordinate ideas in sentences to express your exact meaning and emphasis.

8a Sentence Length

Use sentences of various lengths to create effective paragraph rhythm. A paragraph of short sentences can seem undeveloped and choppy; a paragraph of long sentences can seem dense and difficult.

■ Short Sentences

Although too many short sentences in succession can make writing seem awkward and simplistic, a few well-placed short sentences can enhance variety and add emphasis.

> When you cross New York Harbor by ferry, the *Statue of Liberty* appears in the distance. As the boat grows ever nearer to Liberty Island, the mammoth scale of the statue—all 302 feet—becomes evident. It is awesome.

■ Medium Sentences

Medium-length sentences allow space to connect ideas and add details while remaining clear and easy to read. Medium-length sentences are the most versatile and form the core of most writing.

> A gift from the people of France, the statue was constructed of pounded copper over a framework of steel. Then it was disassembled and shipped to New York City. After its reconstruction on a 151-foot-high base, it was dedicated in 1886.

■ Long Sentences

Because long sentences establish complex interrelationships and include substantial amounts of amplification and clarification, use them selectively to emphasize relationships and to incorporate significant details.

> For more than a century, the *Statue of Liberty,* in all its majesty, has stood at the entrance to New York Harbor, welcoming immigrants, travelers, and returning Americans and symbolizing the freedoms we value.

■ EXERCISE 8.1   Sentence length

Expand, combine, or divide the sentences in the following paragraph to achieve variety and effective expression. (Available on disk.)

Medieval castles, strongly built of native stone, served as homes for the nobility, but in times of brigandage and war they also served as fortresses and as shelters for the peasants who lived nearby. Sometimes castles also served as prisons, treasure houses, or seats of local governments because they were secure and centrally located, although access to castles was sometimes limited because some castles, notably those in central Europe, were built on irregular terrain. Some castles were attractive. Some used drawbridges. Battlements, also called parapets, were the tall, structural walls from which soldiers observed the countryside, and during battles these same soldiers positioned themselves in these lofty places to shoot arrows or hurl rocks at the invaders below. Most people know of castles from films.

8b   Sentence Types

Although the four basic sentence structures are simple, compound, complex, and compound-complex, the effect of these structures varies, depending on the types of sentences used: loose, periodic, or balanced.

■ Loose Sentences

Loose sentences, the most common type, first present major ideas (the subject and verb) and then provide other information. This pattern is satisfying and easy for readers to follow.

> Grover Cleveland was the only president to be elected to serve two nonconsecutive terms, from 1885 to 1889 and from 1893 to 1897.

■ Periodic Sentences

Periodic sentences, less common than loose sentences, create suspense and emphasis by placing the main idea or some part of it at the end of the sentence.

> After months of denying his involvement with the conspiracy, the numerous cover-up attempts, and other related activities, Nixon resigned.

Balanced Sentences

Balanced sentences use parallel elements—words, phrases, and sometimes whole clauses—to create interest and emphasis.

> Theodore Roosevelt was boisterous and excitable, while Franklin Roosevelt was calm and even-tempered.

■ **EXERCISE 8.2   Types of sentences**

Label each of the following sentences as loose, periodic, or balanced; then revise each sentence into one of the other types.

1. Almanacs, published yearly in book or pamphlet form, include calendars, citations for important dates, information about geography and weather, and a myriad of other facts.

2. Almanacs are informative and practical, yet they are also idiosyncratic and entertaining.

3. Though generally associated with colonial American farmers and navigators, almanacs have as their precedents the works of an unsuspected group: Persian astrologers.

4. Over the years, sailors have relied on the *Nautical Almanac,* farmers have used the *Old Farmer's Almanac,* and amateur weather forecasters have depended on the *Ford Almanac.*

5. With its proverbs, its lists of counties and roads, its advice on planting, its selections of verse, and its astrological information, *Poor Richard's Almanack* is probably the best-known early almanac.

6. Contemporary almanacs are best represented by works such as the *Information Please Almanac,* compendiums of widely divergent statistics on thousands of topics.

8c   Sentence Beginnings

Although subjects and verbs in subordinate or independent clauses begin most sentences, writers can create variety by positioning other sentence elements first.

■ **With Adverbs**

Adverbs can appear in many positions in sentences. Using them at the beginning creates variety.

Chillingly,
˄Arthur Miller ~~chillingly~~ dramatized the Salem Witch Trials in *The Crucible.*

■ With Adjectives

When an adjective phrase modifies the subject of the sentence, move it to the beginning of the sentence to create variety.

Articulate and charismatic,

ˏFidel Castro, ~~articulate and charismatic,~~ led the Communist revolution in Cuba.

■ With Prepositional Phrases

Move adverbial prepositional phrases to the beginning of the sentence.

After the publication of <u>Satanic Verses,</u>

ˏSalman Rushdie went into hiding ~~after the publication of~~ ~~*Satanic Verses.*~~

■ With Verbal Phrases

Verbal phrases (gerund, participial, and infinitive phrases) make effective beginnings. Make certain, however, that the phrase modifies the subject of the first clause; otherwise, you will create a *dangling modifier.*

art treasures

Worried that ~~they~~ would be stolen, ~~art treasures~~ from the

the French hid them

Louvreˏ ~~were hidden~~ from the Nazis.

[**The beginning phrase cannot modify** *treasures*; **it is a dangling modifier.**]

■ With Conjuctive Adverbs and Transitional Expressions

Create variety by placing conjunctive adverbs and transitional expressions at the beginning of sentences.

For example,

ˏEconomic sanctions often complicate the lives of regular citizens, ~~for example,~~ without affecting those in political power.

■ With Coordinating Conjunctions

Coordinating conjunctions usually join independent clauses in compound sentences, but they can also be used to introduce a sentence closely related to the one preceding it.

International terrorism has made many world travelers more cautious than they used to be, but some travelers seem naively indifferent to potential threats from terrorists.

■ EXERCISE 8.3   Varying sentence structure and beginnings

Most of the sentences in the following paragraph are loose. To make the writing more varied and interesting, combine some sentences, restructure others into periodic or balanced form, and experiment with different sentence beginnings. (Available on disk.)

Landscaping serves more than an aesthetic function, even if few people realize it. Small shrubs and bushes protect a building's foundation, sheltering it from summer heat and winter cold. Large shrubs and small trees provide windbreaks for buildings, providing protection, especially in the winter, from strong winds that can affect interior temperatures and subsequently heating costs. Large trees shade a building during the summer, keeping the sun's warming rays off the building's roof and consequently keeping the building cool. Landscaping does improve the looks of a building, often enhancing architectural details and softening harsh lines, but the surprise for many people is that landscaping can pay for itself in energy savings, which means it has practical as well as aesthetic benefits.

8d   Coordination and Subordination

■ Coordination

Coordination joins two or more independent clauses with a comma and one of the coordinating conjunctions: *and, but, for, nor, or, so,* and *yet.* The resulting compound sentences bring balance and emphasis to writing.

Linking or Contrasting

To avoid a monotonous series of simple sentences while still giving equal stress to the main ideas, join closely related main clauses with a coordinating conjunction. The resulting compound sentence will give your writing an even, balanced rhythm.

> The Sioux achieved a great victory at the Battle of Little Big Horn, *but* they suffered a tremendous loss at Wounded Knee.

Varying Conjunctions

Each of the seven coordinating conjunctions links ideas in a slightly different way. *But* and *yet,* for example, both indicate contrast and are roughly interchangeable. However, *yet* expresses contrast more strongly and is more formal than *but.*

> Volcanoes may be dormant for decades, ~~but~~ *yet* their threat of potential violence is quite real.

Excessive Coordination

If overused, the balance of clauses in compound sentences creates a monotonous rhythm. Look, for instance, at this series of coordinated sentences:

> In the past, land was often overcultivated, ~~and~~ *Because* crops depleted the nutrients in the soil, ~~and then~~ food production dropped. *If* Farmers then overfertilized, ~~and~~ crop production increased for a short time, but then productivity declined again. Eventually, however, farmers learned to rotate crops, ~~or they would~~ *to* let the land lay fallow.

By the third sentence, an annoying and potentially distracting rhythm has developed. Remember not to rely too much on any one sentence pattern.

Three or more identically structured clauses in a single sentence can effectively link ideas and create interest and an emphatic rhythm. When clauses are dissimilar in structure or meaning, however, try other methods to join the ideas.

Because
  ̂Americans have become concerned about stimulants in foods,

and ~~they~~ have started using products without caffeine, ~~and to~~

~~accommodate them~~ restaurants now regularly serve

decaffeinated coffees and teas *to accommodate them*.
   ̂
[**The clauses in the original sentence lacked balance. The first two explained trends among Americans, but the third described an effect of these trends. The revised sentence effectively subordinates the elements of the sentence.**]

■ **EXERCISE 8.4   Coordination**

Revise the following sentences to achieve effective coordination and to eliminate excessive coordination. (Available on disk.)

1. Many American cities are now concerned with maintaining their architectural characters. Building codes control the development of new buildings.

2. Codes often restrict the kinds and sizes of buildings that can be constructed. Architects must design structures that match the scale of existing buildings.

3. Many cities, such as Boston and San Francisco, need the vast commercial space provided by tall office buildings. These skyscrapers often cannot be built in some areas because of protective codes.

4. City dwellers do not want the severe shadows cast by tall buildings. They do not want small, historical, and architecturally interesting buildings dwarfed by monolithic towers.

5. Citizens are now aware that poorly planned cities become unlivable, and, as a result, they have been supportive of new building codes, but city development is now more challenging than it once was, for cities must now grow by controlled, aesthetically consistent patterns.

■ Subordination

Subordination joins at least one independent clause with at least one subordinate clause, forming a complex sentence that indicates the relative importance of ideas. Different subordinated conjunctions (*after, because, when, until* and others) create differences in meaning and emphasis.

Levels of Importance

To avoid a monotonous series of simple sentences or the awkward rhythm of too many compound sentences, join related clauses with a subordinating conjunction.

> *Because* viewers expect quick overviews with many visual aids, television newswriters must plan brief, attention-getting news stories.
> [**The sentence emphasizes the effect of viewers' expectations on newswriting.**]

Relative Pronouns

Relative pronouns (*that, which, who,* and others) embed clauses within sentences, adding clarity and producing variety. The information in the embedded relative clause is clearly less important than the information in the independent clause.

> One of T. S. Eliot's best poems is "The Love Song of J. Alfred Prufrock," *which* is also one of his earliest.
> [**The relative clause embeds secondary but useful information.**]

Excessive Subordination

When too much secondary information is included in a sentence, ideas can become muddled. The following sentence is grammatically correct but poorly planned. Revision into three sentences improves rhythm and clarity.

~~Although~~ many films about adolescence concentrate on the awkward and often unsatisfying relationships that exist between teenagers and their parents, *however,* most of these films take a satiric approach, presenting parents as fools or tyrants ~~and, as a result,~~ is defus~~ing~~*ed* through laughter much of the tension in the real relationships because the depicted relationships are so extreme, so absurd.

■ **EXERCISE 8.5   Subordination**

Use subordinating conjunctions and relative pronouns to combine the following sets of sentences into a coherent paragraph. (Available on disk.)

1. Some people never visit art museums or exhibitions. Their only contact with art is through "public art." Public art is sculpture and other works displayed in public places.

2. Monuments are one kind of public sculpture. Statues and placards are the most common kinds of monuments. These monuments commemorate historical events or honor individuals or groups of people such as veterans.

3. People often walk through plazas and courtyards near government buildings. Sculpture is often displayed in these areas. This sculpture is frequently commissioned by the government.

4. Most people are comfortable with traditional, realistic statuary of individuals. Many people are less at ease with abstract sculpture.

5. Many people say nonrepresentational sculpture doesn't "look like anything." In time, some grow more accepting. They learn to enjoy modern sculpture's use of form, texture, and material.

6. Sculpture enriches public space. It provides visual and tactile stimulation. It also sometimes provides pleasure. It even supplies topics for conversation.

■ **EXERCISE 8.6　Coordination and subordination**

Revise the following paragraph by using coordination and subordination to indicate the relative importance of ideas and to improve the variety of the sentences.

　　Dermatologists continually warn people about the danger of ultraviolet rays. Many people seem intent on getting dark suntans. During the summer, beaches and pools are crowded with people. These people want to "catch some rays." They smear on creams, lotions, and oils. They can accelerate the sun's natural modification of skin pigments. They want to get deep tans. They lie on towels or stretch out on lounge chairs for hours, defiant of doctors' stern advice. In most cities, tanning salons are quite popular. "California" tans are not always possible everywhere. For a fee, usually between three and ten dollars, people can lie down and subject themselves to artificial sunlight. This artificial sunlight is produced by ultraviolet bulbs. Many people think a tan looks healthy. Overly dark tans, in fact, cause serious skin damage. This damage can last a lifetime. (Available on disk.)

Emphasis underscores the significance of main ideas and makes supporting ideas and details clear and vivid. To control emphasis, therefore, is to control meaning.

Emphatic sentences stress the most important ideas. Control emphasis in the following ways:

▶ Write active sentences to stress the doer of an action.

▶ Write passive sentences to stress the receiver of an action or to stress that the doer of the action is unknown.

▶ Strip sentences of all unnecessary words, phrases, and clauses to highlight words crucial to their meaning.

9a   Active and Passive Sentences

■ Active Sentences

In **active sentences,** the subjects of the sentences act.

```
    subj.          verb                    d.o.
Ralph Nader challenged the American auto industry
      inf. phrase
to make safer cars.
```

■ Passive Sentences

In **passive sentences,** the subject of the sentence is acted upon. A passive verb requires auxiliaries. While a passive sentence does not always specify the person completing the action, when it does, the person is named in a prepositional phrase beginning with *by*.

subj.	verb	inf. phrase

The American auto industry was challenged to make safer cars

prep. phrase

by Ralph Nader.

■ Emphasis

Who or What Acts

An active sentence emphasizes the doer of an action. It establishes a clear, strong relationship between the subject and verb.

The *restorer damaged* a portion of the fresco when he cleaned it.
[**The damage is clearly due to the restorer's error.**]

When the results of an action are more important than the doer or when the doer is unknown, passive sentences effectively express the meaning.

The fresco *was* irreparably *damaged* during its restoration.

The choice of using an active or a passive verb allows subtle but significant shifts in meaning and emphasis.

Active

The 1980 eruption of Mount St. Helens destroyed more than sixty million dollars' worth of property.
[**The use of *eruption* with the active verb *destroyed* emphasizes the violence of nature.**]

Passive

More than sixty million dollars' worth of property was destroyed by the 1980 eruption of Mount St. Helens.
[**This sentence shifts the emphasis to the loss of property.**]

Action

The passive voice emphasizes the action over the doer of the action; thus, it is especially useful for describing universal or widespread conditions or events.

Passive

Open-heart surgery to repair faulty valves is now commonly performed across the United States.
[**The surgical procedure is most important here, not the individual doctors who perform it.**]

Active

Doctors across the United States now commonly perform open-heart surgery to repair faulty valves.
[**This construction emphasizes the doctors who perform the procedures.**]

As a general guide to usage, write active sentences when "who is doing what" is most important. When "what is being done" is most important, passive sentences may better serve your purpose.

■ EXERCISE 9.1   Active and passive sentences

Determine which of the following sentences should be left in the passive voice and briefly state your reasons. Revise the remaining sentences into the active voice. (Available on disk.)

1. Biographies are often written by people who know their subjects well, either from personal contact or through study.

2. The *Life of Samuel Johnson,* a famous early biography, was written by James Boswell, a personal friend of Johnson.

3. In typical fashion, facts, anecdotes, and quotations were recorded in Boswell's diary and then translated into the biography.

4. When people like Benjamin Franklin choose to write their autobiographies, experiences are often presented to create a positive impression of the writer.

5. The lives of famous people like Lincoln were once described reverently by biographers.

6. Balanced treatments of a subject's positive and negative qualities are frequently presented by contemporary biographers.

7. A multifaceted view of the Roosevelts' relationship is presented in *Eleanor and Franklin,* a biography of the couple by Joseph P. Lash.

8. An essentially negative portrait of Pablo Picasso emerges in the Stassinopoulos-Huffington biography of the twentieth-century artist.

9. Contemporary autobiographies are usually written by well-known people with the help of professional writers.

10. *My American Journey,* a recent autobiography, was written by Colin Powell and a cowriter to chronicle Powell's rise within the military establishment.

9b   Concision

Concise writing expresses meaning in as few words as possible. To write concisely, choose concrete, exact words and avoid needless repetition of words, phrases, and clauses that do not add meaning.

■ Unnecessary Repetition

Deliberate, controlled **repetition,** as in the following example, emphasizes important ideas:

> We forget all too soon the things we thought we could never forget.   —Joan Didion

But such effects, if overused, can irritate readers and so should be used selectively.

Avoid unintentional, excessive, or monotonous repetition by deleting unnecessary words and rearranging the sentence to read smoothly.

During the 1930s and 1940s, ~~the~~ MGM studio was renowned for film musicals ~~was MGM studio.~~

Rely on specific word choices to make your ideas clear. Do not elaborate needlessly. **Redundancy,** or repeating ideas, adds useless words.

~~The~~ wide smile ~~on~~ Cuba Gooding's ~~face~~ showed that he was ~~pleasantly~~ elated by winning an Oscar.

■ Wordiness

Expletive Constructions

Sentences beginning with expletive constructions (*it is, here is, here are, there is,* and *there are*) weaken the impact of ideas by obscuring the subject and verb. Consequently, revise your writing by eliminating expletives and using the remaining, substantive words to present the same idea.

~~There are~~ nine planets ~~that~~ form our solar system.

Wordy Expressions

Wordy expressions bog down writing. Phrases like *at this point in time* and *because of the fact that* add unnecessary words without enhancing either sense or sound. Many such expressions can be shortened or have clear, concise substitutes.

Because
~~Due to the fact that~~ an accident blocked the road, I was late.

Concise Alternatives to Wordy Expressions	
Wordy	*Concise*
at this point in time	now
by means of	by
in order to	to
in the event that	if
of the opinion that	think
until such time as	until

Empty Phrases

Phrases such as *in my opinion, I believe, it seems,* and *I suppose* add little meaning to a sentence. Unless your purpose is to compare your opinion with someone else's, such phrases serve no purpose and should be dropped.

~~It seems that~~ athletes in triathlons ~~are~~ *seem* masochistic.

To be *Verbs*

To be verbs add words and deprive sentences of strong verbs. Examine sentences containing *to be* verbs and replace them when possible.

Research assistants ~~are responsible for~~ completing most day-to-day experiments *and recording* the results.

Nonrestrictive Clauses and Modifying Phrases

Reduce nonrestrictive clauses (clauses not essential to the meaning of the sentence) that contain *to be* verbs to appositives (phrases restating a noun or pronoun). Because appositives contain no subject or verb, they are more concise than clauses.

Chemicals found in aerosols have damaged the Earth's ozone layer, ~~which is~~ *our main protection from solar radiation.*

When possible, change prepositional and verbal phrases to one-word or multiword modifiers.

tapestry's   stained-glass

The colors ~~of the tapestry~~ were distorted by a nearby window ~~made of stained glass.~~

■ EXERCISE 9.2 Concision

Through revision, make these wordy sentences concise; note the number of words saved. (Available on disk.)

1. It is known to scientists who study such matters that an average of four trillion gallons of precipitation falls on the United States each and every day.

2. Falling from the overcast sky, heavy rains and snows fill our lakes, rivers, streams, and waterways, as well as replenish water supplies in our reservoirs.

3. There are some areas of the continental United States that are known to receive annually fewer than five inches of rain each year.

4. Other parts of the United States experience the benefit of more than twenty inches of precipitation or rain in a calendar year.

5. Precipitation—which includes rain, snow, sleet, and drizzle—is crucial to the national well-being of the United States.

6. Most of the people who think about it are aware that water is used to satisfy the needs of people, plant life, and animal life; however, they often fail to consider the fact that water is also in use in important industries.

7. I am of the opinion that water distribution should be under the management of a separate and independent national agency.

8. Until such time as we have a national policy for the management of water supplies, we can expect to have imbalances in the supplies of water in this country.

■ EXERCISE 9.3   Concision

Make the following paragraph, bloated with useless words, more concise. (Available on disk.)

To be capable of understanding the development and use of paper and how that use came about, we must make our way back hundreds of years to China. By most estimates, paper was invented by the Chinese, who created it in 105 B.C. As a matter of fact, it was kept as a secret by the state for hundreds of years. As far as we know, most transcriptions were done on bamboo sheets. The Moors discovered the Chinese invention in A.D. 750. They became aware of it when they were at war with the Chinese. The Moors established and forged the link to Europe. In 1100, there was a paper mill for making paper established in Toledo, Spain. Gradually, the use of paper began to spread across Europe in a slow manner. Paper was able to reach Rome in approximately 1200, and it was a cause for the Catholic Church to feel threatened by the "new" invention. The church opposed the introduction of something that was so unfamiliar. According to the church, documents written on paper were not legally binding due to the fact that the church did not consider paper permanent. Still, paper began to be used by people instead of parchment, which was treated animal skin. People were greatly intrigued and fascinated as well by the new medium, which was cheaper and more convenient than parchment had ever been or could ever be. The use of paper reached English soil by 1400, and then it reached America by 1690. Soon, there was no other universally accepted writing surface that was used everywhere by virtually everyone. At this point in time, we take paper for granted and use it daily. We do not even acknowledge the fact that it was once a revolutionary new invention.

Parallelism requires that ideas of equal importance be expressed in similar ways or that words or phrases used together in similar ways appear in identical grammatical form: nouns with other nouns, verbs with other verbs of the same tense, and so on.

QUICK REFERENCE

Use parallelism to stress the balance between similar words, parts of sentences, or entire sentences.

▶ Independent clauses joined by coordinating conjunctions must be parallel.

▶ Clauses and phrases joined by correlative conjunctions must be parallel.

▶ Prepositions, conjunctions, pronouns, and sentence structures arranged in parallel constructions convey meaning clearly and effectively.

10a With Coordinating Conjunctions

Use identical grammatical forms for elements joined by coordinating conjunctions: *and, but, for, nor, or, so,* and *yet.*

To have dreams is important, but ~~living~~ to live them is even more important.
[**To be parallel, both subjects need to be infinitive phrases.**]

10b With Correlative Conjunctions

Use parallel forms for items linked by correlative conjunctions:
both . . . and, either . . . or, neither . . . nor, and *not only . . . but also.*

The aim of a teacher should be both to inspire and ˄educate. *to*
[**To be parallel, the infinitive forms must be repeated after each element of the correlative conjunction.**]

10c Repetition of Sentence Elements

In brief sentences, you may omit prepositions and subordinating conjunctions from the second part of a parallel structure. In longer sentences, repeat prepositions and subordinating conjunctions.

■ **Correctness and Clarity**

Bela Karolyi coached Mary Lou Retton, an exceptional vaulter and ~~who was also~~ an outstanding performer in the floor exercise.
[**To be parallel, the elements must appear in identical form; an alternative would be to add "who was" before the first element.**]

■ **Emphasis and Effect**

Use a series of parallel sentences to create clarity and heighten interest.

His voice quavered audibly; his face blushed hotly; his hand trembled violently.

Consider in detail the parallel structures of these elements:

Possessive pronouns	Subjects	Verbs	Adverbs
His	voice	quavered	audibly;
his	face	blushed	hotly;
his	hand	trembled	violently.

■ EXERCISE 10.1 Parallelism

Revise the following sentences to improve parallelism. (Available on disk.)

1. "As Ye Plant, So Shall Ye Reap" is a moving essay about the plight of migrant workers and which is somewhat controversial.

2. Over the years, César Chávez used his political power to draw attention to the harsh treatment of these workers, to garner support from politicians, and orchestrate boycotts of selected produce.

3. Not only are migrant workers exploited in the Southwest but also in other parts of the Sunbelt.

4. The work of these laborers, extremely tedious and which needs to be controlled by labor laws, is traditionally undervalued.

5. To supply better wages and providing better working conditions should be our goal.

■ EXERCISE 10.2 Parallelism

Locate and correct faulty parallelism in the following paragraph. (Available on disk.)

Americans like to play it safe, so it is not surprising that they want the places where they play to be safe. Not so very long ago, however, amusement parks were poorly supervised, dirty, and they were rather tasteless. On hot summer Saturdays, American families would head to places with names like Chain-of-Rocks Park to have a good time. Once there, they found that the parking facilities were not only randomly planned but also no guards patrolled the area. The parks themselves were poorly maintained, with litter on the sidewalks, with oil running on the sidewalks, and food having been left to spoil on the tables. The attendants appeared to be people with nothing better to do and who wash or shave only infrequently. They seemed to be alternately indifferent, callous, or they sometimes appeared to be threatening. Probably because of these unappealing qualities and other safety concerns, the amusement parks of an earlier time have been replaced by well-maintained, clean, and the attractiveness of today's Six Flags, King's Island, and Disney parks. Yesterday's grimy and chaotic amusement parks have been replaced by today's safe, sanitized theme parks.

To create variety and unity in your writing, substitute pronouns for overused nouns, following accepted patterns of pronoun usage.

A pronoun must refer clearly to a specific noun, its antecedent; otherwise, the meaning of a sentence can become confused.

▶ A pronoun must have one antecedent, not several.

▶ A pronoun's reference must be clear, not vague or general.

▶ Reflexive pronouns must have antecedents in the same sentence.

11a Unclear Pronoun References

Unclear pronoun references result when antecedents are ambiguously placed, broad or vague, or implied rather than stated.

■ Ambiguous References

Ambiguous references result when more than one noun could be a pronoun's antecedent.

Ambiguous

> The scuba instructor gave Patrick a detailed account of the history of the sport. *He* thought the lecture was a waste of time. **[Did the instructor feel dissatisfied, or did Patrick?]**

Clear

> Even though *he* thought the lecture was a waste of time, the
> scuba instructor gave Patrick a detailed account of the history
> of the sport.
> **[The rule of nearness suggests that he refers to the scuba
> instructor.]**

■ Vague References

General or broad antecedents result in **vague references.**

Vague

> The members of Israel's Knesset requested more military aid
> from the United States. *This* was approved by Congress.
> **[Did Congress approve of the request, or did Congress approve
> the aid?]**

Clear

> Upon the request of members of Israel's Knesset, Congress
> approved more military aid.

■ Implied References

An **implied antecedent** suggests a reference but does so confusingly.

Unclear

> The Theater-in-the-Round is not very innovative, but *they*
> usually present technically polished productions.
> **[*They* has no direct antecedent.]**

Clear

> Although the directors at the Theater-in-the-Round are not very
> innovative, *they* usually present technically polished
> productions.

11b Reflexive Pronouns and Subjects of Sentences

Reflexive pronouns serve only as indirect or direct objects.

```
                    reflex.  indirect
         subj.       verb.    obj.     d.o.
Carlotta Monterey gave herself credit for Eugene O'Neill's
```
stability in his last years.

Use a personal pronoun in place of a reflexive pronoun if the subject of the sentence is not the antecedent. A reflexive pronoun should never be the subject of a sentence.

Incorrect

Wilbur and *myself* disagree about the effectiveness of amplified sound on stage.

Correct

Wilbur and *I* disagree about the effectiveness of amplified sound on stage.

11c Clear Pronoun References

When pronouns and antecedents are separated by too many words, references become vague or unclear. To avoid potential confusion, alternate between using a noun and using a pronoun. Such use also helps to avoid monotony.

Charlie Chaplin began his work in American films with the

Keystone Cops. Although ~~Chaplin's~~ _{his} early roles were limited,

they gave him a chance to demonstrate his considerable talents.

Chaplin later showcased his talents in a one-reeler titled

he
The Tramp. In that film, ~~Chaplin~~ introduced the character that

Chaplin
was to win him wide acclaim. ~~He~~ later produced, wrote, directed,

and starred in such films as *The Kid, City Lights,* and *Modern Times.*
[**Although the entire paragraph is about Chaplin and consequently is not confusing, it is improved by alternating Chaplin's name with pronouns.**]

For clarity, observe the convention of restricting pronoun references to sentences within the same paragraph, even when the reference seems clear.

. . . Chaplin later produced, wrote, and starred in such films as

The Kid, City Lights, and *Modern Times.*

Chaplin's
~~His~~ importance in Hollywood soon became clear. In fact,

he, Mary Pickford, and Douglas Fairbanks split from their studios

to form the studio United Artists. . . .

■ EXERCISE 11.1 Pronoun reference

Clarify the pronoun references in the following sentences. (Available on disk.)

Example

Shakespeare
Although *Macbeth* is based on Scottish history, ~~he~~ modified
historical evidence to create a compelling tragedy.

1. In the opening act, the witches tempt Macbeth and Banquo with promises of greatness. They certainly are strange.
2. Teachers have long felt that *Macbeth* is a Shakespearean tragedy that appeals to students. They find *Macbeth* a valuable introduction to Shakespeare's other, more complicated works.

3. Although *Macbeth* has violence at its core, Nedah, Louis, and myself found the Polanski film version bloodier and more perverse than necessary.

4. The elements of Japanese kabuki theater merge well with the symbolic dimensions of *Macbeth*. They make kabuki productions of *Macbeth* very appealing.

5. In the last act of *Macbeth*, it implies that conditions in Scotland will return to normal.

Position **modifiers**—which explain, describe, define, or limit a word or group of words—so that the relationship between them and the words they modify is clear.

QUICK REFERENCE

Modifiers add vividness and specificity to writing when they are effectively positioned in sentences according to these principles:

▶ As often as possible, place modifiers near the words they modify.

▶ Seldom separate subjects and predicates or predicates and complements with long modifiers.

▶ Use modifiers to explain, describe, define, or limit only one word or phrase. If a modifier can conceivably modify several words or phrases, reposition it.

12a Clarity and Smoothness

Place modifiers where they create clear meaning.

■ Long Modifiers

If a long modifier separates the subject from the verb or the verb from the object, reposition the modifier.

Poe's "The Telltale Heart" is, however disturbing its main premise may be, a spellbinding story.

◼ Prepositional Phrases

Because nearness guides modification, place prepositional phrases near the words they modify.

In spite of his successful command of forces in the Pacific,
President Truman relieved Douglas MacArthur of his military
duties.
[**Truman commanded forces in the Pacific?**]

◼ Limiting Modifiers

Place limiting modifiers such as *hardly, nearly,* and *only* with care and double-check to see that the meaning of the sentence is clear.

He simply stated the problem.
[**Stating the problem is all he did.**]

He stated the problem simply.
[**He made the problem easy to understand.**]

◼ Modifiers near Infinitives

Try not to place a modifier between *to* and an infinitive. Although this usage is common, it is best to avoid split infinitives.

After rereading "Ode to a Grecian Urn," Ralph began to quickly prepare his report.

12b Dangling Modifiers

A phrase that appears at the beginning of a sentence but that does not modify the subject of the sentence is a **dangling modifier.** Reposition the misplaced phrases.

, Registering 4.5 on the Richter Scale, the building's inhabitants
felt the effect of the earthquake.

[**The earthquake, not the inhabitants, registered 4.5 on the scale.**]

12c Squinting Modifiers

Squinting modifiers are words or phrases that could modify either the words before them or the words after them. Reposition the element to avoid confusion or use the relative pronoun *that* to clarify your meaning.

The expedition leader said before ten o'clock they would reach the summit.
[This repositioning clarifies a ten o'clock arrival; alternately, moving the phrase "before ten o'clock" to the beginning of the sentence would emphasize the time at which the leader spoke.]

▓ EXERCISE 12.1 Positioning modifiers

The following sentences contain misplaced modifiers. Revise the sentences to make the modification clear and effective. (Available on disk.)

1. The problems of alcoholism, no matter whether they affect adults, adolescents, or even children, need to be honestly addressed.

2. Drinking is, though acceptable within most groups in American culture, socially, physically, and economically costly.

3. Families and coworkers often fail to honestly assess the drinking habits of alcoholics and, as a result, fail to immediately encourage alcoholics to seek professional help.

4. People who drink often have liver trouble, among other medical and social problems.

5. When inebriated, family members endure the emotional and physical abuse of alcoholics.

6. Alcoholics must admit often that their drinking problems are severe before they can get help.

■ **EXERCISE 12.2   Positioning modifiers**

The following paragraph contains a variety of misplaced modifiers.
Revise the sentences to make the modification clear and effective.
(Available on disk.)

Helping my uncle with his one-acre garden taught me that vic-
tories in the garden are won the hard way. My uncle and I, each
morning before it got too hot, would do maintenance work. We
would pull small infestations of weeds by hand and then spray, with
a post-emergent herbicide, larger growths of weeds. Then we would
mulch the plants whose foliage did not protect the soil from the
sun's drying rays. Using straw and sometimes black plastic sheets,
we would, trying not to damage low leaves, encircle the stalks of the
plants. Covered with parasitical bugs, we would sometimes have to
spray plants with a pyrethrin mixture. Once we got started, we
worked often without talking. A few comments seemed to be
enough on the growth of the asparagus or the tomatoes. Once, however, Uncle Charles told me during our work sessions I was a consci-
entious worker when he felt talkative. As the days passed, I began to,
because of my own hard work, realize how much effort goes into
gardening. I must say that grown with so much care, I now appreciate my fruits and vegetables more than I used to.

Diction

Diction, the choice and use of words for effective communication, makes meaning clear to readers. Specific word choices affect the tone of writing, implying your perception of yourself, your readers, your subject, and your purpose in writing.

QUICK REFERENCE

Select appropriate words according to your purpose and audience.

▶ Use formal or informal diction, depending on the desired tone of the paper.

▶ Choose words that your readers will understand.

▶ Select words whose denotations suit your meaning and whose connotations suit your purpose.

▶ Use specific words to convey meaning clearly and efficiently.

▶ Use idioms correctly; note especially the correct preposition in phrasal idioms.

13a Levels of Diction

American English consists of many regional and social dialects that can be broadly classified as standard or nonstandard. **Standard English** is just that: standard, established usage for speaking and writing. Employ its grammatical principles and accepted word choices for most formal writing, including academic and professional; educated readers expect its use in most of what they read. **Nonstandard English**—often used in conversation, fiction, and informal writing—occasionally uses ungrammatical constructions and colloquial, regional, or personal words and expressions.

After planning, organizing, and writing a rough draft, consider word choices carefully. Use the following guidelines, the Glossary of Usage starting on page 525, and your dictionary to choose the words that best convey the meaning and tone you want.

■ Formal Diction

Used in most academic and professional writing, **formal diction** differs somewhat from the word choices of everyday conversation. It generally excludes slang and contractions and uses the third person (*he, she, it, they*). The following paragraph, informal in the first draft, is revised in the second draft to achieve the formal tone suited to the subject.

Informal diction and tone

The effects of divorce on children change with the kids' ages. Little kids, one to four, often don't get it when their parents yell at each other, but they usually know something's wrong. They tend to get down, stopping eating and talking, or to act up, getting loud and wild. Bigger kids, from four to eight, have a better idea of what's going on. Because they don't know any better, they're always asking embarrassing questions like "Why are you and Mommy yelling at each other?" These kids often get edgy, flunk in school, and carry a heavy load of guilt.

Formal diction and tone

The effects of divorce on children vary with the children's ages. Very young children, from one to four, often do not fully comprehend the problems between their parents, but they usually sense the tension. They may become depressed, stop eating or talking, or demand attention through loud misbehavior. Older children, from four to eight, more clearly recognize relationships in turmoil. Lacking social adeptness, they often ask embarrassing and candid questions such as "Why are you and Mommy yelling at each other?" These children may become nervous, do poorly in school, and feel responsible for their parents' problems.

■ Informal Diction

Informal diction is the language of conversation. It often includes contractions and uses first-person pronouns (*I, me, my,* and so on) and sometimes includes slang and regionalisms. The following paragraph, with its personal point of view, effectively employs informal diction.

> When I was about eleven, my parents got a divorce. I wasn't surprised. For months before, I had known something was wrong, although I wasn't sure what. Mom and Dad would alternately argue about trivial matters and then turn silent, not speaking to each other for days. Then one day, Dad just quietly moved out. It was a relief for everyone, and now, ten years later, Mom and Dad are good friends.

■ Diction and Audience

To assess the appropriateness of your diction for your audience, consider these questions:

How well developed are your readers' vocabularies?   Well-educated readers probably have extensive vocabularies, allowing you to use a wide choice of words. On the other hand, if you suspect that your readers' vocabularies are limited, simplify your diction.

Do your readers understand the technical vocabulary of the subject?   Readers familiar with your subject will understand its technical terminology, and you can use it freely. Readers unfamiliar with your subject, however, will need definitions of key words, and you will need to provide everyday equivalents for technical terms.

What level of diction will your readers expect?   Most readers expect standard diction in most writing. Some prefer formal diction; others prefer informal diction; still others expect a well-chosen blend of formal and informal language, a combination often termed **moderate diction.** To answer questions about the level of particular words or phrases, refer to the Glossary of Usage starting on page 525, a general dictionary, or a dictionary of usage.

Although you cannot completely match word choices with readers' knowledge, needs, and expectations, make an effort to analyze your audience and use language that they will understand and appreciate.

■ EXERCISE 13.1   Formal and informal diction

The diction of the following sentences about the novel Native Son *is too informal. Revise the sentences to increase their formality.* (Available on disk.)

1. Many readers are grossed out when Bigger Thomas bashes the rat in the opening scene of the novel.
2. The Daltons, a filthy rich family, had made a bunch of money by ripping off poor tenants in slum housing.
3. Their daughter Mary and her left-wing friends were into hanging out in restaurants in black neighborhoods.
4. Bigger took off after he accidentally did Mary in.
5. Once the cops nabbed Bigger, he was put on trial and then sent up the river.

13b   Denotations and Connotations

Words are defined in two ways, by their denotations and by their connotations.

■ Denotations

Denotations are dictionary meanings—short, specific definitions. They present the explicit meanings of words and exclude the shades of meaning that words acquire in specific contexts.

■ Connotations

Connotations are the secondary and sometimes emotional meanings of words; they suggest meaning beyond the explicit denotation. Make sure that the connotations of your words match your purpose.

Consider Connotations

Two words often share the same denotation (and hence are synonyms) but have distinct connotations, ranging from positive, to neutral, to negative.

Positive connotation

The *delegation* of students protested outside the administration building.
[*Delegation* **implies an orderly, duly constituted, and representative gathering.**]

Negative connotation

The *mob* of students protested outside the administration building.
[*Mob* **suggests a lack of control and implies a threat.**]

Neutral connotation

The *group* of students protested outside the administration building.
[*Group* **simply denotes "a number of people."**]

■ EXERCISE 13.2   Connotations

Revise the following sentences to replace words whose connotations seem inappropriate. (Available on disk.)

1. Airport security has become restrictive during the last few years, as folks who travel a lot have discovered.

2. At every concourse in major airports, people dawdle in lines, waiting to have their carry-on luggage inspected.

3. At these security checkpoints, people sometimes get peeved about passing their stuff through scanning devices, but every once in a while, someone is flabbergasted when his or her luggage sets off the alarm.

4. The security guards interrogate people whose luggage sets off the alarm to see if they have a reasonable excuse, and then the checking continues.

5. Although these security checks are an annoyance, they help to keep air travel inviolate.

13c Abstract or Concrete Words

Abstract words name intangibles, such as concepts, qualities, or conditions: *truth, loyalty, laziness, freedom, poverty.* **Concrete words** name tangibles: *fire hydrant, bagel, razor, rabbit, silo.* Use abstract words to present general ideas and concrete words to add interest and specificity.

Abstract

Poverty demoralizes people.

Concrete

Being unable to pay bills, buy suitable clothing, feed one's children well, and own some small conveniences demoralizes parents who want comfortable homes for their families.

The following table illustrates a simplified continuum of specificity.

Most General ←			→ **Most Specific**
Games	Card games	Wagering card games	Poker
Trees	Fruit trees	Apple trees	Granny Smith apple trees
Animals	Mammals	Marine mammals	Whales

Whales can be made more exact by specifying *blue whales, sperm whales,* or *killer whales.* Although you may not always have this many alternatives, choose the most specific word possible to clarify your meaning.

1. *Women* in *fiction* are sometimes shrewder than *men.*
2. *Heroines* in *novels* are sometimes shrewder than *heroes.*
3. *Romantic heroines* in *nineteenth-century novels* are sometimes shrewder than *their lovers.*
4. *Catherine* in <u>Wuthering Heights</u> is shrewder than *Heathcliff.*

Sometimes a generalization best suits your purpose, in which case the third sentence may be the best. However, do not forget the importance of specificity. Readers of the first sentence could easily and justifiably supply their own details, thinking wrongly, for instance, that the writer means that women in contemporary short stories are sometimes shrewder than their fathers. To avoid such misinterpretation, make your meaning clear by using specific diction.

■ EXERCISE 13.3　Specific words

The following sentences present general ideas. Clarify their meanings by replacing general words with specific ones. (Available on disk.)

1. Politics is expensive.
2. The crowd at the convention was big.
3. Family members of politicians often have personal problems.
4. The candidate won the election.
5. Television influences politics.

13d　Forms of Idioms

Idioms, groups of words that together establish an idiosyncratic meaning, are often illogical if examined word for word. For example, *break it up,* commonly understood to mean "stop fighting," makes little sense when examined one word at a time. Other unanalyzable idioms include *pick up (the house), take a shower, fall in love,* and *catch a cold.* Such idioms have developed along with our language, and although they may not make literal sense, they are understood.

The correct use of many phrasal idioms, such as those in the following list, depends on using the correct preposition. If you are in doubt about which preposition to use, check the list or a dictionary.

Phrasal Idioms

agree with (someone)
agree to (a proposal)
angry with (*not* angry at)
charge for (a purchase)
charge with (a crime)
die of/die from
differ with (meaning "to disagree")
differ from (meaning "to be unlike")
in search of (*not* in search for)
intend to (*not* intend on)
off (*not* off of)
plan to (*not* plan on)
similar to (*not* similar with)
sure to (*not* sure and)
to search for
try to (*not* try and)
type of (*not* type of a)
wait for (someone or something)
wait on (meaning "to serve")

■ **EXERCISE 13.4 Idioms**

Select the appropriate idioms for the following sentences.

1. The National Geographic Society (NGS), founded in 1888, is a (type of a/type of) organization with diverse interests and goals.

2. On the one hand, the NGS often goes (in search of/in search for) exotic flora and fauna to describe in articles and broadcasts.

3. On the other hand, NGS also (tries and/tries to) make Americans aware of simple but subtle differences between peoples of different cultures.

4. Although the format for NGS television programs does not (differ with/differ from) that of other nature documentaries, they are nonetheless uniformly more fascinating.

5. With more than 10.5 million members, NGS will be (sure to/sure and) flourish into the twenty-first century.

13e Slang and Regionalisms

Both **slang** and **regionalisms** are exclusive, informal vocabularies, understood by a restricted group. In the case of slang, the restriction is generally to a social, professional, or cultural group; in the case of regionalisms, the restriction is to a specific geographic area.

Because slang is quickly dated and informal, and its meaning is frequently inexact to those outside the originating group, it should be used sparingly.

When I saw how far ahead I was, I felt *wicked*.
[“Evil”? Wicked good? Wicked bad?]

Because regionalisms are primarily understood within the bounds of a restricted geographic area, they should be used cautiously.

Early in November, we ordered the *tags* for our car.
[**Although *tags* will be clear to readers from some areas of the East, use the more common expression *license plates* to ensure the understanding of readers from other areas.**]

■ **EXERCISE 13.5   Slang and regionalisms**

Make a list of five slang terms or phrases and five regionalisms in current use. Then write two sentences for each one. In the first sentence, use the slang or regionalism; in the second, translate the slang or regionalism into standard English.

Example:

The insurance plan to supplement Medicare was a *rip-off*.

The insurance plan to supplement Medicare was a *fraud*.

13f Euphemisms

Euphemisms are "nice" words substituted for specific words whose connotations are negative. Instead of saying that soldiers were *killed,* a press release might say that they *gave their lives.* Seldom fooled by euphemisms, readers instinctively supply the appropriate translation.

Euphemism	**Translation**
financial enticements	bribes
corporal punishment	spanking
placed in custody	arrested
hair-color enhancer	dye
gave notice	fired

Some euphemisms establish a buffer around painful feelings—
as when *passed away* replaces *died*—but even this use should be
infrequent.

■ **EXERCISE 13.6   Euphemisms**

*Revise the following sentences to eliminate euphemistic words and
phrases.* (Available on disk.)

1. Weddings are often not inexpensive displays by people and for
   people who fail to consider their less-than-genuine behavior.

2. Elaborate and expensive, many weddings must be financed
   through deferred-payment plans.

3. Even brides who are in the family way often wear traditional
   white bridal gowns.

4. Many less-than-honest people who do not attend worship services regularly insist on being married in houses of God.

5. Ironically, many of these marriages—begun with such elaborate
   display—end in marriage dissolutions.

Ineffective word choices—such as clichés, pretentious or sexist language, and jargon—weaken writing by distracting or irritating readers and by obscuring ideas. Be aware of and avoid such problems.

QUICK REFERENCE

Avoid hackneyed or imprecise word choices.

▶ Eliminate clichés and other trite expressions.

▶ Use words to clarify your meaning, not to impress readers; avoid pretentious language and jargon.

▶ Use figurative language to enliven and illuminate your writing; avoid overused, illogical, or mixed figures of speech.

▶ Avoid sexist language; it is often inaccurate and may be offensive.

14a Clichés and Triteness

A **cliché** is an overused expression that has lost its original inventiveness, surprise, and, often, meaning. **Triteness** describes words and phrases that have been overused; they are stale, uninteresting, and frequently vague.

■ Clichés

Using clichés in your writing suggests that you did not take the time to think through ideas or consider original ways to express them.

Phrases such as "last but not least," "in the final analysis," or "red as a rose" are predictable—and boring. Rather than relying on clichés, choose phrases that express your meaning exactly, in your own words.

■ **Triteness**

Using trite words and phrases suggests that your ideas are equally predictable. Instead of using trite words and expressions, select fresh and interesting words.

> included a general preface, a fifteen-chapter text, and six
> appendixes presenting research data.

The report of the Educational Task Force ~~was very thorough.~~ [*Thorough* is so common and used in so many contexts that it hardly clarifies the meaning of the sentence; the use of details improves the clarity of the sentence.]

■ **EXERCISE 14.1   Clichés and trite expressions**

Revise the following sentences to eliminate clichés and trite expressions. (Available on disk.)

1. Some monuments have struck a chord with the American people and can remind each and every one of us of the value of public memorials.

2. The Statue of Liberty is an awe-inspiring national monument, symbolizing how America opened its arms to European emigrants.

3. The simplicity of the Tomb of the Unknown Soldier and the low-key military display put a lump in the throats of many visitors.

4. One out-of-the-ordinary monument, the Gateway Arch, reaches to the sky in a sweeping curve of shiny stainless steel.

5. With its marble as smooth as glass, the Vietnam Memorial is a plain and simple monument honoring the tens of thousands of soldiers who gave their lives for their country.

14b Pretentious Language

Pretentious language tries to impress rather than to communicate with readers. Avoid stilted language, even in formal writing. It is not only dishonest, but it also makes simple ideas difficult to grasp and complicated ideas impossible to understand. If you do not translate pretentious diction into natural words, your readers must do so.

> ~~Before~~
> ~~Prior to~~ the purchase of the ~~abode~~, the Enricos carefully
> ~~thought~~ ~~mortgage~~
> ~~ruminated~~ about how ~~residential~~ payments would affect their
> ~~finances~~
> ~~cash flow~~.
>
> [The stilted word choices here, some poorly chosen synonyms and some jargon, require a translation; the revised sentence is easily understood on the first reading.]

Although referring to a thesaurus, a book of synonyms, may help you to find alternative ways of stating a point, use only words that are a natural part of your vocabulary, avoid clichés, and never choose words whose connotations you do not understand.

■ EXERCISE 14.2   Pretentious language

Revise the following paragraph to eliminate pretentious language and use language that is more natural. (Suggestion: Make this a personal narrative.) (Available on disk.)

When one participates in commencement ceremonies, one is often fraught with a mixture of emotions. One senses relief because one's time in high school is terminating. Conversely, one feels uncertain about what lies ahead. Some students will seek employment immediately, other students will approach matrimony, and yet other students will pursue additional academic studies. For this diversity of students, commencement exercises symbolize an uncertain transmutation in their lives.

14c Jargon

Jargon is the technical vocabulary of a specialized group. Doctors, mechanics, weather forecasters, teachers, carpenters, and publishers all have special words that they use in certain contexts. When writing is directed to a specific group, using the group's jargon may be acceptable (perhaps even necessary). When you write for a wide audience, however, translate jargon into common terms.

Jargon	Translation
urban open space *(city planning)*	a city park
telephone surveillance *(law enforcement)*	wiretapping
discourse community *(communication)*	audience

~~planting trees along streets~~

The city council recommends ~~a systematic program of greening for our arterials~~ as a means to ~~revitalize our declining streetscape.~~

—make them appear less neglected.

■ EXERCISE 14.3 Pretentious diction and jargon

Translate these pretentious, jargon-laden sentences into natural, clear writing. (Available on disk.)

1. An excessive proportion of American citizenry improvidently pass their days ignoring quotidian dangers to health.
2. The abundance of vehicular collisions attests to the fact that the people of the United States of America are oblivious to safety-inducing guidelines for automobile management.

3. The numbers of persons who imbibe an excess of distilled spirits is also a depression-inducing statistic.

4. The inhalation of toxic fumes from smoking materials, although prohibited in most business establishments, continues to have a negative impact on the health aspect of the male and female population sectors.

5. The personal and private ownership and use of firearms and related paraphernalia account for the accidental demise of scores of people in each twelve-month period.

14d Figures of Speech

Figures of speech—whether single words, phrases, or longer expressions—add vitality to writing by making unexpected or suggestive connections between dissimilar things. Metaphors and similes are the most common figures of speech.

Metaphors compare two things, one familiar and one less familiar, to provide a useful or interesting association or insight.

Dr. Mantera's criticism of the proposal was all thunder and no lightning.
[**The implication is that the criticism was mere noise with no illumination or insight.**]

Similes are direct comparisons using the connectives *like, as,* or *as if.*

Cleo is *like a Duracell battery:* She's always starting something, and it lasts longer than we ever expect.

Original and apt figures of speech can enliven your writing, but they should be used to illuminate and clarify your ideas, not to decorate them. Be careful to avoid clichés.

Ron, a *modern Tom Sawyer,* enjoys harmless trickery and mild adventure.

Extended or multiple figures of speech must present a uniform impression, drawing on logically consistent images, locales, experiences, or circumstances. Without this consistency, the image is confused—often laughably so.

Confusingly mixed

Like an agile deer, the politician leaped ~~into the fray~~ over obstacles to the proposal.
[**Agile deer do leap, but they are shy animals unlikely to seek conflict; an agile deer leaping over obstacles is a logical, consistent image.**]

■ EXERCISE 14.4　Figures of speech

Revise the ineffective figures of speech in the following sentences. (Available on disk.)

1. Like good soldiers, athletes get down to the work that training sessions require and rise to the occasion.

2. Swimmers fly through lap after lap during practices, building the tireless endurance necessary in races.

3. Like kangaroos, basketball players jump for balls and then fire them down the court, hoping to hone skills to use in games.

4. With catlike speed, sprinters shoot from starting blocks over and over again, trying to perfect an opening move that will put them miles above the rest.

5. Like trains speeding down the tracks, football linesmen practice rushing and tackling, leaving other players in their wake.

14e　Sexist Language

Sexist language implies, generally through choices of key nouns and pronouns, that the subject applies only to males or only to females. Because it fails to reflect the diversity of contemporary society, sexist language is narrow-minded and inaccurate.

Avoid using gender-specific pronouns when the antecedent is not gender-specific and avoid nouns that arbitrarily restrict meaning to one gender or the other. When choosing nouns, learn to notice the subtle—and sometimes not so subtle—implications of your choices.

> or her
> A psychiatrist is bound by professional oath to keep his^ patients' records confidential.
> [Many psychiatrists are women, a situation which the additional words clarify. Alternately, using the plural forms *psychiatrists* and *their* would also avoid sexist language.]

■ **EXERCISE 14.5   Sexist language**

The following passage was written in 1872, when sensitivity to sexist language was not common. Rewrite the passage to eliminate sexist language—but do not change the meaning of the passage. (Available on disk.)

The blight which threatens theoretical culture has only begun to frighten modern man, and he is groping uneasily for remedies out of the storehouse of his experience, without having any real conviction that these remedies will avail against disaster. In the meantime, there have arisen certain men of genius who, with admirable circumspection and consequence, have used the arsenal of science to demonstrate the limitations of science and of the cognitive faculty itself. They have authoritatively rejected science's claim to universal validity and to the attainment of universal goals and exploded for the first time the belief that men may plumb the universe by means of the law of causation.   —Friedrich Nietzsche, *The Birth of Tragedy*

14f Neologisms and Archaisms

Neologisms, recently coined words or word forms, appear in current speech (and in some journalistic and technical writing). Although some neologisms are so expressive and apt that they become widely used and universally acceptable (*stereo, fallout,* and *refrigerator*), avoid using new terms unless no other word can express your meaning.

Access from one Internet site to another is simplified through a
_{direct electronic connection.}

~~hot connect.~~

[*Internet,* once a neologism, is now standard. *Hot connect* is still
jargon, vague to the uninformed, and colloquial.]

Archaisms, words once in common use but no longer standard, seem affected and disruptive in contemporary writing.
Words no longer in use—like *yon* ("over there") or *betwixt*
("between")—or words no longer used in a given sense—like *save*
in the sense of "except"—make writing artificial and pretentious.

_{while}

We adults sat and reminisced ~~whilst~~ the children played along the
shore.

[**No one says** *whilst* **anymore, and no one should write it.**]

■ **EXERCISE 14.6   Neologisms and archaic words**

*Revise the following sentences to eliminate words or phrases that are
either too new or too old to be standard usage.* (Available on disk.)

1. Methinks that romance novels deserve more attention from
   serious readers than they have often received.

2. Betwixt the covers of romance novels as varied as *Wuthering
   Heights* and *The Lady and the Highwayman,* readers will find
   quickly paced stories of intrigue and love.

3. The heroines and heroes of these novels are ofttimes innocent,
   sincere, and trusting people whose lives are threatened by erst-
   while friends who are really enemies.

4. With their inherent reliance on historical context, these info-
   tainment novels provide readers with knowledge of past societies, as well as reading pleasure.

5. Although the reading of romance novels does not require much
   intellectual input from readers, these books provide innocent
   pleasure and distraction.

Grammar

217

Fragments are capitalized and punctuated as if they were sentences, but instead, they are either subordinate clauses or phrases lacking subjects or verbs.

Although fragments are common in speech, notes, rough drafts, and writing that imitates speech, in formal writing fragments should be used only for special emphasis.

QUICK REFERENCE

Fragments distract readers and shift attention from your ideas to the mechanics of your writing. To avoid this problem, follow these suggestions:

▶ Write sentences that contain subjects and verbs, the basic sentence elements.

▶ Use subordinating conjunctions in complex and compound-complex sentences, not in subordinate-clause fragments.

▶ Use intentional fragments selectively for special effect.

15a Without Subjects or Verbs

Correct fragments that lack subjects or verbs by supplying the missing element or by combining the fragment with a complete sentence.

■ Lacking Subjects

Fragments without subjects may be verb phrases (free-standing predicates and complements); they may also be verbal phrases (phrases using gerunds, participles, and infinitives [see pages

148–52]). Eliminate these fragments by adding a subject or by joining the fragment to an appropriate sentence.

During the Civil War, Clara Barton organized nursing care in

She

makeshift hospitals. ⌃Also founded the American Red Cross.
[**A subject pronoun has been added.**]

Florence Griffith Joyner *'s* ~~had~~ one overriding goal. *was* ⌃To be the
fastest woman in track and field.
[**The infinitive phrase is joined to the sentence.**]

■ **Lacking Verbs**

Fragments without verbs are usually subjects and related modifiers, appositives, or absolute phrases. Correct these fragments by adding a verb or by joining the appositive or absolute phrase to another sentence.

George Washington Carver, the son of slaves⌃ ~~He~~ developed a
wide variety of uses for southern agricultural products like the
peanut.
[**The fragment has been joined to a related sentence.**]

15b Subordinate Clauses

A subordinate clause must be joined to an independent clause to form a grammatical sentence. Correct subordinate-clause fragments by dropping the subordinating conjunction to form a simple sentence or by joining the subordinate clause to an independent clause.

⌃Some students have to postpone starting college. Because the
cost of attending has risen.
[**Here the subordinate clause becomes part of a complex sentence.**]

15c Special Use of Fragments

Fragments can be effective and acceptable when they are used to isolate and thus emphasize a key word or phrase. Use this strategy selectively to achieve emphasis or to supply an answer to a question.

> G, PG, R, X. These symbols are used to classify films and to restrict the audiences that see them. Although the coding system represents an admirable effort to protect children, does it work? No. Many parents disregard the implied advice of the rating system, and few theater owners adhere to its guidelines when selling tickets.

■ EXERCISE 15.1   Fragments

Eliminate the fragments in the following paragraph by adding subjects or verbs or by combining the fragments with complete sentences. (Available on disk.)

The National Board of Teaching Standards was formed to address matters of teacher training and certification. Because of inconsistencies that exist among states. Some states require prospective teachers to take a preprofessional skills test. To establish the reading, writing, and mathematical skills of future teachers. But not others. All states require expertise in content areas. Approximates that of traditional majors in each subject area. States require additional work in educational theory and practice. Usually fifteen to twenty semester hours of work. These pedagogical courses, ones emphasizing general principles of teaching and general patterns of learning. No matter how theoretically sound these courses may be, inconsistencies exist. Since states establish their requirements individually. As a result, teachers moving from one state to the other may not be fully prepared to meet requirements. Future teachers need the coordinated efforts of state departments of education. To develop uniform educational programs. Especially with prospects of taking the National Teacher's Exam.

■ **EXERCISE 15.2   Fragments**

The following paragraph includes a number of fragments. Some are intended for special emphasis, but others are clearly grammatical errors. Correct the ineffective fragments and explain why the others should remain. (Available on disk.)

New York. St. Louis. Knoxville. New Orleans. Los Angeles. These cities have all hosted those pretentious, glorious, overly expensive, and enjoyable activities known as world's fairs. Filled with exhibits, amusements, and restaurants. World's fairs offer people a chance to learn about the world while enjoying themselves. At these large fairs, nations from around the world build pavilions to showcase their national achievements. Often sending examples of their best technology, art, and historical treasures. Dancers, singers, and musicians. Enjoy seeing native costumes and folk dances that illustrate the diversity of the world's cultures. Sometimes, even specialties of individual fairs have become common later on. St. Louis, the city where the ice-cream cone was invented. It has since become a favorite treat worldwide. World's fairs, originally planned to "bring the world closer together." But do they continue to serve this original purpose? Not really. Because people now travel by airplane and can see the countries of the world. They see much more than can be seen in national exhibits at world's fairs.

Comma splices and fused sentences contain two or more independent clauses that are not properly punctuated. In a **comma splice** (also called a **comma fault**), the independent clauses are incorrectly joined with only a comma. In a **fused sentence** (also called a **run-on sentence**), independent clauses are placed one after the other with no punctuation.

Correct comma splices and fused sentences by changing the punctuation or the structure of the sentence.

QUICK REFERENCE

Because they incorrectly merge ideas, comma splices and fused sentences are never acceptable in writing.

▌ Use a period to separate the independent clauses in comma splices or fused sentences.

▌ Use a semicolon, a comma and a coordinating conjunction, or a subordinating conjunction (and a comma if necessary) to join independent clauses.

▌ Remember that conjunctive adverbs do not join independent clauses or sentences as coordinating or subordinating conjunctions do.

16a Forming Two Sentences

To correct a comma splice or a fused sentence, form two sentences.

Many artists and musicians are extremely fashion conscious⊙ they view their clothes as a form of self-expression.

16b   Using a Semicolon

To correct a comma splice or a fused sentence, use a semicolon to separate the independent clauses.

In the 1950s, members of English departments felt their programs were too diverse; they split into departments of literature, composition, linguistics, and speech communication.

16c   Using Coordinating and Subordinating Conjunctions

Use a coordinating conjunction (*and, but, for, nor, or, so,* or *yet*) with a comma to link independent clauses to form a compound sentence. Use a subordinating conjunction (*although, because, since, while,* or others) to join independent clauses to form complex or compound-complex sentences.

Comma Splice

                                because
NASA delayed the shuttle launch, the ground crew wanted to check the on-board computers again.
[**When the subordinate clause ends the sentence, a comma is unnecessary if the meaning is clear.**]

Fused Sentence

Although
Many cabinet members work for only four to eight years with the president they continue to work in Washington as consultants to major firms.
[**When the subordinate clause begins the sentence, a comma is required.**]

16d Conjunctive Adverbs

Conjunctive adverbs (*besides, furthermore, however, nevertheless, still, then, therefore,* and others) connect ideas logically but do not link independent clauses grammatically. When a conjunctive adverb appears in a comma splice or fused sentence, correct the sentence by using a period or semicolon to separate the independent clauses.

Comma splice

Corporate mergers are often like marriages; however, some unfriendly ones are like abductions.
[**The use of a semicolon grammatically separates the two independent clauses.**]

■ **EXERCISE 16.1 Comma splices and fused sentences**

Correct these faulty sentences by changing their punctuation or structure. (Available on disk.)

1. *Rock 'n' roll* is a generic term used to describe a wide variety of musical styles, nonetheless, each musical style remains distinct.

2. The term *pop music* was coined in the 1950s, it describes music that cuts across socio-ethnic lines and appeals to a wide audience.

3. *Acid rock* describes the amplified, electronic music of the mid-1960s artists in this subgenre of rock music were often part of the drug-using counterculture.

4. *Disco's* emphasis on highly synthesized electronic music with an insistent rhythm made it popular dance music, nevertheless, its popularity faded in only a few years.

5. Black American music, sometimes called *soul music* and sometimes *rhythm and blues,* developed from gospel music its acceptance in conservative white culture attests to music's power to break down barriers.

6. With its emphasis on shock value, *punk rock* created a brief sensation in the world of music people soon grew tired of being shocked by performers who often lacked musical skill.

■ **EXERCISE 16.2   Comma splices and fused sentences**

Correct the comma splices and fused sentences in the following paragraph by adding periods, commas and coordinating conjunctions, semicolons, or subordinating conjunctions. (Available on disk.)

Book censorship in American high schools has become a standard practice these days, individuals and groups have applied pressure to school boards everywhere. The books that have been censored range widely in subject they range widely in literary quality as well. No book seems to be beyond the reach of book censors. Books treating sexual situations, like *A Farewell to Arms,* have been banned, books that contain questionable language, like *The Catcher in the Rye,* have been banned, too. *The Grapes of Wrath* has been censored in some communities because of its presentation of socialist ideology, *Lord of the Flies* has been removed from libraries because of its violence. Even a book like *The Adventures of Huckleberry Finn* is now being brought into question it has racially demeaning dialect. The American Library Association has come to the defense of these books, however that has not kept them on bookshelves and reading lists in many American high schools.

Subjects and verbs must agree in number; pronouns and antecedents must agree in number and gender.

QUICK REFERENCE

To correct errors in subject-verb or pronoun-antecedent agreement, apply these principles.

▶ Verbs must agree in number with the subject of the clause or sentence. Do not be misled by intervening words.

▶ Let the meaning of the subject (singular or plural) determine the verb; watch compound subjects with *and* or *or,* indefinite pronouns, collective nouns, and plural words with a singular meaning.

▶ Make sure that pronouns have clear antecedents with which they agree in both number and gender.

▶ Let the intended number of the antecedent guide your choice of pronouns; watch compound subjects with *and* or *or,* indefinite pronouns, collective nouns, and plural words with a singular meaning.

17a Subjects and Verbs

Verbs agree with the subject of the sentence, not with intervening words. Words that separate subjects and verbs, particularly nouns that serve as objects of prepositions, should not influence the choice of verbs.

The *swallows* of Capistrano *are* becoming noticeably less predictable.
[***Capistrano,* a singular noun in a prepositional phrase, does not affect verb choice.**]

■ Compound Subjects Joined by *And*

Compound subjects joined by *and* require plural verbs.

> compound subj.   plural verb
> The defendant and her counsel were both angered by the verdict.

However, compound subjects that are seen as one unit are singular and require a singular verb.

"Tragedy and triumph" describes Britain's lonely resistance to Hitler during the grim days of 1940.

■ Subjects Joined by *Or, Nor, Either . . . Or,* or *Neither . . . Nor*

Or, nor, and so on indicate alternative subjects, not multiple subjects. The verb, therefore, should agree with the number of the individual subjects.

Singular subjects

Either *walking* or *running strengthens* the heart.
[**Walking *strengthens;* running *strengthens.***]

Plural Subjects

As gifts, *recordings* or *books* please most people.
[**Recordings *please;* books *please.***]

When a compound subject contains both plural and singular elements, the verb agrees with the closer element.

Singular and plural elements

Neither the *designer* nor the *engineers like* the prototype.

Plural and singular elements

Neither the *engineers* nor the *designer likes* the prototype.

When a singular noun follows a plural noun in a compound subject, the required singular verb, though grammatically correct, may seem awkward. If a sentence sounds awkward, revise it.

The *prototype satisfies* neither the engineers nor the designer.

■ Indefinite Pronouns

Indefinite pronouns (*anyone, each, either, everybody, none, someone,* and others) have no specific antecedents. Some, such as *both* and *all,* are always plural and require plural verbs, but most are singular and require singular verbs. Be particularly careful using pronouns like *everyone* or *everybody,* which require singular verbs even though *every-* sounds plural; *-one* or *-body* should guide you.

Everyone needs to be tolerant of differences.

Oysters and clams are soft-bodied mollusks. However, *both have* hard shells.

When *every* and *each* are used as adjectives (even with a compound subject), a singular verb is required.

Every man, woman, and child *was* evacuated before nightfall.
[*Every* **emphasizes the people individually, so a singular verb is appropriate.**]

■ Collective Nouns

Collective nouns stressing group unity require singular verbs; collective nouns stressing the individuality of group members require plural verbs.

Group unity

The *committee votes* by a show of hands.
[**The committee as a whole follows this procedure.**]

Group members as individuals

> The *Supreme Court act* according to their individual consciences.
> [**Each member acts separately, so the plural form is correct.**]

If collective nouns stressing individuality sound awkward with plural verbs, revise the sentence by including "members of" or a similar word or phrase that clearly requires a plural verb.

> The Supreme Court *justices act* according to their individual consciences.

■ Expletive Constructions

Expletive constructions (*here is, here are, there is, there are, there was,* and *there were*) depend for meaning on the noun complement (the noun that follows the construction); the verb in the expletive phrase must agree in number with the noun.

> Here *is* the *document* that will demonstrate her innocence.

> There *are* many unimaginative *programs* on television.

■ Relative Clauses

When used as subjects of clauses, relative pronouns (*who, which,* and *that*), agree in number with their antecedents.

> Flooding in the spring is a *threat* that *requires* our attention.
> [***That* refers to *threat*, a singular predicate noun. Consequently, the relative clause requires a singular verb.**]

> People once believed in the *pseudo-sciences* of physiognomy and astrology, which *have* now lost their credibility.
> [***Which* refers to *pseudo-sciences*, a plural object of a preposition. The verb in the relative clause must therefore be plural.**]

■ Linking Verbs

Linking verbs agree with the number of the subject, not the number of the predicate noun.

A major *expense* of operating a school *is* salaries for administrators, teachers, and custodians.
[Although *salaries* is plural, the subject of the sentence is *expense,* a singular noun. Therefore, the verb must also be singular.]

■ Plural Nouns with Singular Meanings

Plural nouns such as *news, politics,* and *electronics* have singular meanings. They require singular verbs.

Fractions, measurements, money, time, weight, and volume considered as single units also require singular verbs.

Plural noun

Geriatrics successfully *discredits* the prejudice that senility is inevitable in the elderly.
[*Geriatrics* is a single discipline and requires a singular verb.]

Plural unit

Twenty-seven million dollars was a small price to pay for the Louisiana Territory.
[The dollar amount, considered *one* price, requires a singular verb.]

■ Titles

Even when the words in a title are plural, the title of a single work requires a singular verb.

Leaves of Grass *illustrates* the best and worst characteristics of nineteenth-century American verse.
[*Leaves of Grass* is the title of one long poem, so a singular verb is required.]

■ Words Used as Words

Words used as words require singular verbs. This rule applies even when the word discussed is plural.

Media is often inaccurately *substituted* for *medium.*
[***Media,*** **a plural noun, requires a singular verb when discussed as a word.**]

■ **EXERCISE 17.1   Subject-verb agreement**

Select the verb that maintains subject-verb agreement.

1. Archaeologists (studies/study) the buildings, tools, and other artifacts of ancient cultures.

2. Every archaeologist, especially field researchers, (know/knows) of a historic site ruthlessly desecrated by treasure seekers.

3. Despite international agreements, unscrupulous museums or a wealthy private collector (compete/competes) for every major artistic discovery, stolen or not.

4. But laws and international policing (reduce/reduces) yearly the number of destroyed sites and stolen artifacts.

5. Excavations—better controlled than ever by teams of university archaeologists, students, local workers, and national representatives—(proceed/proceeds) slowly these days, avoiding the damage inflicted by yesterday's "grave robbers."

6. *Digs* (is/are) the current jargon used to describe excavation sites.

7. Recent decades (has seen/have seen) few finds of the historical significance of the discovery of Tutankhamen's tomb in 1922, but research in various locales (continue/continues).

8. For archaeologists, five or ten years (seem/seems) a reasonable time to work at a single site, so new finds will be made—but more slowly than in the past.

■ **EXERCISE 17.2   Subject-verb agreement**

The following paragraph contains many errors in subject-verb agreement. Correct the misused verbs and then draw arrows to the subjects with which each verb agrees.

There is more and more adults attending college at a later age. Their motives, either to change careers or to get the education they missed, varies. Anyone walking on a college campus see students in their thirties, forties, fifties, and even sixties carrying books and talking with friends. Almost every class and laboratory now include at least one of these "nontraditional" students. Because their home and job situations and their preparedness differs from those of eighteen- to twenty-two-year-olds, these students face problems that surprises a younger student. Some of these adults organizes their schooling around full-time jobs. Others care for families as well as attends class. Nobody going to college and getting a degree find it easy, but an adult student with adult responsibilities have extra problems to cope with. As this situation becomes more common, everyone adjust, however, a process that already have begun. Even the media recognize this trend in American education. With humor and sympathy, the television show *Mad about You* provide insights into the problems adults face when attending college. Who knows? Given a chance today, maybe even Lucy Ricardo or John Walton might enroll in a class or two.

17b Pronouns and Antecedents

Singular antecedents (the words to which pronouns refer) require singular pronouns; plural antecedents require plural pronouns.

```
    sing.              sing.
 antecedent          pronoun
```
Genghis Khan ruled *his* vast empire with great cruelty.

```
   plural                                      plural
 antecedent                                   pronoun
```
Children need encouragement and guidance from *their* parents.

Pronouns must also agree with the gender of their antecedents.

fem.   fem.
antecedent   pronoun

Queen Elizabeth II rules *her* empire as a constitutional monarch.

Plural pronouns do not specify gender, but singular pronouns specify masculine, feminine, or neuter gender.

Pronoun Forms				
	Subjective	*Objective*	*Possessive*	*Reflexive*
Masculine	he	him	his	himself
Feminine	she	her	hers	herself
Neuter	it	it	its	itself

■ Pronoun-Antecedent Agreement and Sexist Language

The masculine pronouns (*he* and its variations) were once used with antecedents whose gender was undetermined. This usage is no longer acceptable.

Use plural antecedents and pronouns when possible or rephrase the sentence. Do not use a plural pronoun like *their* with a singular antecedent; this usage creates a problem in pronoun-antecedent agreement. Another possible solution, using pronouns in pairs (*he or she, his or hers, he/she,* and so on) should be used sparingly since it can lead to distracting repetition and awkward rhythm in sentences.

A good *surgeon* carefully explains procedures to ~~his~~ *their* patients.

or

A good *surgeon* carefully explains procedures to *his or her* patients.

To express generalizations based on individual experiences, use a specific antecedent instead of a general noun. That, in turn, will dictate a specific pronoun choice and help you to avoid sexist language.

Dr. Knepper, like all good surgeons, carefully explains procedures to his patients.

■ Compound Antecedents Joined by *And*

Compound antecedents joined by *and* require plural pronouns.

compound antecedent	plural pronoun

Female *whales* and *dolphins* fiercely protect *their* young.

■ Antecedents Joined by *Or, Nor, Either . . . Or,* or *Neither . . . Nor*

Compound subjects joined by these words present alternative— not multiple—subjects, so pronouns refer to each subject individually.

Singular antecedents

Neither Gladstone nor Disraeli graciously accepted criticism of *his* plans for the British government.
[**Gladstone/***his;* **Disraeli/***his*]

Plural antecedents

Did *the Greeks or the Romans* consider Zeus *their* principal god?
[**Greeks/***their;* **Romans/***their*]

When part of a compound antecedent is singular and part is plural, the pronoun agrees with the closer antecedent.

Singular and plural antecedents

The President or the *members* of Congress must modify *their* terms.
[**members/***their*]

If the construction sounds awkward, place the singular noun first or consider rewriting the sentence.

Correct but awkward

> The members of Congress or the *president* must modify *his* terms.
> [**president/***his*]

Better

> If the *president* will not change *his* terms, the *members* of Congress will have to change *theirs*.
> [**president/***his;* **members/***theirs*]

■ Indefinite Pronouns as Antecedents

Indefinite pronouns (*anyone, each, either, everybody, none,* and others) are usually singular in meaning and take singular pronouns. However, some indefinite pronouns (*all, most, some,* and others) are plural in meaning and take plural pronouns. Let the number of the indefinite pronoun guide you.

> *Anyone* who works as a war correspondent risks *his or her* life frequently.
> [***Anyone* refers to people one at a time, as does the pronoun cluster *his or her*.**]

■ Collective Nouns

When collective nouns stress group unity, they take singular pronouns; when collective nouns stress the group as a collection of individuals, they take plural pronouns.

Group unity

> The *audience* showed *its* approval by applauding loudly.
> [**The audience is perceived as a single unit, creating a unified response.**]

Individuality within the group

> The *audience* raised *their* voices in song.
> [**This sentence stresses the many voices of the audience members.**]

■ **EXERCISE 17.3   Pronoun-antecedent agreement**

Insert appropriate pronouns in the following sentences. (Available on disk.)

1. Greeks, Romans, Egyptians, Indians, and virtually every other civilized group had one or more methods of keeping _____ dwellings cool during summer months.

2. For example, all of these peoples hung water-soaked mats in _____ doorways to develop cooling moisture.

3. Leonardo da Vinci, with _____ usual inventiveness, created the first mechanical fan in about 1500, _____ power provided by running water.

4. The 1838 British House of Commons was the first to enjoy systematic control of ventilation and humidity during _____ sessions.

5. Neither Alfred Wolff (in 1902) nor Willis Carrier (in 1911) realized the impact _____ work would have on later generations.

6. After 1931, a passenger riding on the Baltimore & Ohio Railroad could travel to _____ destination in air-conditioned comfort.

7. When Stuart Cramer first used the phrase *air conditioning* in 1906, _____ almost certainly didn't know that _____ newly coined term would be in universal use today.

8. Few people who live in temperate climates or who work in high-rise buildings would want to give up _____ air conditioning in the summer.

■ **EXERCISE 17.4   Pronoun-antecedent agreement**

Most pronouns in the following paragraph have been omitted. Insert appropriate pronouns, maintaining correct pronoun-antecedent agreement. (Available on disk.)

    Everyone who works in the United States must pay _____ income taxes on or before April 15. An employee of a traditional business has _____ taxes withdrawn during each pay period and at the end of the year receives _____ yearly statement, the W2 form.

Neither employees nor the employer can decide how _____ tax accounts will be handled, but employees determine what percentage of taxes will be taken from _____ wages. For a self-employed taxpayer, the procedure for determining _____ taxes is not so clear. Artists, writers, freelance contractors, and other people whose incomes fluctuate must estimate _____ incomes for the year and pay _____ taxes in installments. Anyone who has ever tried to estimate how productive _____ will be in the next year can appreciate the difficulty a self-employed person has in estimating how much _____ will owe at the end of the year. In the past, the self-employed were grated some leniency in paying _____ taxes. However, in 1987, despite objections from some of _____ constituents, Congress voted to penalize people whose estimated tax payments were less than 90 percent of _____ taxes due.

The **case** of a pronoun indicates the pronoun's grammatical relationship to the other words in the sentence. Pronoun case is indicated by changes in form (*I*, *me*, or *mine*, for example) or by changes in position in the sentence, as in the following example.

subj.   obj.   poss.
case   case case

I gave them his address.

QUICK REFERENCE

Apply these rules and suggestions to determine pronoun case.

▶ Personal pronouns used as subjects in clauses and sentences require the subjective case; pronouns used as objects require the objective case.

▶ Use a personal pronoun in the possessive case to modify a noun or a gerund.

▶ Distinguish among *who* and *whoever* (the subjective-case forms), *whom* and *whomever* (the objective-case forms), and *whose* (the possessive-case form).

▶ Do not confuse possessive-case pronouns (for example, *its*) with contractions (for example, *it's*, which means "it is").

Nouns and pronouns used as subjects or predicate nouns are in the **subjective case.** Nouns or pronouns used as direct objects, indirect objects, or objects of prepositions are in the **objective case.** Nouns or pronouns used to show ownership are in the **possessive case.**

Case Forms of Personal Pronouns			
	Subjective	*Objective*	*Possessive*
Singular			
1st person	I	me	my, mine
2nd person	you	you	your, yours
3rd person	he, she, it	him, her, it	his, her, hers, its
Plural			
1st person	we	us	our, ours
2nd person	you	you	your, yours
3rd person	they	them	their, theirs

Case Forms of *Who* and Related Pronouns		
Subjective	*Objective*	*Possessive*
who	whom	whose
whoever	whomever	

Most pronouns change forms to produce the possessive case (*I, my; she, her*); however, indefinite pronouns (*someone, everybody*) form the possessive by adding *'s* (*someone's, everybody's*).

Do not confuse possessive-case pronouns, which do not use an apostrophe, with contractions that sound the same: *its* and *it's* ("it is"), *theirs* and *there's* ("there is"), and *whose* and *who's* ("who is").

18a Subjective Case

Subjective case

Although *he* got a *D* in freshman composition, Faulkner went on to become one of America's most honored writers.

When a sentence has a compound subject, isolate the parts of the subject to help you choose the appropriate pronoun.

Compound subject

Jimmy Carter and his wife Rosalyn were active in Habitat for Humanity. Carter and *she* not only raised funds, but they also helped to build houses.
[**Carter raised; *she* raised; consequently, *Carter and she* raised.**]

Because a predicate noun restates the subject, it requires the subjective case. If this construction sounds too formal, invert the subject and predicate noun.

At the end of <u>Great Expectations</u>, we discover that Pip's benefactor was *he*.
[**The predicate noun, signaled by the linking verb *was,* must be in the subjective case.**]

At the end of <u>Great Expectations</u>, we discover that *he* was Pip's benefactor.
[**This sentence sounds less formal.**]

18b Objective Case

A direct object answers the question *whom* or *what*. An indirect object answers the question *to whom* or *for whom*. Pronouns that answer these questions should be in the objective case.

Direct object

Susan B. Anthony challenged sexist and racist assumptions; we should respect *her* for that.

Indirect object

Although Rasputin was feared by the Russian nobility, Czar Nicholas and Czarina Alexandra gave *him* their absolute trust.

Object of preposition

The Medici family supported the arts in Renaissance Florence; many of the greatest works of Michelangelo, da Vinci, and Botticelli were created for *them*.

When a preposition has a compound object, isolate the parts of the object to help you select the appropriate pronoun.

Nixon and Kissinger helped to orchestrate the cease-fire in the Vietnam War. Although Kissinger did most of the negotiating, the Nobel Peace Prize was awarded to *him* and Nixon.
[to *him;* to Nixon]

18c Possessive Case

■ Possessive Pronouns Used with Nouns

The possessive pronouns *my, your, his, her, its, our, your,* and *their* modify nouns. They act as adjectives in sentences and are sometimes called pronoun-adjectives.

Geraldine Ferraro was Walter Mondale's vice presidential running mate. *Her* showing in the polls was only slightly better than *his* numbers.
[The pronouns in the possessive case serve as pronoun-adjectives.]

■ Possessive Pronouns Used Alone

The possessive pronouns *mine, yours, his, hers, its, ours, yours,* and *theirs* are sometimes used alone as subjects, predicate nouns, direct objects, indirect objects, or objects of prepositions.

Given Ronald Reagan's immense popularity, the responsibility for the heavy Democratic losses was only partly *theirs*.

■ Possessive Pronouns Modifying a Gerund

When modifying a gerund (an *-ing* verb that functions as a noun), pronouns must be in the possessive case, serving as pronoun-adjectives.

> I was annoyed by *his* talking during the performance.
> [**The annoyance resulted from the person's *talking,* not from the person himself.**]

> The director commented that *their* dancing was the best part of the musical number.
> [**The best part was their *dancing,* not them.**]

18d Appositives and Elliptical Constructions

■ Pronouns in Appositives

When a pronoun in an appositive restates the subject of a clause, use the subjective case. When it restates an object, use the objective case.

> The two assistant managers, Gerald and *he,* were responsible for preparing the quarterly reports.
> [**Because the words *Gerald and he* restates *two assistant managers,* the subject of the sentence, the pronoun must be in the subjective case.**]

> The division head sent out a memo requesting that sales figures be directly reported to the assistant managers, Gerald and *him.*
> [***Gerald and him* restates *managers,* the object of the preposition *to;* therefore, the pronoun must be in the objective case.**]

■ *We* or *Us* with Nouns

When using *we* or *us* with a noun, choose the case that would be correct if the noun were omitted.

The cliché is true: *We* Americans take many of our freedoms for granted.
[**Without** *Americans,* **the pronoun appears correctly in the subjective case.**]

■ Pronouns in Elliptical Constructions

In **elliptical constructions** (constructions in which words are omitted or understood), use the case that would be appropriate if all the words were included. If the pronoun used alone sounds too formal, add the omitted words.

The Piersons arrived twenty minutes later than *we.*
[**The complete thought is that they arrived twenty minutes later than** *we arrived.*]

■ EXERCISE 18.1 Pronoun case

Supply the correct pronouns in the following sentences. (Available on disk.)

1. Hans Christian Andersen, the son of a shoemaker, began _____ adult life as an actor.

2. _____ failed on the stage, but because the king granted _____ a scholarship, Andersen was able to begin _____ writing career.

3. _____ writing of novels, plays, and long poems is almost completely forgotten, but almost everyone knows a few of _____ best fairy tales.

4. Ironically, Andersen did not set out to write fairy tales, but _____ wrote _____ first four to make money quickly.

5. Those stories succeeded beyond _____ expectations, and subsequently European nobility and royalty honored _____ for _____ work.

6. Although Andersen's tales may not be as well known as those of the brothers Grimm, _____ use of irony and humor, rather than violence, makes _____ work very appealing.

7. "The Emperor's New Clothes," one of _____ most ironic tales, alienated _____ from some of _____ noble patrons.

8. Today's readers, however, can enjoy the irony without insult and take delight in what was, for _____, a troublesome piece.

9. The best children's writers—and _____ is among them—delight us as children and intrigue us as adults, providing in simple tales some lessons on life.

10. If you think about Andersen as a failed actor who became a world-famous writer of fairy tales, you'll discover why "The Ugly Duckling" was one of _____ favorites; in a professional sense, at least, it was _____ story.

18e Who and Whoever and Whom and Whomever

■ *Who* and *Whoever*

Use the subjective-case forms *who* and *whoever* as subjects of sentences, clauses, and questions.

> Salvador Dali was an artist *who* took delight in shocking his contemporaries.
> [*Who* is the subject of the clause.]

> Carrie Nation, a turn-of-the-century prohibitionist, would preach abstinence to *whoever* would listen.
> [*Whoever* is the subject of the clause; although the preposition *to* might suggest that the objective case is required, the whole clause, not the word *whoever*, is the object of the preposition.]

■ *Whom* and *Whomever*

Use the objective-case forms *whom* and *whomever* as direct objects, indirect objects, and objects of prepositions.

> *Whom* should we invite to speak about voters' rights?
> [*Whom* is the direct object of *invite*.]

The board will probably approve the appointment of *whomever* we select.
[*Whomever* is the direct object of *select*.]

■ EXERCISE 18.2   Pronoun case

Use who, whom, whoever, *and* whomever *correctly in the following sentences.* (Available on disk.)

1. The Better Business Bureau, a nonprofit organization, was founded to help people _____ are victims of questionable business methods and deceptive advertising.

2. Consumers should first address complaints to _____ has acted in an unbusinesslike manner.

3. The Better Business Bureau is a group to _____ consumers can turn if they still are not satisfied.

4. The Better Business Bureau will answer questions and suggest strategies to _____ calls, but it cannot take legal action against suspected businesses.

5. Since the Better Business Bureau refers cases to government agencies, however, it helps ensure that businesspeople _____ are unethical do not continue to exploit consumers.

■ EXERCISE 18.3   Pronoun case

Indicate whether the italicized pronouns in the following paragraph are in the subjective, objective, or possessive case. Be ready to explain your decisions.

When *I* came out of prison,—for some one interfered, and paid that tax,—*I* did not perceive that great changes had taken place on the common, such as *he* observed *who* went in a youth and emerged a tottering and grey-headed man; and yet a change had to *my* eyes come over the scene,—the town, and State, and country,—greater than any that mere time could effect. *I* saw yet more distinctly the State in which *I* lived. *I* saw to what extent the people among *whom* *I* lived could be trusted as good neighbors and friends; that *their* friendship was for summer weather only; that *they* did not greatly propose to do right; that *they* were a distinct race from *me* by *their* prejudices and superstitions, as the Chinamen and Malays are; that in *their* sacrifices to humanity *they* ran no risks, not even to *their* property; that after all *they* were not so noble but *they* treated the thief as *he* had treated *them,* and hoped, by a certain outward observance and a few prayers, and by walking in a particular straight though useless path from time to time, to save *their* souls. This may be to judge *my* neighbors harshly; for *I* believe that many of *them* are not aware that *they* have such an institution as the jail in *their* village.   —Henry David Thoreau, "Civil Disobedience"

Verb tenses—formed through the use of auxiliary verbs and changes in verb endings—indicate when things happened or existed in relation to when they are described. Tenses also indicate whether an action or state of being continued over time or whether it has been completed.

QUICK REFERENCE

Verbs, along with subjects, form the core of sentences. The use of effective verbs will strengthen your writing.

▶ Use verb tenses and forms to express your meaning accurately.

▶ Use the present tense to describe beliefs, scientific principles, works of art, and repeated or habitual actions.

▶ Use sequences of tenses to clarify the time relations in your writing.

▶ Use verb mood to indicate your opinion on the factuality or probability of your sentence.

19a Verb Forms

■ Regular Verbs

Regular verbs form tenses according to consistent patterns. (For an example of a full conjugation of the verb *to learn*, see page 248.)

To Learn	
Present tense	learn(*s*)
Past tense	learn*ed*
Future tense	*will* learn
Present perfect tense	*have* (or *has*) learn*ed*
Past perfect tense	*had* learn*ed*
Future perfect tense	*will have* learn*ed*
Progressive tenses	
Present progressive	*am (are)* learn*ing*
Past progressive	*was (were)* learn*ing*
Future progressive	*will be* learn*ing*
Present perfect progressive	*has (have) been* learn*ing*
Past perfect progressive	*had been* learn*ing*
Future perfect progressive	*will have been* learn*ing*

■ Irregular Verbs

Irregular verbs form tenses through changes in word form.

To Go	
Present tense	go(es)
Past tense	went
Future tense	will go
Present perfect tense	have (or has) gone
Past perfect tense	had gone
Future perfect tense	will have gone

19b Simple Tenses

The simple tenses are the present, past, and future.

■ Present Tense

Use the **present tense** to describe events occurring or conditions existing in the present.

> Senators *seek* election or reelection every six years.

In addition, there are some special uses of the present tense.

Repeated or Habitual Actions

Use the present tense to describe a habitual or frequently repeated action or series of actions or to explain standard procedures.

> Muslims *make* yearly pilgrimages to Mecca, their holiest city.

General Beliefs and Scientific Principles

Use the present tense to assert accepted beliefs.

> Every child *deserves* adequate nutrition, clothing, housing, and a good education.

Express scientific and other principles in the present tense.

> The force of gravity *determines* the flow of water in rivers and streams.

Descriptions of Works of Art

Use the present tense to describe and discuss works of art—literature, music, dance, and painting.

> Picasso's <u>Guernica</u> *contains* images of chaos and terror.

◼ Past Tense

Use the **past tense** to describe actions completed or conditions that existed in the past.

> Henry Ford *created* the Model T and, more importantly, *perfected* the industrial assembly line.

◼ Future Tense

Use the **future tense** to describe actions or conditions that will or are expected to occur or exist in the future.

> The breakup of the Soviet Union *will affect* global politics for decades.

19c Perfect Tenses

The perfect tenses are the present perfect, past perfect, and future perfect.

◼ Present Perfect Tense

Use the **present perfect tense** to describe actions that occurred or conditions that existed at an unspecified time in the past or that began in the past and continue into the present.

> Since their introduction in the early 1980s, personal computers *have changed* dramatically in power, speed, and price.
> [*Have changed* is in the present perfect tense because the change began in the past and continues in the present.]

◼ Past Perfect Tense

Use the **past perfect tense** to describe past actions or conditions that were completed before some other past action or condition occurred.

Until Lincoln *was elected* in 1860, the Republican party *had achieved* very little since its founding in 1854.
[***Had achieved*** **establishes the limited success of Republicans before the other past event, Lincoln's election.**]

■ Future Perfect Tense

Use the **future perfect tense** to describe actions that will be completed or conditions that will exist in the future but before a specific time.

Most baby boomers *will have retired* by 2020; let's hope that Social Security can survive the financial drain.

19d Progressive Tenses

Progressive tenses stress the continuing nature of actions or conditions.

The Japanese *are sharing* a large part of the costs of operating the United Nations.
[**The present progressive tense shows a continuous action.**]

The American government *has been supporting* the United Nations since its founding.
[**The present perfect progressive tense describes a continuing process that began in the past.**]

To avoid unnecessary wordiness, use the progressive tenses only when necessary to express continuing actions or states.

tried
President Clinton ~~was trying~~ to ensure that all Americans had medical coverage.

19e Relationships among Actions and Conditions

Verb tense signals chronology, indicating when actions occurred or conditions existed in relation to when they are described. Logical sequences of tense clarify the relationships among actions and conditions.

■ Infinitives

Infinitives (*to swim, to subscribe, to record*) assume the tense indicated by the main verb.

> Brainwashing *attempts to convince* people *to give up* their beliefs.
> [**The infinitives coordinate with the present-tense verb** *attempts.*]

■ Present Participles

The **present participle,** like the infinitive, assumes the tense of the main verb.

> *Speaking* to the American people in his first inaugural address, Franklin Roosevelt *reassured* them that "the only thing we have to fear is fear itself."

■ Past Participles and Perfect Participles

Past participles (*hurried, welcomed, driven*) and **perfect participles** (*having hurried, having welcomed, having driven*) indicate that the action or condition they describe occurred before that of the main verb.

> *Having won* a record nine gold medals in Olympic swimming, Mark Spitz *retired* from competition.

■ Tenses in a Subordinate Clause

Past Tense or Past Perfect Tense in a Subordinate Clause

When the verb in an independent clause is in the past or the past perfect tense, the verb in the subordinate clause must also be in the past or the past perfect tense.

> Before bacteria and viruses *were discovered,* diseases *had been explained* in superstitious ways.
> [**The use of the past perfect *had been explained* establishes that nonscientific explanations existed before the scientific ones.**]

Present, Future, Present Perfect, or Future Perfect Tense in a Subordinate Clause

When the verb in the independent clause is in the present, future, present perfect, or future perfect tense, any tense can be used in the subordinate clause.

> Although Molière's Tartuffe *was written* in 1665, its comments on religious hypocrisy and exploitation still *have* meaning today.
> [**Literature of the past still speaks to contemporary audiences.**]

■ **EXERCISE 19.1   Tenses**

Revise the following sentences, written primarily in the present tense, by changing them into the past tense. (Available on disk.)

1. The design team for the theater production meets to review the script for the play.

2. They talk about specific concerns and mention any special needs they should consider.

3. The discussion turns to potential problems in lighting the production, as it always does, because the theater—a renovated movie house—is modified less than is needed.

4. The lighting designer says, once again, that the theater will need major electrical work before a computerized lighting system can be installed.

5. Completing the discussion of lighting, the team turns its attention to the set for the play.

6. The play chosen—*Who's Afraid of Virginia Wolf?*—requires a single set, one room in a history professor's house.

7. The designers describe productions they have seen.

8. The costumer describes a production that was done in Baltimore.

9. The lighting designer remembers a collegiate production she saw in Iowa.

10. The director says he wants this set to be more realistic in its details than others he has seen.

11. As is usually the case, the team leaves after the first meeting, having made only a few key decisions.

■ EXERCISE 19.2 Tenses

Identify the tenses of the numbered verbs in the following paragraphs. Be prepared to explain why each tense is used.

Are owls truly wise? The Greeks (1) *thought* so, identifying them with Athena, goddess of wisdom. In medieval illustrations, owls (2) *accompany* Merlin and share in his sorcery. In fairy tales they rival the fox for cunning. Children's picture books (3) *show* them wearing spectacles, mortarboard, and scholar's gown. Soups and other confections made from owls (4) *have been credited* with curing whooping cough, drunkenness, epilepsy, famine, and insomnia. The Cherokee Indians used to bathe their children's eyes with a broth of owl feathers to keep the kids awake at night. Recipes using owl eggs (5) *are reputed* to bestow keen eyesight and wisdom. Yet these birds are no smarter, ornithologists (6) *assure* us, than most others. A museum guide in Boston once (7) *displayed* a drowsy-looking barn owl on his gloved wrist, (8) *explaining* to those of us assembled there how small the bird's brain actually was. "You (9) *[will] notice* the head of this live specimen appears to be about the size of a grapefruit," he said, "but it's mostly feathers." Lifting his other hand, he (10) *added,* "The skull, you (11) *see,* is the size of a lemon. There's only room enough inside for a birdbrain, not enough for Einstein!" We all laughed politely. But I was not convinced. Sure, the skull (12) *was* small. The lower half was devoted to jaw and most of the upper half to beak and eye-holes. Yet enough neurons could be fitted into the remaining space to enable the barn owl to catch mice in total darkness. They can even snatch bats on the wing, these princes of nighttime stealth. We have to invent sonar for locating submarines, radar for locating airplanes; neither (13) *is* much use with mice or bats. Barn owls can also see dead—and therefore silent—prey in light one-hundredth as bright as we would need. Like the ability to saw a board square or judge the consistency of bread dough, that might not amount to scholarship, but it (14) *is* certainly a wisdom of the body. It (15) *has worked* for some sixty million years.   —Scott Sanders, "Listening to Owls"

19f   Mood

Verbs in English may have one of three **moods:** indicative, imperative, or subjunctive. The word *mood* in the grammatical sense derives from "mode," meaning "manner," the way in which something appears, is done, or happens.

■ Definition and Use of Moods

Use the **indicative mood** to make statements or to ask questions about conditions or actions that are considered facts.

Air travel is one of the safest modes of transportation.

Use the **imperative mood** to make statements (commands) about actions that should or must be done or conditions that should or must become facts.

Fasten your seat belt and *prepare* for take-off.
[**The subject, *you*, is omitted or understood, as is generally the case in the imperative.**]

Use the **subjunctive mood** to make statements or to ask questions about actions or conditions that you doubt, wish for, or consider hypothetical or contrary to fact.

If the terminal *were redesigned*, airport security *would be* easy to maintain.
[**Note that both clauses express conditional, nonfactual states: The terminal has not been redesigned, and security is not easy to maintain.**]

However, clauses beginning with *if* use the indicative when they describe factual conditions, as in the following example:

If the terminal *had been redesigned*, it *was* difficult to see any improvement.
[**Both clauses are in the indicative past tense because they describe actual events and perceptions.**]

■ Forming the Moods

Most expressions in English are in the indicative mood, which is formed using any and all of the verb tenses covered previously in 19a through 19e. The imperative mood is formed using the present tense, as in the example above.

Subjunctive forms of the verb *to be* are *be* (singular, present tense) and *were* (plural, past tense).

If the allegations *be* true, let us act quickly.
[**present tense**]

If she *were* in charge, she would have acted.
[**past tense**]

Subjunctive forms for verbs other than *to be* differ from the indicative only in the third person singular of the present tense, in which the -*s* ending is dropped.

May the weather *continue* clear.

These examples illustrate the formal tone of statements in the subjunctive. Often, a revised version in the indicative can be substituted.

If the allegations *are* true, we should act quickly.

I hope that the clear weather *continues.*

■ EXERCISE 19.3 Mood

Where appropriate, revise the verbs in the following sentences to correct their use of mood. (Available on disk.)

1. Increasingly, working parents in the United States are asking that every employer acknowledges the child-care problem.

2. A single parent often wishes that a company-operated child-care facility was available at or near his or her place of work.

3. Lateness would probably decline if a parent was able to make one trip to a single location, instead of a separate trip to a child-care facility and then the usual trip to work.

4. If Congress was partially to subsidize child-care facilities, many companies might help their employees by providing on-site childcare.

5. But even if a company was to provide on-site childcare, problems in assuring sufficient daycare facilities would still exist.

Using adjectives and adverbs is generally uncomplicated. Occasionally, however, adjectives and adverbs can be misused when modification patterns are confused.

QUICK REFERENCE

Adjectives and adverbs refine the meaning of a sentence, but to do so effectively, they must be used correctly.

▶ Use adjectives to modify nouns and pronouns.

▶ Use adverbs to modify verbs, adjectives, and other adverbs.

▶ Use positive adjective and adverb forms when no comparison is made; use comparative forms to compare two items; use superlative forms to compare three or more items.

▶ Distinguish between troublesome adjective and adverb pairs.

20a Modifying Nouns and Pronouns

Make sure that the word modifying a noun or pronoun is an adjective. When you are uncertain, consult a dictionary to find the correct adjective form.

> <u>Treasure Island</u>, an *exciting* novel by Robert Louis Stevenson, is a classic of *adolescent* fiction.
> [*Exciting* modifies *novel; adolescent* modifies *fiction.*]

20b Modifying Verbs, Adjectives, and Adverbs

Use adverbs to modify a verb. Isolate the pair of words to see if the pair sounds correct. The adverb should make sense when used before or after the verb.

> H. G. Wells, a political and social reformer in Victorian England, is *best* known *today* for two brief works: <u>The War of the Worlds</u> and <u>The Time Machine.</u>
> [***Best*** and ***today*** both modify *is known.*]

Adverbs that modify adjectives and other adverbs are intensifiers, further stressing the primary modifier. Use common intensifiers—*very, especially, really,* and *truly*—only when they are essential to your meaning.

> Unfortunately, Wells's ingenious science fiction has spawned some *very* bad science fiction films.
> [***Very*** intensifies the adjective *bad.*]

This sentence would be improved if the writer substituted a single, stronger adjective (for example, *appalling* or *dreadful*) or a more specific, descriptive adjective (for example, *boring* or *banal*) for *very bad.*

20c Positive, Comparative, and Superlative Adjectives and Adverbs

▦ Positive Adjectives and Adverbs

Positive adjectives and **adverbs** imply no comparisons: *recent, soon, clearly, fortunate.*

adj.   adj.

Completed in 1931, the Empire State Building was *tall* and *stately.*

adv.

Construction was completed *quickly,* in fewer than three years.

■ Comparative Adjectives and Adverbs

Comparative adjectives and **adverbs** establish differences between two similar people, places, things, ideas, qualities, conditions, or actions.

Adjectives and adverbs form comparatives in two ways. One-syllable modifiers add the suffix *-er: sooner, paler.* (See also the table of irregular adjectives and adverbs on page 261.) Multisyllable modifiers use *more* or *less* to form the comparative: *less easily, more recent.*

A number of two- and three-syllable adjectives use the *-er* form for the comparative (and *-est* for the superlative). Use the *-er* and *-est* forms with multisyllable words that have the following characteristics:

L sound in the last syllable: *simple* (*simpler*)

Accent on the last syllable: *severe* (*severest*)

Consult a dictionary if you are unsure of how to form a specific comparative or superlative.

comp. adj.

The Empire State Building was taller than the Chrysler Building, completed only a year before.

comp. adv.

Office space in the building was fully rented more quickly than the owners had anticipated.

■ Superlative Adjectives and Adverbs

Superlative adjectives and adverbs compare three or more people, places, things, ideas, qualities, conditions, or actions.

One-syllable words form the superlative by adding the suffix *-est: soonest, palest.* Multisyllable adjectives and adverbs generally form the superlative by using *most* or *least: least easily, most recent.*

super adj.

Today, the Sears Tower in Chicago is the tallest building in the world, although other structures are taller.

Although other buildings far exceed its height, the Empire State

super adv.

Building remains the most easily recognized of the world's tall buildings.

Positive	Comparative	Superlative
bad	worse	worst
good	better	best
little	less / littler	least / littlest
many / much / some	more	most
well	better	best
badly	worse	worst

■ Double Comparatives and Superlatives

Only one change is needed to form the comparative or superlative of an adjective or an adverb. To use both a suffix and a helping word is unnecessary and incorrect.

Kliban's cartoons of cats are the ~~most~~ funniest ones I have seen.

■ Incomparable Adjectives

Some adjectives—*central, dead, empty, impossible, infinite, perfect, straight,* and *unique*—cannot suggest comparisons of any kind. Use only the positive form of such modifiers.

James Joyce's <u>Ulysses</u> ~~was the *most unique*~~ ^{is a unique} novel ~~I have read.~~
[*Unique* means "one of a kind" and cannot suggest a comparison.]

20d Troublesome Adjective and Adverb Pairs

Use *bad,* the adjective form, to modify nouns and pronouns, even with sensory or linking verbs (*appear, feel, look, smell, taste, sound,* and forms of *to be*); use *badly* only to modify a verb.

That was a *bad* rendition of <u>Rhapsody in Blue.</u>

After sitting in the sun for two hours, Monica felt *bad.*

Use *good,* the adjective form, only to modify a noun or pronoun; use *well* as an adverb to mean *satisfactory* or as an adjective to mean *healthy.*

Louise was a very *good* pianist.

The rehearsal went *well* last night.

Although Anton had a slight fever, he said he felt *well* enough to play in Saturday's game.

Other troublesome adjective and adverb pairs appear in the Glossary of Usage beginning on page 525.

■ EXERCISE 20.1 Adjective and adverb forms

Select the appropriate adjective or adverb forms in the following sentences.

1. Current methods of building construction will make homes (affordable/more affordable/most affordable) than they were in the past, without sacrificing quality.

2. Although prefabricated homes have always been (easily/more easily/most easily) constructed than conventionally built homes, they were not always built (good/well).

3. Now, however, factory construction of major structural elements is (increasing/increasingly) impressive.

4. Many home units—like kitchens and bathrooms—are being constructed with their plumbing and wiring embedded in wall units; then these "core construction blocks" are fitted together (quick/quickly/more quickly) in various ways.

5. Because installing plumbing and wiring is (costly/more costly/most costly) than other phases of construction, these "core blocks" keep on-site construction costs (low/lower/lowest).

6. With the money saved from structural costs, a homeowner can concentrate on architectural trim and interior design work that can make his or her home (unique/more unique/most unique).

■ **EXERCISE 20.2   Adjectives and adverbs**

Correct the errors in adjective and adverb use in the following paragraph. (Available on disk.)

Tapestries, fabrics with pictures woven into them, were used in medieval churches and palaces more often as decorations but sometimes as insulation in the chilly buildings. The most unique tapestries were produced in Arras, France, where the art of weaving pictures reached its perfectest form in the 1400s. The tapestry makers of Arras worked so good that the word *arras* was soon used as a synonym for *tapestry.* The tapestries that have survived from the 1400s and 1500s are in various states of repair. Some, like the set of tapestries called *The Hunt of the Unicorn,* are in real sound condition. Their colors are still vibrant. The more famous panel of the set shows a unicorn sitting within a circular fence, surrounded by flowers and foliage of the brightest colors. Unfortunately, other tapestries have been treated bad over the centuries, and their colors are faded or their yarns damaged. Weaving tapestries is a most complex craft that has been sporadically and more simplistically revived in the last hundred years, but we will probably never approximate the more intricate and reverential nature of tapestries done in the late Middle Ages.

Punctuation

Three marks of punctuation can end sentences: the period (.), the question mark (?), and the exclamation point (!). These marks of punctuation also serve a few other purposes.

End punctuation clearly and simply indicates the end of a sentence and its intended effect.

▶ Use periods to end sentences that make statements, issue commands, or ask indirect questions.

▶ Use question marks to end sentences that ask direct questions.

▶ Use exclamation points to end sentences that express strong feeling.

21a Periods

A period follows a sentence that makes a statement, issues a command, or asks an indirect question.

Statement

Cigarette smoking is hazardous to your health.

Command

Stop smoking today.

Indirect question

The Surgeon General asked whether the students understood the risks of smoking.
[The sentence implies that the Surgeon General asked a question, but the sentence itself is not a question.]

266

21b Question Marks

A question mark is one of two indicators of direct questions; the other is the inverted word order of the subject and any part of the verb.

Question

> Did you know that the Pentagon is the largest federal building in the United States?

Some writers use question marks in parentheses to indicate uncertainty. This usage should be avoided in formal writing.

> The Pentagon houses the central offices of the Army, Navy, and
> Air Force and has office space for twenty-five thousand ~~(?)~~ *approximately* workers.

21c Exclamation Points

An exclamation point may follow a sentence or an interjection to stress strong feeling or indicate special emphasis.

Sentence

> "I know not what course others may take; but as for me, give me liberty or give me death!"   —Patrick Henry

Interjection

> "Well! Some people talk of morality, and some of religion, but give me a little snug property."   —Maria Edgeworth

Exclamation points should be used sparingly since not many sentences or interjections require the emphasis that exclamation points provide.

▩ EXERCISE 21.1   End punctuation

Add the end punctuation required in the following paragraph, capitalizing where necessary to indicate new sentences. (Available on disk.)

Harry Truman, the thirty-third president, was a spirited leader with a penchant for candor he assumed the presidency in 1945, after Franklin Roosevelt's death, and until he left office in 1953 repeatedly challenged assumptions about how presidents ought to behave his presidency was marked by controversy Truman made the decision to drop nuclear bombs on Hiroshima and Nagasaki; he supported the Marshall Plan to help Europe recover from the devastation of World War II; he sent American troops to Korea a sign of his unquestioning acceptance of responsibility for key decisions, one of Truman's favorite slogans became nationally known: "the buck stops here" another of his favorites was "if you can't stand the heat, get out of the kitchen" supporters, using Truman's own flavorful language, often shouted this refrain: "give 'em hell, Harry" Truman made many difficult decisions and never attempted to avoid the controversy that resulted or to blame others for his decisions was he a great president that is a judgment best left to history, but he certainly was an honest and an interesting one.

Commas separate words, phrases, and clauses and clarify the relationships among these elements. If commas do not appear where they are needed, thoughts can merge or overlap confusingly.

> Mark Twain portrayed youthful carelessness in *Tom Sawyer*, and *Huckleberry Finn* allowed him to illustrate a developing conscience.
> **[Without a comma after *Tom Sawyer*, the sentence momentarily suggests that both novels portray youthful carelessness.]**

QUICK REFERENCE

Use commas to clarify and separate sentence elements.

- Use commas to separate items in a series.
- Use commas to separate clauses in compound sentences.
- Use commas to set off introductory subordinate clauses in complex and compound-complex sentences.
- Use commas to set off introductory words and phrases that serve as adverbs.
- Use commas to set off nonrestrictive information.
- Use commas to set off statements that signal direct quotations.

22a Three or More Items in a Series

Separate a series of three or more parallel words, phrases, or clauses with commas. Although the comma immediately preceding the conjunction may be omitted, it is always correct and may prevent confusion.

■ Nouns or Verbs

Nouns

The faces of George Washington, Thomas Jefferson, Abraham Lincoln, and Theodore Roosevelt are carved into Mount Rushmore.

Verbs

A good reporter asks questions directly, listens attentively, and takes notes accurately and quickly.

■ Adjectives and Adverbs

When two or more adjectives independently modify a single noun, use commas to separate each one. Similarly, when several adverbs separately and equally modify a verb or an adjective, separate them with commas. No comma separates the last modifier in the series from the word modified.

The Disney Corporation restored the unused, dirty, and decaying Amsterdam Theatre to its original splendor.
[*unused* Theatre; *dirty* Theatre; *decaying* Theatre; each adjective functions separately.]

The restorers slowly, meticulously repainted the ornate ceiling.
[*Slowly* repainted; *meticulously* repainted; each adverb functions independently.]

To test the independence of modifiers, reverse the order of the modifiers or substitute *and* for each comma. If the sentence still makes sense, the adjectives or adverbs are *coordinate* and should be separated by commas.

The restorers meticulously and slowly repainted the ornate ceiling.
[The modification is clear, and the sentence makes sense.]

■ Phrases and Clauses

Phrases

Letters by Churchill, to Churchill, and about Churchill have become important and valued historical documents.

Clauses

At the turn of the century, the need for social reforms erupted into pitched battles as muckrakers exposed business corruption, industrial leaders challenged their accusations, and politicians sided with the powerful industrialists.

■ **EXERCISE 22.1   Commas**

Insert commas where they are needed in the following sentences. (Available on disk.)

1. Computers are now commonplace equipment in homes schools and businesses.

2. It is amazing how quickly completely and smoothly most people have become acclimated to the new technology.

3. Computerized cash registers are now common in grocery stores at movie houses in discount stores and even at gas stations.

4. Computers in public and private libraries have made it possible for people to search for books print lists of available materials and complete research quickly.

5. Today our mail comes with computer labels our bank statements arrive with spreadsheet accounts of transactions and even our grocery store receipts have computer lists of products we've bought.

22b   Compound and Compound-Complex Sentences

■ **Compound Sentences**

Separate the independent clauses of a compound sentence with a comma. You may omit the comma when the clauses are brief and when no confusion is likely.

Price supports for dairy products greatly help farmers, and consumers benefit as well.
[**Without a comma after** *farmers,* **the initial reading might inappropriately link** *farmers* **and** *consumers* **as direct objects.**]

Making mistakes is common but admitting them is not.
[**Because these clauses are brief and because confusion is
unlikely, the comma may be omitted.**]

Note, however, that conjunctions connecting only two words,
two phrases, or two dependent clauses do not require commas.

■ Complex or Compound-Complex Sentences

When a complex or compound-complex sentence begins with a
subordinate clause, use a comma to show where the subordinate clause ends and the independent clause begins.

> Although she is best known for her work for the Underground
> Railroad, Harriet Tubman also helped the Union cause as a nurse
> and a spy.

■ EXERCISE 22.2 Commas

*Combine these simple sentences to form compound, complex, or
compound-complex sentences. Insert any necessary commas.* (Available on disk.)

1. *Buffalo* is the name usually used to refer to American bison. It is
   a common name used to describe several hundred kinds of
   large wild oxen worldwide.

2. Water buffalo in India have been domesticated for centuries.
   South African buffalo have resisted domestication and run wild.
   Small buffalo on Pacific islands remain wild as well.

3. In North America, especially on the Great Plains, huge herds of
   buffalo once roamed. By 1900, the bison population of approximately 20 million was reduced to fewer than six hundred.

4. William Hornaday, an American zoologist, worked to protect
   the remaining bison. He felt their extinction would be shameful.
   He encouraged the National Forest Service to build fenced areas
   for small herds.

5. Today, bison are kept in captivity. They cannot be trained
   or domesticated. They are of zoological rather than practical
   interest.

22c Introductory Words, Phrases, and Subordinate Clauses

■ Introductory Words

Set off conjunctive adverbs (*however, subsequently,* and others) and nonrestrictive adverbs with commas (see section 22d).

Conjunctive adverb

Consequently, prenatal care is essential for the well-being of both mothers and babies.

A conjunctive adverb used to link compound sentences joined with a semicolon should also be followed by a comma.

Infants acquire language through imitation; therefore, adults should talk coherently to their children from birth.

Adverb

First, children require good nutrition to grow and learn properly.
[**The comma prevents confusion; without it, readers might think that *first* is an adjective modifying *children*.**]

■ Introductory Phrases

Use a comma to set off a transitional expression (*for example, in other words, in fact,* and others) or an opening prepositional or verbal phrase used as an adjective or adverb.

Transitional expression

For example, many rivers, cities, and states are named after Native American tribes.

Prepositional phrase

After a decade of steady increases in stock values, the New York Stock Exchange fell dramatically in 1929.

If an introductory prepositional phrase is brief and if the meaning is clear without a comma, the comma may be omitted.

> In April Americans pay income taxes.

Verbal phrase

> Having learned to communicate through sign language, Helen Keller has been an inspiration to many.

■ Introductory Subordinate Clauses

Use a comma to separate an introductory subordinate clause from the independent clause that follows.

> Because mosquitoes are such a problem in southern coastal cities like New Orleans, city workers spray with insecticides each evening.

■ EXERCISE 22.3 Commas

Insert commas where they are needed in the following sentences. (Available on disk.)

1. Built during the third and fourth centuries the catacombs of Rome are the most famous in the world.

2. Intended for use as burial sites the passages and rooms were used for other purposes too.

3. According to legend early Christians kept the bodies of Saint Peter and Saint Paul hidden for a time in the catacombs.

4. In addition Christians often took refuge in the catacombs because the catacombs were protected by Roman law.

5. Curiously use of the Roman catacombs ceased in A.D. 400.

22d Nonrestrictive Information

Nonrestrictive information—words, phrases, or clauses—adds to but does not substantially alter the meaning of a sentence. Because nonrestrictive information can be omitted, it is set off by commas from the rest of the sentence.

■ Nonrestrictive Words

Conjunctive Adverbs

Use commas to set off conjunctive adverbs. When they appear at the beginning or end of a sentence, use one comma to set them off. When they appear in the middle of a sentence, use two commas.

At end of sentence

Many people admired Kennedy's ready wit and easy manner. They remained suspicious of his politics, however.

In midsentence

In the 1960s, however, reporters did not attack his positions with the vigor they would use today.

The words yes *and* no, *mild interjections, and names in direct address*

Use commas to separate the words *yes* and *no,* interjections, and names in direct address from the rest of a sentence.

Yes *and direct address*

"Yes, Virginia, there is a Santa Claus." —Francis Church
[The comma after *yes* separates it from the rest of the sentence; the comma after *Virginia* separates this name used in direct address.]

Interjection

Okay, so it *was* Franklin who said, "In this world nothing is certain but death and taxes."

■ Nonrestrictive Phrases

Transitional Expressions

Use a single comma if the expression appears at the beginning or end of a sentence; use two commas if it appears in the middle of a sentence.

Jimmy Carter, in fact, seemed more presidential after he left office.

Absolute Phrases

Absolute phrases are nonrestrictive and must be set off by commas. Use a single comma if the phrase appears at the beginning or end of a sentence; use two commas if it appears in the middle of a sentence.

At end of sentence

Franklin Roosevelt was the first president to fly in a commercial airplane, a fact unknown to most people.

In midsentence

Gandhi, the goal of Indian independence having been achieved, retired from public life.

Prepositional and Verbal Phrases

Use commas to set off prepositional and verbal phrases from the rest of the sentence when they supply nonessential information.

Prepositional phrase

J. D. Salinger, above all else, values his privacy.

Verbal phrase

M*A*S*H, challenging idealized assumptions about war, achieved surprising success.

Appositives

Nonrestrictive appositives add clarifying but nonessential information and are set off by commas.

Frank Lloyd Wright, an architect in the early twentieth century, felt that the design of a building should be suited to its surroundings.

■ Nonrestrictive Clauses

Nonrestrictive clauses that begin with a relative pronoun (*which, who, whose, whom, whoever,* and *whomever*) can be omitted without substantially changing the meaning of a sentence. Set them off with commas.

> *The Starry Night,* which is prominently displayed in the Museum of Modern Art in New York, exemplifies van Gogh's use of rich colors applied in bold strokes.

22e Contrasting Sentence Elements

Because words and phrases that provide contrasting details do not function grammatically as parts of a sentence, separate them from the rest of a sentence with commas.

> Shaw's first love was music, not theater.

■ EXERCISE 22.4 Commas

Insert commas where they are needed in the following sentences. (Available on disk.)

1. *Beowulf* which is one of the earliest examples of Anglo-Saxon literature still appeals to those who like adventure stories not only to scholars.

2. The character Beowulf with a combination of heroic and religious qualities goes to the aid of Hrothgar the leader of a noble tribe.

3. The most famous episode of *Beowulf* the battle between Beowulf and the monster Grendel is a marvelous mix of supernatural and traditional Christian elements.

4. *Beowulf* is a historical-literary milestone; it is however a popular classic as well.

5. The plot elements of *Beowulf*—fights with supernatural beasts and tests of moral strength for example—remain standard elements in today's science fiction films perhaps explaining why *Beowulf* remains so popular.

22f Expressions That Signal Direct Quotations

Use commas to separate expressions such as *he said* and *she commented* from the quotations they identify, whether at the beginning, in the middle, or at the end of a quotation.

> In an ongoing battle of wits, Lady Astor once said to Winston Churchill, "Winston, if you were my husband, I should flavor your coffee with poison."
> [**Note that the comma precedes the opening quotation mark.**]

> "Madam," Churchill replied, "if I were your husband, I should drink it."

22g Numbers, Dates, Addresses, Place Names, and Titles

For easy reading, divide numbers of one thousand or more with commas: place a comma between groups of three digits, moving from the right.

> 1,271   1,300,000

Use a comma between the day and the year when dates are written in month-day-year order. In sentences, a comma must also follow the year.

> December 7, 1941, marked the beginning of America's involvement in World War II.

If dates are written in day-month-year order, or if only the month and year are given, no comma is needed.

> Martin Luther King, Jr., was born on 15 January 1929; his birthday has been designated a national holiday.

> The stock market crash of October 1929 precipitated the Great Depression.

Addresses written on one line or within a sentence require commas after the street name and between the city and state. Zip codes follow, with two spaces before and no comma after when written on a single line. When written within a sentence, zip codes appear with just one space before and with a comma after.

709 Sherwood Terrace, Champaign, Illinois 61820

Information on the water rights issue is available by writing the newspaper directly at *Courier-Journal,* 822 Courier Road, Wendel, Vermont 05753, to the attention of the editor.

Use commas to separate parts of place names, even when they include only city and state or city and country. Within a sentence, a comma also follows the last item in the place name.

Baltimore, Maryland   Nairobi, Kenya

Elsa, Illinois, is always 10 to 15 degrees cooler than nearby towns and cities because it is nestled in the bluffs along the Mississippi River.

Set off titles and academic and professional degrees with commas when they follow an individual's name.

C. Everett Koop, M.D., drew attention to the AIDS crisis while serving as Surgeon General.

Commas are required with the abbreviations *Sr.* and *Jr.*

Louis Gosset, Jr., won critical acclaim for his aggressive portrayal of a drill sergeant in *An Officer and a Gentleman.*

When roman numerals follow the name of a private individual, monarch, ship, and so on, no commas are required.

Louis XIV of France was known as the "Sun King" because of the splendor of his court.

■ EXERCISE 22.5   Commas

Insert commas where they are needed in the following paragraphs. (Available on disk.)

A.   Although zoos provide opportunities to see many exotic animals up close the facilities for the animals do not always allow them to pursue or visitors to observe natural habits. Rhesus monkeys very small primates do not seem cramped in small places; they do not appear to suffer or experience any ill effects from their confinement. Chimpanzees however seem noticeably depressed in areas that do not allow them to move about freely. Orangutans highly intelligent primates also seem despondent. However the jungle cats tigers and leopards seem to suffer most. They pace in their cages or lie inactive and inattentive. These large primates and big cats which are usually among a zoo's main attractions require more space and some distance from the crowds of eager spectators. In recent years zookeepers who have the animals' best interests in mind have begun building habitats for these larger animals. Most zoos have paid for these building projects which can be quite elaborate from general funds. Other zoos have launched major advertising campaigns hoping for individual donations. Still others stressing commitment to the community have appealed to major corporations. These large building projects should continue for they provide improved living conditions for large wild animals. As we maintain zoos that entertain and educate people we must also remember that the animals that live there should not suffer for our benefit.

B.   Alaska the forty-ninth state joined the Union on January 3 1959. The largest state geographically covering 586412 square miles Alaska is also the least populated with only 479000 people. In fact the entire state has fewer people than many American cities of moderate size let alone Chicago Los Angeles or New York. Yes the contrast in physical size and population presents an anomaly but Alaska's history is full of such anomalies. Juneau its capital city has approximately twenty thousand people making it roughly the same size as Texarkana Arkansas; Augusta Maine; and Winchester Nevada. Alaska has fewer schools than many other states but has the highest teachers' salaries in the nation. Contradictions such as these have always been present.

In 1867 when William H. Seward secretary of state arranged the purchase of Alaska for $7200000 most people thought the purchase was foolish. But "Seward's Folly" as the acquisition was called turned out to be not at all foolish. Rich deposits of minerals oil and natural gas have made Alaska one of America's greatest assets. (For more information on Alaska write to the Alaskan Chamber of Commerce 310 Second Street Juneau Alaska 99801.)

The use of commas where they are not needed confuses, distracts, and frustrates readers and interferes with the clear communication of ideas.

23a Subjects and Verbs or Verbs and Complements

A comma should not break the subject-verb or verb-complement pattern in a sentence unless it is required by a separate rule.

■ Subject and Verb

Governments in many countries͵ control the prices of consumer goods.
[**The comma interrupts the subject-verb pattern.**]

But:

Governments in many countries, especially those in central Europe, control the prices of consumer goods.
[**The pair of commas is required because a nonrestrictive phrase has been added.**]

■ Verb and Complement

Black markets offer⸴ specialty items in countries where consumer goods are scarce.
[**The comma interrupts the verb-complement pattern.**]

23b Two Words, Phrases, or Dependent Clauses

■ Words

The Federal Reserve controls the twelve Federal Reserve banks⸴ and regulates the prime interest rate.
[**The comma incorrectly separates the elements of a compound verb: controls *and* regulates.**]

■ Phrases

The Federal Reserve's goals are to stabilize the national economy⸴ and to help establish international monetary policies.
[**The comma incorrectly separates two infinitive phrases joined by *and*.**]

■ Clauses

Economists note that low interest rates encourage spending⸴ but that they can also fuel inflation.
[**The comma incorrectly separates two clauses, each beginning with *that*.**]

Remember that a comma *is* required between the independent clauses of a compound sentence.

> Low interest rates encourage spending, but they also fuel inflation.

See Chapter 16 for more information and examples.

23c First or Last Item in a Series

Unless a series is part of a nonrestrictive phrase, no commas should separate the series as a unit from the rest of the sentence.

> To earn extra money, to gain experience, and to make important contacts, are reasons recent graduates in education often work as substitute teachers.
> [**The infinitive phrases form a series that is the subject of the sentence. The commas after *money* and *experience* are appropriate, but the comma after *contacts* separates the compound subject from the verb.**]

23d Cumulative Modifiers

Cumulative modifiers—adjectives and adverbs that build upon each other to create meaning—should not be separated by commas.

> The new, associate director is much younger than her predecessor.
> [**The comma separates cumulative adjectives: *associate* modifies *director,* but *new* modifies the phrase *associate director.*]

To test whether modifiers are cumulative, change their order. If the new order makes no sense, the modifiers are cumulative and no commas should be used. The previous example would not make sense if it were written "The associate new director is much younger than her predecessor."

23e Restrictive Elements

Because restrictive elements—whether they are single words, phrases, or clauses—are essential to the meaning of a sentence, they should not be set off by commas.

■ Words

The musical play⌀*West Side Story*⌀is based on Shakespeare's *Romeo and Juliet*.
[**The commas are incorrect because *West Side Story* is necessary to the meaning of the sentence.**]

■ Phrases

Audience members continued to arrive⌀until well into the first act.
[**Because the phrase is essential to the meaning of the sentence, no comma should be used.**]

■ Clauses

Composers and lyricists⌀who adapt well-known plays⌀usually strive to maintain the spirit of the original works.
[**The commas are incorrect because the relative clause is essential; it identifies a particular group of composers and lyricists.**]

23f Indirect Quotation or a Direct Quotation Introduced by *That*

A quotation preceded by the word *that* or *if* functions as a complement; no comma is required.

Mark Twain commented⌀that Wagner's music is more respected than it should be.
[**The subordinate clause following *commented* is the direct object of *commented*.**]

But:

> Mark Twain commented, "Wagner's music is better than it sounds."

23g *Such As, Like,* or *Than*

Such as and *like* are prepositions that introduce examples in prepositional phrases; commas should not separate prepositions from their objects. *Than* signals a comparative construction; because it is illogical to separate the two items, no comma is required.

> Some humanistic studies such as͜philosophy, art history, and dramatic arts require a more scientific approach͜than most people think.
> [**The comma after *such as* inappropriately separates the preposition from its objects; the comma preceding *than* interrupts a comparative construction. The commas after *philosophy* and *art history* correctly separate items in a series.**]

■ EXERCISE 23.1 Unnecessary commas

The following sentences contain far too many commas. Eliminate those that break the flow of the sentences or that obscure the logical connections between ideas. (Available on disk.)

1. Primary colors like, red, blue, and yellow are the most often used colors in national flags.

2. Interestingly enough, Libya's bright, green, flag is the only solid colored flag, in current use.

3. The small, Arab republic, Qatar, has a simple, black, and white flag.

4. Many countries—such as, Bahrain, Canada, Denmark, Indonesia, Japan, Monaco, Singapore, and Tunisia—use only red, and white, in their flags.

5. Most national flags use three, or four, bold colors, and use simple geometric shapes in their designs.

6. However, the ornate flag, of Sri Lanka, uses four colors, and black, and an elaborate design.

7. Only a few national flags, vary from the traditional, rectangular shape, including those of, Nepal and Switzerland.

8. The most frequently used colors, for flags, are red, white, and blue.

9. The U.S. flag, contains fifty, small, white stars on a blue field, and thirteen, alternating stripes of red and white.

10. As symbols of nations, flags serve, ideological, and political purposes—uniting citizens in times of peace, as well as in times of war.

■ **EXERCISE 23.2   Unnecessary commas**

Delete the unnecessary commas from the following paragraph. (Available on disk.)

   We went fishing, the first morning. I felt the same, damp, moss covering the worms, in the bait can, and saw the dragonfly alight on the tip of my rod, as it hovered a few inches from the surface of the water. It was the arrival of this fly, that convinced me, beyond any doubt, that everything was as it always had been, that the years were a mirage, and there had been no years. The small, waves were the same, chucking the rowboat under the chin as we fished at anchor, and the boat was the same boat, the same color green, and the ribs broken in the same places, and under the floor-boards the same fresh-water leavings and débris—the dead helgrammite, the wisps of moss, the rusty discarded fishhook, the dried blood from yesterday's catch. We stared, silently at the tips of our rods, at the dragonflies that came and went. I lowered the tip of mine into the water, tentatively, pensively dislodging the fly, which darted two feet away, poised, darted two, feet back, and came to rest again a little farther up the rod. There had been no years, between the ducking of this dragonfly and the other one—the one that was part of my memory. I looked at the boy, who was silently watching the fly, and it was my hands that held his rod, my eyes watching. I felt dizzy, and didn't know which rod, I was at the end of.   —E. B. White, "Once More to the Lake"

Semicolons perform various functions, most often acting as periods (separating closely related independent clauses) and sometimes separating items in a series that already contains commas.

A colon, in effect, says, "Notice what follows." Colons formally introduce lists, clarifications, and quotations.

QUICK REFERENCE

Use semicolons and colons selectively according to convention.

▌ Use semicolons to join closely related independent clauses.

▌ Use colons to introduce lists, clarifications, and quotations.

▌ Do not allow colons to separate verbs from complements or prepositions from objects.

24a Independent Clauses

Use a semicolon to emphasize the close relationship between related independent clauses.

> Only a few hundred people in the United States know how to work with neon tubing; most of them are fifty years old or older.

Use a conjunctive adverb in addition to a semicolon to indicate the kind of interrelationship that exists between the independent clauses (*however* for contrast, *moreover* for addition, and so on). Remember, however, that the semicolon provides the technical connection between the clauses.

Neon signs were once common at stores, restaurants, and gas stations across the country; however, in the sixties and seventies these sometimes garish advertisements fell into disfavor.
[**The conjunctive adverb** *however* **emphasizes the contrast.**]

24b Sentence Elements That Contain Commas

■ Items in a Series

Use semicolons to separate items in a series that each contain commas.

Sculptors creating works for outdoor display generally use native stone like sandstone, granite, or limestone; imported stone like marble; metals or alloys like bronze, cast iron, or steel.
[**This use of semicolons helps readers identify the elements of the various series.**]

When a heavily punctuated series becomes awkward to read, break the sentence into briefer, smoother sentences.

Sculptors creating works for outdoor display generally use native stone like sandstone, granite, or limestone. Other frequently used materials include imported marble and metals or alloys like bronze, cast iron, or steel.

■ Independent Clauses

Use a semicolon to mark the connecting point between independent clauses containing commas.

Much of the sculpture commissioned for public plazas is artistically innovative, visually exciting, and technically impressive; but often it does not appeal to the general public because they have grown accustomed to traditional, realistic statuary.
[**The semicolon clarifies the balance of the two-part sentence.**]

Separate clauses into independent sentences if doing so would make them easier to read. Some rewording may be necessary.

Much of the sculpture commissioned for public plazas is artistically innovative, visually exciting, and technically impressive. Nevertheless, it often does not appeal to the general public because they have grown accustomed to traditional, realistic statuary.

24c Incorrect Use

■ With a Subordinate Clause

Use a comma, not a semicolon, after a subordinate clause at the beginning of a complex or compound-complex sentence.

Because it had a strong, centralized government, the Roman Empire was able to maintain relative stability, peace, and prosperity for nearly four centuries.
[**The semicolon obscures the relationship between the subordinate and independent clauses; the isolated subordinate clause is also a fragment.**]

■ To Introduce a List

Use a colon or a dash, not a semicolon or a comma, to introduce a list.

Historians cite several reasons for the decline of Rome: expanded citizenship, the deterioration of the army, barbarian invasions, economic decentralization, and inefficient agriculture.
[**With the semicolon, the closing list is a fragment.**]

24d To Introduce Elements

Use colons selectively to add clarity and emphasis to writing.

■ A Series

An independent clause must precede a colon, and the items in the series should never be direct objects, predicate nouns or adjectives, or objects of prepositions.

The names of six of the Seven Dwarfs reflect their personalities and habits: Bashful, Dopey, Grumpy, Happy, Sleepy, and Sneezy. [**The colon emphasizes the list; the words that precede the colon form a complete sentence.**]

■ An Independent Clause That Explains the Preceding Clause

When a complete sentence is needed to explain the meaning of the preceding sentence, use a colon to clarify the relationship. The first word following the colon usually begins with a lower-case letter, which identifies the clause as a clarification. However, the first word following the colon may begin with a capital letter.

Good song lyrics are like good poetry: both express ideas in rhythmic, elliptical form. [**Without the second sentence, the meaning of the first would not be completely clear; the colon points to the explanatory relationship.**]

■ An Appositive at the End of a Sentence

Use colons to add special emphasis to appositives (restatements of nouns or pronouns). This use of the colon stresses the appositive as a necessary explanation of a key word in the main sentence.

Early astronomers and astrologers assigning names to planets drew primarily on one source: mythology.

■ A Direct Quotation

Use colons to introduce direct quotations formally. Both the introduction and the quotation must be independent clauses. The first word of the quotation is capitalized (see section 29a).

The educational sentiment that Mark Twain articulated would shock many humorless educators: "It doesn't matter what you teach a boy, so long as he doesn't like it."
[**The colon, preceded by a complete sentence, emphasizes Twain's comment.**]

24e Numerals

Use a colon to separate hours and minutes when time references are given in numerals. When the reference is to hours only, spell out the number.

The next flight to Tel Aviv leaves at 2:15 A.M.

We expect to be home by nine o'clock.

Use a colon to separate chapter and verse in citations of books of the Bible.

Genesis 3:23   Luke 12:27

Separate titles and subtitles with a colon.

Henry Louis Gates, Jr.'s, *Figures in Black: Words, Signs, and the "Racial" Self*

24f Verbs and Complements or Prepositions and Objects

Do not separate basic sentence elements with colons. To test the accuracy of colon placement, change the colon to a period and drop the words that follow. If the remaining sentence is complete, the colon is correctly placed. If the remaining sentence is incomplete, delete or move the colon or rephrase the sentence.

The names of Enrico's cats are: Winston Churchill, T. S. Eliot, Eudora Welty, and Eleanor Roosevelt.
[*The names of Enrico's cats are* is a fragment; the colon separates the verb from its complement.]

■ **EXERCISE 24.1 Semicolons and colons**

Correct the errors in semicolon and colon usage in the following sentences. (Available on disk.)

1. The Mediterranean Sea is bordered to the south by: Egypt, Libya, Tunisia, Algeria, and Morocco.

2. The major ports on the Mediterranean Sea are: Barcelona; Spain, Marseille; France, Naples; Italy, Beirut; Lebanon, Alexandria; Egypt, and Tripoli; Libya.

3. Because the Bering Sea borders both Russia and the United States; it is often patrolled by military ships from each country.

4. In the Western Hemisphere, gulfs are more common than seas: however, several seas are located off the northernmost coasts of North America.

5. Four seas are named for colors; the Yellow Sea, the Red Sea, the White Sea, and the Black Sea.

■ **EXERCISE 24.2 Semicolons and colons**

The following paragraph uses the semicolon as its primary form of internal punctuation. Revise the punctuation, reserving the semicolon for places where it works better than any other mark of punctuation. (Available on disk.)

Ninety-six percent of Americans have eaten at one of the McDonald's restaurants in the last year; slightly more than half of the U.S. population lives within three minutes of a McDonald's; McDonald's has served more than 55 billion hamburgers; McDonald's commands 17% of all restaurant visits in the U.S. and gets 7.3% of all dollars Americans spend eating out; McDonald's sells 32% of all hamburgers and 26% of french fries; McDonald's is the country's largest beef buyer; it purchases 7.5% of the U.S potato crop; McDonald's has employed about 8 million workers—which amounts to approximately 7% of the entire U.S. work force; and McDonald's has replaced the U.S. Army as America's largest job training organization.   —John Love, *McDonald's: Behind the Arches*

Use apostrophes to show possession (usually with an added *s*) and to indicate the omission of letters or numbers from words or dates.

QUICK REFERENCE

Apostrophes have two uses: to show possession and to indicate omission.

▶ Use an apostrophe or an apostrophe and an *s* to form the possessive case, depending on the singular noun or pronoun.

▶ Use only an apostrophe to form the possessive of plural nouns ending in *s*.

▶ Use an apostrophe to indicate the omission of letters in contractions and numbers in dates.

▶ Do not use apostrophes with possessive pronouns (*yours, theirs*); do not confuse the possessive pronoun *its* with the contraction *it's* ("it is").

25a Possessive Case

■ Singular Nouns

Form the possessive of a singular common noun by adding *'s* or only an apostrophe if the word ends in *s*; form the possessive of a singular proper noun by adding *'s*, regardless of the noun's ending letter.

Common Nouns	**Proper Nouns**
stereo's features	Gunter Grass's novels
bus' emissions	Mother Teresa's legacy
building's dimensions	New Orleans's night life

■ Plural Nouns

Form the possessive of plural nouns ending in *s* (either common or proper) by adding an apostrophe only; an additional *s* is unnecessary. Irregular plural nouns that do not end in *s* (*children,* for example) form the possessive by adding an apostrophe and an *s*.

Teachers' lounge   a United Nations' task force

but:

children's theater   women's rights

   To check whether a possessive form is correct, eliminate the apostrophe and the *s* or just the apostrophe. The word remaining should be the correct one for your meaning. For example, the phrase *earthquake's destruction* without the apostrophe and *s* refers to only one earthquake; the phrase *earthquakes' destruction* without the apostrophe refers to multiple earthquakes.

■ Compound Words and Joint Possession

Show possession in compound words or joint possession in a series by adding an apostrophe and *s* to the last noun only.

brother-in-law's objection

General Motors, Ford, and Chrysler's combined profits

If possession in a series is not joint but individual, each noun in the series must be possessive.

Young Sook's, Bert's, and Tess's fingerprints
[**Each person has a separate set of fingerprints.**]

25b Omission of Letters and Numbers

Use contractions and dates with numbers omitted in informal writing only. In formal writing, present words and dates fully.

With apostrophe	*Complete form*
shouldn't	should not
I'll	I will *or* I shall
the '98 champions	the 1998 champions

25c Not with Possessive Pronouns

Possessive pronouns do not require the addition of an apostrophe. Do not be confused by those (*yours, ours, his,* and others) that end in *-s.*

Emily Dickinson published few poems during her lifetime; the fame that might have been her's held no value for her.

[**The apostrophe in *her's* would indicate a contracted form—*her is*—which is nonsensical. Clearly, the possessive pronoun is correct.**]

■ EXERCISE 25.1 Apostrophes

Correct the use of apostrophes in the following sentences. Add needed apostrophes and delete unnecessary ones. (Available on disk.)

1. Even before people kept record's or conceived of science as a field of study, chemistry exerted its influence on their lives.

2. Early civilizations understanding of elements was primitive—the Greeks and Romans four elements were air, earth, fire, and water—but their applications of chemical principles were sophisticated.

3. Today, perhaps, its difficult to understand how much the development of the alloy bronze revolutionized human's lives.

4. During the Middle Ages, alchemists discovered how many chemical compounds work, even though trying to turn metals to gold was a chief preoccupation of their's.

5. By the seventeenth century, scientists studies were more methodical and practical, as was illustrated by Robert Boyles studies' of gases, for example.

6. Even before the development of sophisticated microscopes, John Daltons' theories of atomic elements explained chemical's reactions.

7. Dmitri Mendeleev, Russias foremost early chemist, explained the relationships among elements and devised the periodic tables that still appear on student's tests in classes' in introductory chemistry.

8. Marie Curie's and Pierre Curie's discovery of radium in 1898 further expanded scientist's understanding of chemistry.

9. Alfred B. Nobels' bequest of $9 million made possible awards in science and literature; one of the first five prizes in 1901 was an award for achievement in chemistry.

10. Chemist's work today is aided by sophisticated technology, but their search for knowledge has been shared by scientists' of generation's past.

Use dashes, hyphens, parentheses, brackets, and ellipsis points to create stress and establish meaning.

QUICK REFERENCE

Use specialized marks of punctuation to emphasize elements of your sentences and to clarify your meaning.

▶ Use dashes to introduce parenthetical information, to set off material that contains commas, and to mark interruptions in thought, speech, or action.

▶ Use hyphens to divide words, to form some compound words, and to join some prefixes and suffixes to root words.

▶ Use parentheses in pairs to introduce parenthetical information and numbered or lettered sequences.

▶ Use brackets to indicate alterations to direct quotations.

▶ Use ellipsis points to indicate omissions in direct quotations and to indicate hesitation or suspended statements.

26a Dashes

A dash, made by typing two hyphens with no space before or after, introduces parenthetical information emphatically and clearly, sets off a series at the beginning or end of a sentence, and marks interruptions in thought, speech, or action.

■ Parenthetical Comments

Parenthetical comments—single words, phrases, or clauses—are inserted into sentences to explain, amplify, or qualify ideas. Because they are grammatically independent of the rest of the sentence, they may be set off with dashes for special emphasis.

American military advisers did not acknowledge the strength and tenacity of the Viet Cong—a costly error.

The reports of atrocities—in particular the My Lai Massacre—changed American attitudes about the war.

Appositives (phrases renaming nouns or pronouns) that contain commas should be set off by dashes for greater clarity.

Several presidents—Eisenhower, Kennedy, Johnson, and Nixon—were embroiled in political debates about the necessity of American involvement in Vietnam.
[**Because the appositive contains three commas, dashes mark the appositive more clearly than commas would mark it.**]

■ A Series

A list of items placed at the beginning of a sentence for special emphasis is followed by a dash.

The Tiger, the Mako, the Great White—these "man-eating" sharks deserve our respect more than our fear.

A dash may be used to introduce a list informally.

Jaws portrayed most people's reactions to sharks—ignorance, fear, and irrationality.
[**In formal writing, use a colon to introduce a list.**]

■ Shifts or Breaks in Thought, Speech, or Action

Andrew Wyeth's monochromatic paintings—why does he avoid color?—are popular with the American public.
[**The dashes mark a shift in thought.**]

Because of cover stories and related articles in scholarly and popular magazines, interest in Wyeth's "Helga" paintings and drawings was intense for several months—and then suddenly subsided.
[**The dash marks a break in action.**]

■ Selective Use

Because the overuse of dashes can disrupt the rhythm of writing, use them selectively. Often, other punctuation serves as well—or better.

The thunderstorm—coming from the southwest—looked

threatening—with black and blue clouds and flashes of lightning.

Within a matter of minutes—five to be exact—it was upon us.
[*five*]

Around our house, the trees—delicate dogwoods, tall maples,

and stout pines—bent in the heavy winds—their branches

swaying violently. The black sky, the growing roar, the shaking
[*and*]

house—all signaled the approach of a tornado—we headed for

the basement.

[**Only one use of the dash is required in this paragraph, with the appositive in the third sentence. The other uses are technically correct, but the use of fewer dashes would call less attention to the mechanics of the paragraph and allow readers to focus on the events described.**]

■ EXERCISE 26.1   Dashes

Use dashes to combine each set of sentences into a single sentence.
(Available on disk.)

1. The Distinguished Service Cross, the Navy Cross, the Silver Star, the Distinguished Flying Cross, the Bronze Star, and the Air Medal are awards given to members of the armed forces. These awards all recognize heroism.

2. Soldiers may be recognized for heroic behavior several times. They do not receive additional medals. Instead, they receive small emblems to pin on the first medal's ribbon.

3. Since 1932, the Purple Heart has been awarded to members of the armed forces who were wounded in combat. The medal is gold and purple, heart-shaped, and embossed with George Washington's image.

4. General George Washington established this military decoration in 1782. It was called the Badge of Military Merit. It wasn't given between 1800 and 1932.

5. The Congressional Medal of Honor is our nation's highest military award. The award was authorized in 1861 for the navy and in 1862 for the army.

26b Hyphens

■ Compound Forms

A compound noun—a pair or group of words that together function as a single noun—may be open (*beer mug*), closed (*headache*), or hyphenated (*hurly-burly*). If you are unsure about how to present a compound noun, consult a dictionary. If the compound does not appear, it should be left open.

father figure	snowmobile	mother-in-law
medical examiner	notebook	razzle-dazzle

When modifiers preceding a noun work together to create a single meaning, hyphens emphasize their unity. When the same modifiers follow the noun, hyphens are not needed.

Hyphens necessary	Hyphens unnecessary
out-of-the-way resort	a resort that is out of the way
long-term investment	an investment for the long term

When an adverb ending in *-ly* is the first word of a compound, omit the hyphen.

Margaret Atwood is a highly inventive writer.

When spelled out, fractions and cardinal and ordinal numbers from twenty-one through ninety-nine require hyphens.

two-thirds of the taxpayers

seventy-six CDs

forty-first president

■ Prefixes and Suffixes

Use hyphens to form words with the prefixes *all-*, *ex-*, and *self-* and with the suffix *-elect*. Other prefixes (*anti-*, *inter-*, *non-*, *over-*, *post-*, *pre-*, and *un-*) and suffixes (*-fold*, *-like*, and *-wide*) are generally spelled closed.

Hyphenate	Spell closed
all-consuming ambition	antibody
self-restraint	postpartum
president-elect	unequivocal

Prefixes joined to proper nouns or compounds consisting of more than one word require hyphens.

un-American

non-native speakers

When a prefix has the same last letter as the first letter of the root word (or when a suffix has the same first letter as the last letter of the root word), hyphens add clarity.

anti-intellectual

bell-like

When the omission of a hyphen would result in ambiguity, a hyphen should be used.

release	re-lease
["let go"]	**["to lease again"]**
reform	re-form
["to improve"]	**["to form again"]**

■ Word Division

Although word processing has all but eliminated hyphenation in typed manuscripts, follow these principles when needed. Use hyphens to divide words that do not fit in their entirety at the ends of typed or printed lines. Divide words by syllable but do not isolate one or two letters on a line or divide proper nouns. When it is not possible or acceptable to hyphenate a word, move the entire word to the next line.

Because of excavation difficulties, the archaeologist ~~thou~~⁀
thought
~~ght~~‿he'd quit the project.

Every year some natural disaster seems to strike ~~Bo~~⁀
Bolivia
~~livia~~‿.
[Proper names should not be divided; two letters should not be isolated on a single line.]

■ EXERCISE 26.2 Hyphens

Add or delete hyphens to correct the use of hyphens in the following sentences. (Some of the hyphens are used correctly.) (Available on disk.)

1. In the United States, senators are elected to six year terms, presidents (and their vice presidents) to four year terms, and members of Congress to two year terms.

2. Although these electoral guidelines are un-changed, little else about modern day elections has remained the way our national founders conceived them.

3. In pre-computer elections, hand-tabulated ballots were the norm, and results often were not certain for days.

4. Today, with computer-aided counting, officials post fully three fourths of election returns by mid-night of election day.

5. Television-networks quickly project the results of today's elections, usually on the basis of less than one fiftieth of the ballots cast.

6. Consequently, presidents elect now make victory speeches before mid-night on election day, rather than at mid-morning on the following day. Times have clearly changed.

26c Parentheses

■ Parenthetical Comments

Use parentheses to set off casually related information from ideas in the rest of the sentence; essential information deserves direct presentation. Do not include long explanations parenthetically.

> Joan of Arc (only seventeen at the time) led military troops to help return the rightful king of France to the throne.
> **[The information about Joan of Arc's age supplements the main idea; it is appropriately set off by parentheses.]**

Because parentheses are more disruptive than dashes, the overuse of parentheses makes writing seem uneven, incoherent, or immature. Consequently, use parentheses only when no other strategy or punctuation will serve your purpose.

The compass (scratched and cracked) should have been replaced (years ago), but Joaquín (reluctant to spend the money) preferred to keep it as it was.
[**The rhythm of the sentence is broken by the disruptive use of parenthetical details, some of which should be incorporated within the main sentence.**]

Sparingly add clarifications of elements in parentheses using brackets, as in the following example:

HMS ("Her [or His] Majesty's Ship") *Reliant*

■ Numbered or Lettered Sequences

Use parentheses with the numbers or letters that clarify lists of information.

Freezing green beans involves six steps: (1) snap the ends off the beans; (2) wash the beans thoroughly in water; (3) blanch the beans for two to three minutes in boiling water; (4) cool them in ice water; (5) drain them for several minutes and then pack them into freezer containers; (6) seal the containers, label them, and put them in the freezer.

26d Brackets

Use brackets to indicate alterations in quoted material.

■ Clarification

When quotations out of context are not clear, use brackets to add clarifying information. Add only information that makes the original meaning clear.

Davies commented, "The army nurses' judgment in triage [where the medical staff decides which patients to treat first] is paramount, for they must determine a soldier's medical stability in a matter of seconds."
[The bracketed material explains a key term, and the brackets indicate that the writer, not Davies, defined *triage*.]

"If architectural preservationists are unsuccessful in their efforts, most [theaters built in the early 1900s] will probably be demolished by the end of the century," Walter Aspen noted.
[In place of the bracketed material, the original read "of these fascinating buildings," an unclear reference outside of the original context.]

■ Alteration of Syntax

Use brackets to indicate changes in the syntax of a quoted passage. Make only minor changes—changes in verb tense, for instance—that allow you to insert a passage smoothly into the context of your writing. Do not alter the meaning of the original.

Immigrants were sometimes confused or ambivalent about a new life in the United States. As a journalist noted in 1903, "Each day, thousands of immigrants [moved] through the turnstiles at Ellis Island, uncertain but hopeful."
[The brackets show a change from the present tense *move*, which was appropriate in 1903, to the past tense *moved*, which is appropriate in current contexts.]

■ Notation of Error

When a direct quotation contains an error in grammar or fact, indicate to readers that you recognize the error and have not introduced it yourself by inserting the word *sic* (Latin for "thus") in brackets.

Adderson noted in her preface, "The taxpayers who [sic] the
legislation will protect are the elderly, the handicapped, and
those in low-income families."
[*Sic* notes that the writer recognized Adderson's misuse of *who*
for *whom*.]

26e Ellipsis Points

Use ellipsis points—three *spaced* periods—to indicate that you
have omitted material from a quotation. Other marks of punctuation (periods, question marks, exclamation points, commas,
and so on) are separated from ellipsis points by one space.

■ Omissions from Quoted Material

Use ellipsis points placed within brackets to indicate where you
have omitted information, details, or clarifications in quoted
material. Maintain the original meaning of a source.

Original version

> "The Ninth Street Station is a superb example of ornate
> woodworking and stonework. Typical of Steamboat-Gothic
> architecture, it was designed in 1867 by Fielding Smith. It is a
> landmark we should endeavor to preserve."

Acceptable shortened version

> "The Ninth Street Station is a superb example of ornate
> woodworking and stonework. [. . .] It is a landmark we should
> endeavor to preserve."
> [**Note the retention of the period at the end of the first
> sentence.**]

Original version

> "This is a great movie if you enjoy meaningless violence,
> gratuitous sex, inane dialogue, and poor acting. It is offensive by
> any standards."

Dishonest shortened version

"This is a great movie [. . .] by any standards."
[**This is clearly a misrepresentation of the original quotation.**]

■ Hesitating or Incomplete Statements

Use ellipses points sparingly to indicate hesitating or incomplete thoughts and statements.

Woody Allen's *Stardust Memories* was . . . boring.

■ EXERCISE 26.3 Parentheses, brackets, and ellipsis points

Correct the faulty use of parentheses, brackets, and ellipsis points in the following sentences. (Available on disk.)

1. To install a cable converter, simply follow these directions: 1) remove the converter from the box; 2) attach the blue adapter wires to your television set; 3) plug the converter into an electrical outlet; 4) select a channel and test the equipment by turning it on.

2. "The benefits (for those who subscribe to cable services) are amazingly varied, from more programs to better programs," explained Ms. Abigail Fitzgerald, a cable network spokesperson.

3. Most cable subscribers would agree that they are offered more . . . , but is it better?

4. Professor Martínez, media specialist at ASU, commented: "Much of what's offered is junk . . . When *Mr. Ed, Car 54,* and *The Munsters* make it to national rebroadcast, we have to question the uses to which cable is put. Of course, that's the long-standing issue (in television broadcasting)."

5. Then again, people (the American people in particular) have always enjoyed (really enjoyed) some mindless entertainment (*unchallenging* is, perhaps, a better word) to relieve the tension (and frustration) of the day.

■ EXERCISE 26.4   Punctuation review

Punctuate the following paragraph. (Available on disk.)

The Postal Reorganization Act signed into law by President Nixon on August 12 1970 created a government owned postal service operated under the executive branch of the government the new US Postal Service is run by an eleven member board with members appointed by the president of the Senate for nine year terms the Postmaster General who is no longer part of the president's cabinet is selected by the members of the board since 1971 when the system began operating four men have served as Postmaster General Winton M Blount E T Klassen Benjamin F Bailar and William F Bolger but has the postal system changed substantially since the PRA went into effect on July 1 1971 no not to any great extent first class second class third class and fourth class these still represent the most commonly used mailing rates however some services have been added for instance Express Mail which tries to rival Federal Express Purolator and other one day delivery services guarantees that packages will arrive at their destinations by 300 the day after mailing the prices are steep as one might expect in addition the Postal Service has instituted nine digit zip codes in some areas for all practical purposes however the business at 29990 post offices throughout the US continues in much the same way it did before the PRA

Mechanics

313

Use capitals to indicate the beginnings of sentences, to signal proper nouns and proper adjectives, and to identify important words in titles. Capitalization creates clarity, but unnecessary capitalization is confusing and annoying to readers. Capitalize a word only when an uppercase letter is required.

QUICK REFERENCE

Use capitals to create special emphasis.

▶ Capitalize the first word in every sentence.

▶ Capitalize proper nouns and proper adjectives.

▶ Capitalize first, last, and important words in titles.

27a The First Word in Every Sentence

Subtitles in foreign films can be as distracting as they are helpful.

Apply this rule when quoting a complete sentence.

The senator remarked, "*Initiating* dialogue among national leaders is an important step in solving problems in the Middle East."

In long, interrupted quotations, only words that begin sentences are capitalized.

"*Prospects* for peace in the Middle East exist," the senator reiterated, "only if leaders negotiate in good faith."

When a complete sentence follows a colon, capitalizing the first word is optional.

The Declaration of Independence presents an idea we should remember: *All* people are created equal.

27b Proper Nouns and Proper Adjectives

Proper nouns and proper adjectives refer to specific people, places, and things and are therefore capitalized.

The *Grammy Award* nominations are always announced in *January*.
[specific name and month, capitals required]

But:

The award nominations are always announced in the winter.
[general nouns, no capitals required]

Names of specific individuals, races, ethnic groups, nationalities, languages, and places

Proper Nouns: Eva Perón, Caucasian, Chicano, Canadian, Zaire

Proper Adjectives: Shakespearean sonnet, Egyptian border, Chinese traditions, Mexican trade, Belgian lace

Registered trade names and trademarks, even those for common objects, must be capitalized.

Coke   Scotch tape   Kleenex   Xerox

Names of historical periods, events, and documents

the Age of Reason   the Battle of Bull Run

the Declaration of Independence

Names of days, months, and holidays

Monday   August   Presidents Day

Do not capitalize the names of seasons (*winter, spring, summer,* and *autumn/fall*).

Names of organizations and government branches and departments

Phi Beta Kappa   National Wildlife Federation

the House of Representatives   the Department of Transportation

Names of educational institutions, departments, specific courses, and degrees

University of Chicago	Department of Psychology
Aviation Technology 421	Bachelor of Arts

General references to academic subjects (*psychology*) do not require capitals unless they are languages (*English, Italian*) or use proper nouns or proper adjectives (*American history*). Course titles including numbers, however, require capitals.

Thomas earned an *A* in every speech course he took, but he was proudest of his *A* in *Speech 363.*

Religious names, terms, and writings

Judaism	Torah	Allah
Islam	Koran	Krishna
Buddhists	Ramadan	Christmas

Titles used with proper names

Professor Angélica Sànchez	Dr. Martin Luther King, Jr.
President Jefferson	
but: my history professor	the former president

Abbreviations, acronyms, and call letters

100 B.C. [or **b.c.**]	7:30 P.M. [or **p.m.**]
NAACP	Schedule SE
WZZQ radio	KTVI-TV

27c Titles and Subtitles

Capitalize the first and last words in titles and subtitles, as well as nouns, pronouns, verbs, adjectives, adverbs, and subordinating conjunctions. Unless they begin or end a title or subtitle, do not capitalize articles, prepositions, coordinating conjunctions, or *to* in an infinitive.

The House of Mirth
[**a novel**]

Pulp Fiction
[**a film**]

Nick of Time
[**an album**]

"Sailing to Byzantium"
[**a poem**]

How to Make Yourself Miserable: Another Vital Training Manual
[**a book title and subtitle**]

■ **EXERCISE 27.1   Capitalization**

Add the capital letters required in the following sentences. (Available on disk.)

1. art 426 (or english 426) is an interdisciplinary course that offers a survey of important artists and writers.

2. the course is team-taught by dr. nicholas bradford of the english department and ms. marlene jacobs of the art department.

3. during the fall of last year, i took the course to fulfill a humanities requirement.

4. we read a portion of dante's *divine comedy*—but not in italian—and saw slides of michelangelo's frescoes on the ceiling of the sistine chapel, both presenting perspectives on italian religious views.

5. we saw numerous paintings depicting the nativity, the crucifixion, and the ascension and read several religious poems.

6. turning our attention from europe, we saw *habuko landscape* by sesshu, a sixteenth-century japanese painter, and read samples of haiku poetry to learn of the spare but elegant images both create.

7. italian and flemish artists dominated the months of october and november.

8. we learned, however, that by the 1800s, neo-classicism had emerged and artistic dominance had shifted to france, where it remained for over a century; we read corneille's *phaedre* and saw representative paintings by david and ingres.

9. Over thanksgiving break, i took an optional field trip with ms. jacobs and several other students; we went to the art institute of chicago, her alma mater, to view their collection.

10. by the time we studied abstract art, national and artistic boundaries had been broken, and painters like picasso and poets like t. s. eliot could be said to draw upon the same aesthetic traditions.

11. when ms. jacobs first said, "the fine arts are symbiotic, each reciprocally influencing the other," i wasn't sure i understood what she meant. now i think i know.

Use italics to distinguish titles of complete published works: books; journals, magazines, and newspapers; works of art; the specific names of ships, trains, aircraft, and spacecraft; foreign words used in English sentences; and words or phrases requiring special emphasis.

Italics are indicated with slanted type (*like this*) or with underlining (like this). The meaning is the same.

QUICK REFERENCE

Use italics to create your intended meaning.

▶ Use italics to distinguish some titles, generally those of lengthy published works.

▶ Italicize the specific names of ships, trains, aircraft, and spacecraft.

▶ Italicize unfamiliar foreign words and phrases.

▶ Italicize words used as words, letters as letters, and numbers as numbers.

▶ Italicize words to create special emphasis.

28a Titles of Lengthy Published Works

Use italics with the titles of books, journals, magazines, newspapers, pamphlets, plays, and long poems. Titles of long musical compositions, albums, films, radio and television programs, paintings, statues, and other works of art are also italicized.

Books:
  Joseph Heller's *Catch-22*, Zora Neale Hurston's *Their Eyes Were Watching God*

The Bible, books of the Bible (Song of Solomon, Genesis), and legal documents (the Constitution) are not italicized, although they are capitalized.

Magazines and journals:
Time, American Scholar

Newspapers:
the *Boston Globe,* the *New York Times*

Long poems:
John Milton's *Paradise Lost,* Walt Whitman's *Leaves of Grass*

Long musical compositions:
Igor Stravinsky's *Firebird Suite,* Giacomo Puccini's opera *Madame Butterfly*

Recordings:
the Beatles's *Abbey Road,* Linda Ronstadt's *What's New?,* Dwight Yoakam's *Just Lookin' for a Hit*

Plays:
Edward Albee's *Zoo Story,* Wendy Wasserstein's *The Heidi Chronicles*

Films:
Sense and Sensibility, The Wizard of Oz

Radio and television programs:
All Things Considered, The Today Show

Although italic type is required for the name of a television series, the titles of episodes (daily, weekly, or monthly segments) are enclosed in quotation marks.

"Antarctica: Earth's Last Frontier" airs Tuesday on *NOVA.*

Paintings:
Pablo Picasso's *Three Musicians,* Georgia O'Keeffe's *Black Iris III*

Statues:
Rodin's *The Thinker,* Michelangelo's *David*

Pamphlets:
NCTE's *How to Help Your Child Become a Better Writer,* Roberta Greene's *'Til Divorce Do You Part*

28b Specific Names of Ships, Trains, Aircraft, and Spacecraft

Only specific names are italicized and capitalized. The names of vehicle types and models are capitalized but not italicized. Abbreviations such as *SS* ("Steamship") and *HMS* ("Her [or His] Majesty's Ship") are not italicized.

Ships:
   Queen Elizabeth II, HMS *Wellington*

   but: Starcraft Marlin, cruiser series XL

Trains:
   Orient Express, Stourbridge Lion

Aircraft:
   The Spirit of St. Louis, The Spruce Goose

   but: Boeing 707

Spacecraft:
   Apollo XIII, Sputnik II

28c Unfamiliar Foreign Words and Phrases

If a foreign word or phrase is likely to be unfamiliar to your readers, italicize it.

   Andrea Palladio made frequent use of *trompe l'oeil* effects and murals in his villa designs.

When terms—such as *coffee, coupon, kasha, cliché,* and *kindergarten*—are fully assimilated into standard American usage, they do not require italics. However, recently imported or unfamiliar words or phrases (*perestroika*) should be italicized. When using any but the most common foreign terms, follow conventions of spelling and include the accents and diacritical marks found in the original language.

28d Words Used as Words, Letters Used as Letters, Numbers Used as Numbers, and Symbols Used as Symbols

"The *s* was put in *island,* for instance, in sheer pedantic ignorance." —Bergen Evans

According to numerology, the numbers *5, 7, 12,* and *13* have occult significance.

28e For Emphasis

Use italics selectively to emphasize words, to signal a contrast, and to ensure careful examination of words by the reader.

"It makes a world of difference to a condemned man whether his reprieve is *upheld* or *held up.*" —Bergen Evans

Overuse of italics dilutes emphasis and may distort the tone of your writing. (See also section 29d.)

▦ EXERCISE 28.1   Italics

Supply italics where they are needed in the following sentences. (Available on disk.)

1. E. D. Hirsch's Cultural Literacy: What Every American Needs to Know—especially its appended list—has created a fascinating controversy since its publication.

2. For instance, Herman Melville's name is on the list, but his famous novel Moby Dick is not.

3. The statues David and the Pietà in St. Peter's Church in Vatican City are listed, but their creator Michelangelo does not appear.

4. Many of the foreign phrases—including ancien régime, bête noire, coup d'état, déjà vu, faux pas, fin de siècle, and tête-à-tête—are French, although a large number are Latin.

5. The Niña, Pinta, and Santa Maria do not appear, but the unfortunate Lusitania and Titanic do.

6. The maudlin poem Hiawatha and its author Henry Wadsworth Longfellow both appear, but Paradise Lost, the brilliant epic poem, appears without its author, John Milton.

7. Birth of a Nation is the only film on the list not produced first as a book or play with the same name.

8. The absence of I Love Lucy, The Dick Van Dyke Show, The Mary Tyler Moore Show, All in the Family, and M*A*S*H makes it clear that popular television culture does not concern Hirsch.

9. Oddly enough, the ampersand (&) appears on the list.

10. Including the novel Tobacco Road on the list but not the play Who's Afraid of Virginia Woolf? seems arguable, but the enjoyment of lists is in disagreeing with them.

Use quotation marks to set off direct quotations and dialogue and to identify the titles of unpublished and short works and chapters and other sections of long works.

29a Direct Quotations and Dialogue

■ Direct Quotations

Direct quotations represent spoken or written words exactly. Use quotation marks to indicate where the quoted material begins and ends. In contrast, indirect quotations—often introduced by *that* for statements or *if* for questions—report what people say or ask without using their exact words. Do not use quotation marks with indirect quotations.

> John Kenneth Galbraith commented, "In the affluent society no useful distinction can be made between luxuries and necessities."
> **[Galbraith's exact words are enclosed in quotation marks.]**

But:

> Galbraith argues that the necessary and the desirable become inextricably mixed in a wealthy society.
> [**The paraphrase of Galbraith's comment needs no quotation marks, though it does require attribution and documentation.**]

■ Dialogue

Use quotation marks to indicate the exact words used by speakers in dialogue. By convention, each change of speaker begins a new paragraph.

> Mrs. Moss, my landlady, asked me one Sunday morning:
> "Son, what is this you keep on reading?"
> "Oh, nothing. Just novels."
> "What you get out of 'em?"
> "I'm just killing time," I said.
> "I hope you know your own mind," she said in a tone that implied that she doubted if I had a mind.   —Richard Wright, "The Library Card"

29b Punctuation with Quotation Marks

■ Periods and Commas

Place periods and commas before closing quotation marks.

> One of Flannery O'Connor's most haunting stories is "The River."

> "The Circus Animals' Desertion," a late poem by William Butler Yeats, describes his growing frustration with poetry.

■ Semicolons and Colons

Place semicolons and colons after closing quotation marks.

As a young poet, T. S. Eliot showed his brilliance in "The Love Song of J. Alfred Prufrock"; readers and critics responded to it enthusiastically.

One word describes Lewis Carroll's "Jabberwocky": nonsense.

■ Question Marks and Exclamation Points

Place question marks and exclamation points to maintain the meaning of the sentence. If the material contained within quotation marks (whether a direct quotation or a title) ends with a question mark, then the closing quotation mark appears last. If your sentence is a question that contains material in quotation marks, then the question mark appears last. The same principles apply to the use of exclamation points with quotation marks.

Was it Archibald MacLeish who wrote "A world ends when its metaphor has died"?
[**The quotation is contained within the question.**]

Have you read Ralph Ellison's "Did You Ever Dream Lucky?"
[**The question mark inside the quotation marks serves both the question in the title and the question posed by the sentence.**]

If a quotation ends with a question mark or exclamation point, any other punctuation normally required by the sentence structure may be omitted.

I just read Ralph Ellison's "Did You Ever Dream Lucky?"

"Which is the correct road?" he asked, but he received no reply.
[**A comma is unnecessary following the question mark.**]

29c Titles of Brief Works, Parts of Long Works, and Unpublished Works

Place the titles of articles, short stories, short poems, essays, and songs in quotation marks. Chapter or unit titles and episodes of television series require quotation marks because they are parts of long works. Titles of unpublished papers or dissertations of any length are also placed in quotation marks.

Articles

"Good News Is No News" in *Esquire*

"The New World through New Eyes" in *Smithsonian*

Short stories

Bobbie Ann Mason's "Shiloh"

Isaac Bashevis Singer's "Gimpel the Fool"

Poems

Sylvia Plath's "Lady Lazarus"

Theodore Roethke's "My Papa's Waltz"

Essays

Joan Didion's "Why I Write"

James Thurber's "University Days"

Songs

Sarah Vaughn's "How Long Has This Been Going On?"

Lyle Lovett's "West Texas Highway"

Chapter or unit titles

"Theatre of the Orient" in O. G. Brockett's *History of the Theatre*

"Nightmare" in *The Autobiography of Malcolm X*

Episodes of television programs

"Chuckles Bites the Dust" from *The Mary Tyler Moore Show*

"Take My Ex-Wife, Please" from *Taxi*

Unpublished papers and dissertations

"Prohibition in the New England States"

"The Poetic Heritage of John Donne"

29d Ironic or Other Special Use of a Word

Use quotation marks sparingly to represent irony or to indicate the potential inappropriateness of slang, regionalisms, or jargon. (See also section 28e.)

Ironic use

> Who needs enemies with "friends" like these?
> [**Clearly *friends* is being used ironically.**]

Disavowal

> The negotiator asked for our "input."
> [**Placing *input* in quotation marks suggests that the writer knows the word is jargon. Unless you are quoting directly, use a better word such as *reactions, responses,* or *thoughts.***]

▧ EXERCISE 29.1   Quotation marks

Place the necessary quotation marks in the following sentences. Pay attention to their positioning with other punctuation. (Available on disk.)

1. Running on Empty? an article in *National Wildlife,* stresses that water management should be a universal concern.

2. The opening chapter of *The Grapes of Wrath* contains this central image: The rain-heads [thunderclouds] dropped a little spattering and hurried on to some other country. Behind them the sky was pale again and the sun flared. In the dust there were drop craters where the rain had fallen, and there were clean splashes on the corn, and that was all.

3. Dry as Dust, a local documentary on the plight of the Depression farmers, had special meaning in 1994, when water shortages occurred throughout the midwestern states.

4. The very real fear of drought was softened during the Depression by ironic songs like What We Gonna Do When the Well Runs Dry?

5. Nadene Benchley's dissertation, Deluge or Drought: The Crisis in Water Management, ought to be published, for it contains information many people need to know.

Use numbers and abbreviations according to convention.

▶ In most instances, write out numbers expressible in one or two words.

▶ Use figures for exact numbers starting with 101.

▶ Use figures for measurements, technical numbers, percentages, and fractions.

▶ Use abbreviations sparingly in formal writing; if you use them, use standard abbreviations and forms.

30a Numbers

■ Numbers Expressible in Words

Unless you are preparing scientific or technical material, write out cardinal and ordinal numbers expressible in one or two words. This rule applies to numbers *one* through *one hundred* (*first* through *one hundredth*) and to large round numbers like *four thousand* (*four thousandth*) and *nine million* (*nine millionth*).

> Russia has two cities—Moscow and St. Petersburg—with populations of more than two million.

Numbers from *twenty-one* through *ninety-nine* must be hyphenated.

Spell out numbers at the beginning of a sentence—no matter how many words are needed. If the number is long and awkward, revise the sentence.

One hundred fifteen
~~115~~ seniors attended graduation.

329

■ Numbers Expressible in Figures

Use figures for cardinal and ordinal numbers starting with *101*.

The Rogun Dam, the tallest in the world, stands 1,066 feet high.

Other Numbers Expressible in Figures	
Addresses	316 Ridge Place, 1111 West 16th Street
Dates	24 December 1948 (or December 24, 1948), 150 B.C., A.D. 1066
Divisions of books and plays	chapter 3, volume 9, act 2, scene 4
Exact dollar amounts	$3.12; $546 million; $7,279,000
Measurements	8 by 10
Identification numbers	332-44-7709, UTC 88 22495
Percentages	82 percent, 100 percent
Fractions	3/4
Scores	101 to 94
Times	3:15 A.M., 7:45 P.M. (but four-thirty in the morning; nine o'clock)

30b Abbreviations

Use only the most commonly recognized abbreviations (*Ms., Mr., JFK, NBA*) in formal writing. If you are unsure whether your readers will recognize an abbreviation, spell out the words.

If you choose to use a common abbreviation for a person or organization in formal writing, the first mention should include the full name, followed by the abbreviation in parentheses. Because many common abbreviations may be written without periods, check your dictionary for acceptable forms.

The Potato Chip/Snack Food Association (PC/SFA) is an international trade association. Like other trade associations, the PC/SFA monitors government actions that affect the business of its members.

Certain specialized writing situations—technical directions, recipes, entries for works-cited pages, résumés—use abbreviations to save space, but academic writing should not. Instead, write the words out completely.

Acceptable Abbreviations (in Prose)	
Well-known personal names	LBJ (Lyndon Baines Johnson), FDR (Franklin Delano Roosevelt)
Personal titles	John Walton, Jr.; Ms. Ella Beirbaum; Harold Blankenbaker, M.D.; Dr. Asha Mustapha; Rev. Joshua Felten; Gov. George Wallace (*but* Governor Wallace)
Names of countries	USA, US (*or* U.S.A., U.S.); UK (*or* U.K.); USSR (*or* U.S.S.R.)
Names of organizations and corporations	UNESCO, GE, FAA, AT&T
Words with figures	no. 133 (*or* No.)
Time of day	1:05 P.M. (*or* p.m.)
Dates	1200 B.C., A.D. 476

Unacceptable Abbreviations (in Prose)		
	Not	*But*
Business designations	Co. Inc.	Company Incorporated
Units of measurement	lb. cm	pound centimeter
Names of days and months	Fri. Oct.	Friday October
Academic subjects	psych. Eng.	psychology English
Divisions of books and plays	p. chap. sc. vol.	page chapter scene volume
Names of places	L.A. Mass.	Los Angeles Massachusetts
Personal names	Wm. Robt.	William Robert

■ EXERCISE 30.1　Numbers and abbreviations

Correct the misuse of number forms and abbreviations in the following sentences. (Available on disk.)

1. Doctor Ruth Waller, an econ. prof. at UCLA, has written 26 articles and 2 books about Asian-American trade relations.

2. 1 of her books and 14 of her articles are on reserve at the ISU library—to be read by students in Econ. two-hundred and thirty-six.

3. Statistics in one article show that Japan's labor force is well diversified, with eleven percent in agriculture, thirty-four percent in manufacturing, and forty-eight percent in services.

4. Statistics also show that the Am. labor force is not as well diversified: we have seventy percent in services, with close to one-third of those in info. management.

5. By Fri., Dec. twelfth, each of us in the class must prepare a report on a US co. that is affected by Asian-American trade.

■ **EXERCISE 30.2   Numbers and abbreviations**

Correct the misuse of number forms and abbreviations in the following paragraph. (Available on disk.)

Walter E. Disney, better known as Walt, was born Dec. fifth, 1901, in Chicago. After early work at the Chicago Academy of Fine Arts and at a commercial art firm in MO, he moved to Hollywood in nineteen-twenty-three. It was there that he revolutionized US entertainment. 1928 was the year he produced "Steamboat Willie," a short cartoon that introduced Mickey Mouse as well as the use of soundtracks with cartoons. 10 years later, his studio produced the 1st feature-length animated cartoon, *Snow White and the 7 Dwarfs,* and 2 years later, *Pinocchio.* The success of Disney's films stemmed from their innovations—that is, their use of animated forms, color, music, voices, and story. After more than 12 successful films, Disney began work in television in 1950. In 55, Disneyland opened outside L.A., and Disney's theme parks created a new standard for amusement parks. Few would have suspected, in nineteen-twenty-six, that the man whose first cartoon creation was Oswald the Rabbit would change entertainment in the US of A.

Although familiar spelling rules (for example, *i* before *e*, except after *c*) can solve some spelling problems, spelling rules in English have many exceptions because English words derive from so many language groups.

31a General Rules

Although rules for spelling in English have many exceptions, a few basic rules are helpful.

■ Plurals

The letters that end a singular word dictate how its plural is formed.

Ending Letters	Plural Ending	Samples	
Consonant plus o	Add -*es*	potato	potatoes
		fresco	frescoes
Vowel plus o	Add -*s*	radio	radios
		stereo	stereos
Consonant plus y	Change *y* to *i* and add -*es*	victory	victories
		melody	melodies
Vowel plus y	Add -*s*	monkey	monkeys
		survey	surveys
s, ss, sh, ch, x, *or* z	Add -*es*	bonus	bonuses
		by-pass	by-passes
		dish	dishes
		catch	catches
		tax	taxes
		buzz	buzzes
Proper name with y	Add -*s*	Gary	Garys
		Germany	Germanys

■ Prefixes

Some prefixes (*dis-*, *mis-*, *non-*, *pre-*, *re-*, *un-*, and others) do not change the spelling of the root word.

similar   dissimilar   restrictive   nonrestrictive

See pages 304–05 for exceptions to this rule.

■ Suffixes

The pattern for adding suffixes depends on the letters that end the root word and those that begin the suffix.

Last Letter of Root Word	First Letter of Suffix	Pattern	Examples
Silent e	Consonant	Retain the *e*	achiev*e*ment, resolut*e*ly
Silent e	Vowel	Drop the *e*	gri*e*ving, sizable
Silent e *preceded by a "soft"* c *or* g	Vowel	Retain the *e*	notic*eable*, chang*e*able
Single consonant in one-syllable word with one vowel	Vowel	Double the consonant	si*tt*ing, cli*pp*ing

■ *Ie* and *Ei*

This familiar, useful poem explains the order of *i* and *e*.

> Write *i* before *e*
> Except after *c*
> Or when sounded like *ay*
> As in *neighbor* and *weigh*.

31b Dictionaries

■ Spelling Dictionaries

Spelling dictionaries provide the correct spellings of thousands of words. These specialized dictionaries dispense with pronunciation guides, notes on word origins, definitions, and synonyms. They generally indicate syllable breaks, however. Spelling dictionaries offer a quick way to confirm, for example, that *separate* is spelled with two *a*s and two *e*s and *develop* does not end with an *e*.

■ Standard Dictionaries

Words that sound alike, such as *pail* and *pale,* may have very different meanings and spellings. Knowing which word has your intended meaning will lead you to the correct spelling. To determine that a word has your intended meaning and that you have spelled it correctly, use a standard dictionary. Be sure to read *all* the definitions to find the word and spelling you need.

The sample from *The American Heritage Dictionary, Third College Edition* (Boston: Houghton, 1993) shown in Figure 1 illustrates common features of a dictionary entry.

Figure 1 A sample dictionary entry

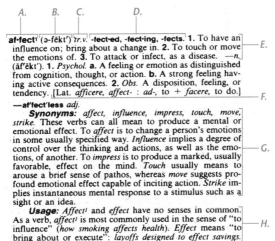

A. *Spelling and syllabification*
B. *Pronunciation (guide at bottom of dictionary page)*
C. *Part of speech*
D. *Spelling variations (past tense, present participle, plural)*
E. *Numbered definitions*
F. *Word origins*
G. *Synonyms and antonyms*
H. *Usage note*

31c   Technical Words and British Variants

■ Technical Words

Check specialized words individually. Their spellings are some-times difficult to remember because we use such words infre-quently. Keep a note card handy with a list of the correct spelling of any technical words that you use often.

■ British Variants

Dictionaries list alternative spellings for some common words, and many times any choice is acceptable if applied consistently. When alternatives are identified as *American (Am.)* and *British (Brit.),* however, use the American spelling.

American Words with British Variants	
American	*British*
center	centre
color	colour
encyclopedia	encyclopaedia
judgment	judgement

However, when using a proper name, maintain the original spelling.

> Great Britain's *Labour Party* favors the nationalization of many industries.
> **[Although the American spelling is *labor,* the proper name of the political party uses the British spelling.]**

The advice in this chapter concerns acclimating yourself to the contexts of writing within the American culture, even though it also addresses a number of important technical issues related to the study of English as a Second Language (ESL).

QUICK REFERENCE

▶ Recognize the contexts for writing in the American culture.

▶ Recognize special ESL needs when learning the writing process.

▶ Learn about the technical issues of writing from general discussions.

▶ Consider some special concerns for ESL students.

32a Writing in the American Culture

Having arrived in the United States to study, you are well aware of the ways that American culture differs from your own. Yet as a student in an American college, you will be expected to communicate—both in writing and in speaking—in an American fashion, and that requires practice.

As you begin to strengthen your writing through classroom experiences, consider the following contexts for your writing.

Individuality. In the United States, individuals assert their unique identities, even when they consider themselves to be members of groups.

Personal experience. Because of the emphasis on individuality, personal experiences are highly valued in American culture, even while recognizing that those experiences are limited.

Directness. American culture is, to a great extent, a direct one. To ensure that your ideas are understood, you will need to state your ideas in clearly expressed topic sentences and thesis statements.

Diversity. Because America includes many subcultures (immigrant groups have increased American diversity), you must realize the importance of differences among people.

Linear organization. Because Americans are generally direct people, you will need to develop organizational skills that present your ideas in a straightforward, uncluttered fashion.

Explanations of unfamiliar material. Because students in American colleges and universities come from a broad spectrum of society, you will not be able to assume that they share the same kinds of experiences. As a result, you will need to explain your ideas, information, experiences, and insights with care.

Growth and development. American education is, in large part, founded on the principles of growth and development, not finite results. Consequently, within a writing course, you will be judged on improvement: if your writing matures and your control of technical issues increases, teachers will recognize your development.

Available tutoring. American colleges and universities are committed to providing help with writing instruction. Often affiliated with departments of English, writing centers frequently provide free tutoring to help you work to improve your skills.

Teachers. American teachers are, for the most part, willing to work with students on an individual basis. Do not feel embarrassed to ask for available help during teachers' scheduled office hours; they will help you isolate writing problems and discuss ways to solve those problems.

Computers. Computers are available on most college campuses in the United States, and they can provide you with special opportunities to improve your writing.

32b General Issues of Writing

The first five chapters of this handbook deal with the composing process—the strategies and techniques that help writers to put their ideas into written form. As an ESL writer, you may benefit from approaching those materials with these suggestions in mind.

■ Planning

Write about what you know. Use your unique experiences to your advantage. Teachers and classmates, who may know little about your culture, will be interested in the ideas and experiences you have to share.

Consider your readers carefully. If you write about your experiences in another culture—or write about your new experiences in American culture—remember what your readers know and do not know. Provide details and clear explanations, rather than allowing readers to rely on stereotypes.

Solicit reactions to your work. Ask your teacher, a classmate, or a tutor to respond to your planning and outline. Seeking reactions at this early stage will help you to avoid problems later in the composing process.

■ Drafting

Outline your ideas fully. Consider preparing your outline by using full sentences to describe each element. Although such a strategy will take longer than creating an outline using words and phrases, you will discover appropriate ways of expressing your ideas while working in stages.

Concentrate on the ideas in your paper. Because you have spent so much time learning the technical issues of English, you may find it difficult to ignore them, even for a short while. However, you will compose more fluently if you concentrate first on explaining the ideas in your paper.

Work in stages. Divide your writing into small blocks of time, working steadily but never too long during one sitting. You will be less frustrated—and more productive—if you relax between stages of writing.

Be patient and realistic. Remember that learning to write well is a difficult process for *all* writers. Consequently, you must allow yourself some mistakes and recognize that you cannot solve all problems at once. In particular, remember that the more language skills you assimilate during your studies, the better your writing will become. Relax and allow yourself time to improve.

Solicit reactions to your work. Ask your teacher, a classmate, or a tutor to read through an early draft of one of your paragraphs. A response at this stage will indicate where you are succeeding with your writing and where you need more work.

■ Revising

Give special attention to content. Revise your draft by looking first at its content. Have you described the people, places, actions, and ideas with care? Could you explain them more fully? Have you provided useful explanations of your central ideas? Have you expressed them plainly?

Consider grammatical issues. Once you have reviewed the ideas of the paper, revise your sentences as needed. Make sure that your sentences are complete and that your verbs are in the proper tenses. Examine the order of adjectives and adverbs. Looking at these matters slowly and carefully—apart from your review of content—will allow you to concentrate on grammatical issues one sentence at a time.

Consider issues of usage. Once you have double-checked your sentences to ensure that they are grammatical, examine your word choices to determine whether they reflect current American usage. Have you included modifiers that are in the correct word forms? Have you double-checked idiomatic structures?

Consider mistakes you frequently make. Based on responses to your earlier written work, give special attention to matters that have caused you problems before. If you have consistent difficulty with verb tense, examine your verb tenses in every sentence. If you sometimes confuse words, use the Glossary of Usage (page 525) to make sure that you have selected the appropriate word to convey your meaning.

Solicit reactions to your work. Ask your teacher, a classmate, or a tutor to review your work with you. Select the feature (grammar or usage, for example) that has caused you the most consistent trouble and ask someone to respond only to that feature.

By dividing your work on a paper into stages, you will be able to concentrate on improvements one at a time. This pattern will make the work less frustrating and more productive than it would be if you tried to revise all the features at once. Also, remember that your papers will improve as you gain experience in composing in English. Patience, practice, and perseverance are qualities you will want to develop.

32c Technical Issues of Writing

Chapters 6–31 of this handbook discuss the technical issues of writing—from sentence development and word choice to grammar, punctuation, and mechanics. Use these discussions from the main portion of the handbook to find answers to many of your technical questions. This outline of topics, with brief descriptions, will help you to locate the sections that will be of most use to you:

Parts of Speech (Chapter 6).   Turn to this chapter for a review of the parts of speech: nouns, pronouns, verbs, adjectives, adverbs, conjunctions, prepositions, and interjections. For brief definitions, also consult the Glossary of Grammatical Terms (539–53).

Sentence Structures (Chapter 7).   For a review of how sentences are formed in English, read this chapter. You will find discussions of the parts of sentences (subject and predicate) and the kinds of sentences (simple, compound, complex, and compound-complex). The Glossary of Grammatical Terms also includes brief definitions and samples.

Sentence Elements (Chapters 8–12).   For a review of the elements that will improve the effectiveness of your sentences (variety, emphasis, parallelism, pronoun reference, and positioning modifers), read the discussions in these chapters.

Word Choices (Chapters 13–14).   To explore the possibilities for improving your individual word choices, review these chapters to learn about how your word choices affect the meaning of your sentences. Give particular attention to abstract and concrete words, idioms, jargon, and sexist language. The Glossary of Usage also contains discussions of frequently confused words and words used in special contexts.

Grammar (Chapters 15–20).   Because effective grammar is at the heart of effective writing, use these chapters to eliminate fragments, comma splices, and fused sentences from your writing. Address issues of subject-verb and pronoun-antecedent agreement, pronoun case, and verb tense. Follow the advice in these chapters to ensure that you use adjectives and adverbs in their proper forms.

Punctuation (Chapters 21–26).   These six chapters include discussions of how to use three kinds of end punctuation (periods, question marks, and exclamation points) and a wide variety of in-sentence punctuation (commas, semicolons, colons, apostrophes, dashes, hyphens, parentheses, brackets, and ellipsis points).

Mechanics (Chapters 27–31). These five chapters describe technical matters that relate to writing in American English: capitalization, italics (or underlining), quotation marks, number style, abbreviations, and spelling.

Research (Chapters 33–35; Appendix B, pages 477–94). Offering advice on how to plan, research, write, and document a research paper, these chapters describe a wide variety of technical issues. The discussions pertain to the documentation style of the Modern Language Association, although Appendix B discusses the documentation style of the American Psychological Association.

Glossary of Usage (pages 525–38). Located at the back of the handbook, this glossary explains the usage of potentially confusing words and phrases. Many commonly confused word pairs (*accept/except, among/between, fewer/less,* and others) are included in this simple reference guide.

Glossary of Grammatical Terms (pages 539–53). Located at the back of the handbook, this glossary provides brief definitions of all grammatical terms used in the book.

32d Special Concerns

As an ESL student, you may have some special concerns related to irregularities of the English language. You may also be concerned about issues that native speakers develop intuitively and that are therefore discussed infrequently in textbooks for English speakers. Many of these matters are discussed in other sections of this handbook, but several unique issues are discussed next.

■ Articles (*a, an,* or *the*)

A and *an* are indefinite articles. Use *a* before a word that begins with a consonant sound; use *an* before a word with a vowel sound. For words beginning with *h,* use *a* when the *h* is voiced (sounded) and *an* when the *h* is unvoiced (unsounded). Uses of either *a* or *an* suggest that the noun or pronoun that follows is nonspecific and that it can be counted.

A passport is required for travel in *a* foreign country.
[**In both instances, the use of *a* signals a nonspecific noun.**]

An honest person is not always *a* helpful one.
[**In the first instance, the *h* is unvoiced, so *an* is required. The voiced *h* in the second instance requires the use of *a*.**]

When nonspecific nouns are plural, they do not require the use of an article, as the next sample illustrates:

Chi Li and Miko took vacations three times a year.

But:

Miguel took *a* vacation last year.

Use *the,* a definite article, with a noun that is specific and countable. The use of *the* suggests that readers are familiar with the specific noun or that other words in the sentence make it particular.

The travel agent whom Sasha recommended provided excellent help.
[**The use of *the* indicates that readers are able to identify the particular travel agent.**]

But:

I prefer to consult *a* travel agent who is not too aggressive.
[**This general use requires the indefinite article *a* since it is nonspecific.**]

■ Modal Auxiliary Verbs

Modal auxiliaries are used along with the infinitive of a verb to create special meanings. By using modals, you can indicate ability, intention, permission, possibility, necessity, obligation, or speculation. The following examples illustrate the various meanings that modal auxiliaries create.

Meaning	Modals	Sample
Ability	can, could	You *can* pick up your tickets any time after 5:00 P.M.
Intention	will, would, shall	Jamal *will* study law next year.
Permission	can, could, may, might	Renters *may* keep small pets as long as they are not noisy.
Possibility	may, might, can, could	Ian's family *can* afford to travel, but they don't.
Necessity	must, have to	Nakia *must* work to help pay for her college expenses.
Obligation	should	Parents *should* read to their children on a regular basis.
Speculation	would	If we had a longer break, I *would* visit my family.

■ Idioms

In English, as in most other languages, some expressions create meaning collectively, even when the words do not make complete sense when considered individually. Consult the following list to ensure that you are conveying your intended meaning.

Idiom	Meaning
break down	stop functioning
break up	separate
call off	cancel

Idiom	Meaning
check into	investigate
figure out	understand
fill out	complete
find out	discover
get over	recover from
give up	stop trying
hand in	submit
hand out	distribute
leave out	omit
look after	take care of
look into	examine
look up	locate
look up to	admire
look forward to	anticipate
pick out	choose
point out	show
put off	postpone
run into	meet by chance
turn down	refuse

You can often avoid the potential confusion of using American idioms by using the single words or the descriptive phrases that convey the same meaning.

■ Order of Modifiers

In English, multiple words that modify a noun must appear in a specific sequence. When you include multiple modifiers, include them in this order:

1. Articles, possessives, and demonstratives (*the* computer, *her* apartment, *this* assignment)
2. Order (*third* speaker)
3. Number (*sixteen* candles)
4. Description (*beautiful* park)
5. Size (*enormous* lake)
6. Shape (*spiral* staircase)
7. Age (*middle-aged* teacher)
8. Color (*red* rose)
9. Origin (*Chinese* vase)
10. Material (*wooden* bowl)

The pattern for combining modifiers works in this way:

the fourth white house
[**article, order, color**]

a dozen long-stemmed roses
[**article, number, shape**]

a talented young dancer
[**article, description, age**]

an ancient Egyptian statue
[**article, age, origin**]

In most instances, restrict the number of modifiers used to describe a noun. More than three modifiers often make a sentence seem overloaded with information.

Research

351

As you begin work on a research paper, consider topics related to your fields of study, topics related to your personal interests, or topics that raise questions you would like to explore. Whatever your final choice, make sure you are committed to the topic because you will spend hours reading, thinking, and writing about it.

QUICK REFERENCE

▌ Choose a general subject that is interesting, specific, and challenging.

▌ Narrow the subject to a specific topic by restricting its time period, locale, or special circumstances.

▌ Write a working thesis statement to guide your research.

▌ Compile a preliminary list of sources and evaluate their potential usefulness.

▌ Take clear, consistent, and complete notes.

▌ Avoid plagiarism by taking accurate notes.

Research papers can be informative or interpretive, depending on their purpose. Informative research papers are factual, objective surveys of all material available on a topic. Interpretive research papers are analyses of selected evidence to support the writer's viewpoint and ideas. Since most college research papers are of the second type, this text focuses on interpretive research papers. Writers of such papers must be thorough and fair, even though they support a single position on their material. Part of the challenge—and pleasure—of research is the constant need to reexamine your evidence in the light of new evidence and your ideas in the light of new ideas.

As you gather and read materials related to your topic, you will be taking notes to record information and ideas to use when you write the final paper.

33a Subject to Topic

■ A General Subject

Begin your research work by selecting a general subject. Your major or minor field of study or an academic subject that you enjoy or know well can provide a useful, broad subject. Any general subject that you know well or have an interest in can also lead you to a good topic.

Assessing General Subjects

- The subject should be interesting enough for you to spend hours reading, thinking, and writing about it.

- The subject should be of a scope broad or narrow enough to be treated adequately in a paper of the required length.

- Enough material should be available to research the subject completely within the time available. (Very recent events sometimes do not make good subjects because adequate materials may not be available.)

- The subject should be challenging but should not require special knowledge that you do not have and do not have time to acquire.

- The subject should not be overused. If a subject is overused, source materials may be unavailable because of high demand.

After selecting a general subject that meets the previous requirements, consult with your instructor to be sure that it meets the requirements of the assignment.

Angela, a history education major, considered these general subjects:

```
presidential impeachment

plagiarism and the Internet

the Smithsonian
```

Angela eliminated the first subject because it was too complex for a brief paper while the third topic was too broad. *Plagiarism and the Internet* was also broad, but it could be narrowed easily, and with Internet access and the recent attention to the topic, she knew she would be able to find a wide range of materials.

■ EXERCISE 33.1   General subjects

List five possible subjects for a research paper. Test them against the guidelines given on page 353. (Consider skimming the index of a textbook in your major or minor field for interesting subjects.)

Example

1. Government subsidies
2. High-grossing films
3. The Federal Reserve Board
4. Museums
5. Childcare

■ A Specific Topic

Continue your work by narrowing your general subject to a specific topic. Doing so will help you to avoid wasting valuable research time reviewing and reading materials unsuited to the final paper. An hour or two spent skimming reference books to narrow a subject often saves many hours later.

Read general sources in the library's reference room—encyclopedias, specialized dictionaries, and fact books—to discover the scope and basic themes and details of your general subject. (See the selected list of general reference works on pages 360–65). Use this information and the following strategies to narrow your subject to a specific topic:

- **Time:** Limit the scope of your paper to a specific, manageable time span. For example, restrict the topic *assembly-line automobile production* to the *1920s* or *1990s.*

- **Place:** Limit the scope of your topic to a single, specific location. For example, focus the topic *revitalization of cities* on *midwestern cities* or *St. Louis.*

- **Circumstance:** Limit your topic to a specific set of circumstances. For example, the topic *the U.S. presidency* might focus on *the U.S. presidency in wartime.*

These strategies can be combined to achieve even greater focus. For example, a student might research *assembly-line automobile production in Japan in the 1990s* or *the U.S. presidency during the conflict in Vietnam.*

    To obtain a basic knowledge of plagiarism and the Internet and to find some themes or details to help her narrow the general subject, Angela skimmed some general reference materials in her college library, working with the print collection, as well as with the electronic databases. She found that the subject of plagiarism was indeed a broad topic. By joining the subject *plagiarism* with the Internet, she had already established a time frame extending back less than a decade; and as she knew, the Internet extends worldwide. However, she could concentrate her attention on her paired subjects in the United States, the area that interested her most.

    Angela also found that she had many special circumstances that applied to her subject. For example, she discovered that examples of plagiarism ranged from literature to scientific studies, student papers, political speechmaking and filmmaking, as well as to other topic groups. Even after narrowing the subject to the last ten years in the United States, Angela discovered that she had numerous additional topics: old- versus new-styled plagiarism, penalties, preventions, implications, psychological motivations, and others. She found that she could effectively narrow her topic by addressing any one of these areas.

As a future teacher, Angela was most interested in three specific and related topics: what motivates students to plagiarize papers, the ease with which they can acquire papers through the Internet, and the strategies to deter this practice. She was unsure about whether she would treat all three of these areas, but she decided to begin by researching them all, knowing that she could narrow her topic further if she found a great deal of information on one of these areas of focus.

■ **EXERCISE 33.2   Specific topics**

Select three subjects from your responses to Exercise 33.1 and write three focused topics by identifying a particular time, place, or special circumstance.

Example

1. Government subsidies for the dairy industry (special circumstance)

2. Museums and innovative programs in the last twenty years (special circumstance and time)

3. Childcare in the inner city (place)

33b A Working Thesis Statement

In the same way that a working thesis statement guides the planning and drafting for other papers (see pages 19–22), it guides the planning and drafting for a research paper. For a research paper, which involves intensive reading and thinking, the working thesis statement also helps you to select and evaluate materials.

Your focused topic, presented as a complete statement or question and anchored with details derived from your preliminary research, should yield an effective working thesis statement.

A student working with the focused topic *the U.S. presidency during the conflict in Vietnam* might develop the following thesis:

> During the conflict in Vietnam, the presidency was forced to a new level of accountability by the peace movement and the media.

After writing your working thesis statement, evaluate its effectiveness. (For more information on thesis statements, see section 1e.) An effective thesis statement has three essential characteristics and may have three optional characteristics:

Essential Characteristics

Identify a specific, narrow topic.

Present a clear opinion on, not merely facts about, the topic.

Establish a tone appropriate to the topic, purpose, and audience.

Optional Characteristics

Qualify the topic as necessary, pointing out significant opposing opinions.

Clarify important points, indicating the organizational pattern.

Acknowledge your readers' probable awareness of the topic.

A thesis statement can make research seem a deductive process, one beginning with a general conclusion to support. But research should also be inductive, shaped by and building to a conclusion based on discovered information. When researching, allow new ideas and unexpected information to lead you in promising new directions. Keep an open mind by using your working thesis not as something to be proved but as a controlling idea to be confirmed, refuted, or modified on the basis of your reading in the weeks or months ahead.

After her general reading and discussions with a college history teacher and other history education students, Angela decided to research the strategies teachers can use to deter Internet plagiarism. Before beginning her focused search for specific, relevant materials, she reviewed her preliminary research notes and formulated this working thesis statement:

```
Because the Internet has made the process of
plagiarizing papers easy for students, teachers
must take informed, active steps to deter it.
```

Angela planned to use this working thesis statement to guide her research. It would help her to eliminate sources that treated unrelated aspects of plagiarism and direct her toward relevant sources. She kept in mind, however, that her thesis statement would likely change as she learned more about her topic.

■ EXERCISE 33.3　Working thesis statements

Type three working thesis statements with which you might begin your research. Discuss them with other students or with your instructor to determine which one promises to lead to the most productive research and the best paper.

Example

1. Although the federal government first subsidized the dairy industry during the Great Depression to ensure its survival, the threat is long since past, and the time has come for the dairy industry to operate without subsidies.

2. Although museums have long been seen as formidable, formal institutions, today's curators challenge this assumption by hosting innovative exhibits.

3. Before government agencies can fairly expect parents on welfare to work, they must provide affordable, acceptable childcare.

33c The Library

■ Library Facilities

If you have not done so already, tour your college library. As part of a group or on your own, locate and explore all areas of your library.

These typical facilities should be included in your tour:

- *The Circulation Area* (where you will check out and return books)
- *The Reference Area* (where encyclopedias, dictionaries, fact books, yearbooks, indexes, and other sources are collected)
- *The Current Periodicals Area* (where recent issues of journals, magazines, and newspapers are available)
- *The Stacks* (where books and other bound materials are stored)
- *Special Collections* (where rare books and archival materials are housed)
- *Departmental Libraries* (where individual departments maintain their own collections)
- *The New-Book Area* (where the most recent acquisitions are kept until they are added to the general collection)
- *The Government Documents Area* (where materials produced by government agencies are located)
- *The Microform (Microfilm, Microfiche) Area* (where reduced-image versions of materials are kept)
- *The Multimedia Area* (where videotapes, audiotapes, CDs, and other nonprint materials are located)
- *The Interlibrary Loan Area* (where requests for materials from other libraries are processed).
- *The Reserve Area* (where faculty can put materials on hold for special, short-term use)
- *The Preshelving Area(s)* (where books are temporarily placed before being returned to collections)
- *The Photocopy Areas* (where you can make copies of print materials)
- *Group Study Rooms* (where you can study or collaborate with other students)

■ Computer Clusters

Give particular attention to the computer areas in your library, for they will provide you with access to online catalogs, electronic indexes, Internet sources, and CD-ROM collections. Most libraries now have large clusters of computers in areas where they once housed their card catalogs, as well as in other high-use locations like the reference area. These heavily used computer clusters are generally monitored by experienced librarians and staff members who can answer most of your questions, making these excellent areas in which to work if you have limited experience using electronic search systems. To provide you with even more options, most libraries have additional, smaller computer clusters located throughout the building.

If you have questions about the library's facilities, resources, or services (such as questions about specialized instruction), talk to a librarian or a staff member.

■ General Reference Works

The reference area in your library contains many useful general reference works: major encyclopedias, almanacs, atlases, dictionaries, and compendia of biographies, etymologies, and quotations, some of which are available in electronic formats. The following lists indicate the variety of material available.

General References

> *Contemporary Authors.* Detroit: Gale, 1962 to date. Also electronic.
>
> *Current Biography.* New York: Wilson, 1940 to date. Also electronic.
>
> *Facts on File: A Weekly World News Digest.* New York: Facts on File, 1940 to date. Also electronic.
>
> *National Geographic Atlas of the World.* 6th rev. ed. Washington, DC: Natl. Geographic, 1996.

Who's Who. London: Black, 1849 to date. Also electronic.

Who's Who among African Americans. 9th ed. Detroit: Gale, 1999.

The World Almanac and Book of Facts. New York: Newspaper Enterprise, 1868 to date.

Encyclopedias

Academic American Encyclopedia. 21 vols. 1998 ed.

Collier's Encyclopedia. 24 vols. 1996 ed.

Encyclopedia Americana. 30 vols. 1998 ed.

The New Encyclopaedia Britannica. 32 vols. 1997 ed. Also electronic.

Art and Music

Abraham, Gerald. *The Concise Oxford History of Music.* New York: Oxford UP, 1985.

Baker's *Biographical Dictionary of Musicians.* Ed. Nicholas Slonimsky. 8th ed. New York: Macmillan, 1992.

The Concise Oxford Dictionary of Art and Artists. Ed. Ian Chilvers. New York: Oxford UP, 1990.

New Grove Dictionary of Music and Musicians. Ed. Stanley Sadie. 20 vols. Washington, DC: Grove's, 1995.

The Pelican History of Art. 50 vols. in progress. East Rutherford, NJ: Penguin, 1953 to date.

Economics and Business

Concise Dictionary of Business. New York: Oxford UP, 1992.

Freeman, Michael J., and Derek Aldcroft. *Atlas of the World Economy.* New York: Simon, 1991.

The HarperCollins Dictionary of Economics. Ed. Christopher Pass et al. New York: Harper, 1991.

Rutherford, Donald. *Dictionary of Economics.* New York: Routledge, 1992.

Terry, John V. *Dictionary for Business and Finance.* 2nd ed. Fayetteville: U of Arkansas P, 1990.

History

American Decades. Ed. Matthew J. Bruccoli, Richard Layman, and Karen L. Rood. 9 vols. Detroit: Gale, 1996.

Britannica Book of the Year. Chicago: Britannica, 1938 to date.

Brownstone, David M., and Irene M. Franck. *Dictionary of Twentieth-Century History.* New York: Prentice, 1990.

Encyclopedia of American History. Ed. Richard B. Morris and Jeffrey B. Morris. 6th ed. New York: Harper, 1982.

Grum, Bernard. *The Timetables of History: A Horizontal Linkage of People and Events.* 3rd ed. New York: Simon, 1991.

Newsmakers: *The People behind Today's Headlines.* Ed. Louise Mooney Collins. New York: Gale, 1985 to date.

Rand McNally Atlas of World History. Rev. ed. Chicago: Rand, 1993.

The Times Atlas of World History. Ed. Geoffrey Barraclough. 3rd ed. Maplewood, NJ: Hammond, 1989.

Language and Literature

Cambridge Encyclopedia of Language. Ed. David Crystal. New York: Cambridge UP, 1987.

Cambridge Guide to Literature in English. Ed. Ian Ousby. New York: Cambridge UP, 1988.

Cambridge Handbook of American Literature. Ed. Jack Salzman. New York: Cambridge UP, 1986.

Crystal, David. *An Encyclopedia Dictionary of Language and Languages.* Oxford: Blackwell, 1992.

Holman, C. Hugh, and William Harmon. *Handbook to Literature*. 7th ed. New York: Macmillan, 1996.

The Oxford Companion to American Literature. Ed. James D. Hart. 6th ed. New York: Oxford UP, 1995.

The Oxford Companion to English Literature. Ed. Margaret Drabble. Rev. ed. New York: Oxford UP, 1995.

Oxford English Dictionary. Ed. J. A. Simpson and E. S. C. Weiner, 2nd ed. 20 vols. New York: Oxford UP, 1989. Also electronic.

Philosophy and Religion

Cohn-Sherbok, Dan. *Dictionary of Judaism and Christianity*. Philadelphia: Trinity, 1991.

Contemporary Religions: A World Guide. Ed. Ian Harris et al. Harlow, Eng.: Longman, 1992.

Copleston, Frederick Charles. *A History of Philosophy*. Rev. ed. 9 vols. New York: Image, 1993.

Lacey, Alan R. *A Dictionary of Philosophy*. 3rd ed. London: Paul-Methuen, 1996.

Science and Math

Ashworth, William. *Encyclopedia of Environmental Studies*. New York: Facts on File, 1991.

Cambridge Encyclopedia of Life Sciences. Ed. E. Adrian Faraday and David S. Ingram. Cambridge: Cambridge UP, 1985.

Concise Dictionary of Physics. New York: Oxford UP, 1990.

The Concise Oxford Dictionary of Earth Sciences. Ed. Ailsa Allaby and Michael Allaby. Oxford: Oxford UP, 1990.

The Concise Oxford Dictionary of Ecology. Ed. Michael Allaby. Oxford: Oxford UP, 1994.

Encyclopedia of Earth System Science. Ed. William A. Nierenberg. 4 vols. San Diego: Academic-Harcourt, 1992.

Encyclopedia of Mathematics and Its Applications. 31 vols. in progress. Reading, MA: Addison; Cambridge: Cambridge UP, 1976 to date.

The Encyclopedia of Physics. Ed. Robert Besancon. 3rd ed. New York: Van Nostrand, 1990.

Encyclopedic Dictionary of Mathematics. Ed. Kiyoshi Ito. 2nd ed. 2 vols. Cambridge, MA: MIT P, 1993.

Hale, W. G., and J. P. Margham. *The HarperCollins Dictionary of Biology.* New York: Harper, 1991.

McGraw-Hill Encyclopedia of Physics. Ed. Sybil P. Parker. 2nd ed. New York: McGraw, 1993.

McGraw-Hill Encyclopedia of Science and Technology. 20 vols. New York: McGraw, 1992.

Van Nostrand Reinhold Encyclopedia of Chemistry. Ed. Douglas M. Considine and Glenn D. Considine. 4th ed. New York: Van Nostrand, 1984.

Social Sciences

The Encyclopedia of the Peoples of the World. Ed. Amiram Gonen. New York: Holt, 1993.

Encyclopedia of Sociology. Ed. Edgar F. Borgatta and Marie L. Borgatta. 4 vols. New York: Macmillan, 1992.

Evans, Graham, and Jeffrey Newnham. *The Dictionary of World Politics: A Reference Guide to Concepts, Ideas, and Institutions.* New York: Simon, 1990.

Harvard Encyclopedia of American Ethnic Groups. Ed. Stephan Thernstrom, Ann Orlov, and Oscar Handlin. Cambridge, MA: Belknap-Harvard UP, 1980.

Jary, David, and Julia Jary. *The HarperCollins Dictionary of Sociology.* New York: Harper, 1991.

Multiculturalism in the United States: A Comparative Guide to Acculturation and Ethnicity. Ed. John D. Buenker and Lorman A. Ratner. New York: Greenwood, 1992.

Political Handbook of the New World. New York: McGraw, 1975 to date.

Winthrop, Robert H. *Dictionary of Concepts in Cultural Anthropology.* New York: Greenwood, 1991.

■ Online Catalogs and Electronic Search Systems

Online catalogs and electronic search systems have revolutionized research, increasing the efficiency of finding sources and providing mechanisms for searching selectively. Most libraries provide a combination of search options, some specific to your library and some provided through electronic access to commercial and academically supported databases.

Online Catalogs for Books

The online catalog at your library will provide you with information about each kind of material in the library's collection: author's name, title, call number, publication information, technical information, subject classification, cataloging information, and, in some cases, brief summaries of the source's content. These technical descriptions will familiarize you with a source before you search for it in the collection.

Each source in the library's collection is cataloged in multiple ways: by author, by title, by key words, by subject, and by call number. You can, consequently, locate a source using alternative strategies. To take fullest advantage of these search capabilities, familiarize yourself with your library's online catalog for books. Take advantage of specialized training sessions or use the instructional handouts available near computer terminals. Although online systems vary, most offer a variety of on-screen options to guide you, including the following:

Search Results.   When your search retrieves records for sources in your library's collection, a list of sources will appear. If the number of sources is small, a *short list* will appear on the screen; in some systems, each item is numbered (for example, 1–12). If the number of sources is large, a *long list* will appear, with items grouped (1–12, 13–24, 25–36) so that you can select from among the groups. As systems become more sophisticated, more options such as marking sources and initiating related searches are made available.

Display Options.   Online search systems allow you to select how much information you want to see on each source. One option, the short record (brief view), includes the book's title, author, publishing information, description, subject classifications, location, call number, and status (whether checked out or not). (See Figure 1.) The other option, the long record (long view), includes all information in the short record but also includes edition numbers, descriptions of indexes, bibliographies (and their length), volumes, previous titles, series information, and selected information about the content. (See Figure 2, page 369.)

No Entries Found.   A message will indicate when a search does not produce a "match," meaning that the system cannot locate a corresponding entry. Some systems will describe the common causes for failure: search procedures are inaccurate or the item is not in the library's collection.

Help Options.   These pull-down options explain procedures, often describing commands in detail and providing alternative ways to work within a search. Many online systems now provide search capabilities from within a help option. These support features are frequently tailored to your library's system and collection.

Print or Save Options.   Current systems provide alternative ways for you to create records of your searches. One common option is to print your results, but it is now possible to save results on a disk or have them e-mailed to your account for later use.

Electronic Indexes (for Periodicals)

Periodicals may be indexed along with books, in which case your search procedures will be the same as for books. However, periodicals may also be indexed in separate electronic systems.

Figure 1 Short record (brief view)

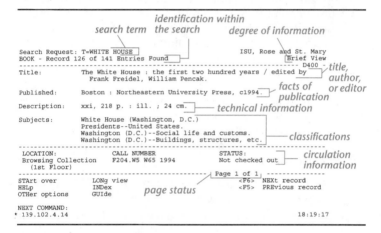

```
                          identification within
             search term  the search           degree of information

Search Request: T=WHITE HOUSE                        ISU, Rose and St. Mary
BOOK - Record 126 of 141 Entries Found                       Brief View
--------------------------------------------------------------- D400 -  title,
Title:        The White House : the first two hundred years / edited by       author,
              Frank Freidel, William Pencak.                    facts of   or editor
Published:    Boston : Northeastern University Press, c1994.    publication
Description:  xxi, 218 p. : ill. ; 24 cm.         technical information
Subjects:     White House (Washington, D.C.)
              Presidents--United States.
              Washington (D.C.)--Social life and customs.
              Washington (D.C.)--Buildings, structures, etc.    classifications
----------------------------------------------------------------------
LOCATION:          CALL NUMBER        STATUS:               circulation
Browsing Collection F204.W5 W65 1994  Not checked out        information
  (1st Floor)
-----------------------------------------------/ Page 1 of 1 / --------------
STArt over         LONg view                    <F6>  NEXt record
HELp               INDex          page status   <F5>  PREvious record
OTHer options      GUIde

NEXT COMMAND:
* 139.102.4.14                                                18:19:17
```

These electronic indexes for periodicals (journals, magazines, and newspapers), available either through CD-ROM technology or through the Internet, provide an impressive array of research options.

Because electronic indexes are compiled according to kind of source (*Readers' Guide to Periodical Literature* for magazines, for example), subject (*Education Index, Biography Index*), or source (*The New York Times Index*), begin your search by selecting the index or indexes that correspond to your topic.

Although indexing systems for periodicals differ in some ways, partly because of the sources themselves and partly because of the electronic providers, most supply the following information about each source: author, article title, special information (about illustrations, bibliographies, maps, and other special features), and publication information. In addition, most electronic indexes also include abstracts (brief summaries) of articles.

You can search for periodical articles using the author, title, key word, or subject. And given the range of periodical material available, your search will probably provide a large number of sources. However, because your library probably will not subscribe to all of the sources listed, you must verify whether the periodical is available. Some systems are directly linked to the library's online catalog and can provide you with immediate information about the library's holdings of journals, magazines, and newspapers. If your library does not have that option, then you will have to check the catalog.

You will also have a host of other options available which will enhance your work:

- *Year Identification:* Most systems allow you to designate the year or years from which to select articles.

- *Marking Options:* Most systems allow you to identify citations for further use.

- *Search History:* Many systems allow you to review your searches, letting you reexamine your search patterns and results.

- *Print and Save Options:* Most systems allow you to create alternative records of your searches: you can print results, save them on disk, or e-mail them to your account.

Internet Searching

With the introduction of the Internet, research options have expanded dramatically and continue to do so. Providing an astonishing array of material—some excellent, some worthless—the Internet has expanded the scope of research.

Search engines—Yahoo!, WebCrawler, Alta Vista, InfoSeek, Excite, Hotbot, and many others—will link you to web sites. The initial process is really rather simple: select a search engine, type in your search term, click on "search," and wait for results. But an unsystematic search will produce a sea of materials: citations in the thousands, which you cannot possibly review. Consequently, choose your search terms carefully, making them as specific as possible. Also, experiment with different search engines to see which one best matches your needs. Some search engines identify the most popular sites, some indicate the percentage of "match" with the search topic, and others simply list (and sometimes re-list) anything associated with the term. Therefore, take some time to explore the Internet before you begin researching.

Figure 2 Long record (long view)

degree of information

```
Search Request: T=WHITE HOUSE                    ISU, Rose and St. Mary
BOOK - Record 126 of 141 Entries Found                        Long View
-------------------------------------------------------------- D400 -
Title:          The White House : the first two hundred years / edited by
                Frank Freidel, William Pencak.

Published:      Boston : Northeastern University Press, c1994.
Description:    xxi, 218 p. : ill. ; 24 cm.

Notes:          Includes bibliographical references (p. 209-210) and index.

Contents:       Roles of the president's house / Daniel J. Boorstin --
                Becoming a national symbol: The White House in the early
                nineteenth century / Robert V. Remini -- America's house:
                The bully pulpit on Pennsylvania Avenue / Richard Norton
                Smith -- "This damned old house": The Lincolns in the White
                House / David Herbert Donald -- Disability in the White
                House: The case of Woodrow Wilson / John Milton Cooper, Jr.
-----------------------------------------------  + Page 1 of 3 --------------
STArt over      BRIef view                            <F8>  FORward page
HELp            INDex                                  <F6>  NEXt record
OTHer options   GUIde                                 <F5>  PREvious record

NEXT COMMAND:                                                    18:20:52
* 139.102.4.14
```

additional information

page status

full description of the book; it continues onto the second and third screens

33d A Preliminary List of Sources

■ **Compiling a Preliminary List of Sources**

In the process of compiling a preliminary list of sources, you will make several useful discoveries about your topic. First, you will discover how much material is available. If you find too much information, your topic is probably too broad. If you find too little information, then your topic is probably too narrow. Second, you will discover imbalances in your research strategies. If you discover that you have selected only books and magazine articles, you will need to expand your research to include a wider range of sources. Therefore, as you begin to compile a preliminary list of sources, remember that a mix of print, nonprint, and electronic sources is essential.

Print Sources

You should incorporate a representative sampling of print sources in your research. Books will provide the longest, most detailed, and most comprehensive discussions of your topic. Make sure that you select a reasonable variety of books that represent different positions, publishers, and time periods. Journals, the publications of professional organizations, will present knowledgeable discussions of your topic that are written by specialists. Articles from journals will be technical and scholarly. Magazines, publications intended for general readers, will provide informative discussions for nonspecialists; such writing will usually be nontechnical. Newspapers, daily or weekly publications for wide reading audiences, publish current, timely discussions of recent events for general readers; these articles will be nontechnical.

The traditional mix of books and articles from journals, magazines, and newspapers has served researchers very well. By selecting all four kinds of print sources, you will have materials that range from comprehensive to current, from specialized to general.

Nonprint Sources

Research should not be confined to the library, however, nor should you feel constrained by print materials. Instead, use those important research tools but move beyond them to discover other interesting and often personal perspectives on your topic. Consider these possibilities:

- *Radio and television:* Use informational programming that is available on the ever-expanding constellation of networks.

- *Interviews:* Conduct interviews with local experts on your subject, either in person, by telephone, or by e-mail. Also consider interviewing informed nonspecialists.

- *Questionnaires and Surveys:* Construct one of these research tools and administer it locally (or via e-mail) to gather highly personal reactions to your topic.

- *Film and Television:* View and use artistic treatments that in some way connect with your topic.

- *Recordings:* Consider how musicians have interpreted your topic.

- *Visual Art:* Use visual art related to your topic to create impact within your paper.

By broadening your research to include some of these interesting approaches, you will discover information and ideas that will complement traditional print materials.

Electronic Sources

Electronic sources have radically altered research techniques and have made materials available in formats that are new and potentially useful. Take advantage of the technology, expand your research, and consider these options:

- *Discussion (Interest) Groups:* Use e-mail to gain access to the ongoing discussions of groups of people also interested in your topic.

- *News Groups:* Through your Usenet provider, review the collected postings of individuals.

- *Individual Correspondence:* Note the e-mail addresses of people who post interesting or helpful comments on discussion groups or news groups and correspond with them individually.

- *Database Vendors:* For a fee, you can have vendors gather information from restricted and limited-access databases.

- *CD-ROM Sources:* Although CD-ROM sources will soon be supplanted by online research tools, they presently offer many useful directories, statistical collections, and full-text collections.

- *World Wide Web:* Take full advantage of WWW, one of the most promising research tools available. Use your Internet provider to initiate key-word searches related to your topic and prepare yourself for a flood of information. Much of it will be repetitive, but the possibilities of finding useful information keep expanding.

Much of the information available through electronic sources is so new that it is unavailable in print forms. By taking advantage of electronic sources, you can ensure that your research is as current as possible.

In addition, electronic sources like the World Wide Web often provide print materials in readily accessible formats. Television interviews and news broadcasts are now instantaneously available at web sites supported by news organizations. Traditional print publications now provide online versions—sometimes condensed—of their journals, magazines, and newspapers. In these instances—and others—you will not be limited by the resources available at your library.

A List of Sources

Using 3-by-5-inch note cards (or, alternately, paper or your computer), record information about each prospective source. For books, note the call number, author, and title. For articles, write down the complete index or bibliography entry. For interviews, documentaries, class notes, and so on, indicate the date, title, speaker or producer, and any other relevant identifying information. For electronic sources, note the author (when known), title, access information, and date. In addition to identifying information and location, note any special features, such as maps or bibliographies, that might make the source particularly useful.

■ **Evaluating a Preliminary List of Sources**

Review your preliminary list of sources by applying the following guidelines to evaluate their potential usefulness:

Does the author have special credentials?   An *M.D., M.A., Ph.D.,* or notice of an affiliation with a university or other credible organization generally indicates authority and expertise.

Does the title of the work suggest a focus appropriate to your topic? The phrasing of a title or subtitle can indicate the author's subject and his or her attitude or approach to the subject.

Is the publishing company a reputable one?   Most of the books you will use are published by university, academic, or trade presses. You will soon recognize the important publishers in your field.

Are the periodicals well respected?   Consider periodicals with professional affiliations or national distribution. For example, *English Journal,* because of its affiliation with the National Council of Teachers of English, provides thoughtful interpretations of issues. Similarly, the *New York Times* or *Washington Post* are often more authoritative than local newspapers. Also note which periodicals are most frequently cited in the notes and bibliographies of the works you consult.

Is the publication date recent?   Although the currentness of sources is unimportant for some topics, most topics require sources from the last ten or fifteen years.

■ Special Concerns for Internet Sources

Because the Internet provides opportunities for people and organizations to distribute materials widely without the intervening steps of review and traditional publication, you will need to be selective about what materials you use. Other concerns—questions about an author's credentials, focus, current relevance, and so on—also apply when you evaluate the usefulness of an Internet source, but some source-specific issues require special attention:

Is the site affiliated with a reputable organization or institution? Examine the site for the sponsoring group. Such affiliations mean that the site represents a credible organization—though you will still need to consider its quality. Sites maintained by individuals can be extremely good, but you must realize that they may represent idiosyncratic perspectives.

Is the scholarship reasonable? Examine the ways in which the site documents its information: Is documentation provided? Is it complete? Are the sources of documentation varied?

Is the site cross-linked to other credible sites? Today's electronic links are like the bibliographies in books and articles: consistent linkage or reference implies the usefulness of the site or source.

Using these guidelines, Angela evaluated Thomas Mallon's *Stolen Words: Forays into the Origins and Ravages of Plagiarism.* The title of the book suggested an appropriate focus, but the 1989 publication dated troubled her. Clearly, the book would contain no material related to the Internet, but would that situation make it unusable? Was its information too dated? After a brief review of the book—skimming the table of contents, the preface, and one chapter—Angela decided that *Stolen Words* provided useful historical information, creating a context for a discussion of Internet plagiarism. Later in her research, Angela discovered that Mallon's work is cited in many other sources, suggesting that the book, though not directly related to Internet plagiarism, is seen as a central source in the discussion of the broader subject of plagiarism.

■ **EXERCISE 33.4   Preliminary list of sources**

Prepare a preliminary list of sources. Using the online catalog, find at least four books on your topic, including one published within the last two years and one providing an overview of the topic. Using electronic indexes, find at least six articles on your topic, making sure to include journals, magazines, and newspapers. Using the nonprint resources of your library and other local resources—such as businesses, government agencies, and civic and cultural organizations— find two nonprint sources, including one potential interview. Finally, find at least four electronic sources.

33e Evaluating Sources

Before you read carefully, leaf through your sources quickly, noting their organization, content, and any tables, maps, photographs, or other illustrations. Do not read each source thoroughly or take notes at this stage. Instead, follow the guidelines listed next to assess the usefulness of your collected materials. With a general sense of your sources, you can then read carefully and take complete and consistent notes (see section 33f).

■ Evaluating Books

Books generally provide the most thorough coverage of a subject, but you should evaluate each one quickly to see whether it meets your research needs.

Consider the title and subtitle carefully and look for information about the author's credentials and other writings. Also, review the table of contents, noting the book's arrangement and coverage of your topic.

Skim the preface, introduction, or first chapter to get a sense of the author's general style and perspective. Frequently, authors explain their reasons for writing, their strategies for presenting information, or their general interpretations of material here. Such explanations will help you to assess the source's potential value.

Examine any special sections or appended materials: in-text illustrations, tables, charts, graphs, or diagrams; bibliographies; or sections containing special supporting material such as case studies or lists of additional readings. Nontextual materials can provide details, illustrations, and references to other sources.

Skim a portion of the text that relates specifically to your topic. Note the author's development. For example, does the author use examples and facts or narration and description based on personal experience? Does the author explain and support assertions, document facts, and present balanced discussions? Is the author's style varied, lively, and interesting? How technical is the vocabulary? A quick analysis of content and style can reveal whether a source will suit your research needs. (For more information about evaluating sources and forms of argument, see Chapter 5, "Critical Thinking and Writing.")

■ **Evaluating Articles**

Articles in periodicals generally provide the most current information on a subject, but you should evaluate the article's potential usefulness.

First, examine the title and subtitle carefully, assessing what they reveal about the author's content, approach, and tone. Check for notes about the author (at the bottom of the first page or at the end of the article), especially affiliations or credentials.

Read headings that separate sections of the article, noting whether they indicate content specifically related to your topic.

Without pausing over details, skim the article to see if it is specific, current, and complete, and whether its style indicates a useful approach to the topic.

Also check for related materials in the same periodical. Sometimes lists of suggested readings or of people or organizations to contact appear with an article. If an issue is organized around a theme, a number of articles may relate to your topic.

■ Evaluating Electronic Sources

Follow the same basic procedures for evaluating an electronic source as you would for an article—looking at its authors, affiliations, development, structure, currency, completeness, and so on. Then consider using these additional strategies.

One of the most interesting and useful ways to understand the perspectives provided by Internet sources is to consider the *domains,* the brief designations in electronic addresses that indicate the kind of web site:

edu indicates an affiliation with an educational institution. Although this implies a reasonable level of sophistication and trustworthiness, you need to consider that affiliated individuals can construct private pages.

com indicates a commercial site. Although materials found on commercial sites can be extremely helpful, you should keep in mind that the primary function of commercial groups is to make money—so remember that what you find on a commercial site is part of a sales-driven organization. Be critical.

gov indicates a government site. These sites present consistently trustworthy information (statistics, facts, reports, and so on). They are less useful in interpretive matters, probably since there is often a sense of self-justification in government rationales.

mil indicates a military site. Again, the technical information on these sites is consistently useful, but interpretive material frequently justifies a single, promilitary position.

net indicates an independent, unaffiliated site. Use the materials on these sites only after considering them carefully. The possibilities of finding valuable information is balanced by the possibility of finding questionable material.

org indicates an organizational site. Since organizations by their natures serve to advance political, social, financial, educational, and other specific agendas, you will need to review these materials with care. Don't discount what you find, but consider, when appropriate, the biases that will influence the ways in which information on such a site is used and interpreted.

■ **EXERCISE 33.5 Evaluating a source**

Look briefly at three sources—one book, one article, and one web site—and write a brief paragraph describing each. Note particularly each source's potential usefulness for your paper.

33f Taking Notes

Establish a uniform system for taking notes. Consider using 4-by-6-inch index cards because they are large enough to hold complete notes and easy to distinguish from 3-by-5-inch source cards. (For more on source cards, see section 33d.) Consider the generous space of legal pads or loose-leaf paper. Consider taking notes on a computer to save time during later stages of typing.

If you use cards, use a new card for each new idea. During planning, this will make it easier for you to organize—and reorganize—your notes. If you use another format, leave several spaces between notes. At the top of each note, record the following information to identify sources easily and to avoid plagiarism: the author of the source, the title (if you are using more than one source by an author), and the page number of the material. Make notes on one side of the card or paper only so that later you do not overlook information. Fit material on one card if possible, but if additional cards are necessary, note the author's name, the number of each card, and the total number of cards at the top (for example, "Johnson, Card 2 of 3").

Having your working thesis statement nearby will help you to maintain your focus as you take notes. However, be alert to unexpected information and ideas that alter or expand your working thesis in new and interesting ways.

As you take notes, look for relevant information (facts, examples, and details) and for ideas (the thoughts and conclusions offered by your sources). You can take notes on both types of material in three helpful ways: summaries, quotations, and paraphrases.

■ Summaries

Summaries present the substance of a passage in condensed form. A useful means of recording facts, summaries are presented best in a list or other abbreviated form (see Figure 3). Examples should be briefly noted, perhaps as a sketch of the original (see Figure 4). A long argument should be noted in outline form.

Summaries should be entirely in your own words. When taking notes, read the passage carefully, determine what information and ideas to record, and express them in lists of words, brief phrases, or short sentences. Do not use any of the original passage without enclosing it in quotation marks.

■ Quotations

Quotations reproduce a writer's work word for word, maintaining the original spelling and punctuation. Assess the value of a quotation before you copy it by asking yourself the following questions:

- Is the author's style so distinctive that I could not say the same thing as well or as clearly in my own words?
- Is the vocabulary technical and therefore difficult to translate into my own words?
- Is the author so well known or so important that the quotation will lend authority to my argument?
- Does the author's material raise doubts or questions or make points with which I disagree?

If you answer "yes" to any of these questions, then copy the quotation.

Always enclose the quoted material within quotation marks and double-check your note against the original. The copy must be *exact*. Figure 5 shows a sample quotation note in computer format.

Figure 3 Summary note (card format)

Rubin, William B./_Faultline_   salaries

— 1990 figures: men with high school diploma
   ($28,911) and college diploma ($44,554);
   women with high school diploma ($18,954) and
   with college diploma ($28,043)//

— 1979-89: 2% increase in real earnings;
   1989-92: 1.6% decrease

                              p. 128-29

Figure 4 Summary note (paper format)

Larson/<u>Naked Consumer</u>   mailing lists

Equifax and TRW (major marketing firms) compile
lists—the book's example is people with credit cards
with spending limits over $5,000—and sell them
to direct-market retailers. That way retailers can
target people with, the assumption is, large
discretionary spending habits—the $5,000 figure
would generatate a list of several million people.
                                        p. 76

Figure 5 Quotation note (computer format)

Robinson/<u>Critics</u>   influence

"Freud has fundamentally altered the way we think.
He has changed our intellectual manners, often without
our even being aware of it. For most of us [,] Freud
has become a habit of mind--a//bad habit, his critics
would be quick to urge, but a habit now too deeply
ingrained to be broken. He is the major source of our
modern inclination to look for meanings beneath the
surface of behavior--to be always on the alert for the
'real' (and probably hidden) significance of our actions."
                                        p. 270-71

When a quotation continues from one page to the next in a source, indicate in your note where the break occurs. A double slash (//) is a useful indicator for such a break. This notation of a page break is important because if you use only part of a long quotation, you must cite the single page only.

■ Paraphrases

Paraphrases restate a passage in another form and in other words, but unlike summaries, they contain approximately the same amount of detail and the same number of words as the original. If a passage contains an important idea but does not meet the requirements for quotation, restate the idea in your own words, sentence structure, and sequence. When you finish the paraphrase, check it against the original passage to be sure the idea has been completely restated. If you use any phrases or sentences from the original, place them in quotation marks. Figure 6 shows a sample paraphrase card.

Figure 6 Paraphrase note (card format)

Mitford/_American Way_   c-sections

The rates of caesarian sections increase or decrease depending on how doctors are paid and how patients pay their bills. When doctors bill separately for procedures and when patients have their own insurance, the rates of caesarian sections increase to roughly one-third of births (33-39%); hospitals with the lowest c-section rates are those where doctors do not receive special fees and where bills are not itemized.

                              p. 152

■ **EXERCISE 33.6 Taking notes**

*Using the books and articles from your preliminary list of sources,
begin taking notes. Summarize, directly quote from, and paraphrase
your sources. Make sure that each note accurately reflects the source
and provides full identifying information.*

33g Plagiarism

Plagiarism is the use of someone else's words, ideas, or line of
thought without acknowledgment. Even when plagiarism is
inadvertent—the result of careless note taking, punctuating, or
documenting—the writer is still at fault for dishonest work, and
the paper will be unacceptable. To avoid plagiarizing, learn to
recognize distinctive content and expression in source materials
and to take accurate, carefully punctuated, and documented
notes.

■ Common Knowledge

Some information—facts and interpretations—is known by
many people and is consequently described as **common knowledge.** That U.S. presidents are elected for four-year terms is
commonly known, as is the more interpretive information that
the U.S. government is a democracy with a system of checks and
balances among the executive, legislative, and judicial branches.
But common knowledge extends beyond such general information to more specific information within fields of study. In English studies, for example, it is commonly known that George
Eliot is the pseudonym of Mary Ann Evans, and a commonly
acknowledged interpretation is that drama evolved from a Greek
religious festival honoring the god Dionysus. Documenting
these facts in a paper would be unnecessary because they are
commonly known in English studies, even though you might
have just discovered them for the first time.

When researching an unfamiliar subject, distinguishing common knowledge that does not require documentation from special knowledge that does require it is sometimes difficult. The following guidelines may help.

What Constitutes Common Knowledge

Historical facts (names, dates, and general interpretations) that appear in many general reference books. For example, George Washington was the first president of the United States, and the Constitution was adopted in 1787.

Literature that cannot be attributed to a specific author. Two examples are *Beowulf* and the Bible. However, the use of specific editions or translations still requires acknowledgment.

General observations and opinions that are shared by many people. For example, a general observation is that children learn by actively doing, not by passively listening; and a commonly held opinion is that reading, writing, and arithmetic are the basic skills to be learned by an elementary-school child.

Unacknowledged information that appears in multiple sources. For example, it is common knowledge that the earth is approximately 93 million miles from the sun and that the *gross national product* is the market value of all goods and services produced by a nation in a given year.

If a piece of information does not meet these guidelines or if you are uncertain about whether it is common knowledge, always document the material.

■ EXERCISE 33.7 Common knowledge about your topic

Make a list of ten facts, ideas, or interpretations that are commonly known or held about your topic. Beside each item, note into which category of common knowledge it falls.

■ Special Qualities of Source Materials

To acknowledge your use of an author's words and ideas—without inadvertently plagiarizing—learn to recognize the distinctive qualities of your sources:

Special Qualities of Sources

Distinctive prose style: the author's choices of words, phrases, and sentence patterns

Original facts: the result of the author's personal research

Personal interpretations of information: the author's individual evaluation of his or her information

Original ideas: those ideas that are unique to that author

As you work with sources, be aware of these distinguishing qualities and make certain that you do not appropriate the prose (word choices and sentence structures), original research, interpretations, or ideas of others without giving them proper credit.

Look, for example, at these paragraphs from Joyce Appleby, Lynn Hunt, and Margaret Jacob's *Telling the Truth about History* (New York: Norton, 1994):

> Interest in this new research in social history can be partly explained by the personal backgrounds of the cohort of historians who undertook the task of writing history from the bottom up. They entered higher education with the post-Sputnik expansion of the 1950s and 1960s, when the number of new Ph.D.s in history nearly quadrupled. Since many of them were children and grandchildren of immigrants, they had a personal incentive for turning the writing of their dissertations into a movement of memory recovery. Others were black or female and similarly prompted to find ways to make the historically inarticulate speak. While the number of male Ph.D.s in history ebbed and flowed with the vicissitudes of the job market, the

number of new female Ph.D.s in history steadily increased from 11 percent (29) in 1950 to 13 percent (137) in 1970 and finally to 37 percent (192) in 1989.

Although ethnicity is harder to locate in the records, the GI Bill was clearly effective in bringing the children of working-class families into the middle-class educational mainstream. This was the thin end of a democratizing wedge prying open higher education in the United States. Never before had so many people in any society earned so many higher degrees. Important as their numbers were, the change in perspective these academics brought to their disciplines has made the qualitative changes even more impressive. Suddenly graduate students with strange, unpronounceable surnames, with Brooklyn accents and different skin colors, appeared in the venerable ivy-colored buildings that epitomized elite schooling.

Now look at the following examples of plagiarized and acceptable summaries and paraphrases.

Summaries

Plagiarized

—A historian's focus is *partially explained by* his or her *personal background.*

—Because of their experiences, *they have a personal incentive* for looking at history in new ways.

—Large numbers were important, but the change in viewpoint *made the qualitative changes even more impressive.*

[The italicized phrases are clearly Appleby, Hunt, and Jacob's, even though the verb tenses are changed. To avoid plagiarism, place key words in quotation marks or rewrite them entirely in your own words and form of expression.]

Acceptable

—A historian's focus and interpretation are personal.

—For personal reasons, not always stated, people examine the facts of history from different perspectives.

—Large numbers were important, but the change in viewpoint "made the qualitative changes even more impressive."

[Here the words and phrases are the writer's, not Appleby, Hunt, and Jacob's. Quotation marks enclose a selected phrase by the authors.]

Paraphrases

Plagiarized

Even though ethnic background is not easily found in the statistics, the GI Bill consistently helped students from low-income families enter the middle-class educational system. This was how democracy started forcing open college education in America.

[Changing selected words while retaining the basic phrasing and sentence structure of the original is not acceptable paraphrasing. Appleby, Hunt, and Jacob's thought patterns and prose style still mark the passage.]

Acceptable

Because of the GI Bill, college wasn't only for middle-class children anymore. Even poor children could attend college. For the first time, education was accessible to everyone, which is truly democracy in action. The GI Bill was "the thin end of a democratizing wedge prying open higher education."

[The revised paraphrase presents Appleby, Hunt, and Jacob's idea but does not mimic their sentence structure; the quoted material records a single phrase for possible use later. Remember that summaries and paraphrases, as well as facts and quotations, require full citations.]

Avoiding plagiarism takes conscious effort, but through careful and complete note taking and documenting, you can ensure that your work is acceptable.

■ **EXERCISE 33.8   Practice in note taking**

For practice, take notes on the following paragraphs as if you were researching their subjects. Include a summary, a quotation, and a paraphrase from each set. (Check your notes to confirm that you have not inadvertently plagiarized any part of the paragraphs.) Then, in groups of three or four, discuss both your techniques for note taking and the ideas and information gleaned from these passages.

Collier, James Lincoln. *Jazz: The American Theme Song*. New York: Oxford UP, 1993.

[The following paragraphs appear on pages 22 and 23; a double slash (//) indicates the page break.]

Furthermore, the feminism that was an integral part of the new spirit was critical to the acceptance of jazz. Until middle-class women were able to go out drinking and dancing, their boyfriends and husbands would not be able to do so either, more than occasionally. But now, by 1920, they could. So the middle class began visiting speakeasies, cabarets, roadhouses, and dance halls where the new music was played. Their financial support was critical, for it was only the middle class and the class above that could afford to patronize places // like the Cotton Club, where Duke Ellington developed his music and became celebrated; the Club Alabam, which provided the first home for the Fletcher Henderson Orchestra; Reisenweber's, where the Original Dixieland Jazz Band introduced jazz to mainstream America; the colleges where Beiderbecke, Oliver, and other groups got much of their employment in the early 1920s.

We have to understand, then, that while a substantial proportion of the American middle class did not like jazz—was indeed threatened by it—probably the majority at least tolerated it, and a large minority were excited by it. Conversely, a great many religious blacks, and religious working people in general, were as hostile to the music as was the middle-class opposition. Jazz was astonishingly democratic: both its friends and its foes came from the whole spectrum of the American class system.

Worster, Donald. *An Unsettled Country: Changing Landscapes of the American West.* Albuquerque: U of New Mexico P, 1994.

[**The following paragraphs appear on page 27.**]

Westerners of many stripes want to lay claim to [John Wesley] Powell, because they sense that he shared their interest in, their loyalty toward, the West. He was, in a sense, the father of their country. But today he would be a most bewildered old fellow if he came back to look at the West we have been making: a West that is now the home of 77 million people, ranging from Korean shopowners in Los Angeles to African-American college students in Las Vegas, from Montana novelists and poets to Colorado trout fisherman and skiers, from Kansas buffalo ranchers to Utah prison guards. How to make a regional whole of all that? And how to turn the life and ideas of the nineteenth-century frontier dirt farmer become explorer-geologist become environmental reformer into a prophet for all those people today?

What those 77 million still have in common, despite the demographic and cultural changes, is the land itself. Even today questions about how that land ought to be used, exploited, or preserved continue to dominate western conversations and public-policy debates. Much of that land is still in public title, despite all the access that has been allowed to private users. Perhaps the most distinctive feature of the West, after aridity, is the fact of extensive public ownership of that land, hundreds of millions of acres in all, a feature that ties the past to the present. In New Mexico the federal government owns 33 percent of the state, in Utah 64 percent, in Nevada 82 percent, though in my own state of Kansas it owns about 1 percent.

Careful documentation and a complete works-cited list provide readers with full information on sources cited in the paper. (See section 35d for information on in-text citations.)

To be useful to readers, citations must be clear and consistent. Therefore, very specific rules of documentation have been devised and must be applied.

QUICK REFERENCE

Using the following formats, begin preparing your works-cited entries as soon as you begin taking notes. Use a new 3-by-5-inch card for each entry or create a works-cited file on your word processor.

▶ A book by one author

Author's last name, first name. <u>Book title</u>. Additional information. City of publication: Publishing company, publication date.

▶ An article by one author

Author's last name, first name. "Article title." <u>Periodical title</u> Date: inclusive pages.

Guidelines for preparing entries for other types of sources appear on the pages that follow.

34a Citation Format

Most researched writing in English and other humanities courses uses the documentation format described in Joseph Gibaldi's *MLA [Modern Language Association] Handbook for*

Writers of Research Papers, fifth edition (New York: MLA, 1999). This documentation format, known as MLA style, is simple, clear, and widely accepted.

Other subjects, however, may require other styles of documentation, so always ask instructors, especially in nonhumanities courses, whether MLA style is acceptable. In addition to the *MLA Handbook,* a number of other style guides are frequently used.

■ Frequently Used Style Guides

The Chicago Manual of Style. 14th ed. Chicago: U of Chicago P, 1993.

Publication Manual of the American Psychological Association. 4th ed. Washington, DC: APA, 1994.

Scientific Style and Format: The CBE [Council of Biology Editors] Manual for Authors, Editors, and Publishers. 6th ed. Chicago: Cambridge UP, 1994.

Turabian, Kate L. *A Manual for Writers of Term Papers, Theses, and Dissertations.* Rev. John Grossman and Alice Bennett. 6th ed. Chicago: U of Chicago P, 1996.

The most widely used of these alternate styles is that of the American Psychological Association (APA), often the preferred style for writing in the social sciences. Guidelines for using APA style appear in Appendix B.

34b Accuracy and Completeness

Because works-cited entries direct readers to sources used in researched writing, they must be as complete as possible and presented in a consistent and recognizable format. If the following guidelines do not cover a source you want to use, consult the *MLA Handbook.*

To complete a citation, leaf through the following samples until you find the one that most closely corresponds to your source, remembering that some citations combine information according to the guidelines that follow. Prepare your citations using 3-by-5-inch index cards (one citation per card), sheets of paper, or a computer. If you prepare citations on a computer, use a separate file with an easily recognizable name (for example, *paper2.cit, research.cit,* or *aviation.cit*). Since a citation file will remain comparatively small, you can retrieve it quickly, add to it and delete from it, and then append the complete works-cited file to the final draft of your paper.

Whichever pattern you choose—index card, paper, or computer—record complete and accurate citations. If you do not record full information when you first use a source, you will have to return to it at a later—and potentially less convenient—time to supply the missing information.

■ Information for MLA Citations

MLA citations present information in an established order. When combining forms (to list a translation of a second edition, for example), follow these guidelines to determine the order of information:

1. *Author(s).* Use the name or names with the spelling and order shown on the title page of books or on the first page of articles, without degrees, titles, or affiliations. If no author (individual or organization) is named, list the work by title in the works-cited entry.

2. *Title.* List titles from part to whole: the title of an essay (the part) before the book (the whole), the title of an article before the periodical title, an episode before the program, or a song before the compact disc. Use complete titles, including subtitles, no matter how long they are.

3. *Additional information.* In the order noted next, include any of the following information listed on the title page of the

book or on the first page of an article: editor, translator, compiler, edition number, volume number, or name of series.

4. *Facts of publication.* For books, find the publisher's name and the place of publication on the title page and the date of publication on the copyright page (immediately following the title page). Use the publisher's name in abbreviated form (see samples in sections 34c–34f), use the first city listed if more than one is given, and use the most recent date shown. When a city is unfamiliar, abbreviate the state by using two capital letters without a period. For periodicals, find the volume number, issue number, and date on the masthead (at the top of the first page of newspapers or within the first few pages in journals and magazines, often in combination with the table of contents).

5. *Page numbers.* When citing a part of a book or an article, provide inclusive page numbers without page abbreviations. Record inclusive page numbers from one to ninety-nine in full form (8–12, 33–39, 68–73); inclusive numbers of one-hundred or higher require at least the last two digits and any other digits needed for clarity (100–02, 120–36, 193–206).

■ Format for MLA Citations

MLA citations follow these general formatting guidelines:

- Begin the first line of each entry at the left margin and indent subsequent lines one half-inch (five spaces).

- Invert the author's name so that it appears with the last name first (to alphabetize easily). If sources are coauthored, list additional authors' names in normal, first-then-last order.

- Italicize or underline titles of full-length works (the meaning is the same), but do not underline the period that follows the title. Be consistent throughout the paper.

- Separate major sections of entries (author, title, and publication information) with periods and one space, not two. When other forms of end punctuation are used (when titles end with question marks or exclamation points, for example), the period may be omitted. Punctuation that is part of a title must be italicized (or underlined).
- Double-space all entries.

34c Books

■ A Book by One Author

```
Freemuth, John C. Islands under Siege: National
     Parks and the Politics of External Threats.
     Lawrence: UP of Kansas, 1991.
```

[**The period with the author's middle initial substitutes for the period that normally follows the author's name. The letters UP, without periods or a space, abbreviate *University Press*.**]

■ A Book by Two or More Authors

Authors' names appear in the order in which they are presented on the title page, which may or may not be alphabetical. A comma follows the initial author's first name; second and third authors' names appear in normal order.

```
Scott, John Paul, and John L. Fuller. Genetics
     and the Social Behavior of the Dog. Chicago:
     U of Chicago P, 1965.
```

When a book has four or more authors, include only the first author's name in full form; substitute *et al.* (meaning "and others," not italicized or underlined) for the names of additional authors.

```
Gershey, Edward L., et al. Low-Level Radioactive
     Waste: From Cradle to Grave. New York: Van
     Nostrand, 1990.
```

■ A Book with No Author

When no author is named, list the work by title. Alphabetize books listed by title using the first important word of the title, not the articles *a, an,* or *the.*

```
United Press International Stylebook: The
     Authoritative Handbook for Writers, Editors,
     and News Directors. 3rd ed. Lincolnwood, IL:
     Natl. Textbook, 1992.
```

[Because the city of Lincolnwood is not commonly recognized, the state abbreviation is required. Note that *national* is abbreviated when it is part of a publisher's name.]

■ Multiple Works by the Same Author

When citing multiple works by the same author, present the first citation completely. Subsequent entries, alphabetized by title, are introduced by three hyphens and a period and alphabetized by title. Coauthored works require full names and are alphabetized after those with single authors.

```
Ehrenreich, Barbara. "Battered Welfare Syndrome."
     Time 3 Apr. 1995: 82.
---. Fear of Falling: The Inner Life of the
     Middle Class. New York: Pantheon, 1989.
Ehrenreich, Barbara, Elizabeth Hess, and Gloria
     Jacobs. Re-Making Love: The Feminization of
     Sex. Garden City, NY: Anchor-Doubleday,
     1986.
```

[Notice that the publisher of the last selection includes a two-part name: the imprint and the major publisher (see An Imprint, page 400, for an additional sample).]

■ A Book with an Organization as Author

When an organization is both the author and the publisher, present the name completely in the author position and use an abbreviation in the publisher position.

```
Gemological Institute of America. The Diamond
     Dictionary. Santa Monica, CA: GIA, 1977.
```

■ An Edition Other than the First

The edition number, noted on the title page, follows the title of the book. When a book also has an editor, translator, or compiler, the edition number follows that information. (See also 360 and 392–93.) Edition numbers are presented in numeral-abbreviation form (*2nd, 3rd, 4th*).

```
Mano, M. Morris. Digital Design. 2nd ed. Engle-
     wood Cliffs, NJ: Prentice, 1991.
```

■ A Reprint

A reprint, a newly printed but unaltered version of a book, is identified as such on the title page or copyright page. The original publication date precedes the facts of publication, and the date of the reprinted edition follows the publisher's name.

```
Palmer, John. The Comedy of Manners. 1913. New
     York: Russell, 1962.
```

■ A Multivolume Work

A multivolume work may have one title, or it may have a comprehensive title for the complete work and separate titles for each volume. When you use the entire set of volumes, use the collective title and note the number of volumes. If volumes are published over several years, provide inclusive dates (1993-95); if the work is still in progress, include the earliest date, a hyphen, one space, and the closing period (1996- .).

Perspectives on Western Art: Source Documents

and Readings from the Renaissance to the

1970s. Ed. Linnea H. Wren. 2 vols. New York:

Icon-Harper, 1994.

To emphasize a single volume, first cite the volume as a separate book. Then add the volume number, the collection title, and the total number of volumes.

Direct Solar Energy. Ed. T. Nejat Veziroglu.

New York: Nova, 1991. Vol. A of Energy and

Environmental Progress. 7 vols.

[Volumes identified by letters should be presented that way in the citation.]

■ A Work in a Collection

To cite a work in a collection, include the name of the selection's author, the title of the specific selection (appropriately punctuated), the collection title, publication facts, and the inclusive page numbers for the selection (without page abbreviations). To cite more than one selection from the collection, prepare separate citations (see Multiple Selections from the Same Collection, page 398).

Modelski, George, and William R. Thompson.

"Long Cycles and Global War." Handbook of

War Studies. Ed. Manus I. Midlarsky. Ann

Arbor: U Michigan P, 1993. 23-54.

■ A Previously Published Work in a Collection

To indicate that a selection has been previously published, begin the citation with original facts of publication. *Rpt.*, meaning "reprinted," begins the second part of the citation, which includes information about the source you have used.

Wallace, Mike. "Mickey Mouse History: Portraying
    the Past at Disney World." <u>Radical History</u>
    <u>Review</u> 32 (1985): 33-55. Rpt. in <u>Customs</u>
    <u>in Conflict: The Anthology of a Changing</u>
    <u>World</u>. Ed. Frank Manning and Jean-Marc
    Philbert. Peterborough, ON: Broadview, 1990.
    304-32.

■ Multiple Selections from the Same Collection

To cite several selections from the same collection, prepare a citation for the complete work—beginning either with the editor's name or with the collection title. Additional references begin with the author of the individual selection and its title. However, instead of providing full publication information, include the editor's name or a shortened version of the title; provide inclusive page numbers for the selection. Notice that all citations are alphabetized.

Gilbert, Sandra, and Susan Gubar. "The Parable
    of the Cave." Richter 1119-26.
James, Henry. "The Art of Fiction." Richter
    420-33.
Richter, David H., ed. <u>The Critical Tradition:</u>
    <u>Classic Texts and Contemporary Trends</u>. New
    York: Bedford, 1989.

■ **An Article in an Encyclopedia or Other Reference Work**

Use an author's name when it is available. If only initials are listed with the article, match them with the name from the list of contributors. Well-known reference books require no information other than the title, edition number (if any), and date. Citations for less well-known or recently published reference works include full publication information. Page numbers are not needed when a reference work is arranged alphabetically.

```
Angermüller, Rudolph. "Salieri, Antonio."

     The New Grove Dictionary of Music and

     Musicians. 1980 ed.
```

[This twenty-volume set is extremely well known and consequently needs no publication information.]

```
Gietschier, Steven. "Paige, Satchel."

     The Ballplayers: Baseball's Ultimate

     Biographical Reference. Ed. Mike Shatzkin.

     New York: Arbour, 1990.
```

[Since this source is relatively new, full publishing information is required.]

When no author's name or initials appear with an article, begin with the title, reproduced to match the pattern in the reference book. Other principles remain the same.

```
"Glenn, John Hershel, Jr." Who's Who in Aviation

     and Aerospace. US ed. Boston: Natl.

     Aeronautical Inst., 1983.
```

■ **A Work in a Series**

Names of series (collections of books related to the same subject, genre, time period, and so on) are typically found on a book's title page and should be included just before the publishing information. Abbreviate the word *Series* (Ser.) if it is part of the series title.

```
Morley, Carolyn. Transformation, Miracles,
    and Mischief: The Mountain Priest Plays
    of Kyogen. Cornell East Asia Ser. Ithaca,
    NY: Cornell UP, 1993.
```

When volumes in a series are numbered, include both the series name and number, followed by a period.

```
Forster, E. M. Passage to India. Everyman's
    Library 29. New York: Knopf, 1992.
```

■ An Imprint

An imprint is a specialized division of a larger publishing company. When an imprint name and a publisher name both appear on the title page, list them together (imprint name first), separated by a hyphen and no additional spaces.

```
African Rhapsody: Short Stories of the
    Contemporary African Experience. Ed. Nadezda
    Obradovic. New York: Anchor-Doubleday, 1994.
```

[Anchor is the imprint; Doubleday is the publisher.]

■ A Translation

A translator's name must always be included in a citation for a translated work because he or she prepared the version that you read. To emphasize the original work (the most common pattern), place the abbreviation *Trans.* (for "translated by," not italicized) and the translator's name after the title (but following editors' names, if the translator translated the entire work).

```
Esquivel, Laura. Like Water for Chocolate: A
     Novel in Monthly Installments, with Recipes,
     Romances, and Home Remedies. Trans. Carol
     Christensen and Thomas Christensen. New
     York: Doubleday, 1992.
```

If selections within a collection are translated by different people, then each translator's name should follow the appropriate selection.

```
Salamun, Tomaz. "Clumsy Guys." Trans. Sonja
     Kravanja. The Pushcart Prize XVII: Best of
     the Small Presses. Ed. Bill Henderson et al.
     New York: Pushcart, 1993. 443.
```

■ A Government Document

Congressional Record

Citations for *Congressional Record* are exceedingly brief: the italicized and abbreviated title, *Cong. Rec.,* the date (presented in day-month-year order), and the page number. Page numbers used alone indicate Senate records; page numbers preceded by an *H* indicate records from the House of Representatives.

```
Cong. Rec. 15 June 1993: 7276+.
```

[This simple citation is for a Senate record. The plus sign (+) following the page number indicates that the discussion continues on several pages.]

```
Cong. Rec. 7 Oct. 1994: H11251.
```

[Note the page reference, with the H indicating that this citation is for a House record.]

Committee, Commission, Department

Information to describe government documents is generally presented in this order: (1) country, state, province, or county;

(2) government official, governing body, sponsoring department, commission, center, ministry, or agency; (3) office, bureau, or committee; (4) the title of the publication, italicized; (5) if appropriate, the author of the document, the number and session of Congress, the kind and number of the document; (6) the city of publication, the publisher, and the date.

When citing more than one work from the same government or agency, use three hyphens and a period to substitute for identical elements.

```
United States. Commission on Migrant Education.
     Invisible Children: A Portrait of Migrant
     Education in the United States. Washington:
     GPO, 1992.
```

[The Government Printing Office, the publisher of most federal documents, is abbreviated to save space.]

```
---. Cong. Budget Office. An Analysis of the
     Managed Competition Act. Washington: GPO,
     1994.

---. ---. ---. Federal Financial Support for
     High-Technology Industries. Washington: GPO,
     1985.
```

[The three sets of three hyphens indicate that this source also was prepared by the United States Congressional Budget Office.]

```
---. ---. Senate. Committee on Aging. Hearings.
     101st Cong., 1st sess. 1989. Washington:
     GPO, 1990.
```

[The use of only two sets of hyphens indicates that only the first two elements correspond to the preceding citation: this source was prepared by the United States Congress, but the Senate affiliation requires the introduction of new, clarifying information in the third position.]

■ A Preface, Introduction, Foreword, Epilogue, or Afterword

To cite material that is separate from the primary text of a book, begin with the name of the person who wrote the separate material, an assigned title (if applicable) in quotation marks, a descriptive title for the part used (capitalized but not punctuated), the title of the book, the name of the book's author (introduced with *By*, not italicized), publication facts, and inclusive page numbers for the separate material. Note that most prefatory or introductory material is paged using lowercase roman numerals.

Dabney, Lewis M. "Edmund Wilson and The Sixties."
Introduction. The Sixties: The Last Journal,
1960-1972. By Edmund Wilson. New York: Far-
rar, 1993. xxi-xlvii.

Finnegan, William. Epilogue. Crossing the Line:
A Year in the Land of Apartheid. New York:
Harper, 1986. 401-09.

■ A Pamphlet

When pamphlets contain clear and complete information, they are cited like books. When information is missing, use these abbreviations: *N.p.* for "No place of publication," *n.p.* for "no publisher," *n.d.* for "no date," and *N. pag.* (with a space between the abbreviations) for "no page."

Adams, Andrew B. Hospice Care. New York:
American Cancer Soc., 1984. 9-16.

America's Cup? The Sober Truth about Alcohol
and Boating. Alexandria, VA: Boat/U. S.,
n.d.

■ A Dissertation

A citation for an unpublished dissertation begins with the author's name, the dissertation title in quotation marks, the abbreviation *Diss.* (not italicized), the name of the degree-granting school (with *University* abbreviated as *U*), and the date.

```
Stevenson, David Stacey. "Heat Transfer in
     Active Volcanoes: Models of Crater Lake
     Systems." Diss. Open U, UK, 1994.
```

[When the university's location is unfamiliar, include the state, province, or country.]

A published dissertation is a book and should be presented as such. However, include dissertation information between the title and the facts of publication.

```
Salmon, Jaslin U. Black Executives in White
     Businesses. Diss. U of Illinois-Chicago,
     1977. Washington, DC: UP of America, 1979.
```

■ Sacred Writings

Citations for sacred writing follow patterns similar to those of other books, with several notable variations. First, titles of sacred writings (the parts or the whole) are neither placed in quotation marks nor italicized; they are capitalized only. Second, full facts of publication are not required for traditional editions. When appropriate, include additional information according to the guidelines for the element.

```
The Bhagavad Gita. Trans. Juan Mascaró. New
     York: Penguin, 1962.
```

[Include translators when appropriate.]

```
The Holy Bible.
```

[This citation is for the King James version of the Bible, the traditional edition.]

```
The New Oxford Annotated Bible. Rev. Standard
    Version. Ed. Herbert G. May and Bruce M.
    Metzger. New York: Oxford UP, 1973.
```

[This citation provides full information, highlighting a version other than the King James and the editorial work that it includes.]

34d Periodicals

■ An Article in a Monthly Magazine

To cite an article in a monthly magazine, include the author's name, the article's title in quotation marks, the magazine's name (italicized), the month (abbreviated) and year, and the inclusive pages of the article (without page abbreviations).

```
Frosch, Robert A. "The Industrial Ecology of the
    Twenty-First Century." Scientific American
    Sept. 1995: 178-81.
```

[Note that the period comes before the closing quotation marks of the article's title, that one space (but no punctuation) separates the periodical title and the date, and that a colon separates the date and the pages.]

■ An Article in a Weekly Magazine

Citations for articles in weekly magazines are identical to those for monthly magazines, with one exception: the publication date is presented in more detailed form, in day-month-year order (with the month abbreviated).

```
Morrow, James. "Watching Web Speech." U.S. News
    and World Report 15 Feb. 1999: 32.
```

[Even though magazines often use special typography (as in *U.S. News & World Report*), such material is standardized in citations.]

■ An Article in a Journal with Continuous Paging

Journals with continuous paging number the issues sequentially for the entire year. For this kind of journal, place the volume number after the journal title, identify the year in parentheses, follow it with a colon, and then list page numbers.

```
Enstad, Nan. "Fashioning Political Identities:

     Cultural Studies and the Historical

     Construction of Political Subjects."

     American Quarterly 50 (1998): 745-82.
```

■ An Article from a Journal with Separate Paging

For journals that page each issue separately, follow the volume number with a period and the issue number (without spaces).

```
Hardy, Janice V. "Teacher Attitudes toward and

     Knowledge of Computer Technology." Computers

     in the Schools 14.3-4 (1998): 119-36.
```
[When issues are combined, list both numbers separating them with a hyphen without additional spaces.]

■ An Article in a Newspaper

Citations for newspapers resemble those for magazines: they include the author's name, article title (in quotation marks), newspaper title (italicized), the date (in day-month-year order, followed by a colon), and inclusive pages.

However, when newspapers have editions (*morning, evening, national*), they must be identified. After the year, place a comma and describe the edition, abbreviating common words.

When sections of newspapers are designated by letters, place the section letter with the page number, without a space (*A22, C3, F11*). If sections are indicated by numerals, place a comma after the date or edition (rather than a colon), include the abbreviation *sec.* (not italicized), the section number, a colon, a space, and the page number (*sec. 1: 22, sec. 3: 2, sec. 5: 17*).

When an article continues in a later part of the paper, indicate the initial page, use a comma, and then add the subsequent page. If the article appears on more than three separated pages, list the initial page, followed by a plus sign (*22*+, A17+, sec. 2: 9+).

Weekly newspapers are cited just like daily newspapers.

```
Brody, Jane E. "Americans Gamble on Herbs
     as Medicine." New York Times 9 Feb. 1999:
     D1, 7.
Snyder, Jeffrey B. "Star Wars Toys: A Force to
     Reckon With." Antique Week 25 Jan. 1999: A1,
     43-44.
```

▮ An Editorial

The citation for an editorial resembles that for a magazine or newspaper article, with one exception: the word *Editorial* (not italicized), with a period, follows the title of the essay.

```
McCormick, David M. "The Draft Isn't the
     Answer." Editorial. New York Times 10 Feb.
     1999: A31.
```

▮ A Letter to the Editor

Letters to the editor follow a very simple format. Include the author's name, the word *Letter* (not italicized), the name of the publication (magazine, journal, or newspaper), and appropriate facts of publication. Do not record descriptive, attention-getting titles that publications, not authors, supply.

```
Trivedi, Apaar. Letter. Business Week 25 May
     1998: 12.
```

["Counting Chickens before They Hatch" served as the functional title of this letter to the editor, but it is not used in the citation.]

■ **A Review**

A citation for a review begins with the author's name and the title of the review (if one is provided). The abbreviation *Rev. of* (not italicized) follows, with the name of the book, film, recording, performance, product, or whatever is being reviewed, followed by clarifying information. Publication information ends the citation, incorporating elements required for different kinds of sources.

```
Siegel, Lee. "A Writer Who Is Good for You."
        Rev. of Jane Austen: A Biography by Claire
        Tomalin and Jane Austen: A Life by David
        Nokes. Atlantic Monthly Jan. 1998: 93-98.
```

34e Nonprint Sources

Finding documentation information for nonprint sources is usually easy but sometimes requires ingenuity. Compact disc booklets provide the manufacturers' catalog numbers and copyright dates. Printed programs for speeches or syllabuses for course lectures provide names, titles, locations, and dates. Information about films or television programs can be obtained from opening or closing credits or from reference books such as *Facts on File* or web sites such as *All-Movie Guide* (<http://allmovie.com>). If you have difficulty finding the information to document nonprint sources clearly, ask your instructor or a librarian for help.

■ **A Lecture or Speech**

A citation for a formal lecture or speech includes the speaker's name, the title of the presentation (in quotation marks), the name of the lecture or speaker series (if applicable), the location of the speech (convention, meeting, university, library, meeting hall), the city (and state if necessary), and the date in day-month-year order.

Branch, Tayler. "Democracy in an Age of Denial."
    Humanities on the Hill Ser. Washington, DC,
    7 May 1992.

Mitten, David M. "Greek Art and Architecture in
    the West: Southern Italy, Sicily, and Campa-
    nia." Class lecture. Harvard University.
    Cambridge, 15 May 1989.

**[For class lectures, provide as much of this information as
possible: speaker, title of lecture (in quotation marks), a
descriptive title, the school, the city (and state if necessary),
and the date.]**

Quayle, J. Danforth. "The Most Litigious Society
    in the World." American Bar Assn. Annual
    Meeting. Atlanta, 13 Aug. 1991.

■ A Work of Art

When artists title their own work, include this information:
artist's name; the title (italicized); the museum, gallery, or collection where the work of art is housed; and the city (and state,
province, or country if needed for clarity).

Cézanne, Paul. Houses along a Road. The Her-
    mitage, St. Petersburg, Russia.

When an artist has not titled a work, use the title that art
historians have given to it (without quotation marks), followed
by a brief description of the work. The rest of the citation is the
same as those for other works of art.

Amateis, Edmond Romulus. Jonas Edward Salk.
    Sculpture in bronze. Natl. Portrait Gallery,
    Washington, DC.

**[*Jonas Edward Salk* is the attributed title of the statue of this
famous scientist.]**

■ A Map, Graph, Table, or Chart

Maps, graphs, tables, and charts are treated like books. If known, include the name of the author, artist, designer, scientist, person, or group responsible for the map, graph, table, or chart. Then include the title (italicized), followed by a separately punctuated descriptive title. Also include any other necessary information.

> Lewis, R. J. [Noninteractive and Interactive]
>
> Telecommunication Technologies. Table.
>
> Meeting Learners' Needs through
>
> Telecommunication: A Directory and Guide
>
> to Programs. Washington, DC: American Assn.
>
> for Higher Education, 1983. 75.

[Clarifying information can be added within brackets.]

■ A Cartoon

Begin with the cartoonist's name, the title of the cartoon in quotation marks, and the word *Cartoon* (not italicized), followed by a period. Then include the citation information required for the source.

> Davis, Jack, and Stan Hart. "Groan with the
>
> Wind." Cartoon. Mad Jan. 1991: 42-47.

[This cartoon appeared in a monthly magazine.]

■ A Film

To cite a film as a complete work, include the title (italicized), the director (noted by the abbreviation *Dir.*, not italicized), the studio, and the date of release. If you include other people's contributions, do so after the director's name using brief phrases (*Screenplay by, Original score by*) or abbreviations (*Perf.* for "performed by," *Prod.* for "produced by") to clarify their roles.

```
On the Waterfront. Dir. Elia Kazan. Perf. Marlon
     Brando and Eva Marie Saint. Horizon-Columbia,
     1954.
```

To emphasize the contribution of an individual (rather than the film as a whole), place the person's name first, followed by a comma and a descriptive title (beginning with a lowercase letter). The rest of the citation follows normal patterns.

```
Coppola, Francis Ford, dir. Apocalypse Now. Perf.
     Martin Sheen, Marlon Brando, and Robert
     Duvall. United Artists, 1979. Suggested by
     Joseph Conrad's Heart of Darkness.
```

■ A Television Broadcast

List a regular program by the title (italicized), the network (CBS, CNN, Fox), the local station (including both the call letters and the city, separated by a comma), and the broadcast date (in day-month-year order).

Include other people's contributions after the program title, using brief phrases (*Written by, Hosted by*) or abbreviations (*Perf.* for "performed by," *Prod.* for "produced by") to clarify their roles.

```
X-Files. Perf. Gillian Anderson and David
     Duchovney. Fox. WXIN, Indianapolis. 20 June
     1999.
```

To cite a single episode of an ongoing program, include the name of the episode in quotation marks before the program's title. Other elements are presented in the same order as used for a regular program.

```
"The Understudy." Seinfeld. Perf. Bette Midler.
     NBC. WTHR, Indianapolis. 18 May 1995.
```

List special programs by title, followed by traditional descriptive information. If a special program is part of a series (for example, Hallmark Hall of Fame, Great Performances, or American Playhouse), include the series name without quotation marks or italics immediately preceding the name of the network.

> The Sleeping Beauty. Composed by Peter Ilich
>
>   Tchaikovsky. Choreographed by Marius Petipa.
>
>   Perf. Viviana Durante and Zoltan Solymosi.
>
>   Great Performances. PBS. WFYI, Indianapolis.
>
>   24 Dec. 1995.

■ A Radio Broadcast

A citation for a radio broadcast follows the same guidelines as those for a television broadcast.

> The War of the Worlds. WCBS, New York. 30 Oct.
>
>   1938.

■ A Recording

Citations for recordings usually begin with the performer or composer, followed by the title of the recording (italicized except for titles using numerals for musical form, key, or number), the recording company, the catalog number, and the copyright date.

List other contributors after the title, using brief phrases or abbreviations (*Cond.,* the abbreviation for conductor; *Perf.* for "performed by"; *Composed by*) to clarify their roles. Orchestras (abbreviated *orch.*) and other large musical groups are listed without clarifying phrases, usually following the conductor's name.

When appropriate, include recording dates immediately following the title. Compact discs (CDs) are now the standard recording format; indicate other formats, when necessary, after the title.

Notation of multidisc sets, similar to the pattern for multivolume books, appears immediately preceding the record company.

```
The Beatles. Live at the BBC. 2 discs. Capital,
    C2-31796-2, 1994.

Mahler, Gustav. Symphony no. 1 in D major.
    Record. Cond. Georg Solti. Chicago Symphony
    Orch. London, 411731-2, 1984.
```

[Since this selection is titled by musical form and key, it is not italicized. As noted after the title, this is a record, not a CD.]

To cite a single selection from a recording, include the selection title in quotation marks followed by the title of the complete recording. All else remains the same.

```
Clapton, Eric. "Tears in Heaven." Eric Clapton
    Unplugged. Reprise, 9 45024-2, 1992.
```

To cite liner notes, the printed material that comes with many recordings, list the name of the writer and the description *Liner notes* (not italicized), followed by a period. The rest of the citation follows normal patterns.

```
McClintick, David, and William Kennedy. Liner
    notes. Frank Sinatra: The Reprise Collection.
    4 discs. Reprise, 020373, 1990.
```

■ An Interview

Citations for personally conducted interviews include the name of the person interviewed, the type of interview (personal or telephone), and the interview date.

```
Otwell, Stephen. Personal interview. 11 Nov. 1998.
```

Citations for broadcast or printed interviews include the name of the person interviewed, the descriptive title *Interview* (not italicized), and information necessary to describe the source.

```
Stewart, Jimmy. Interview. Reflections on the
    Silver Screen. A&E. 5 Nov. 1994.
```

■ A Transcript

Transcripts of programs are presented according to the source of the original broadcast, with clarifying information provided. The entry ends with information about availability.

```
Watkins, Terri, et al. "McVeigh Said to Have
    Mentioned Other Bombings in Letter."
    Transcript. Daybreak. CNN. 28 Apr. 1995.
    Available: Journal Graphics Online.
```

34f Electronic Sources

Electronic sources, including Internet sources and CD-ROMs, provide a wide array of materials for current researchers. However, because of their variety, providing clear documentation for electronic sources can be a challenge. It is, nevertheless, a challenge worth meeting.

Be both resourceful and patient as you gather citation information for electronic sources. Information does not always appear in the same place in each source, a situation which can be confusing, and some sources do not provide all of the information you might want, a situation which can be frustrating. Provide as much information as possible on each source, following the patterns described in this section.

■ Internet Sources

Internet sources exist in widely varied forms, from online books to personal web sites, making the process of citing them complicated. However, using the following list, you should be able to provide the information necessary to complete an accurate and helpful citation for each of your Internet sources. Provide, in this order, all information pertinent to your source:

1. Author (or editor), last name first
2. Title (of article, poem, and so on) from a scholarly project, database, or periodical, in quotation marks; title of discussion-group posting, in quotation marks (followed by the phrase *Online posting,* not italicized); title of book, italicized (underlined)
3. Additional information: editor, compiler, or translator, preceded by the appropriate abbreviation
4. Facts of publication for material available in print form
5. Date of electronic publication (or most recent updating or posting)
6. Name of subscription service (or listserv or forum)
7. Number of pages or paragraphs when they are identified (7 pp. or 36 pars.)
8. Name of sponsoring institution or organization
9. Date you gained access to the source
10. Electronic address enclosed in angle brackets

Professional Site

    Law Student Division. American Bar Association.
        11 Feb. 1999 <http://www.abanet.org//lsd/
        home.html>.

Article in a Magazine

    Begley, Sharon, and Martha Brant. "The Real
        Scandal." Newsweek 15 Feb. 1999. 16 Feb.
        1999 <http://www.newsweek.com/nw=srv/
        printed/int/socu/sp0107_7.htm>.

Article in a Journal

> Miller, Donald E. "Experiencing Homelessness."
> <u>Journal of Contemporary Ethnography</u> 27
> (1998): 5 pp. 13 Feb. 1999 <http:proquest.
> umi.com/pqdweb>.

Article in a Reference Database

> "Expenditures for Health Care Plans by Employers
> and Employees." <u>Bureau of Labor Statistics</u>.
> 7 Dec. 1998. Bureau of Labor Statistics. 17
> Feb. 1999 <http://stats.bls.gov/pub/
> news.release/nce.txt>.

Book

> Lofting, Hugh. <u>The Voyages of Doctor Dolittle</u>.
> Project Gutenberg. Jan. 1998. U of Illinois.
> 2 Feb. 1999 <ftp://uiarchive.cso.uiuc.edu/
> pub/etext/gutenberg/etext98/vdrdl10.txt>.

Poem

> Dickinson, Emily. "I felt a funeral in my
> brain." <u>Emily Dickinson: Poems</u>. Project
> Bartleby Archives. Columbia U. 31 Jan. 1999
> <http://www.columbia.edu/acis/bartleby/
> dickinson4.html#30>.

Scholarly Project

> Austen, Jane. <u>Sense and Sensibility</u>. Project
>
> Gutenberg. Sept. 1994. U of Illinois. 4 Feb.
>
> 1999 <ftp:/uiarchive.cso.uiuc.edu/pub/etext/
>
> gutenberg/etext94/sense11.txt>.

Posting to a Discussion Group

> Dungarvin Parent Association of Delaware.
>
> "Developing Programs for Adults with
>
> Autism." Online posting. 14 June 1998. 3
>
> Feb. 1999 <grnlks@alltell.net>.

■ CD-ROM Sources

Although CD-ROMs are being phased out in many libraries because Internet sites provide more easily updated materials, it is possible that you will still need to cite a CD-ROM source.

If a CD-ROM source reproduces material available in print form, begin the citation with full print information: author (or editor), title, and facts of publication (see pages 394–414 for complete citation patterns). If the material is not available in print form, begin the citation with identifying information: author (if given), title (in quotation marks), and the date of the material (if appropriate). Citations for both kinds of materials then include information about the CD-ROM source in this order:

1. The title of the database, italicized
2. The description *CD-ROM,* not italicized
3. The city (if known) and the name of the company that produced the CD-ROM
4. The date of electronic publication

Available in Print Form

```
"On the Brink: An Interview with Yitzhak Rabin."
     Jerusalem Post 23 Apr. 1994: 16. PAIS
     International. CD-ROM. Silverplatter, 1995.
```

Electronic Only

```
"National Rifle Association of America (NRA)."
     Encyclopedia of Associations. CD-ROM.
     Detroit: Gale, 1994.
```

If a CD-ROM source is not regularly revised or updated, the citation follows a pattern similar to that for a book, with one exception: the description *CD-ROM* (not italicized) precedes the publishing information.

```
Welmers, William E. "African Languages." The
     New Grolier Multimedia Encyclopedia. 1994
     ed. CD-ROM. New York: Grolier, 1994.
```

■ EXERCISE 34.1   Compiling a works-cited page

From the following sets of scrambled information on sources related to Toni Morrison's Beloved, *produce correct sample works cited entries and arrange them alphabetically.* NOTE: *Some information is included for the sake of clarity only; it will not be incorporated into the citations.* (Available on disk.)

1. Produced by Harpo Productions; released in 1998; the movie *Beloved;* directed by Jonathan Demme; distributed by Touchstone Pictures; starring Oprah Winfrey and Danny Glover.

2. Published by Alfred A. Knopf, Incorporated; written by Toni Morrison; published in 1987; the novel *Beloved;* winner of the Pulitzer Prize for fiction; New York City, New York.

3. Published in 1998; written by Missy Dehn Kubitschek; published by Greenwood Press; the book *Toni Morrison: A Critical Companion;* 224 pages long; Westport, Connecticut; part of the Critical Companions to Popular Contemporary Writers Series.

4. Directed by Jonathan Demme; a review written by Richard Corliss; the review "Bewitching *Beloved*"; published in *Time* magazine; a review of the film *Beloved;* with performances by Oprah Winfrey and Danny Glover; appearing on pages 74, 75, 76, and 77; published on October 5, 1998.

5. Written by Dinita Smith; the article "Toni Morrison's Mix of Tragedy, Domesticity, and Folklore"; appearing in section E; published in the *New York Times;* appearing on page 1 and on four more separated pages; published January 8, 1998; appearing in a late edition.

6. A collected set of information titled "Historical Events Affecting Characters in *Beloved*"; appearing in an online posting; posted from the University of Texas; first posted on October 30, 1998; retrieved February 12, 1999; compiled by Ali Lakhia, Glenn Schuetz, Katie Gilette, and Scott Lloyd; available at <http://www.cs.utexas.edu/users/lakhia/morrison/history.html>.

7. Appearing on pages 92–110; in a collection edited by Donna Bassin; New Haven, CT; published by Yale University Press; written by Marianne Hirsch; a chapter titled "Maternity and Rememory: Toni Morrison's *Beloved*"; part of a book titled *Representations of Motherhood*; published in 1991.

8. Published in 1991; appearing on pages 153–69; published in *Journal of Narrative Technique,* which uses continuous pages throughout a volume; written by Eusebio L. Rodrigues; an article titled "The Telling of *Beloved*"; appearing in volume 21.

9. Published in the journal *Religion and Literature,* which uses separate pages with each issue; appearing on pages 119–29; appearing in issue 1 of volume 27; an article titled "Who Are the Beloved? Old and New Testaments, Old and New Communities of Faith"; written by Danille Taylor-Guthrie; published in 1995.

10. Published by Gale Publishers, Incorporated; the 9th edition; an entry titled "Morrison, Toni"; published in 1999; published in *Who's Who among African Americans.*

11. Appearing on page 14 and on five additional, separated pages; published December 1987; an article titled "Telling How It Was"; written by Geoffrey C. Ward; published in *American Heritage.*

12. A book titled *Conversations with Toni Morrison;* published in 1991; edited by Danille Taylor-Guthrie; published in Jackson, Mississippi; published by the University Press of Mississippi.

Organizing and writing are exciting stages in your research work because you now are ready to bring your information and your ideas together in a clear and convincing paper.

QUICK REFERENCE

▷ Reread your notes and organize them into groups that correspond to logical divisions of your topic.

▷ Write a rough draft based on this organization, working with one group of notes at a time.

▷ Integrate source material smoothly with your ideas.

▷ Use parenthetical notes to document your use of sources.

▷ Revise the rough draft to clarify organization and content, to improve style, and to correct technical errors. (See Chapter 3, "Revising," for revision checklists.)

▷ Prepare and submit the final copy.

35a Organization

The basic patterns of organizing a research paper resemble patterns used for other papers. (See Chapter 4, "Paragraphs," to review patterns of organization.) Your note taking has given you a wealth of material; now you need to arrange that material in the way that will best present your thesis.

■ Reread Your Notes

Begin by reviewing your notes. Though time consuming, rereading all notes will help you to see the scope of your materials and the connections among ideas. A complete grasp of your materials is crucial as you revise the thesis statement, prepare an outline, and sort materials.

■ Revise Your Thesis Statement

Examine your working thesis statement. Based on the information gathered during your research, test its validity:

- Does it identify the topic clearly?
- Does it present a valid judgment?
- Does it incorporate necessary qualifications and limitations?
- Does it state or imply that you have acknowledged opposing views?
- Is it worded effectively?

If you cannot respond "yes" to all of these questions, revise your thesis statement.

■ Develop a Rough Outline

Once you have revised the thesis statement to ensure that it is clearly and effectively worded, print or type a clean copy and use it to help you to construct a rough outline. Identify major categories derived from your thesis statement and use them as the basis of a rough outline.

After reviewing her working thesis statement, Angela decided that she had established a reasonable cause and effect relationship that would support the point she wanted to make in her paper: the need to deter Internet plagiarism. Knowing that she could refine the thesis statement further if necessary, Angela felt that she could begin organizing the paper.

Allowing for an introduction and conclusion, Angela created this rough outline to arrange the ideas of her paper:

```
Introductory paragraph (Thesis statement:

Because the Internet has made the
```

```
process of plagiarizing papers easy for
students, teachers must take informed,
active steps to deter it.)
```

History of plagiarism

    --Borrowings

    --Printing (17th century)

    --Ownership and careers in writing

    --20th-century issues

Paper mills

    --Advertisements

    --Conditions

    --Costs

    --Troublesome

Internet paper sites

    --Copies of papers (to download)

    --Free or purchased (costs)

    --Easy

The teacher's role--controlling the
project

    --Simple suggestions

    --Explore the sites

    --Discuss plagiarism

    --Review Internet samples

    --Divide projects into stages

    --Grade the process

Concluding paragraphs--the good and the
bad

Remember that you can revise your outline later if you discover a better way to arrange the materials as you write the rough draft.

■ Sort Your Notes

Using the major headings of the rough outline, sort your notes. Consider making label cards for each major topic of your outline and then sort your notes into appropriately labeled topic groups.

If a note fits into more than one group, place it in the most appropriate group and create a cross-reference note (for example, "See Parker quotation, p. 219—in *childhood*") for each of the other groups. Expect to have a stack of notes that do not logically fit into any group. Label these notes *miscellaneous* and set them aside. You may see where they fit as you continue working. Use paper clips, binder clips, rubber bands, or envelopes to keep groups of notes together.

Because organizing and perhaps reorganizing involves analyzing, reconsidering, and rearranging, expect temporary chaos.

■ Prepare a Formal Outline

After organizing your notes into major topics, use the topics to arrange information within the sections of your paper. Take each group of notes and organize them into a clear, logical sequence: creating a formal outline is generally the most useful way to accomplish this. (To review outlining, see section 2b.)

Through a formal, detailed outline derived from her notes, Angela evolved the structure of her paper. It included chronological organization of material on the history of plagiarism and topical organization of material on methods for deterring Internet plagiarism. Her formal outline appears on pages 446–48.

35b A Rough Draft

With notes, revised thesis, and formal outline in hand, you are ready to begin writing. The rough draft of a research paper, like the rough draft of any paper, will be messy and inconsistent, sketchy in some places and repetitive in others. That is to be expected. To help with the process of drafting your research paper, remember the drafting strategies that you developed in writing other kinds of papers. (For a complete discussion, see section 2c.)

General Drafting Strategies

- Gather all your materials together.
- Work from your outline.
- Remember the purpose of your paper.
- Use only ideas and details that support your thesis statement.
- Remember your readers' needs.
- Do not worry about technical matters.
- Rethink and modify troublesome sections.
- Reread sections as you write.
- Write alternative versions of troublesome sections.
- Periodically take a break from writing.

Beyond these general principles, which apply to all writing, the following specific principles apply to writing a research paper and take into account its special requirements and demands.

Drafting Strategies for Research Papers

Allow ample time to write. Begin writing as soon as possible and write something every day.

Think of your paper by section, not by paragraph. Because of the complexity of material in a research paper, discussions of most topics will require more than one paragraph. Keep that in mind and use new paragraphs to present subtopics.

Work on one section at a time. Work steadily, section by section. When you come to a section that is difficult to write or that needs more information, leave it for later and move to the next section. Remember to look for necessary new material as soon as possible.

Use transitions to signal major shifts within your work. The multiparagraph explanations required for key points can make it difficult for readers to know when you have moved from one key point to another. Consequently, emphasize transitions in your draft; you can refine them during revision if they are too obvious.

Incorporate your research notes so that they are an integral part of your paper. Material from sources should support, not dominate, your ideas. Incorporate source material as it is needed to support your thesis; do not simply string notes together with sentences. (For a complete discussion of incorporating research notes, see section 35c.)

Give special attention to introductory and concluding paragraphs. Ideas for introductory and concluding paragraphs may occur at any time during the writing process. Consider several strategies and select the one most clearly matched to the tone and purpose of your paper.

Pay special attention to technical language. Define carefully any technical language required in your paper. Thoughtful definition and use of important technical terms will help you to clarify ideas as you draft your paper.

As you write, remember that a research paper should present your views on a subject as based on outside reading and interpretation, not just show that you can collect and compile what others have written or said. Develop your own ideas fully. Be a part of the paper: add comments on sources and disagree with them when necessary. Be a thinker and a writer.

35c Incorporating Notes

The information from your note taking—summaries, quotations, and paraphrases—must be incorporated smoothly into your research paper, providing clarifications, explanations, and illustrations of important ideas. (Section 35d, Parenthetical Notes, will explain how to document the information.) Use your notes to substantiate your points, not simply to show that you have gathered materials, and to provide your own commentary on the central ideas.

■ Facts and Summaries

Incorporate facts and summaries into your own sentences; use parenthetical notes (see section 35d) to identify the sources of the information, as in this example:

```
Unlike productions from earlier generations,
current musicals are extravaganzas, developed by
multinational groups and presented in multiple
venues. One useful example is Les Misérables,
based on the novel by Victor Hugo. Produced in
France, England, and the United States in 1989,
it had eighteen companies touring worldwide,
bringing in $450 million (Rosenberg and Harburg
65).
```

> [Rosenberg, Bernard, and Ernest Harburg. *The Broadway Musical: Collaboration in Commerce and Art.* New York: New York UP, 1993.]

Hugo's authorship is an example of commonly known information that does not require an identifying note. (see section 33g for a discussion of common knowledge).

■ Paraphrases

Include paraphrased material wherever it will support the ideas of the paper. A one-sentence paraphrase should be followed immediately by a parenthetical note; longer paraphrases, especially background information taken from a single source, should be placed in a separate paragraph with parenthetical documentation at the end. For added clarity, identify the author and source at the beginning of the paragraph, as in this example:

```
In School Choice: The Struggle for the Soul of
American Education, Peter W. Cookson, Jr., pro-
vides a useful summary of why people have come
to question the government's monopoly in public
education. According to Cookson, high dropout
rates, in-school violence, disintegrating facil-
ities, low educational standards, and cultural
fragmentation have all contributed to educa-
tion's decline. However, he contends that it was
media attention to these troubles, coupled with
the conservative backlash of the Reagan years,
that gave the school choice movement its momen-
tum (2-7).
```

[Cookson, Peter W., Jr. *School Choice: The Struggle for the Soul of American Education.* New Haven, CT: Yale UP, 1994.]

■ Quotations

Use quotations selectively to add clarity, emphasis, or interest to a research paper, not to pad its length.

Never include a quotation without introducing or commenting on it: readers may not understand why you find it important. Always introduce the quotation to place it in a context and then follow it with an evaluative comment, no matter how brief. Numerous verbs may be used to introduce quotations.

Some Verbs Used to Introduce Quotations		
add	explain	reply
answer	mention	respond
claim	note	restate
comment	observe	say
declare	reiterate	stress
emphasize	remark	summarize

The examples given below and on pages 430–36 demonstrate an effective pattern for introducing a quotation: identify the author and source and explain the quotation's relevance to the discussion.

The way in which you present a quotation—either prose or poetry—depends on its length.

Brief Prose Quotations

Include prose quotations of four or fewer typed lines within the paragraph text. Enclose the words in quotation marks. For example:

No community is free from the effects of news as business. As Doug Underwood observes in When MBAs Rule the Newsroom: How the Marketers and Managers Are Reshaping Today's Media: "In this era of conglomerates and concentrated ownership, the tentacles of the big media companies are reaching everywhere, connecting with their electronic competitors and entertainment combines,

```
plugging up the remaining independent media
outlets, and extending their hold even into our
smallest communities" (181). The result is,
quite logically, less local control.
```

For variety, place identifying material at the end of the quoted material—or in the middle if it is not disruptive. For example:

```
No community is free from the effects of news as
business. "In this era of conglomerates and con-
centrated ownership," Doug Underwood observes in
When MBAs Rule the Newsroom: How the Marketers
and Managers Are Reshaping Today's Media, "the
tentacles of the big media companies are reach-
ing everywhere, connecting with their electronic
competitors and entertainment combines, plugging
up the remaining independent media outlets, and
extending their hold even into our smallest com-
munities" (181). The result is, quite logically,
less local control.
```

To use only a phrase or part of a sentence from a source, incorporate the material into your own sentence structure. Although derived from the same passage as the quotation used previously, this example uses only a small portion of the original:

```
No community is free from the effects of news as
business. In When MBAs Rule the Newsroom: How
the Marketers and Managers Are Reshaping Today's
Media, Doug Underwood suggests that national and
international media companies are "plugging up
```

```
the remaining independent media outlets, and
extending their hold even into our smallest com-
munities" (181). The result, quite logically, is
less local control.
```

[Underwood, Doug. *When MBAs Rule the Newsroom: How the Marketers and Managers Are Reshaping Today's Media.* New York: Columbia UP, 1993.]

Punctuate such quotations according to the requirements of the entire sentence. Do not set such quotations apart with commas unless the sentence structure requires commas.

Brief Verse Quotations

Incorporate verse quotations of one or two lines within the paragraph text. Use quotation marks, indicate line divisions with a slash (/) preceded and followed by one space, and retain the poem's capitalization. Cite poetry using line numbers, not pages.

```
In "Morning at the Window," T. S. Eliot offers a
familiar, foggy image, the distant musings of a
person who observes life but does not seem to
live it: "The brown waves of fog toss up to me /
Twisted faces from the bottom of the street"
(5-6). The poem continues with other similar
images, each one building on the earlier ones.
```

[Eliot, T. S. "Morning at the Window." *The Complete Poems and Plays: 1909–1950.* New York: Harcourt, 1971. 16.]

Long Prose Quotations

Incorporate prose quotations of five or more typed lines by setting the quotation off from the body of the paragraph. Indent the quotation one inch (ten spaces) from the left margin (the right margin is not indented). Double-space the material but do not enclose it within quotation marks. If a clause introduces the quotation, follow it with a colon, as in this example:

```
Anthropologists and social scientists are now
realizing that a broader range of information
must be collected in order for us to understand
the diversity of ethnic and social groups. Rhoda
H. Halperin offers this rationale in "Appalachi-
ans in Cities: Issues and Challenges for
Research":

        Family histories that reveal the dynam-
        ics of intergenerational relationships
        in all of their dimensions (education,
        economic, psychological)--the constant
        mentoring and tutoring, the patience of
        grandmothers with grandbabies--must be
        collected. We need as researchers to
        collect data that avoid the patronizing
        "we" (urban professionals) who know what
        is best for "you" or "them" (the poor
        people). (196)

Current studies, as a result, are developed in a
multidimensional way.
```

[Halperin, Rhoda H. "Appalachians in Cities: Issues and Challenges for Research." *From Mountains to Metropolis: Appalachian Migrants in American Cities.* Ed. Kathryn M. Borman and Phillip J. Obermiller. Westport, CT: Bergin, 1994. 181–97.]

Long Verse Quotations

To quote three or more lines of poetry, follow the pattern for long prose quotations: indent one inch (ten spaces), double-space the lines, and omit quotation marks. Follow the poet's line spacing as closely as possible, as in this example:

```
In "Poem [1]," Langston Hughes offers a spare,

critical assessment of western culture:

            I am afraid of this civilization--

                So hard,

                    So strong,

                        So cold. (4-7)

In only twelve words, Hughes provides a sharp,

insightful look at the world around him.
```

[Hughes, Langston. "Poem [1]." *The Collected Poems of Langston Hughes. Ed.* Arnold Rampersad and David Roessel. New York: Knopf, 1994.]

Punctuation Within Quotations

SINGLE QUOTATION MARKS.　To indicate an author's use of quotations within a passage, follow one of two patterns. In a brief passage, enclose the full quotation in double quotation marks (" ") and change the source's punctuation to single quotation marks (' '), as in this example:

```
In Tribes: How Race, Religion, and Identity

Determine Success in the New Global Economy,

Joel Kotkin emphasizes the influence of immi-

grants in American culture and business: "Even

blue denim jeans, the 'uniform' of the gold

rush--and indeed, the American West--owe their

origination and popular name to Levi Strauss, a
```

```
gold rush-era immigrant to San Francisco" (57).
This is but one example among many.
```

[Kotkin, Joel. *Tribes: How Race, Religion, and Identity Determine Success in the New Global Economy.* New York: Random, 1993.]

In a long quotation—one indented one inch (ten spaces) and therefore not enclosed within quotation marks—the author's quotation marks remain double, as in this example:

```
James Sellers, in Essays in American Ethics,
suggests that self-identity is often inextrica-
bly linked to one's nationality:

        National identity need not always be in
        the forefront of one's awareness of who
        he [or she] is. But in America, it is.
        The United States is the "oldest new
        nation," we are often told by political
        scientists; and the national heritage,
        while it has certainly not turned out to
        be a "melting pot," has become a power-
        ful background influence upon the iden-
        tity of Americans, reshaping even the
        ways in which they express their ethnic-
        ity or their religion. (97)

Whatever our race, religion, or ethnicity, we
are, perhaps most obviously, Americans.
```

[Sellers, James. *Essays in American Ethics.* Ed. Barry Arnold. New York: Lang, 1991.]

BRACKETS. Use brackets to clarify words or phrases in a quotation. For example, in the following passage, the bracketed phrase "value-destroying industries" (a commonly understood phrase in economic studies) substitutes for the phrase "one of these firms," which has no clear referent in the quotation or in its introduction.

> In "The Disintegration of the Russian Economy,"
> Michael Spagat explains a major industrial
> dilemma: "Workers in these industries are
> receiving more wages than the wealth they are
> creating for society. So if [value-destroying
> industries] were closed down, money would be
> saved but the savings would not be enough to pay
> full unemployment compensation" (52). This has
> been one of the primary concerns as Russia has
> shifted to a private economy.

[Spagat, Michael. "The Disintegration of the Russian Economy." *Russia's Future: Consolidation or Disintegration?* Ed. Douglas W. Blum. Boulder, CO: Westview, 1994. 47–67.]

Bracketed information can substitute for the original wording, as in the previous example, or appear in addition to the original material: "she [Eleanor Roosevelt]" or "he [or she]." If a quotation requires extensive use of brackets, use another quotation or express the information in your own words.

ELLIPSES. Use ellipsis points (three spaced periods) placed within brackets to show where words are omitted from a quotation. Omissions from the middle of a sentence do not require any punctuation other than the ellipses within brackets. To indicate an omission from the beginning or end of a sentence, retain the sentence's punctuation.

> Robert I. Williams stresses the social
> dimensions of comedy in <u>Comic Practice:</u>
> <u>Comic Response</u>: "Humor is a guide. It is
> largely culture bound. Chinese Communist
> jokes do not do well here, just as ours tend
> to be duds in Beijing. [. . .] Yet there is
> a range of humor that works for a broad,
> variegated audience. The very existence of
> comic films is testimony" (56-57). This is
> probably why some comics appeal to many peo-
> ple, while others appeal to only a few.

[Omitted: "The humor of a Chicago street gang will not work in a retirement home, even one in Chicago. Regional, age, gender, and social differences all enter in."]

[Williams, Robert I. *Comic Practice: Comic Response.* Newark: U of Delaware P, 1993.]

When clarity is not compromised, ellipsis points within brackets are unnecessary at the beginning or end of a quotation because readers understand that quotations come from more complete sources.

35d Parenthetical Notes

Documentation identifies material from sources and indicates where facts, quotations, or ideas appear in original sources. In some documentation styles (University of Chicago, for example), note numbers (one half-space above the line) at the end of sentences correspond to full citations placed either at the bottom of the page (footnotes) or gathered at the end of the paper (endnotes).

Acknowledging the repetitive nature of full-note citations, the Modern Language Association (MLA) has followed the lead of the American Psychological Association (APA) and now provides documentation in parentheses.

■ Consistency of Reference

Parenthetical references must correspond to entries in the list of works cited. If a works-cited entry begins with an author's name, then the parenthetical reference in the text must also cite the author's name—not the title, editor, translator, or some other element. Readers then match the information within the parenthetical references with the information in the works-cited entries.

■ Basic Forms of Parenthetical Notes

To avoid disrupting the text, parenthetical notes use the briefest possible form to identify the relevant source: the name of the author (or in some instances the title) and, for print sources, a page number (without a page abbreviation). No punctuation follows the author's name. For example:

```
Soon after Johnson was inaugurated in 1965,
Operation Rolling Thunder began; ultimately
American planes dropped 643,000 tons of
explosives on North Vietnam (Brownmiller 20).
```

In the interests of clarity and economy, you may incorporate some of the necessary information into your sentences; this information is then omitted from the note.

```
Brownmiller notes that soon after Johnson
was inaugurated in 1965, Operation Rolling
Thunder began; ultimately American planes
dropped 630,000 tons of explosives on North
Vietnam (20).
```

[Brownmiller, Susan. *Seeing Vietnam: Encounters of the Road and Heart.* New York: Harper, 1994.]

In special cases, however, the rule of using the author's last name and the page reference is superseded:

Special Circumstance	Rule and Sample
Two authors with the same last name	Include first and last name: (John Barratt 31), distinct from (Theresa Barratt 2–4)
Two works by the same author	Include the title or a short-ened version of the title, separated from the author's name by a comma: (Morrison, *Sula* 116), distinct from (Morrison, *Solomon* 13)
Two authors	Include both last names: (Scott and Fuller 213–14)
Three authors	Include all last names, sepa-rated by commas: (Jarnow, Judelle, and Guerreiro 58)
Four or more authors	Include the first author's last name and *et al.,* not italicized: (Gershey et al. 22)
Corporate author	Include the abbreviated name of the organization as the author: (AMA 117)
Multivolume works	Include the volume number after the author's name, followed by a colon and one space: (Tebbel 4: 89–91)

Special Circumstance	Rule and Sample
Reference works	Include the author's name or a shortened form of the title, depending on how the work appears in the works-cited list; no page numbers are required for alphabetically arranged sources: (Angermüller) or ("Manhattan Project")
Poetry or drama in verse	Include the author's name, a short title (if necessary), and line (not page) numbers: (Eliot, "Waste Land" 173–81)

Nonprint Sources

Cite nonprint sources, for which no page numbers can be given, by "author" (lecturer, director, writer, producer, performer, or interview respondent) or title, as they appear in the works-cited list.

```
The isolation and despair of patients with AIDS

are captured in these haunting images:

            I walked the avenue till my legs felt

            like stone

            I heard the voices of friends vanished

            and gone

            At night I could hear the blood in my

            veins

            Black and whispering as the rain.

              (Springsteen, "Streets")
```

Such citations, however, are often clearer if incorporated into the text of the paper.

> The isolation and despair of patients with AIDS
> are captured in these haunting images from Bruce
> Springsteen's "Streets of Philadelphia":
>
>> I walked the avenue till my legs felt
>> like stone
>> I heard the voices of friends vanished
>> and gone
>> At night I could hear the blood in my
>> veins
>> Black and whispering as the rain.

**[Springsteen, Bruce. "Streets of Philadelphia." *Philadelphia.*
Soundtrack. Epic, 7464-57624-2, 1993.]**

Because nonprint sources require limited information in parenthetical notes, incorporate all needed information in the written text when possible.

■ Positioning Parenthetical Notes

Without disrupting your text, place parenthetical notes as close as possible to the material they document—usually at the end of the sentence but before the end punctuation. Allow one space before the opening parenthesis.

Facts, Summaries, and Paraphrases

> Congressionally approved military assistance to
> foreign nations gradually increased from $2 bil-
> lion per year during Kennedy's administration to
> $7 billion a year during the Reagan administra-
> tion (Hinckley 122-23).

[Hinckley, Barbara. *Less than Meets the Eye: Foreign Policy Making and the Myth of the Assertive Congress.* Chicago: Twentieth Century-U of Chicago P, 1994.]

Brief Quotations

For brief quotations, place the notes *outside* the quotation marks but *before* the end punctuation, in contrast to the usual placement of end punctuation before closing quotation marks.

```
Economic and political power are intertwined
because "together, the politically strong and
our legislators devise measures to limit [eco-
nomic] competition from those who are politi-
cally weaker" (Adams and Brock 118). This should
come as no surprise.
```

[Adams, Walter, and James W. Brock. *Antitrust Economics on Trial: A Dialogue on the New Laissez-Faire.* Princeton: Princeton UP, 1991.]

Long Quotations

For long, set-off quotations (those indented ten spaces and not enclosed by quotation marks), place a period at the end of the quotation. Then add the parenthetical note without additional punctuation.

```
Unlike the traditional "hard" sciences, the
study of past cultures must, by nature, be some-
what intuitive. As Rachel Harry suggests in
"Archaeology as Art":
          Objectivity in archaeology is at once
          both an easy and an impossible target to
          shoot down because it simply does not
```

exist. Archaeologists cannot <u>choose</u>
objectivity. We will find what we look
for, and are left with what by chance is
revealed to us. (133)

Balance, then, must be achieved by reviewing a
variety of archaeological studies, not just one.

[Harry, Rachel. "Archaeology as Art." *Archaeological Theory:
Progress or Posture?* Ed. Iain M. Mackenzie. Worldwide
Archaeological Ser. Brookfield, VT: Avebury, 1994. 131–39.]

35e Revision

After writing the draft of the paper, set it aside; two or three days is usually long enough for you to gain critical distance. Then reread it carefully. Consider the paper's organization, content, and style. Your ideas should be clearly expressed, logically organized, and effectively supported with appropriate and illuminating facts, quotations, and paraphrases. All documented material should be smoothly and accurately incorporated.

Allow time to rework your paper, strengthening undeveloped sections by expanding them, clarifying confusing sections by rewriting them, and focusing overly long sections by cutting unnecessary material. For more information on this stage of the writing process, see Chapter 3, "Revising."

■ Evaluate the Rough Draft

Using the following guidelines, assess the rough draft yourself or ask another student from your class to peer-edit the draft. Make revisions according to an honest assessment of the paper's strengths and weaknesses.

Introduction

- Is the title interesting, accurate, and appropriate?
- Is the introductory strategy interesting and suited to the tone and subject of the paper?
- Is the thesis statement effectively and unambiguously worded?
- Is the thesis statement located near the end of your introductory paragraphs?
- Is the length of the introduction proportionate to the length of the entire paper?

Organization

- Is the organizational pattern suitable for the subject?
- Are topics and subtopics clearly related to the thesis?
- Is the background information complete, relevant, and well integrated?

Content

- Is the thesis statement effectively developed throughout?
- Are topics adequately supported by facts, ideas, and quotations?
- Is material from sources smoothly and accurately incorporated?

Style

- Is the tone of the paper consistent and suitable for a college paper?
- Are the sentences clear and logical?
- Are the sentences written in the active voice whenever possible?
- Are the sentences varied in length and type?
- Are the word choices diverse, precise, and interesting?
- Are unfamiliar terms sufficiently explained?

Mechanics

- Are the grammar and usage standard?
- Is the spelling accurate, especially the technical language and any proper nouns?
- Are capitals, italics, and punctuation used correctly?
- Are parenthetical notes appropriately placed and punctuated?

Conclusion

- Does the conclusion summarize the main ideas of the paper without repetition?
- Does the concluding strategy leave the reader with the impression of a thorough, thoughtful paper on a meaningful subject?

■ Prepare the List of Works Cited

Separate the source cards containing the works-cited entries for *sources used in the paper* and alphabetize them. Double-check the form of the entries (see section 34b) and then type the works-cited list, starting on a new page. (See pages 461–63 for an illustration of the correct format.)

If you have prepared your citations on the computer, simply add the heading "Works Cited" (without quotation marks), alphabetize the entries, and double-check the form of each entry.

35f A Final Manuscript

The manuscript format for the research paper varies only slightly from that for other papers. (See Appendix A, Word Processing and Manuscript Form.) The margins, the heading, and the pagination are the same, and double-spacing is still required throughout. Because the research paper has additional parts and because parenthetical notes complicate typing, however, allow extra time to prepare the final copy. Do not assume that typing and proofreading a research paper can be a one-night process.

■ Typing

Type at an unhurried pace, proofreading and correcting pages as you work. When the final copy is complete, run the spell-check program, proofread carefully for errors that spell checkers will not identify (inverted words, homonyms, wrong words, unique spellings of names, and so on), and make necessary corrections.

■ Submitting the Paper

Submit the final paper according to your instructor's directions. If you receive no specific guidelines, secure the pages with a paper clip (in the upper-left corner) and place lengthy papers in a 9-by-12-inch manila envelope with your name and course information typed or written on the outside.

Be aware that instructors may require a disk copy of the paper. In such a case, submit a copy of the final paper on a separate disk that is clearly labeled with your name and course information. Also keep a disk version for yourself.

35g A Sample Research Paper

The following paper demonstrates many important aspects of writing and documenting a research paper.

Rios 1

Angela Rios

Dr. Robert Perrin

English 307

February 26, 1999

Beg, Borrow, or Buy?
The Wide World of Internet Plagiarism

INTRODUCTION

Thesis Statement: Because the Internet
has made the process of plagiarizing
papers easy for students, teachers must
take informed, active steps to deter it.

I. Context for discussion of plagiarism

A. Brief history

1. Middle Ages

2. Printing (seventeenth century)

3. Careers in writing

4. Twentieth-century issues

B. Paper mills

1. Advertisements

2. Conditions

3. Costs

4. Troublesome issues

Rios 2

    C. Internet paper sites

        1. Availability

        2. Downloadable formats

        3. Ease of acquisition

Roman numeral for second major division

II. Antiplagiarism suggestions

    A. Simple suggestions

        1. Knowledge of students

        2. Frequent writing assignments

        3. Clear assignments

    B. Exploration of Internet sites

        1. Major sites

        2. Familiarity with offerings

        3. Knowledge as a deterrent

Uppercase letters for a series of subdivisions

    C. Discussions of plagiarism

        1. Orientations

        2. Introductions to classes

        3. Introductions of paper assign-
           ments

        4. Sharing information

    D. Review sample Internet papers

        1. Use of Internet examples

        2. Quality of samples

        3. Demonstrated awareness of sites

    E. Projects into stages

        1. Developed in steps

        2. Evidence of students' work

        3. Timeliness

    F. Emphasis on the process

        1. Oral presentations

        2. Submitting all materials

        3. Grading the steps

        4. Grading the finished product

Conclusion: separated from the outline, without Roman numerals

CONCLUSION

Angela Rios

Dr. Robert Perrin

English 307

February 26, 1999

Beg, Borrow, or Buy?
The Wide World of Internet Plagiarism

Geoffrey Chaucer; William
Shakespeare; George Washington; John F.
Kennedy; Martin Luther King, Jr.; Alex
Haley; George Harrison; Stevie Wonder;
Steven Spielberg. Besides being famous,
what else do these men have in common?
They have all been accused of plagiarism, attempting "to use or pass off as
one's own (the ideas or writings of
another)" ("Plagiarize"). But they're
not the only ones to help themselves. At
high schools and colleges across the
country, students by the score use
papers that they have gotten from
friends, from roommates, from fraternity
buddies, or from siblings. In the past,
the lazy, fearful, or desperate could
resort to buying papers from what were

Last name and page number on every page, one-half inch from top

Identification information, one inch from top of page

Title in conventional capitalization, centered

Left margin one inch

Right margin one inch

No page number for reference works

called "paper mills"; these days, however, the Internet provides access to
thousands of papers, and plagiarism is

A lead-in to the thesis statement

on the rise. What's a serious student to
do? What's a teacher to do? To reassure
hard-working students that lazy or
indifferent students are not getting by
with passing off other people's work as
their own, teachers must do something.

The thesis statement

Because the Internet has made the
process of plagiarizing papers easy for
students, teachers must take informed,
active steps to deter it.

Historical context

Using other people's words and
ideas wasn't always considered wrong. As

Quote introduced with author's name and title; page number for print source

Julia Keller notes in "Aspects of Ambiguity," "During the Middle Ages, using
other peoples' ideas and phrases was
desirable; it showed that you had done
your homework. Originality wasn't
prized" (5). But as more people became
educated, the amount of "shared" material increased, and the printing press
made more written materials available
to a large audience. As writers began
to live on their earnings, they became

Rios 3

concerned about ownership; their writing
did, after all, produce their incomes.
Consequently, statutes were enacted in
England, beginning in 1710, to protect

Fact incorpo-
rated; author and
page required for
print source

authors' works (Mallon 39). In the following centuries, writers lobbied for
the protection of their work, and copyright laws because progressively
stricter. Today, appropriating someone
else's writing is generally considered
wrong. But instances of plagiarism still
exist, and in schools across the country
the problem is getting worse.

Explanation of
how papermills
work

Acquiring, rather than writing,
papers is an unsavory tradition. Paper
mills have for years advertised in magazines, in newspapers, and on school bul-

No citation for
common knowl-
edge

letin boards. For fees, students could
acquire an already prepared paper, or,
for additional fees, they could get cus-

Author's name
and title to intro-
duce quotation

tom research and writing. In "The Cheating Industry," D. Keith Mano describes
his dealings with a service called Crib
Corp., which asked in a magazine advertisement, "TERM PAPER BLUES?" and
offered the unsettling assurance that

Rios 4

it had "Over 16,000 Available" (50). But
Mano's experience was in the "old days":
1987. When Mano called the company, he
discovered that he would get a photocopied version of the paper to retype,
with this advice from the Crib Corp.
representative: "You can add words of
your own to make it sound authentic.
Feel free to call us if there's anything
in the paper you don't understand" (52).
Shady though the process was, it did
require some effort and was notably slow.

Explanation
of Internet
plagiarism

However, with the development of
the Internet, the world of plagiarized
papers has changed dramatically. Materials are now available in downloadable
formats, making it possible for students
to copy articles in the same way some
fifth graders copy school reports from
World Book Encyclopedia. But there are
two differences: (1) high school and
college students aren't eleven years old
and should know better, and (2) those
who don't know better--or don't care--
don't even have to write or type. They
just download and print.

Rios 5

Because of the proliferation of Internet sites and the tendency of some students to use them, the teacher's role must change to involve active supervision of writing projects. Even Kenny Sahr, the operator of <u>School Sucks</u>, a well-known web site, notes that "nobody will dare cheat if [teachers] are giving good assignments and paying attention to their students" (Wice). So what steps can teachers take?

Some antiplagiarism suggestions are so sensible that they barely need discussing: (1) teachers must get to know their students; (2) teachers must have students write more than just one lengthy, final research paper; (3) teachers should give clear, well-focused, specific assignments. These are things that all teachers should do anyway, but other suggestions move in new and interesting directions, with modifications of old principles and the creation of new ones.

One of the most practical suggestions is for teachers to familiarize

Quotation introduced with speaker's name; found in another source themselves with the sites that make Internet plagiarism possible; in other words, teachers should do some personal research. Several web sites are particularly helpful for preparing a tour of the major sites. GroupWeb.com's page on term papers provides a listing of what are euphemistically called "term paper resources," including Absolutely Free Online Essays, Cheater.com, Cheathouse.com, Genius Papers, Research Papers Online, School Sucks, and others. Cheaters Paradise (note the missing apostrophe) also provides a listing of web sites. Teachers should explore these sites to discover what they offer. Professor Leon Geyer, advisor to Virginia Polytechnic Institute and State University's honor system, suggests that Internet plagiarism is easy, but that once teachers become familiar with the process of computer cheating, it is "easy to detect--and students haven't figured out the latter" (B11). Quite simply, learning more about the Internet will help teachers to be prepared to detect and deal with plagiarism.

No page number for an Internet source

Quotation introduced with speaker's name; found in a newspaper

Another important strategy is to
include discussions of plagiarism during
student orientations and introductions
to classes. David K. Wright, Assistant
to the Vice President for Student
Affairs at Indiana State University,
notes that "faculty involved in the two-
day orientation course [for entering
freshmen] do address the area of academic dishonesty." But schools should go
further, and teachers should discuss in
very specific ways the consequences of
plagiarism as part of the introduction
to any major writing assignment. Many
sites on the Internet now post information that schools across the country
provide to their students: definitions
and clarifications of plagiarism, statements on academic integrity, clarifications of penalties, and so on. Ignoring
the problem or simply complaining about
it in a general way has not helped to
solve it, so perhaps this active approach
will emphasize to students that teachers
are aware of these Internet sources.

In "How Teachers Can Reduce Cheating's Lure," Mark Clayton suggests that

No page number for an e-mail interview

No citation required for summary of general information

teachers "download a few papers, [and] discuss their strengths and weaknesses. Let students know that you know what is out there--and that most of it is not very good." For example, examine the opening sentences of a paper on <u>The Great Gatsby</u>, available through <u>Absolutely Free Online Essays</u>:

An extended example to illustrate the writer's point

1 inch (10-space) indention for a long quotation

> Characters in books can reveal the author feeling toward the world. In The Great Gatsby Fitzgerald suggested the moral decline of the period in American history through the interpersonal relationships among his characters. The book indicates the worthlessness of materialism, the futile quest of Myrtle and Gatsby, and how moral values had diminished. Despite his newly acquired fortune, Gatsby's monitory means could not afford his only true wish, therefore, he cannot buy everything which is important to Daisy. (Fitzgerald, page 42)

Analysis of the
example

A teacher could highlight the numerous problems in this paper: lack of underlining or italics, problems with possessive forms, faulty documentation, comma difficulties (including a comma splice), lack of focus, and other matters. It would be useful for students to see that what is available from the Internet isn't necessarily worth the academic risk. Further, Tom Rocklin, in "Downloadable Term Papers: What's a Prof. to Do?" observes, "it seems unlikely that students will hand in as their own papers downloaded from a site that the instructor has obviously inspected."

Another strategy is to require that work be completed in stages. Rocklin stresses the process of writing the paper, requiring students to turn in topics, outlines, drafts, and revisions, all before submitting their final papers. Working in stages establishes several safeguards. First, it provides teachers with evidence throughout the term of the quality of students' work, and second, it requires students to

begin working early. The second goal
is especially important. Miguel Roig
and Laureen DeTommaso, writing for
Psychological Reports, present these
easy-to-predict research findings: "students who score high on academic pro-
crastination may be more likely to
engage in plagiaristic practices" (694).
Requiring work in stages, then, will not
allow students to delay their work until
they are desperate enough to plagiarize.
Rocklin adds, "If students have been
turning in interim evidence of their
work throughout the semester, they are
less likely to panic at the last
moment."

Yet another technique involves comprehensive evaluation of writing and
research processes, not just papers.
Gary Galles, a professor at Pepperdine
University, suggests that teachers
require "graded oral presentations of
papers, with students required to answer
questions and defend their arguments."
Heyward Ehrlich of Rutgers University
insists that students submit all elements of their research work: "original

Page references
required for print
source

Affiliations
included to
establish
credibility

handwritten notes, marked photocopies or printouts, and copies of all computer disk files." In addition, Ehrlich recommends that teachers refuse to accept papers that have not gone through monitored research procedures since he asserts that "they are much more likely to be plagiarized. Proposals that mysteriously arise from nowhere and reach an unexpected conclusion are to be suspected." This cluster of grading strategies works well with the sequential approach previously noted, providing students with the credit they deserve for learning the research process, as well as for producing the final paper.

Summary, with connection to earlier section

Transition from body of the paper

Although teachers should not assume that all students plagiarize, they cannot afford to believe that no students plagiarize. It becomes important, then, for teachers to take active steps to ensure that the papers they require are the work of the students who will receive the grades. By becoming familiar with Internet sites, discussing issues of plagiarism, and reviewing sample papers, teachers will make students

Summary of major points

aware of the full context in which they work. By dividing writing projects into stages and then grading based on the submitted materials, teachers will ensure that students work within the appropriate contexts.

The Internet brings with it both promises and problems. On the one hand, it allows us to gather information in ways that are, even today, amazing. On the other hand, we have learned that much of what can be gathered is of questionable value or will be put to questionable use. If we are to help future students to make the best use of the technology, we must teach them to use it responsibly. As John N. Hickman notes in "Cybercheats," "To get the benefits of online technology, [schools] have to cope with the costs. The only real solution to cyberplagiarism, then, is old-fashioned vigilance" (15).

Quotation as concluding strategy

Name and page numbers continue on works-cited pages

Heading, centered

The entire list is alphabetized.

Electronic addresses for online sources

Clarifying information within citation

Works Cited

Clayton, Mark. "How Teachers Can Reduce
    Cheating's Lure." <u>Christian Science</u>
    <u>Monitor</u> 27 Oct. 1997. 9 Feb. 1999
    <http://csmonitor.com/durable/1997/
    10/27/feat/learning.3.html>.

Ehrlich, Heyward. "Plagiarism and Anti-
    Plagiarism." 26 Sept. 1998. 11 Feb.
    1999 <http://newark.rutgers.edu/
    ~ehrlich/plagiarism598.html>.

Galles, Gary M. "Copy These Strategies
    to Stop Plagiarism by Students." 28
    Sept. 1997. 12 Feb. 1999 <http://
    www.chron.com/content/chronicle/
    editorial/97/09/28/galles.
    0-0.html>.

"The Great Gatsby." Student Essay.
    <u>Absolutely Free Online Essays</u>. 12
    Feb. 1999 <http://www.elee.calpoly.
    edu/~ercarlso/papers.htm>.

<u>GroupWeb.com.</u> 5 Feb. 1999
    <http://www.groupweb.com/education/
    term_papers.htm>.

Hickman, John N. "Cybercheats."
    <u>New Republic</u> 23 Mar. 1998: 14-15.

Keller, Julia. "Aspects of Ambiguity."
     Chicago Tribune 25 Nov. 1998, sec.
     2: 4-5.

NOTE: First lines
begin at the reg-
ular margin; sub-
sequent lines are
indented.

Mallon, Thomas. Stolen Words: Forays
     into the Origins and Ravages of
     Plagiarism. New York: Ticknor, 1989.

Mano, D. Keith. "The Cheating Industry."
     National Review 5 June 1987: 50-53.

"Plagiarize." The American Heritage
     College Dictionary. 3rd ed. 1993.

Rocklin, Tom. "Downloadable Term Papers:
     What's a Prof. to Do?" Aug. 1996. 5
     Feb. 1999 <http://www.uiowa.edu.80/
     ~centeach/newslet...nline-exclusives/
     term-paper-download.html>.

Roig, Miguel, and Lauren DeTommaso.
     "Are College Cheating and Plagia-
     rism Related to Academic Procrasti-
     nation?" Psychological Reports 77
     (1995): 691-95.

Wice, Nathaniel. "Copy and Paste: Term
     Paper Mills on the Web." Slackers
     and Hackers Jan. 1997. 6 Feb. 1999
     <http://www.zdnet.com/yil/content/
     mag/9701/wice9701.html>.

Wright, David K. E-mail interview. 12
    Feb. 1999 <studavid@amber.
    indstate.edu>.

Zack, Ian. "Universities Finding a
    Sharp Rise in Computer-Aided Cheat-
    ing." New York Times 23 Sept. 1998,
    late ed.: B11.

APPENDIXES

465

APPENDIX A Word Processing and Manuscript Form

Word processing has altered the ways in which people compose. It's that simple. Many people—probably most people—now write at a keyboard, using a word-processing program and taking advantage of the increasing number of features to develop and modify manuscripts of increasing sophistication.

If you are not currently generating your papers using a word processor, consider the ways in which word processing could improve your work.

- **Efficiency.** Although typing at a computer keyboard is no faster than typing at a typewriter, revising a disk version of a manuscript is so much more efficient that, in the entire process of composing, the work is faster.

- **Improved Revision.** Because materials can be saved in an electronic form, you can modify them easily. For example, you can add, delete, move, reformat, and create different versions of materials. The simplicity with which you can perform these operations can enhance your productivity.

- **Effective Storage.** Since today's disks store so much information, you can keep electronic copies of all your written work—even the early stages.

- **Flexibility.** With current software and hardware, you can create alternative versions of your written work which you can use in different ways.

You should, of course, take full advantage of the equipment and the opportunities they provide, but you should also understand some tendencies that follow from the use of word processors.

- **Less Planning.** Since word processors allow you to generate materials quickly, it is easy to step past early, integral stages of planning. Although revision allows you to adjust quickly generated work, effective planning should still precede typing.

- **Lazy Use of Support Features.** The technical support that comes with word-processing programs—spell checkers and grammar checkers in particular—is helpful but limited. You should not expect such features to solve all of your technical troubles. Spell checkers and grammar checkers will highlight potential errors, but *you* must still understand key principles of spelling, grammar, and sentence formation in order to select the correct options wisely.

- **Sophisticated Look.** One advantage that can become a disadvantage is the professional look of word-processed manuscripts. Because printed versions—especially with today's laser and inkjet printers—look so good, it is easy to be satisfied with a paper that is more attractive than it is good.

Even with these potential problems, word processing has enhanced the writing process. You must take advantage of the opportunities while recognizing that you, not the equipment, remain the most important element in the equation.

Features to Explore

Current word-processing programs provide a wide range of features, which will enable you to create manuscripts whose polished appearance will complement your effective presentation of ideas. Take advantage of the full range of features your program provides, these among them.

- **Font Selection.** Fonts (designed versions of letters and numbers) allow you to create different "looks" for your manuscripts. Fonts with serifs (cross marks on the ends of letters) like Times Roman replicate the look of traditional printed materials, while sans serif fonts (those without cross marks on the ends of letters) like Helvetica create the look of technical materials. For most academic writing, select attractive fonts that are not too unusual.

- **Font Size.** Fonts are measured in points, ranging from extremely small (4 points) to extremely large (70 points or larger). For most academic purposes, select fonts between 10 and 14 points in size, with the understanding that 12-point fonts are the most commonly used.

- **Format.** With a word processor, you can select line spacing (single-spacing, space-and-a-half, double-spacing, and others), and you can create headers (information repeated at the top of pages) or footers (information repeated at the bottom of pages). You can select justification patterns: full justification (even margins on both the left and right), flush left (even only on the left side), flush right (even only on the right), or centered (indented on both sides). Word-processing programs also allow you to set margins (usually one or one and one-half inches for academic work); to center titles automatically; to use italics (slanted type), rather than underlining, to identify titles and to create emphasis; and to use boldface for emphasis.

- **Block Indents.** In those instances when you need to set in information from the margins—for example, the ten-space indentions required for quotations—a word processor will allow you to do this automatically, simply by selecting the appropriate key or icon. This feature is especially convenient for researched writing.

- **Cut-and-Paste.** Word processors allow you to block information—a word, a sentence, a paragraph, or a whole section of a paper—and then extract it to move to another area within the same file or in another file. As a writer, you will discover the advantage of this feature during revision, when you want to rearrange material to improve the presentation of your ideas.

- **Copy.** Word processors allow you to block information and, while leaving the original information in the text, copy it to another place in the same file or in another file. This feature is particularly helpful when you want to produce several versions of the same material.

- **Spell Check.** Current word-processing programs include a spell check feature, which can conveniently review your document for obvious errors in spelling and sometimes the repetition of words. When you use this feature, be aware of its limitations. Spell check will not catch a wrong word (for example, *exit* for *exist*) if the word is correctly spelled; spell check will also only include a limited selection of proper nouns and technical language. For these reasons, you must still read your manuscript carefully to ensure that the correct words convey your meaning.

- **Grammar Check.** Many word-processing programs now contain features to check the grammatical correctness of your writing. However, these programs can check grammar in only the most general way. So when using a grammar checker, expect it to draw attention to potential problems but do not expect it to correct your paper. For example, a program may provide this kind of notation: "This sentence may need a verb" or "This word normally appears in plural form," but only you can determine—in the context of your writing—whether your writing is correct or not. However, a grammar checker will isolate possible problems for your consideration—and therein lies its usefulness.

- **Thesaurus.** Many word-processing programs now include a thesaurus, a dictionary of synonyms. Use this electronic resource in the same way you would use a print thesaurus: select *only* words that are part of your writing vocabulary, being especially sensitive to context and connotation.

- **Graphics.** Most systems provide options for creating visual interest in a manuscript—although such features should be used only when they enhance the readability of your work. Consider the use of horizontal and vertical lines to divide elements of your work; use textboxes (lines that surround print material) to draw attention to selected information; use tables and charts and graphs to present technical, statistical information; use graphics features to add accents (é) or diacritical marks (ç).

- **Scanning.** If equipment is available, you can scan illustrations and graphic materials (charts, tables, diagrams, and so on) to incorporate within your text. Having these materials in digital form makes incorporating them easier than it once was, and cut-and-paste features allow you to experiment with their placement within your manuscript.

- **Footnotes.** Most word-processing programs allow you to introduce footnotes in your text when you need to provide clarifications or if you are required to use a documentary style that requires footnotes. When using the footnote feature, simply position the note number in the text, and the program will automatically position the corresponding note at the bottom of the page, with appropriate spacing.

- **Outlining.** Many programs provide options for outlining information. The program, once directed to the outlining feature, will allow you to introduce information, which is then formatted and spaced appropriately.

To take full advantage of word-processing, experiment with the options that are available to you, take a course, or attend a workshop at your campus. Because of their enhanced capabilities, word processors can improve your composing process—but only if you become a fluent user of the technology.

■ Manuscript Preparation

Writers in language-related disciplines should follow these guidelines—based on the principles adopted by the Modern Language Association—for preparing and presenting manuscripts. If a paper or project provides you with special challenges or if you are required to follow other style guidelines, consult with your instructor.

Paper

Use white, medium-weight, 8-1/2-by-11 inch paper. Avoid unusual paper—onion-skin, erasable, or colored paper—for most projects.

Printing Formats

Use the best printer available. Laser or inkjet printers produce the highest-quality printing, but dot-matrix printers are still acceptable, providing that you use the correspondence-quality (double-strike) mode.

Use a standard, nondecorative font (Courier, Times Roman, Helvetica, Palatino, or some other) in a conventional size (12 point is standard, but easily readable fonts may be as small as 10 point or as large as 14 point). Avoid unusual fonts for most academic writing.

Do not justify the right margins of your papers. Such justification creates unusual spaces between words and after punctuation and, consequently, can distort the look of your prose and create inaccuracies in the internal spacing of the works-cited entries of a research paper.

Take advantage of the italics feature of your word processor to set titles, foreign words, and words for emphasis in slanted type when possible. However, since underlining and italics mean the same thing, you may choose to use the underlining feature. Whichever form you choose, be consistent throughout the paper.

Spacing

Double-space everything: the heading, the title (if it requires more than one line), the text, set-in quotations, notes, the works-cited page, and any appended material.

Margins

Leave one-inch margins on the left, right, and bottom of the main text; paging (which appears at the top) determines the top margin (example on page 474). Most word-processing programs have default margins of one inch; if yours does not, reset the margins.

Indent paragraphs one-half inch (five spaces) using the "tab" feature. To indent the second and subsequent lines of works-cited entries, use the "indent" feature of your word processor; this feature will "hold" the one-half inch (five space) indention until you enter a hard return.

Indent set-in quotations one inch (ten spaces), using the "indent" feature; if the indent feature of your word processor works in half-inch (five space) increments, click it twice to achieve the ten spaces. This feature will "hold" the one-inch (ten space) indent until you enter a hard return.

Paging

In the upper-right corner of each page, one half-inch from the top, type your last name, a space, and the page number (without a page abbreviation). Two spaces below, the text of the paper continues (whether it is the heading on the first page or the text on subsequent pages). Word-processing programs provide you with easy-to-set options for creating these headers; check under "format" on the tool bar.

Heading and Title

A paper in MLA style has no separate title page. Instead, in the upper-left corner of the first page, two spaces below the header, type on separate lines your name, your instructor's name, the course number, and the date. Two lines below the date, center the paper's title. Capitalize all important words in the title (see 316–17) but do not italicize it, place it in quotation marks, or follow it with a period. Two lines below the title, begin the first paragraph of the paper.

Tables, Graphs, Charts, Maps, or Illustrations

Place graphic materials—tables, charts, maps, or other illustrations—within the text of your paper, as close as possible to the discussion they illustrate, not at the end of the paper.

A table is a visual presentation of statistical data, generally presented in columns. Label tables with word *Table* (not italicized), the table number and the table title. Type this identifying information above the table and flush with the left margin; you should also set the table flush with the left margin and use horizontal lines, as necessary, to provide clarity. Below the table, introduce the source of the data with the word *Source* (not italicized) and a colon, as in the sample on page 475.

1/2" Clark 1

1"

Nakia Clark

Dr. C. Martin

1"

English 231

10 September 2000

Title of the Paper

1"

1"

1/2" Clark 2

1"

1"

Table 1

Poverty Thresholds in 1998 by Family Size and Number of Children

Size of Family Unit	0 children	1 child	2 children	3 children
One person	8,480			
Two persons	10,915	11,235		
Three persons	12,750	13,120	13,133	
Four persons	16,813	17,088	16,530	16,588
Five persons	20,275	20,570	19,940	19,453
Six persons	23,320	23,413	22,930	22,468
Seven persons	26,833	27,000	26,423	26,020
Eight persons	30,010	30,275	29,730	29,253

Source: United States, Bureau of the Census
<http://www.census.gov/hhes/poverty/threshld/thresh98.html>.

Place graphs, charts, maps, line drawings, photographs, and other illustrations in the paper with descriptive material below the illustration. Type the abbreviation *Fig.* (short for *figure,* not italicized) under the illustration with a number and descriptive title or caption, as in the following sample.

Times Roman	COPPERPLATE GOTHIC
Arial	Courier
Abadi MT Condensed	*Present Bold*
Arrus BT	PMN Caecilia
Book Antiqua	**Verdana**
Century Gothic	*Caflisch Script Semibold*

Fig. 1. Alternative Fonts

Most word-processing programs now include features to create tables, charts, and graphs in a uniform and efficient way. If you are preparing a paper that requires a variety of these illustrations, experiment with these options.

■ Submitting the Paper

Submit manuscripts according to your instructor's directions. If you receive no specific guidelines, secure the pages with a paper clip in the upper-left corner. Place lengthy papers in a 9-by-12-inch manila envelope with your name and course information typed or written on the outside. Always keep a photocopy of the paper before submitting it.

Be aware that instructors may ask for a disk copy of the paper. In that case, submit a copy of the final paper on a separate disk, clearly labeled with your name and course information. Keep a disk version for yourself.

Appendix B APA Documentation Style

In fields such as psychology, education, public health, and criminology, researchers follow the guidelines given in the *Publication Manual of the American Psychological Association*, fourth edition (Washington, DC: APA, 1994) to document their work. Like MLA style (see Chapters 34 and 35), APA style encourages brevity in documentation, uses in-text parenthetical citations of sources, and limits the use of numbered notes and appended materials.

The following information is a brief overview of APA style. If your major or minor requires APA style, you should acquire the APA manual and study it thoroughly.

■ Paper Format

Title Page

Include a descriptive title, your name, and your affiliation (course or university), with two spaces between elements; center this information left to right and top to bottom. In the upper-right corner, include the first few words of the paper's title, followed by five spaces and the page number (without a page abbreviation). Two lines below, at the left margin, type the words *Running head* (not italicized), a colon, and a brief version of the title (no more than fifty letters and spaces) in all capital letters. The title page is always page 1.

Abstract

On a separate page following the title page, type the label *Abstract* (capitalized but not italicized). Two lines below, include a paragraph describing the major ideas in the paper; it should contain no more than 960 characters (including punctuation and spaces).

Introduction

Include a paragraph or series of paragraphs to define the topic, present the hypothesis (or thesis), explain the method of investigation, and state the theoretical implications (or context).

Body

Incorporate a series of paragraphs to describe study procedures, results obtained, and interpretations of the findings.

In-Text Documentation

In parentheses, include the author and date for summaries and paraphrases; include the author, date, and page number for quotations and facts.

List of Sources

Cite sources fully identified in a listing titled "References."

Appendix

Include related materials (charts, graphs, illustrations, and so on) that cannot be incorporated into the body of the paper.

■ Manuscript Format

Fonts

Use any standard font with serifs (cross lines on the ends of individual letters). Sans serif fonts like Helvetica are used only for labeling illustrations, not for text. Underlining is used instead of italics.

Spacing

All elements of the paper are double-spaced.

Margins

Use one-inch margins at the top and bottom and on the left and right. Indent paragraphs five to seven spaces; indent long quotations five spaces.

Paging

Put the first two or three words of the title (no more than fifty letters and spaces) in the upper-right corner; after five spaces, include the page number without a page abbreviation.

Headings

Whenever possible, use headings to label divisions and subdivisions of the paper.

Number Style

Express numbers one through nine in words and all other numbers in numeral form. When numbers are used for comparisons, all must appear in numeral form.

■ Citation Format

The following samples illustrate a number of basic citation forms. If you are using other kinds of sources, consult the APA style guide.

■ Reference List Format

A Book by One Author

        Freemuth, J. C. (1991). <u>Islands under</u>
<u>siege: National parks and the politics of</u>
<u>external threats.</u> Lawrence: University Press of
Kansas.

[Use initials for the author's first name. After the author's name, place the publication date in parentheses, followed by a period. Capitalize only the first word of the title and of the subtitle and any proper nouns and proper adjectives. Spell out the names of university presses. For other publishers, retain only the words *Books* and *Press*.]

A Book by Two or More Authors

> Freedman, D., Pisani, R., Purves, R., & Adhikari, A. (1991). <u>Statistics</u> (2nd ed.). New York: Norton.

[Invert the names of all authors. Insert an ampersand (&) before the last author.]

A Book with an Organization as Author

> American Psychological Association. (1994). <u>Publication manual of the American Psychological Association</u> (4th ed.). Washington, DC: Author.

[When the organization is also the publisher, use the word *Author* (not italicized) in the publisher position.]

A Work in a Collection

> Graham, B. J. (1988). Tall buildings as symbols. In L. S. Beedle (Ed.), <u>Second century of the skyscraper</u> (pp. 117-147). New York: Van Nostrand.

[Do not enclose the title of a short work in quotation marks. *In* introduces its source. Provide the editor's name, the abbreviation *Ed.* (capitalized and placed in parentheses) followed by a comma, the collection title, and inclusive page numbers for the short work (given in parentheses). Abbreviate *pages.*]

An Article in a Monthly Magazine

> Gould, S. J. (1989, March). The wheel of fortune and the wedge of progress. <u>Natural History, 98,</u> 14-21.

[Give the year of publication followed by a comma and the month and day (if any). When appropriate, follow the magazine title with a comma, one space, the volume number, and another comma (all underlined). Do not use a page abbreviation.]

An Article in a Journal with Separate Paging

```
Felix, J. W., & Johnson, R. T. (1993).
Learning from video games. Computers in the
Schools, 9 (2-3), 119-134.
```

[Underline the name of the journal, the comma that follows it, and the volume number. The issue number (or numbers) in parentheses immediately follows the volume number; no space separates them. No abbreviation for pages accompanies the inclusive page numbers. Note that inclusive numbers appear in their full forms.]

An Article in a Newspaper

```
Leatherman, C. (1994, September 28). Free
speech or harassment? The Chronicle of Higher
Education, p. A22.
```

[Invert the date. Do not include information about the edition or section. When sections are indicated by letters, present them along with the page numbers with no intervening space.]

A Lecture or Speech

```
Branch, T. (1992, May 7). Democracy in an
age of denial. Speech presented for the Humani-
ties on the Hill lecture series, Washington, DC.
```

[Underline the title of the speech. Follow the title with the name of the sponsoring organization and the location, separated by commas.]

Nonprint Materials

> Apted, M. (Director). (1994). <u>Nell</u> [Film].
> Beverly Hills: 20th Century-Fox.

[List entries by the name of the most important contributor (director, producer, speaker, and so on); note the specific role in full in parentheses following the name. Identify the medium (film, filmstrip, slide show, tape recording) in brackets after the title. The place of production precedes the name of the production company.]

Electronic Sources

> National Rifle Association of America
> (NRA). (1994). <u>Encyclopedia of associations.</u>
> [CD-ROM]. Available: Gale: Encyclopedia of
> Associations.

[This citation is for a CD-ROM source that is prepared independently from a printed version. Since the materials are arranged in alphabetical order and can be accessed from an electronic index, no item number is required—but a closing period is.]

> Ladew, J. (1995, May 29). Hyperlexia,
> autism, and language [Discussion], [Online].
> Available: Internet Newsgroup
> bit.listserv.autism

[The descriptive title is taken from the "message" line of the electronic correspondence; the date indicates when Ladew's information was posted on the newsgroup.]

■ Text Citation Format

One Author

> Greybowski (1995) noted that . . . .

Or:

In a recent study at USC (Greybowski, 1995),
participants were asked to . . . .

Multiple Authors: First Citation

Cadrillo, Thurgood, Johnson, and Lawrence (1967)
found in their evaluation . . . .

Multiple Authors: Subsequent Citations

Cadrillo et al. (1967) also discovered . . . .

Corporate Authors: First Citation

. . . a close connection between political
interests and environmental issues (Council on
Environmental Quality [CEQ], 1981).

Corporate Authors: Subsequent Citations

. . . in their additional work (CEQ, 1981).

■ Quotations Within the Text

First Option

She stated, "The cultural awareness of a student
depends, by implication, on the cultural awareness of the parents" (Hermann, 1984, p. 219).

Second Option

Hermann (1984) added that "enrichment in our
schools is costly and has little bearing on the
later lives of the students" (pp. 230-231).

text

Third Option

"A school's responsibility rests with providing
solid educational skills, not with supplementing
the cultural education of the uninterested,"
stated Hermann (1984) in her summary (p. 236).

A required title
page
Short title and
page number

Identification of
the running head

Running head: MUSIC THERAPY

Identifying
information,
centered on the
page

Music Therapy: An Art of Communication

Shingo Endo

Indiana State University

The abstract is
labeled.

Abstract

A required
abstract of no
more than 960
characters

Although many people realize that music alters moods, they do not realize that it provides useful treatment for mentally and physically impaired people.

Beginning in ancient times, music has been used for therapy. In the twentieth century--especially in the United States--music has been used to alter moods and influence behavior. Currently, music therapy is used to treat patients with schizophrenia, Alzheimer's disease, autism, and asocial behaviors. Studies indicate that further uses will be found for music therapy in treating various disorders.

Music Therapy: An Art of Communication

For many people, listening to their favorite music at the end of a busy day or going to a concert on a weekend is an essential aspect of their lives. Most people know that being involved with music, either playing or listening, is a rewarding and pleasurable experience because music relieves stress effectively.

However, it is often forgotten, or not known, that beyond its entertainment value music has a salutary effect on people with illness and distress, a fact once underestimated by mainstream medicine (Weiss, 1994, p. WH11). In the United States, so many people think of music as a mood modifier that this view overshadows the medical effects of music (Weiss, 1994, p. WH11). Yet because music possesses a power to reach a level of awareness that goes beyond verbal and physical communication, it offers important treatment for mentally or physically impaired people.

The text of the paper begins on page 3.
Title, centered

Citation with no previous mention of author

Music Therapy 4

Music therapy, though itself a
rather new medical discipline, can be
traced back to 1500 BC in Egypt, where
magicians used sound and music to communicate directly with what they believed
to be the evil spirits in a patient's
body (Alvin, 1966, <u>Music Therapy</u>,
pp. 21–23). Later, the Greeks developed
a systematic use of music to alleviate
disorder, and now they are most often
regarded as the founders of music therapy (Bunt, 1994, p. 10). However, it was
not until after World War II that doctors began sustained and rigorous experimentation in music therapy (Bunt, 1994,
p. 11).

Two early, successful examples of
music therapy in the United States are
worth noting. One is the result of concerts by community music groups. When
groups performed in hospitals for
injured veterans of World War II, staff
noted that many patients responded to
the music and "perked up and got better"
(Weiss, 1994, p. WH11). And in 1959,
dentists first used music as a way to

A citation for one
of several
sources by a
single author

minimize pain during surgery--a technique that allowed them to use lower

Citation for coau-thored source

dosages of nitrous oxide when treating
their patients (Scofield & Teich, 1987,
p. 70). Since then, hundreds of research
studies have demonstrated the positive
effects of music on a wider range of
symptoms, and research has helped to
establish music therapy as a behavioral
science (Bunt, 1994, p. 11).

Yet a central question remains:
What, then, is music therapy? It is
self-explanatory that therapists use
music to heal people--but how? In what
situations? And how effective is it?
These factors are less known.

Underlining, not italics, is used in APA style.

Awakenings, a popular film based
on the writings of neurologist Oliver
Sacks, presents the lives of post-
encephalitic patients, who were cata-
tonic as well as partially paralyzed, in
a mental ward in the 1960s. In one
scene, an elderly female patient, who is
otherwise immobile, reacts to a recording of an aria from La Bohème. At first,
her eyes are unfocused, but gradually

they narrow, and as the melody reaches
its familiar climax, the patient appears
to be in a state of catharsis. As a further experiment with music therapy, a
male nurse plays big-band music for
elderly patients as an accompaniment to
their meals. The music provides a stimulus for the patients and somehow prompts
them to begin eating on their own. The
charge nurse later reports to the doctor: "It's not just any music; it has to
be music that's right for them"

A film, cited by
director
(Marshall, 1990). These examples, from a
well-known film, only hint at the uses
of music therapy.

Juliette Alvin, a renowned British
music therapist, explains that severely
regressed patients, with whom contact is
difficult, sometimes react when they
hear music that was recorded when they
were young (Alvin, 1961, Introduction,
p. 7). And Florence Tyson (1981), in
Psychiatric Music Therapy: Origins and
Development, says that music is "especially effective as a psychological
stimulus in a total hospital environment
when used as an accompaniment to meals,

When the author is mentioned in the text, only the page is required.

calisthenics, and remedial exercises" (p. 8).

During the years from 1950 to 1970, many state mental hospitals had full-scale music programs, incorporating activities such as these:

Long quotes are double-spaced and idented five spaces.

> small orchestra, band, chamber music, chorus; music-listening appreciation; ward and auditorium concerts; musical quiz, variety and talent shows; staging of Broadway-type musicals; individual music study, including creative musical writing; folk and square dancing, religious choir, holiday pageants; maintenance of musical instruments, construction of simple instruments; maintenance of representative library records. (Tyson, 1981, p. 12)

Note following closing punctuation

Larol Merle-Fishman, a New York music therapist, states in The Music within You, that "either playing an instrument or joining a singing group builds confidence, nurtures creative self-expression, and helps you to under-stand who you are" (Scofield & Teich,

1987, p. 76). Tyson (1981) describes a range of patients' responses to those activities: "clapping hands, sudden smiling, humming, singing or dancing, which often provided the opening toward contact with reality and resocialization" (p. 9).

[End of excerpt.]

Heading,
centered

References

The entire list is
alphabetized.

Alvin, J. (1961). Introduction to
music therapy. London: The Society for
Music and Remedial Music.

Alvin, J. (1966). Music therapy.
New York: Basic Books.

Bunt, L. (1994). Music therapy: an
art beyond words. London: Routledge.

Article title with-
out quotation
marks

Hardie, A. (1994, March 12). Old
songs strike right note. The Atlanta
Journal and Atlanta Constitution,
p. El.

Clarifying infor-
mation in paren-
theses and
brackets

Marshall, P. (Director). (1990).
Awakenings. [Film]. Burbank, CA: Columbia.

Michel, D. (1976). Music therapy:
an introduction to therapy and special
education through music. Springfield,
IL: Thomas.

Milloy, C. (1992, February 9).
"A healing force in London prison."
The Washington Post, p. C3.

Both authors'
names are
inverted.

Nordoff, P., & Robbins, C. (1968).
Improvised music as therapy for autistic
children. In E. Gaston (Ed.), Music

Running head on
reference pages

Music Therapy   10

therapy (pp. 191-193). New York:

Macmillan.

Priestley, M. (1975). Music therapy

in action. New York: St. Martin's.

Scofield, M., & Teich, M. (1987).

Mind-bending music. Health, 19, 69-76.

Spender, N. (1980). Music therapy.

In S. Sadie (Ed.), The New Grove

dictionary of music and musicians.

Tyson, F. (1981). Psychiatric

music therapy: origins and development.

New York: Creative Arts Rehabilitation

Center.

Weiss, R. (1994, July 5). Music

therapy: doctors explore the healing

potential of rhythm and song. The

Washington Post, pp. WH11-12.

Pages are not
required for ref-
erences that are
alphabetized.

APPENDIX C Essay Exams

To study for an essay exam, reread course materials, review important concepts, and memorize specific information related to major topics. This work is best done over a period of days or weeks.

When writing the exam, consider the following strategies for producing effective responses.

■ Point Values

Apportion the time you spend writing responses according to their point values. For instance, a question worth ten points out of a possible one hundred deserves no more than ten percent of the total exam time for your response; a question worth fifty points out of one hundred is worth half of the exam time.

■ Multiple Questions

To respond to two or more essay questions, pace your writing. Decide, on the basis of point values, how much time each question deserves and write accordingly. An extended response to one question worth ten points and a brief, superficial response to another worth ten points may yield only fifteen points, whereas balanced discussions of both questions would probably yield more total points.

■ Optional Topics

When given alternative questions, construct a brief topic outline for each choice to see which essay would be most substantial. A few moments spent outlining will help you to select the questions to which you can respond most completely and effectively.

■ Careful Reading

Many essay questions provide an implied topic sentence for a paragraph-length essay or a thesis statement for a longer essay. Focus your work by developing the idea presented in the question. Follow instructions carefully. Describe, illustrate, compare, contrast, evaluate, analyze, and so on according to instructions.

■ Style and Technical Matters

To guarantee that responses are, as much as possible, grammatically correct, well worded, complete, and free from errors in punctuation and mechanics, adjust your writing strategies. Either write slowly—to make your sentences clear, complete, and free from errors in a first draft—or allow time to make corrections and revisions after you have written your response. For either approach, pacing is crucial.

■ Organization and Development

A response to an essay question is like a brief paper: It should include an introduction, a body, and a conclusion, although the development and length of each part will depend on the question and its point value. A ten-point and a fifty-point essay on the same question would share the same structure *but* would require very different degrees of development.

Before an essay exam, review the patterns of development in Chapter 4 (description, examples, facts, comparison and contrast, analogy, cause and effect, process analysis, classification, and definition). Recognize the explicit or implicit patterns required by different kinds of questions.

Varied Organization

For an illustration of how the organizational pattern of an essay question response varies with the form of the question, examine the following topic outlines. The first question implicitly requires a comparison and contrast structure. The second explicitly requires an analysis structure.

Question

Which is the more effective: the personal interview or the e-mail interview?

Introduction (thesis): Although each has its strengths, the e-mail interview is more convenient for busy people.

I. Personal interview

    A. Special time

    B. Specific place

    C. Flexible questioning

    D. Interaction

II. E-mail interview

    A. Any time

    B. Any place

    C. Less flexible questioning

    D. Less interaction

Conclusion: E-mail interviews have some problems, but they are best for busy people.

Question

In what ways are nonverbal signals important in spoken communication?

Introduction (thesis): Because nonverbal signals influence listeners, sometimes positively and sometimes negatively, speakers should avoid extreme nonverbal signals.

I.   Gestures

    A. Too few

    B. Too many

II. Facial expressions

    A. Immobile

    B. Too animated

III. Body movement

    A. Statuelike

    B. Too dramatic

III. Tone of voice

    A. Monotone

    B. Overly theatrical

<u>Conclusion:</u> By being aware of extreme nonverbal signals, speakers can improve the effectiveness of their communication.

Degree of Development

For an illustration of the similar structures but different degrees of development of essay responses with different point values, examine the following samples prepared as part of an hour-long exam.

Question

As a writer, what concerns should you have as you analyze your audience?

Ten-point response

Analyzing your audience is important as you plan a paper because what you discover about the audience will determine, to some degree, what you include and how you include it. For example, you should try to determine the audience's age and probable level of education. Additionally, you should consider the experiences and interests of the audience. And finally, you should consider the audience's probable language preferences. By thinking about these issues and adjusting what you write, you can present a paper that will meet your readers' needs.

Forty-point response

Deciding on your role and purpose is important when planning a paper because those two activities will make you self-aware. But because what you write is intended for readers, analyzing your audience is also important as you plan a paper. What you discover from an analysis of your audience will determine, to some degree, what you include and how you include it.

First, you should try to determine the audience's age. Although people cannot be categorized by age alone, certain patterns are predictable. If you're writing about music for an older audience, Frank Sinatra would likely be a better choice than the Beastie Boys.

Second, you should think about the audience's probable level of education. If you're writing a paper on standardized tests, someone who's been to college will have taken several and will understand the procedures you describe, whereas someone who's only finished high school may not have taken the standardized tests you discuss.

Third, you should consider the audience's experience. If you want to write about dog sledding, you should determine whether your reading audience may have been dogsledding or have even read about dog sledding. If you decide they haven't, then you will need to describe equipment and explain procedures carefully.

Fourth, you should consider the audience's interests. Although it's sometimes hard to tell what audiences may or may not care about, making a reasonable guess is a good idea. If you decide that your audience will want to read about your subject of fly fishing, then you can build on that interest; if you decide they will not, then you need to find another topic.

Finally, you should think about the audience's probable language preferences. Some readers like informal language patterns while others prefer more traditional patterns. If your audience is the more traditional sort, you'll want to avoid contractions, slang, fragments (even intentional ones), and other questionable language patterns.

By thinking about these issues and adjusting what you write and how you write it, you can present a paper that will meet your readers' needs. After all, if you are taking the time to plan, draft, and revise a paper, it's a good idea to consider the person or people who will read and, you hope, enjoy it.

■ Timed Practice

Before writing an essay exam, practice composing under time pressure. Using notes from class, write and respond to sample essay questions. Use a timer and write several practice responses over several days' time. Practice will quicken your writing pace while also helping you to study for the exam.

APPENDIX D Business Writing

■ The Résumé

A résumé is a brief listing of important information about your academic credentials, work experience, and personal achievements. The title *Résumé, Curriculum Vitae,* or *Data Sheet* may, but does not have to, appear as a heading at the top of the page. A résumé is commonly submitted with a job application letter to obtain an interview and is sometimes submitted with admissions or scholarship applications, funding requests, project proposals, and annual personnel reports and in other situations when you need to document your accomplishments.

Begin work on a résumé by analyzing your goals and background and by gathering pertinent information. Modify the format and content of the samples shown in Figures 1 and 2 to emphasize your individual strengths.

Sections

HEADING.   Center your name at the top of the page. Use capitals, underlining, italics, boldface, or a special font to make your name stand out.

ADDRESS.   List your current mailing address in standard postal form, including zip code; your full phone number, including area code; and an electronic-mail address or a fax number. If you expect to change addresses soon, or if you spend time in two places (such as at college and at home), include both addresses and indicate when you use each.

PERSONAL INFORMATION.   Include information on age, marital status, health, height, weight, and so on *only* if it in some way is pertinent to your objective (for example, if the job has requirements about physical size such as those for a police officer or flight attendant).

STATEMENT OF OBJECTIVES. When applying for a specific position or purpose, state your immediate objectives and long-range goals. This statement serves as the "thesis" for the résumé, and all information should be relevant to your objective. Include the job title(s) of the position(s) you are seeking, the types of skills you possess or the types of duties you can perform, and your career goals. If the purpose of the résumé is simply to list information, the statement of your career objective may be omitted.

EDUCATION. Students or recent students with little work experience generally describe their education before their work experience. Specify degrees, majors, minors, names and locations of schools, month and year of graduation (your anticipated date of graduation is acceptable), and grade point average. If you have a college degree, you need not mention high school unless you did exceptionally well (such as being class valedictorian) or the school is prestigious or might interest the employer for some other reason (because it is in the same city, for instance).

List honors and awards either with education or in a separate section for emphasis. In addition, you can include extracurricular activities, internships, co-op training, observation programs, conference workshops, and so on.

WORK EXPERIENCE. Describe work experience either before or after education, depending on the emphasis you want to create. Arrange work experience either chronologically (to show progress or promotion) or in descending order of importance. List job titles, names of businesses or organizations (including the military), locations (not necessarily full addresses), dates of employment, and duties. Provide specific details about relevant skills you possess—including technical skills such as methods (double-entry accounting) and equipment (computers) used. If your work experience is not directly relevant to the objective of your application, mention responsibilities and accomplishments involving such general skills as communication, leadership, organization, problem solving, and money handling.

ACTIVITIES, INTERESTS, AND HOBBIES.   Include memberships in professional, fraternal, and community organizations; mention special participation, contributions, and official positions. List your involvement in organized sports, challenging hobbies, reading preferences, and cultural interests if they demonstrate your habits and character.

REFERENCES.   List two to four recent employers and teachers who are willing to describe your qualifications and recommend your work. Supply their full names, titles, work addresses, phone numbers, and electronic-mail addresses. Secure their permission before using them as references.

If you do not want to list your references on the résumé (perhaps because of limited space), note that references are available upon request.

Format

LENGTH.   For most purposes, limit your résumé to one page. If you must go to a second page, arrange the information so that you have two full and evenly balanced pages, not a full first page and half of a second page.

GENERAL APPEARANCE.   Make the résumé attractive, balanced, and scannable. Use consistent indentation, alignment, capitalization, boldface, underlining, parentheses, and other devices that identify similar kinds and levels of information. Use lists and columns, but make minimal use of patterns that create obvious vertical lines. Leave at least one-inch margins and double-space between sections, avoiding blocks of "white space" (large unused areas).

HEADINGS.   Use clear, descriptive headings for each section. Position the main headings at the left margin or center them.

Subheadings can further indicate and emphasize areas of special interest, but too many levels of headings may make the résumé look choppy.

ARRANGEMENT.   Arrange the sections and the items within each section in a logical and emphatic order. Chronological order is appropriate when you have only a few items to mention (two part-time jobs, for instance). Reverse chronological order is effective when you have many degrees, experiences, or activities to present—especially if the most recent ones are the most important. Alphabetical order might be useful for listing references, organizations, and courses.

STYLE.   Abbreviate sparingly, using only standard abbreviations (such as two-letter abbreviations for state names in addresses) and acronyms (such as professional organizations). Use active verb phrases. Instead of saying, "I was responsible for training new crew members," you need only write "Trained new crew members."

Typing

PRINTING.   Use a word processor and print the final résumé on a laser printer if possible. Use a standard font (Times Roman or Helvetica) in 10–12 point size. Single-space within and double-space between sections.

Photocopying

Have high-quality photocopies made at a reliable copy shop. Consider having your résumé copied on fluorescent white bond paper, "parchment" paper, or some other special-purpose paper so that it will be distinctive. Spending a little extra money may be worth the investment.

Figure 1. Standard Résumé Format

SANDRA K. BOYER

Present Address

363 Maehling Terrace
Alton, IL 62002
(618) 465-7061
E-mail: sboyer@coral.freemont.edu

After May 15, 2000

431 N. Seventh St.
Waterloo, IL 62298
(618) 686-2324

CAREER OBJECTIVE

Music teacher and orchestra director, eventually leading to work as a music
program coordinator for a school district.

EDUCATION

Bachelor of Science in Education : May 2000. Freemont College, Alton, IL.
Major: Music education. Minors: Music theory and business. G.P.A.: 3.87 on a
4.0 scale. Alpha Alpha Alpha, music honorary society (secretary, 1999-2000).
Division 1 Ratings : violin, viola, clarinet; Division 2 Ratings : cello, oboe

MUSICAL EXPERIENCE

Waterloo Community Orchestra (1994-1996): first violin, 1996; 10-17 performances each year, Waterloo Arts Festival; classical and popular music
Waterloo Community String Ensemble (1996): coordinator; 8 performances each
year. Waterloo Arts Festival; classical music
Freemont College Orchestra (1997-present): second violin, 1997-1998; first
violin, 1998-present; student conductor, 2000; 10-20 performances each year;
conducted 3 concerts; classical and popular music

WORK EXPERIENCE

Appointment secretary and sales clerk. Carter's Music Shop, Waterloo, IL
(1996-1997): coordinated 65 lessons each week; demonstrated and sold instruments and music. Sales clerk. Hampton Music, Alton, IL (1997-present):
demonstrated and sold instruments and music

REFERENCES

Available upon request from the Career Center, Freemont College, Alton, IL
62002, (618) 461-6299, extension 1164; file #39261

Figure 2. Alternate Résumé Format

RÉSUMÉ

Sandra K. Boyer

Address

School: Home:
363 Maehling Terrace   431 N. Seventh St.
Alton, IL 62002   Waterloo, IL 62298
School phone: Home phone:
(618) 465-7061   (618) 686-2324
E-mail: sboyer@coral.freemont.edu

EDUCATION

1992-1996: Benjamin Thomas High School, Waterloo, IL
1996-2000: Freemont College, Alton, IL
           Major: Music education. Minors: Music theory and business

EXTRACURRICULAR ACTIVITIES

1992-1996: Benjamin Thomas High School Orchestra (1st violin, 1994-1996)
           Benjamin Thomas High School String Ensemble (student coordinator,
           1994-1996)
1996-2000: Freemont College Orchestra (2nd violin, 1997-1998; 1st violin,
           1998-present; student conductor, 2000), Alpha Alpha Alpha, music
           honorary society (secretary, 1999-2000)

WORK EXPERIENCE

1996-1997: Carter's Music Shop, Waterloo, IL 62298; part-time appointment
           secretary and sales clerk
1997:   Hampton Music, Alton, IL 62002 (837 Telegraph and Alton Square
           shops); sales clerk

REFERENCES

Dr. Glendora Kramer, Professor of Music and Orchestra Director, Freemont
  College, Alton, IL 62002, (618) 461-6299, extension 2110,
  <gkramer@music.freemont.edu>
Mr. Philip Sheldon, Manager, Hampton Music, 837 Telegraph, Alton, IL 62002,
  (618) 466-6311, <psheldon@hampmus.com>
Mrs. Rhonda Travis, Music Instructor, Benjamin Thomas High School, Waterloo,
  IL 62298, (618) 686-5534, <r_travis@bthomashs.edu>

■ Business Letters

Although business letters differ from papers in format and purpose, they should be clearly organized, carefully written, and support a thesis.

When writing business letters, be sensitive to tone. In most instances, a moderate tone, formal but friendly, will work best.

The following sample, in block style, illustrates a form appropriate for most purposes.

your address	363 Maehling Terrace Alton, IL 62002
date	March 20, 2000
inside address	Dr. Geoffrey Timmons, Chairperson Department of Music Carlson University Springfield, IL 62710
salutation	Dear Dr. Timmons:
introductory paragraph: (why you're writing)	Through the Career Center at Freemont College, I learned that you are looking for an Assistant in Music Pedagogy. Because I have enjoyed working both with music and with young children, I would like to be considered for that position.
body paragraph or paragraphs: (appropriate details and information; descriptions and explanations)	In May 2000, I will receive a Bachelor of Science in Education degree, with a major in Music Education and minors in Music Theory and Business. Through my course work, my field work, and my extracurricular experiences, I have had many opportunities to work with young students. During my student teaching, for example, I taught general music classes (ninth through twelfth grades), as well as directed the student string ensemble. In addition, as part of my

work as student conductor of the
Freemont College Orchestra, I participated in several workshops for young
students. A review of my enclosed résumé
will show my long-standing interest in
music and music education.

closing
paragraph:
(other-useful
information)

If you feel that my qualifications satisfy your needs, I would be pleased to
meet with you for an interview at your
convenience. I can be reached at my
school address until May 15, after which
I can be reached at my home address. My
complete credentials (transcripts and
letters of recommendation) are available
through the Career Center (618-461-
6299), file number 39261.

Thank you for your consideration.

closing

signature

typed name

Sincerely,

Sandra K. Boyer

Sandra K. Boyer

■ Envelope Format

Sandra K. Boyer
363 Maehling Terrace
Alton, IL 62002

Dr. Geoffrey Timmons, Chairperson
Department of Music
Carlson University
Springfield, IL 62704

APPENDIX E Writing about Literature

▪ Preparing to Write

Preparing to write can be just as important as actually writing the paper. Good preparation simplifies the writing process and helps you to write a better paper.

Choosing What to Write About

Not everyone responds to every literary work in the same way. You will like some pieces but not others, and some works will leave you ambivalent. Acknowledging these mixed reactions, most teachers will allow you to select authors, literary works, and topics to write about.

However, even when you have been assigned a specific author or literary work, certain aspects of that author's writing or certain elements within the work are likely to appeal to you. Those features could become the basis for a well-focused paper about literature.

Reading Critically

Once you have chosen an author or a literary work about which to write, you need to read critically, looking for material that seems especially meaningful or significant.

MARKING PASSAGES.   Underline passages that seem significant and make notes in the margins as you proceed. This method keeps the work and your notations about it directly linked.

USING INDEX CARDS.   Use index cards to record meaningful and significant details and your responses to them. Include page or line number notations on each card for later reference.

PHOTOCOPYING.   Photocopy selected pages of a work for reference and make notes on the photocopied sheets, rather than in the book itself.

As you read critically and make notes—in whatever form suits your needs—look at traditional elements of literary analysis. These basic elements will provide you with a focus, but also note anything else that interests you:

• language	• tone
• symbolism	• dialogue
• irony	• character
• structure	• description
• plot movement	• setting
• imagery	• theme development

It is better to mark a passage when you first read it than to hunt later for something that you vaguely remember. Also, while examining your notations, you may find the way to proceed with your paper.

■ Approaches

Having chosen a literary work and having read it critically, determine the approach you will take in writing about it. Most literary essays fall into one of three categories: explication, analysis, or comparison/contrast.

Although the approaches differ, all have one element in common: they demonstrate your assessment of how the author has presented his or her work.

Asking yourself a series of questions based on the list of literary elements previously noted will help you discover what you want to discuss and how you want to discuss it.

1. How has the author used **language** (word choice, connotation, figures of speech) to express his or her meaning?

2. Does the author use **symbols** in a unique or interesting way?

3. How has the author used **irony** to express his or her meaning?

4. How does the **structure** of the work affect its meaning?

5. How is the **tone** of the work significant to the reader's understanding of the message?

6. How is **dialogue** used to express the action or meaning?

7. What is particularly significant about the **characters** and **characterization?**

8. How does the author use **description** to convey his or her message?

9. Through what means does the author develop the **plot** of the work?

10. What **images** in the work are particularly notable?

11. How is **setting** used in the work?

12. What is the **theme** of the work? Is there more than one major theme?

13. How do any or all of these elements work together to create the author's **meaning?**

Explication

An **explication essay** requires that the writer explain a meaning or meanings in a work of literature. An essay based on this approach moves carefully through a work of literature—most often a poem—line by line or sometimes passage by passage, calling attention to details and noting the developing meaning.

Because explication concentrates on detail, it generally is not the best approach to use when writing about entire short stories, novels, or plays, unless you focus on selected passages or scenes.

Because explication involves explaining and analyzing, its organization should follow the organization of the work: start at the beginning of the work or passage and proceed to the end.

Analysis

An **analysis essay** looks not at the entire work but rather at how the author has used one or several elements to create meaning.

Two basic methods of organization work well and can be easily modified to suit the purpose of the paper.

ONE-ELEMENT ORGANIZATION. The writer discusses the ways in which one important element or technique is used to develop the work.

SEVERAL-ELEMENTS ORGANIZATION. The writer discusses several elements or techniques that the author uses to develop the work.

*Comparison/Contrast**

A **comparison-contrast essay** may show how two subjects are alike (compare), how two subjects are different (contrast) or how two subjects are both alike and different (compare-contrast).

An essay based on this approach may deal with two subjects within one literary work, two or more works with the same subject or theme, two or more works by the same author, and so on.

Begin by identifying several ways in which the subjects can be compared or contrasted. It is important to identify clearly the manner in which the subjects will be compared or contrasted. Otherwise, your discussion may go off in too many directions and be confusing to the reader.

Then consider which of the following two patterns of comparison-contrast will best suit your purpose.

WHOLE-TO-WHOLE METHOD. Using this organization, a writer first discusses one of the subjects under consideration according to the identified points of comparison-contrast and then discusses the second subject according to the same points.

---

* A more complete discussion, with sample paragraphs, appears on pages 73–74.

PART-TO-PART METHOD. Using this organization, a writer discusses each point of comparison-contrast, giving examples from the two subjects.

Although one approach should provide the basic structure for your paper, remember that these basic patterns overlap. A comparison-contrast paper may include explication as well as some analysis, and an analysis paper may include explication and comparison-contrast.

■ The Structure

A paper about literature, like any other type of essay, has a three-part structure: (1) an introduction with a thesis statement, (2) a body made up of several supporting paragraphs, and (3) a conclusion. By asking yourself a series of questions, you can ensure that your paper will have a clear and effective organization.

The Introduction and Thesis Statement

1. Have I opened my discussion with an introductory strategy that leads to my thesis statement?

2. Does my introduction explicitly identify the work of literature to be discussed and its author?

3. Does my introduction narrow the focus, directing readers' attention to a clear and narrow thesis statement?

The Body

1. Have I selected an appropriate number of main points to support my thesis effectively?

2. Have I provided clear and sufficient support for my thesis in each body paragraph?

3. Are my paragraphs coherent?

4. Has each body paragraph explained (explication), analyzed (analysis), or compared or contrasted (comparison-contrast) the work(s) or author(s) under discussion, according to the approach I have selected?

5. Have I supported the topic of each paragraph with material from the work(s) under discussion?

6. Does the body of my paper have continuity, and does it flow logically from one point to the next, employing clear transitions?

The Conclusion

1. Do I summarize in some fashion the general idea of my thesis?

2. Have I used a concluding strategy to draw my discussion to a close?

■ Quotation and Documentation

Literary papers are most often presented in MLA documentation style, the style treated in Chapters 34 and 35 (pages 390–463). Before writing a literary paper, you should first read those chapters and learn the principles they explain.

Writing about literature, however, incorporates several special principles that require particular attention:

VERB TENSE: Discussions of literature use the present tense in order to indicate that the circumstances depicted in the literature always exist in the present.

> In Hurston's <u>Their Eyes Were Watching God,</u> Janie at first *lives* a life determined by other people and then, in rebellion, *chooses* the path she *wants* to follow.

QUOTATIONS: Because works of literature generally use language so effectively, you should quote from the original text whenever possible to let the author's words help to make your point. Summaries work well for explaining plot developments, and paraphrases can effectively present simple ideas. But when ideas and impressions depend on subtleties of language, you should use the author's own words. Importantly, however, you should not simply quote a line or passage and expect readers to understand your point automatically. Rather, you should first introduce the quotation and direct your reader's attention; then, after the quotation, you should provide a brief analysis of, not merely a restatement of, the quotation.

DOCUMENTATION: Different genres require different citation patterns. Familiarize yourself with the important differences (see also Chapters 34 and 35).

Prose   (short fiction, essays, and novels) requires citation by page number only.

> Poe's narrator observes, "It is impossible to say how first the idea entered my brain; but once conceived, it haunted me day and night" (37).

Poetry   (both brief and long) requires citation by line number only.

> Frost's use of sound repetitions is easily illustrated by these lines: "The only other sound's the sweep / Of easy wind and downy flake" (11–12).

Drama   (both brief and long, classic and contemporary) requires citation by act and scene. If a play is written in verse, as many classic plays are, they also require line numbers.

> A desperate, ordinary man, Willy Loman asserts his imagined uniqueness: "I am not a dime a dozen! I am Willy Loman, and you are Biff Loman" (2.1421).

> Hamlet's now-famous musings include "There are more things in heaven and earth, Horatio, / Than are dreamt of in your philosophy" (1.5.166–67).

■ **Student Paper**

Christin Scott

Dr. Perrin

English 308

January 22, 1999

Definition or Defamation of Character

F. Scott Fitzgerald's novel The Great Gatsby
(New York: Scribner-Simon, 1992) is, in many
ways, an American novel of the times. It is a
characterization of the twenties in all their
gore and glory, replete with dominant stereo-
types--judge, bully, dreamer, downtrodden, social
climber, ice queen, and flibbertigibbet. Though
all of the characters seem to have had equal
introduction by the end of the second chapter,
Tom Buchanan alone has his fate as a character
sealed. His characterization, at this point, is
the only one accomplished through his own
actions as much as through dialogue and description. The most revealing aspect of Tom's characterization is its general consistency. Unlike
the slowly developing, fluid introductions of
the other characters, there is no question about
the road Tom walks: each description and deed
supports the image Fitzgerald builds of this
brutally fractious wastrel.

Scott 2

    The narrator Nick provides the initial image
of Tom Buchanan. Nick first implies that Tom is
someone to be pitied, a man who "drifted here
and there unrestfully [. . .] forever seeking a
little wistfully for the dramatic turbulence of
some irrecoverable football game" (10). This
anticlimactic life is in direct contradiction to
Nick's physical description of Tom--a man with a
"cruel body," a voice expressive of his irrita-
ble nature who, like the "valley of ashes," is
dominated by "two shining, arrogant eyes [. . .
giving] him the appearance of always leaning
aggressively forward" (11). Near the end of the
first chapter, Nick states that he is less surprised by Tom's affair than he is that Tom has
"been depressed by a book [. . .] making him
nibble at the edge of stale ideas as if his
sturdy physical egotism no longer nourished his
peremptory heart" (25). Nick's ironic interpretation of Tom's behavior is worth noting, but
Tom's unrest seems to lie beyond ideas, perhaps
in his inability to control all of the world
around him.

    Tom's need for control is further exempli-
fied in Daisy's accusatory comments about him.
When Daisy accuses Tom of being "a brute of a
man, a great big hulking physical specimen," his

only reply is, "I hate the word hulking" (16).
That Tom does not also reject the term <u>brute</u>
implies that he both acknowledges and accepts
his aggressive nature. When Daisy pouts about
Tom "<u>getting</u> profound" due to reading "deep
books with long words in them," she unknowingly
asserts how unaccustomed he is to thought in
contrast to action (17).

Yet Tom's actions--toward Daisy and the
other characters--truly clarify that others' comments about him are accurate. Tom shows his need
to control people and to be the center of attention by cutting Daisy off in midconversation
(14). Similarly, he interrupts George Wilson,
his mistress' husband, and establishes his dominance over him when he says, "If you feel that
way about it, maybe I'd just better sell [the
car] somewhere else after all" (29). So, too,
Tom's control has already begun to envelop Nick,
who reports: "He jumped to his feet and taking
hold of my elbow, literally forced me from my
car. [. . .] 'I want you to meet my girl' "
(28). The aggressiveness implied by Tom's leaving the train is boldly explicit by the end of
the second chapter. Nick describes a disagree-
ment between Tom and his mistress Myrtle, which
ended abruptly: "Making a short deft movement,

Tom Buchanan broke [Myrtle's] nose with his open hand" (41).

Ultimately, however, Tom's selfish brutality goes beyond his obvious characterization. It is not necessarily the fact that Tom has a mistress, since this was a common practice for men of his class during the period. Rather, the cruelty lies in the fact that Daisy knows that he has a mistress and that his mistress' calls are accepted during a traditional family time. Tom's treatment of his mistress' husband George is also extremely callous; it is a game of dark humor for Tom to stroll into the garage to arrange a meeting with Myrtle right in front of her husband. But perhaps the most unsettling display of Tom's brutish control is the way in which he both expects and undervalues his "ownership" of Daisy and Myrtle: Daisy is the silent, respectable jewel that shines in his crown. Myrtle, on the other hand, is his pet--the playful pup begging for scraps whom Tom kicks when she gets too close to his table. By the conclusion of the second chapter, Fitzgerald has created in Tom Buchanan a truly despicable man, one whose darkness is revealed through both his words and his deeds.

■ **Literary Terms**

Allusion   A reference to another work of art, a person, or an event.

Analysis   A method by which a subject is separated into its elements as a means of understanding the whole.

Character   An imagined person appearing in a work of fiction, poetry, or drama.

Characterization   The method by which characters in a work of literature are made known to the reader.

Comparison   A discussion concerning how two or more persons or things are alike.

Conflict   A struggle among opposing forces in a literary work.

Connotation   The set of implications and associations that a word carries in addition to its literal meaning.

Contrast   A discussion concerning how two or more persons or things are different.

Dialogue   A conversation between characters.

Drama   A play.

Explication   A method of explaining.

Fiction   Stories that are at least partially imagined and not factual.

Figures of speech   Words that mean, in a particular context, something more than their dictionary definitions.

Imagery   The use of words or groups of words that refer to the senses and sensory experiences.

Irony   An effect created when statements or situations seem at odds with how things truly are.

Metaphor   An implicit comparison of a feeling or object with another unlike it. *Example:* He is a snake in the grass.

Metaphorical language   Language that draws comparisons between things that are essentially dissimilar. Metaphorical language is most often created through the use of metaphor, simile, and personification.

Narrator   The person telling the story in a work of literature.

Novel   A long fictional narrative.

Personification   A figure of speech in which nonhuman things or beings are said to have human characteristics. *Example:* The car died on the hill.

Plot   The sequence of events in a literary work.

Poetry   A form of writing in which the author writes in lines using either a metrical pattern or free verse.

Point of view   The position of the narrator in relation to the events that occur.

Prose   Any form of writing that is not poetry.

Setting   The background against which a literary work takes place. Time, place, historical era, geography, and culture are all part of the setting.

Short story   A brief fictional narrative.

Simile   A comparison of a feeling or object with another unlike it, using the term *like* or *as. Example:* He eats like a horse.

Symbol   Something concrete that represents something abstract.

Symbolism   The use of symbols to give a literary work a message greater than its literal meaning.

Theme   The message, or main idea, of a literary work.

Tone   The expression of a writer's attitude toward a subject in a literary work and the creation of a mood for that work.

GLOSSARY OF USAGE

This brief glossary explains the usage of potentially confusing words and phrases. Samples illustrate how the words and phrases are used. Consult a dictionary for words or phrases not included here.

a, an   Use *a* before a consonant sound; use *an* before a vowel sound. For words beginning with *h*, use *a* when the *h* is voiced and *an* when it is unvoiced.

a locket   **a** historical novel [voiced]

an oration   **an** honest mistake [unvoiced]

accept, except   *Accept* means "willing to receive"; *except* means "all but."

Hoover rightfully would not **accept** the blame for the Stock Market Crash of 1929.

No elected official in the United States earns more than $200,000 **except** the president.

accidentally, accidently   Use *accidentally,* the correct word form. The root word is *accidental,* not *accident.*

The curator **accidentally** mislabeled the painting.

advice, advise   *Advice,* a noun, means "a suggestion or suggestions"; *advise,* a verb, means "to offer ideas" or "to recommend."

Lord Chesterfield's **advice** to his son, though written in 1747, retains its value today.

Physicians frequently **advise** their cardiac patients to get moderate exercise and to eat wisely.

affect, effect   *Affect,* a verb, means "to influence"; *effect,* a noun, means "the product or result of an action;" *effect,* a verb, means "to bring about" or "to cause to occur."

The smallness of the audience did not **affect** the speaker's presentation.

One **effect** of decontrol will be stronger competition.

To **effect** behavioral changes in some house pets is no small task.

agree to, agree with   *Agree to* means "to accept" a plan or proposal; *agree with* means "to share beliefs" with a person or group.

Members of the Writer's Guild would not **agree to** the contract's terms.

Although I **agree with** the protesters' position, I cannot approve of their methods.

all ready, already   *All ready* means "all prepared"; *already* means "preexisting" or "previous."

Ten minutes before curtain time, the performers were **all ready.**

Volumes A through M of the *Middle English Dictionary* are **already** in print.

all right, alright   Use *all right,* the correct form.

The Roosevelts clearly felt that it was **all right** for their children to be heard as well as seen.

all together, altogether   *All together* means "all acting in unison"; *altogether* means "totally" or "entirely."

Synchronized swimming requires participants to swim **all together.**

Life in a small town is **altogether** too peaceful for some city dwellers.

alot, a lot   Use *a lot,* the correct form. Generally, however, use more specific words: *a great deal, many,* or *much.*

The senator's inflammatory comments shocked **a lot** of his constituents.

The senator's inflammatory comments shocked **many** of his constituents.

among, between   Use *among* to describe the relationship of three or more people or things; use *between* for two.

Disagreements **among** the lawyers disrupted the proceedings.

Zoning laws usually require at least forty feet **between** houses.

amount, number   Use *amount* for quantities that cannot be counted separately; use *number* for items that can be counted. Some concepts, like time, use both forms, depending on how elements are described.

The **amount** of money needed to restore Ellis Island was surprising.

The contractor could not estimate the **amount** of time needed to complete the renovations.

We will need a **number** of hours to coordinate our presentations.

In the 1960s, a large **number** of American elm trees were killed by Dutch elm disease.

an   See **a.**

and/or   Generally avoid this construction. Instead, use either *and* or *or.*

anxious, eager   *Anxious* means "apprehensive" or "worried" and consequently describes negative feelings; *eager* means "to anticipate enthusiastically" and consequently describes positive feelings.

For four weeks, Angie was **anxious** about her qualifying exams.

Lew was **eager** to see the restaging of *La Bohème.*

as, as if, like   Use *as* or *as if,* subordinating conjunctions, to introduce a clause; use *like,* a preposition, to introduce a noun or phrase.

Walt talked to his cocker spaniel **as if** the dog understood every word.

Virginia Woolf's prose style is a great deal **like** that of Leslie Stephens, her father.

as, because, since   *As,* a subordinating conjunction, establishes a time relationship; it is interchangeable with *when* or *while. Because* and *since* describe causes and effects.

As the train pulled out of the station, it began to rain.

Because (Since) the population density is high, housing is difficult to find in Tokyo.

awful   Generally avoid using this word, which means "full of awe," as a negative description. Instead, use *bad, terrible, unfortunate,* or other similar, more precise words.

bad, badly   Use *bad,* an adjective, to modify a noun; use *badly,* an adverb, to modify a verb.

Napoleon's winter assault on Russia was, quite simply, a **bad** plan.

Although Grandma Moses painted **badly** by conventional standards, her work had charm and innocence.

because, due to the fact that, since   Use *because* or *since; due to the fact that* is merely a wordier way of saying the same thing.

Beef prices will rise **because** ranchers have reduced the size of their herds.

before, prior to   Use *before* in almost all cases. Use *prior to* only when the sequence of events is drawn out, important, and legalistic.

Always check your appointment book **before** scheduling a meeting.

Prior to receiving the cash settlement, the Jacobsons had filed four complaints with the Better Business Bureau.

being as, being that, seeing as   Use *because* or *since* instead of these nonstandard forms.

beside, besides   *Beside* means "next to"; *besides* means "except."

In Congress, the vice president sits **beside** the Speaker of the House.

Few of Georgia O'Keeffe's paintings are well known **besides** those of flowers.

between   See **among.**

borrow, lend, loan   *Borrow* means "to take something for temporary use"; *lend* means "to give something for temporary use"; *loan* is primarily a noun and refers to the thing lent or borrowed.

People seldom **borrow** expensive items like cars, furs, or electronic equipment.

Many public libraries now **lend** compact discs and video tapes.

The **loan** of $5,000 was never repaid.

bring, take   *Bring* means "to transport from a distant to a nearby location"; *take* reverses the pattern and means "to transport from a nearby location to a distant one."

Croatian dissidents **bring** to the United States tales of harsh treatment and inequity.

American scholars working in central Europe must **take** computers with them because the machines are not readily available at many European universities.

can, may   *Can* means "is able to"; *may* means "has permission to." *May* is also used with a verb to suggest a possible or conditional action.

Almost anyone **can** learn to cook well.

Foreign diplomats **may** travel freely in the United States.

I **may** learn to like escargot, but I doubt it.

can't help but Avoid this phrase, which contains two negatives, *can't* and *but;* instead rewrite the sentence, omitting *but.*

We **can't help** wondering whether the new curriculum will help or hinder students.

center around, center on Use *center on. Center around* is contradictory because *center* identifies one position and *around* suggests many possible positions.

If we can **center** our discussions **on** one topic at a time, we will use our time productively.

compare to, compare with *Compare to* stresses similarities; *compare with* stresses both similarities and differences.

Jean Toomer's novel *Cane* has been **compared to** free verse.

In reviews, most critics **compared** the film version of *Amadeus* **with** the original play by Peter Shaffer.

complement, compliment *Complement,* normally a noun, means "that which completes"; *compliment,* either a noun or a verb, means "a statement of praise" or "to praise."

A direct object is one kind of **complement.**

One of the highest forms of **compliment** is imitation.

The renovators of the Washington, D.C., train station should be **complimented** for their restraint, good taste, and attention to detail.

continual, continuous *Continual* means "repeated often"; *continuous* means "without stopping."

In most industries, orienting new workers is a **continual** activity.

A **continuous** stream of water rushed down the slope.

could of, should of, would of Use the correct forms: *could have, should have,* and *would have.*

The athletic director **should have** taken a firm stand against drug use by athletes.

council, counsel *Council,* a noun, means "a group of people who consult and offer advice"; *counsel,* a noun or a verb, means "advice" or "to advise."

The members of the **council** met in the conference room of the city hall.

Following the meeting, they offered their **counsel** to the mayor.

Ms. Reichmann **counsels** the unemployed at the Eighth Avenue Shelter.

different from, different than Use *different from* with single complements and clauses; use *different than* only with clauses.

Most people's life styles are **different from** those of their parents.

Our stay in New Orleans was **different than** we had expected.

disinterested, uninterested *Disinterested* means "impartial" or "unbiased"; *uninterested* means "indifferent" or "unconcerned about."

Olympic judges are supposed to be **disinterested** evaluators, but most are not.

Unfortunately, many people are **uninterested** in classical music.

due to the fact that See **because.**

each and every Generally avoid this repetitious usage. Use *each* or *every,* not both.

eager See **anxious.**

effect See **affect.**

enthusiastic, enthused Use *enthusiastic,* the preferred form.

William was **enthusiastic** about his volunteer work for the Special Olympics.

etc. Except in rare instances, avoid the use of *etc.,* which means "and so forth." Normally, either continue a discussion or stop. The phrase *and so on* may also be used sparingly.

every day, everyday *Every day,* an adjective-and-noun combination, means "each day"; *everyday,* an adjective, means "typical" or "ordinary."

Nutritionists suggest that people eat three balanced meals **every day.**

Congested traffic is an **everyday** problem in major cities.

except See **accept.**

farther, further *Farther* describes physical distances; *further* describes degree, quality, or time.

Most people know that it is **farther** to Mars than to Venus.

The subject of teenage pregnancy needs **further** study if we intend to solve the financial and social problems that it creates.

fewer, less   Use *fewer* to describe physically separate units; use *less* for things that cannot be counted.

Fewer than ten American companies have more than one million shareholders.

Because the cost-of-living raise was **less** than we had anticipated, we had to revise our budget.

finalize, finish   Generally use *finish* or *complete,* less pretentious ways of expressing the same idea.

fun   As an adjective, *fun* should be used in the predicate-adjective position, not before a noun.

White-water rafting is dangerous but **fun.**

further   See **farther.**

good, well   Use the adjective *good* to describe someone or something; use the adverb *well* to describe an action or condition; use the adjective *well* to describe someone or something.

A **good** debator must be knowledgeable, logical, and forceful.

We work **well** together because we think alike.

She isn't **well.**

has got, have got   Simply use *has* or *have.*

Major networks **have** to rethink their programming, especially with the challenge of cable networks.

he or she, him or her, his or hers, himself or herself   Use these paired pronouns with indefinite but singular antecedents; avoid awkward constructions like *he/she* or *s/he.* Generally, however, use plurals or specific nouns and pronouns when possible.

Each person is responsible for **his or her** own actions.

People are responsible for **their** own actions.

President Clinton was responsible for **his** and **his staff's** actions.

hopefully, I hope   Use *hopefully,* an adverb, to describe the *hopeful* way in which something is done; use *I hope* to describe wishes.

Marsha **hopefully** opened the envelope, expecting to find a letter of acceptance.

I hope the EPA takes stronger steps to preserve our wildlife.

imply, infer *Imply* means "to suggest without stating"; *infer* means "to reach a conclusion based on unstated evidence." They describe two sides of a process.

Chancellor Michaelson's awkward movements and tentative comments **implied** that he was uncomfortable during the interview.

We **infer,** from your tone of voice, that you are displeased.

in, into *In* means "positioned within"; *into* means "moving from the outside to the inside." Avoid using *into* to mean "enjoys," an especially nonsensical colloquialism.

Investments **in** the bond market are often safer than those **in** the stock market.

As the tenor walked **into** the reception room, he was greeted by a chorus of "bravos."

infer See **imply.**

irregardless, regardless Use *regardless,* the accepted form.

Child custody is usually awarded to the mother, **regardless** of the father's competence.

its, it's, its' *Its,* a possessive pronoun, means "belonging to it"; *it's,* a contraction, means "it is"; *its'* is nonstandard.

After the accident, the quarter horse favored **its** right front leg.

It's unlikely that the federal government will increase educational spending.

kind of, sort of Use *rather, somewhat,* or *to some extent* instead.

lay, lie *Lay* means "to place something"; *lie* means "to recline." Some confusion is typical because *lay* is also the past tense of *lie.*

In hand-treating leather, a tanner will **lay** the skins on a large, flat surface.

People with migraine headaches generally **lie** down and stoically wait for the pain to subside.

Nina **lay** awake all night worrying about her interview.

lead, led   *Lead* is the present-tense verb; *led* is the past-tense form.

The clergy used to **lead** quiet lives.

Montresor **led** the unsuspecting Fortunato into the catacombs.

learn, teach   *Learn* means to "acquire knowledge"; *teach* means "to give instruction." These are two sides of the same process.

Children **learn** best in enriched environments.

Experience **teaches** us that hard work is often the key to success.

less   See **fewer.**

lie   See **lay.**

like   See **as.**

loan   See **borrow.**

loose, lose   *Loose,* an adjective, means "not tight or binding"; *lose,* a verb, means "to misplace."

In tropical climates, people typically wear **loose,** lightweight garments.

Overcooked vegetables **lose** vitamins, minerals, texture, and color.

may   See **can.**

may be, maybe   *May be,* a verb, means "could be"; *maybe* means "perhaps."

The use of animals in research **may be** legal, but it raises ethical questions.

Maybe van Gogh was mad; if so, his work is the result of an inspired madness.

myself   Use *myself* only to create emphasis in a sentence with *I* as the subject; *myself* cannot stand alone as the subject of a sentence.

I always type my papers **myself.**

number   See **amount.**

off of   Use *off* by itself; it is perfectly clear.

During re-entry, a number of tiles came **off** the first space shuttle.

on account of   Use *because* or *since,* briefer ways of saying the same thing.

passed, past   Use *passed* as a verb; use *past* as a noun, adjective, or preposition.

Malcolm X **passed** through a period of pessimism to reach a time of optimism in his last months.

The **past,** as the saying goes, helps to determine the present.

Thoughtful people often reflect on their **past** actions and inactions.

The ambulance raced **past** the cars, hurrying from the site of the fire to the hospital.

people, persons   Use *people* when referring to a group, emphasizing anonymity; use *persons* to emphasize unnamed individuals within the group.

People who lobby for special-interest groups must register their affiliations with Congress.

Several **persons** at the hearing criticized the company's environmental record.

percent, percentage   Use *percent* with a number; use *percentage* with a modifier.

More than fifty **percent** of the government's money is spent on Social Security and defense.

A large **percentage** of divorced people remarry.

persons   See **people.**

pretty   *Pretty* means "attractive" or "pleasant looking"; do not use it to mean "rather" or "somewhat."

principal, principle   *Principal,* an adjective, means "main" or "highest in importance"; *principal,* a noun, means "the head of a school"; *principle,* a noun, means "a fundamental truth or law."

The **principal** difficulty of reading the novels of Henry James is sorting out his syntax.

The **principal** in the satiric novel *Up the Down Staircase* seems oblivious to the needs of his students.

The **principle** of free speech is vital to American interests.

prior to   See **before.**

quotation, quote   *Quotation,* the noun, means "someone else's material used word for word"; *quote,* the verb, means "to use a quotation." In informal contexts, *quote* is often used as a noun.

In his speeches and essays, Martin Luther King, Jr., frequently incorporated **quotations** from the Bible.

In his poem "The Hollow Men," T. S. Eliot **quotes** from *The Heart of Darkness,* a brief novel by Joseph Conrad.

reason, reason why, reason that, reason is because   *Reason,* used by itself, is sometimes unclear; *reason why* or *reason that,* more complete expressions, are generally preferred.

Literature about AIDS often explores the **reasons why** the general public reacts so irrationally to the disease.

respectfully, respectively   *Respectfully* means "showing respect" or "full of respect"; *respectively* means "in the given order."

George Washington **respectfully** declined to be named king of the newly independent colonies.

These cited passages were submitted by Joshua Blaney, Andreas Church, and Joanna Meredith, **respectively.**

seeing as   See **being as.**

set, sit   *Set* means "to place or position something"; *sit* means "to be seated."

The photographer **set** the shutter speed at 1/100th of a second.

Many civil rights demonstrators refused to **sit** in segregated sections of buses, theaters, and government buildings.

shall, will   *Shall,* which indicates determination in the future tense, was once clearly distinguished from *will,* which merely describes future actions or conditions. Past distinctions between these forms are disappearing, and *will* is now used in almost all cases. *Shall* remains standard, however, for questions using the first person.

Many animals raised in captivity **will** die if released into the wild.

"**Shall** I compare thee to a summer's day?"   —Sonnet 18, William Shakespeare

should, would   Use *should* to explain a condition or obligation; use *would* to explain a customary action or wish.

Universities **should** not invest funds in companies whose policies conflict with their own.

When asked a pointed question, John Kennedy **would** often begin his response with a humorous remark to ease the tension.

should of   See **could of.**

since   See **as, because.**

sit   See **set.**

sort of   See **kind of.**

suppose to, supposed to   Use *supposed to,* the standard form.

Affirmative action policies are **supposed to** ensure fair hiring practices nationwide.

take   See **bring.**

teach   See **learn.**

that, which, who   Use *that* to refer to people or things, but usually to things; use *which* to refer to things; use *who* to refer to people.

The musical work **that** set the standard for CD size was Beethoven's Ninth Symphony.

O'Neill's *Long Day's Journey into Night,* **which** won the 1957 Pulitzer Prize, was published posthumously.

People **who** cannot control their tempers are irritating and sometimes dangerous.

their, there, they're   *Their,* a possessive pronoun, means "belonging to them"; *there,* usually an adverb, indicates placement; *they're,* a contraction, means "they are."

Legislation is pending to give artists royalties whenever **their** work is sold for profit.

Put the boxes over **there,** and I will open them later.

Let them sit wherever **they're** comfortable.

theirself, theirselves   Use *themselves,* the standard form.

The members of Congress did not hesitate to vote **themselves** a raise.

there   See **their.**

they're   See **their.**

threw, through, thru   *Threw,* the past tense of the verb *throw,* means "hurled an object"; *through* means "by way of" or "to reach an end"; *thru* is a nonstandard spelling of *through.*

Quite by accident, Tasha **threw** the invitation away.

Blue Highways is a picaresque account of William Least Heat-Moon's travels **through** the United States.

till, until, 'til   Both *till* and *until* are acceptable; though archaic, *'til* is also admissible.

There will be no peace in the Middle East **till (until)** religious groups there become more tolerant of each other.

to, too, two   *To* is a preposition or part of an infinitive; *too* is a modifier meaning "in extreme" or "also"; *two* is the number.

In Cold Blood was Truman Capote's attempt **to** create what he called a nonfiction novel.

James Joyce's *Finnegan's Wake* is **too** idiosyncratic for many readers.

China gave the Washington Zoo **two** pandas who were promptly named Yin and Yang.

try and   Use *try to,* the accepted form.

Producers of music videos **try to** recreate the essence of a song in visual form, with mixed success.

uninterested   See **disinterested.**

until   See **till.**

use to, used to   Use the standard form: *used to.*

Artists **used to** mix their own paints from pigments, oils, and bonding agents.

utilize, utilization   Generally use *use,* a shorter, simpler way of expressing the same idea.

wait for, wait on   *Wait for* means "to stay and expect"; *wait on* means "to serve."

In Beckett's famous play, Vladimir and Estragon **wait for** Godot.

Because of severe bouts of asthma and allergies, Marcel Proust was frequently bedridden and had to be **waited on** most of his life.

weather, whether   *Weather* means "conditions of the climate"; *whether* means "if."

In the South, rapid changes in the **weather** can often be attributed to shifts in the Gulf Stream.

Citizens must pay taxes **whether** they like them or not.

well See **good.**

whether See **weather.**

which See **that.**

who See **that.**

who/whom, whoever/whomever Use *who* and *whoever* as subjects; use *whom* and *whomever* as objects.

Doctors **who** cannot relate well to patients should go into research work.

Whoever designed the conference program did a splendid job.

To **whom** should we submit our report?

Contact **whomever** you wish. I doubt that you will get a clear response.

who's, whose *Who's,* a contraction, means "who is" or "who has"; *whose,* a possessive pronoun, means "belonging to someone unknown."

We need to find out **who's** scribbling graffiti on the walls.

A spelunker is someone **whose** hobby is exploring caves.

will See **shall.**

would See **should.**

would of See **could of.**

GLOSSARY OF GRAMMATICAL TERMS

absolute phrase   See **phrase.**

abstract noun   See **noun.**

active voice   See **voice.**

adjective   A word that modifies or limits a noun or pronoun by answering one of these questions: *what kind, which one, how many, whose.*

Distilled water makes the best ice cubes.

A **regular adjective** precedes the word it modifies:

The **velvet** dress cost two hundred dollars.

A **predicate adjective** follows a linking verb but modifies the subject of the sentence or clause:

Ladders should be **sturdy** and **lightweight.**

An **article** (*a, an, the*) is considered an adjective:

A good friend is **a** good listener.

A **demonstrative adjective** can show closeness (*this, these*) or distance (*that, those*) and singularity (*this, that*) or plurality (*these, those*):

All of **these** books will not fit in **that** bookcase.

A **pronoun adjective** is a pronoun that modifies a noun:

Somebody's car is parked in **my** space.

adjective clause   See **clause.**

adjective phrase   See **phrase.**

adverb   A word that modifies a verb, adjective, adverb, clause, phrase, or whole sentence by answering one of these questions: *how, when, where, how often, to what extent.*

Roberto enunciates **carefully.** [*Carefully* modifies *enunciates*, telling how.]

He is **usually** soft-spoken. [*Usually* modifies *is*, telling when.]

He sometimes speaks **too** softly. [*Too* modifies *softly*, telling to what extent.]

Frequently, he has to repeat comments. [*Frequently* modifies the whole sentence, telling how often.]

adverb clause   See **clause.**

adverbial conjunction   See **conjunctive adverb.**

agreement   The matching of words according to number (singular and plural) and gender (masculine, feminine, and neuter). A verb takes a singular or plural form depending on whether its subject is singular or plural. A pronoun must match its antecedent (the word to which it refers) in gender as well as in number. A demonstrative adjective must match the number of the word it modifies (*this* and *that* for singular, *these* and *those* for plural).

antecedent   The word to which a pronoun refers.

Debra changed the tire herself. (*Debra* is the antecedent of the reflexive pronoun *herself.*)

appositive   A word or group of words that restates or defines a noun or pronoun. An appositive is positioned immediately after the word it explains.

Nonrestrictive appositives clarify proper nouns and are set off by commas:

Crest, **the best-selling toothpaste,** is recommended by many dentists.

Restrictive appositives are themselves proper nouns and require no commas:

The toothpaste **Crest** is advertised frequently on television.

article   See **adjective.**

auxiliary verb   Same as helping verb. See **verb.**

balanced sentence   See **sentence.**

case   The form that a noun or pronoun takes according to its grammatical role in a sentence.

Subjective case describes a word used as a subject or predicate noun:

She drives a Honda Civic LX.

Objective case describes a word used as a direct object, indirect object, or object of a preposition:

The small size is just right for **her.**

Possessive case describes a word used to show ownership:

Her Civic is cherry red.

Most nouns and pronouns change only to form the possessive case (by adding an apostrophe and *s: cat's, someone's*). Personal, relative, and interrogative pronouns, however, change form for all three cases.

clause A group of words that has a subject and a predicate.
An **independent clause** is grammatically complete; when used separately, it is indistinguishable from a simple sentence:

Dinosaurs had small brains.

An independent clause can be joined to another clause with a coordinating conjunction, a subordinating conjunction, or a semicolon.
A **subordinate clause** also has a subject and a predicate, but it is not grammatically complete; it must be joined to an independent clause:

Although dinosaurs had enormous bodies, they had small brains.

A subordinate clause can function as an adjective, an adverb, or a noun.
An **adjective clause** modifies a noun or pronoun:

We want a television **that has surround-sound.**

An **adverb clause** modifies a verb, an adjective, another adverb, a clause, a phrase, or a whole sentence:

Adam gets up earlier **than I usually do.**

A **noun clause** functions as a noun:

Whoever finds the wallet will probably return it.

collective noun See **noun.**

comma fault See **comma splice.**

comma splice Independent clauses incorrectly joined by a comma:

Einstein's brain has been preserved since his death**,** the formaldehyde has damaged the tissue.

common noun See **noun.**

comparative degree See **degree.**

complement Words or groups of words that complete the meaning of a sentence.

Jason is **my best friend.**

A **direct object** follows a transitive verb and answers these questions: *what, whom:*

Jason rented some **skis.**

An **indirect object** follows a transitive verb, is used with a direct object, and answers these questions: *to what, to whom:*

Jason gave **me** skiing lessons.

A **predicate noun** follows a linking verb and restates the subject of the sentence or clause:

Jason is a patient **instructor.**

A **predicate adjective** follows a linking verb and modifies the subject of the sentence or clause:

Nevertheless, the lessons were **frustrating.**

complete predicate   See **predicate.**

complete subject   See **subject.**

complex sentence   See **sentence.**

compound   Two or more words, phrases, or clauses that work together as one unit. **Compound words:** *dining room, razzle-dazzle.* **Compound subject:** Shimita and **Amir** were married on Tuesday. **Compound verb:** We **attended** the wedding but **skipped** the reception.

compound-complex sentence   See **sentence.**

compound sentence   See **sentence.**

compound subject   See **compound.**

concrete noun   See **noun.**

compound verb   See **compound.**

conjunction   Words that join words, phrases, and clauses. Conjunctions link compound words, explain alternatives, show contrast, clarify chronology, and explain causal relationships.
A **coordinating conjunction** (*and, but, for, nor, or, so,* or *yet*) links equivalent sentence parts:

Stenographic **and** typing skills are required for the job.

A **subordinate conjunction** (*although, because, until,* and others) introduces a subordinate clause in a sentence:

Although Todd could type, he could not take shorthand.

A **correlative conjunction** (*either . . . or, neither . . . nor,* and others) links equivalent sentence parts and provides additional emphasis:

He will **either** learn shorthand **or** look for other work.

conjunctive adverb   Though used to link ideas logically, a conjunctive adverb does not make a grammatical connection as a traditional conjunction does and must therefore be used in an independent clause:

The experiment lasted two years; **however,** the results were inconclusive.

coordinating conjunction   See **conjunction.**

correlative conjunction   See **conjunction.**

dangling modifier   An introductory modifier that does not logically modify the subject of the sentence:

Charred from overcooking, **we** could not eat the steaks.

degree   The form that adjectives and adverbs take to show degrees of comparison. **Positive degree** is a direct form with no comparison: *simple.* **Comparative degree** compares two items: *simpler.* **Superlative degree** compares three or more items: *simplest.*

demonstrative adjective   See **adjective.**

demonstrative pronoun   See **pronoun.**

dependent clause   Same as subordinate clause. See **clause.**

direct address   The use of a noun to identify the person or people spoken to; the noun is set off by commas and restricted to speech or writing that approximates speech:

Friends, it is time for us to voice our opinions.

direct object   See **complement.**

direct quotation   Using someone's exact words, taken from speech or writing, in speech or writing. Quotation marks indicate where the quoted material begins and ends:

Professor Mullican often says, **"Writing is never finished; it is only abandoned."**

An **indirect quotation** reports what people say without using direct wording; an indirect quotation is often introduced with *that* for statements and *if* for questions:

Professor Mullican asked **if I understood what he meant.**

double negative   Nonstandard use of two negative words within one construction. See also **can't help but** in the Glossary of Usage.

He **didn't** do **no** work on the project.

elliptical construction   A construction that omits words (usually verbs and modifiers) that are considered understood:

Gorillas are more intelligent than chimpanzees [are].

expletive construction   A construction (*here is, it is, there are,* and *there is*) that functions as the subject and verb of a sentence or clause but depends on a complement to create meaning:

There are too many desks in this office.

fragment   A group of words improperly presented as a sentence, with a capital letter at the beginning and with end punctuation. A fragment can lack a subject or a verb:

Left her baggage in the terminal.

It can be an unattached subordinate clause:

Although the clerk had said the bags were ready.

It can be an unattached phrase:

Stood at the baggage claim area for ten minutes.

fused sentence   Two or more independent clauses placed one after the other with no separating punctuation:

The vegetables at Trotski's Market are always fresh those at Wilkerson's are not.

future perfect tense   See **tense.**

future tense   See **tense.**

gender   Three classes of nouns and pronouns based on sex: masculine (*Roger, he*), feminine (*Martha, she*), and neuter (*tractor, it*).

gerund   See **verbal.**

gerund phrase   See **phrase.**

helping verb   Same as auxiliary verb. See **verb.**

imperative mood   See **mood.**

indefinite pronoun　See **pronoun.**

independent clause　Same as main clause. See **clause.**

indicative mood　See **mood.**

indirect object　See **complement.**

indirect quotation　See **direct quotation.**

infinitive　See **verbal.**

infinitive phrase　See **phrase.**

intensive pronoun　Same as reflexive pronoun. See **pronoun.**

interjection　A word that expresses surprise or emotion or that provides a conversational transition:

Well, I don't want to go either.

interrogative pronoun　See **pronoun.**

intransitive verb　See **verb.**

irregular verb　See **verb.**

linking verb　See **verb.**

loose sentence　See **sentence.**

main clause　Same as independent clause. See **clause.**

misplaced modifier　A modifier incorrectly placed in a sentence; the word, phrase, or clause it modifies is not clear:

Anthony said **before midnight** he would have his paper done.

modifier　A word, phrase, or clause used as an adjective or adverb to limit, clarify, qualify, or in some way restrict the meaning of another part of the sentence.

mood　A verb form that allows writers to present ideas with proper meaning.

Indicative mood presents a fact, offers an opinion, or asks a question:

The baby **has** a fever.

Imperative mood presents commands or directions:

Call the doctor.

Subjunctive mood presents a conditional situation or one contrary to fact:

I wish she **were feeling** better.

nominative case   Same as subjective case. See **case.**

nonrestrictive element   An appositive, phrase, or clause that supplies information that is not essential to the meaning of a sentence. A nonrestrictive element is separated from the rest of the sentence by commas:

Cabaret, **my favorite film,** is on Cinemax next week. [appositive]

Michael York, **with charm and humor,** played the leading male role. [phrase]

Marisa Berenson, **who was better known for her modeling than for her acting,** played the wealthy Jewish woman who came for English lessons. [clause]

noun   A word that names a person, place, thing, idea, quality, or condition. A **proper noun** names a specific person, place, or thing: *Elijah P. Lovejoy, Versailles, the Hope Diamond.* A **common noun** names a person, place, or thing by general type: *abolitionist, palace, jewel.* A **collective noun** names a group of people or things: *team, herd.* A **concrete noun,** either common or proper, names something tangible: *Mrs. Mastrioni, clinic, credit card.* An **abstract noun** names an intangible quality or condition: *honesty, nervousness.*

noun clause   See **clause.**

noun marker   Same as article. See **adjective.**

number   Two classes of nouns, pronouns, and verbs: singular (one) and plural (two or more). A noun in the plural form usually ends with *s: problem* (singular), *problems* (plural); a verb in the third-person-singular form ends with *s: she cares* (singular), *they care* (plural); a demonstrative pronoun in the plural form ends with *se: this rabbit* (singular), *these rabbits* (plural).

objective case   See **case.**

object of a preposition   A noun or pronoun that a preposition links to the rest of the sentence:

The electrical outlet is behind the **couch.** [*Couch* is linked to *is,* telling *where.*]

parallelism   The use of the same form for equivalent verbs in the same tense, a series of similar verbals or predicate nouns, and so on:

Congressman Abernathe **denied** the charges, **questioned** the evidence, **produced** full records, and **received** a formal apology. [all past-tense verbs]

parenthetical expression A word or group of words that interrupts the pattern of a sentence, separating elements and adding secondary information. Such expressions are separated by parentheses or dashes:

Seeing *Arcadia* in New York was expensive—**the tickets were fifty-five dollars each**—but worthwhile.

participial phrase See **phrase.**

participle See **verbal.**

parts of speech The classification of words into eight categories according to their use in sentences: noun, pronoun, verb, adjective, adverb, conjunction, preposition, and interjection. Each part of speech is separately defined in this glossary.

passive voice See **voice.**

past participle See **verbal.**

past perfect tense See **tense.**

perfect tenses See **tense.**

periodic sentence See **sentence.**

person Three classes of nouns, pronouns, and verbs that indicate the relationship between the writer and the subject. **First person** (*I am, we are*) indicates that the writer writes about himself or herself; **second person** indicates that the writers write to people about themselves (*you are*); **third person** indicates that the writer is writing to an audience *about* someone else (*she is, they are, Mitch is, the researchers are*).

personal pronoun See **pronoun.**

phrase A group of words that cannot function independently as a sentence but must be part of a sentence. A whole phrase often functions as a noun, adjective, or adverb.
A **prepositional phrase** consists of a preposition (*above, during, under,* and others), its object, and any modifiers: *above the front doorway, during the thunder storm, under the subject heading.* A prepositional phrase can function as an adjective or adverb:

The woman **next to me** read **during the entire flight.** [*Next to me* is adjectival, modifying *woman; during the entire flight* is adverbial, modifying *read.*]

A **gerund phrase** combines a gerund and its complements and modifiers; it functions as a noun:

Conducting an orchestra requires skill, patience, and inspiration. [*Conducting an orchestra* is the subject of the sentence.]

A **participial phrase** combines a participle and its modifiers; it functions as an adjective:

From her window, Mrs. Bradshaw watched the children **playing under her maple tree.** [*Playing under her maple tree* modifies *children.*]

An **infinitive phrase** combines an infinitive and its complements and modifiers; it functions as a noun, an adjective, or an adverb:

To succeed as a freelance artist is difficult. [noun]

Supplies **to use in art classes** are costly unless I get them wholesale. [adjective]

To make ends meet, I work part time at a bank. [adverb]

An **absolute phrase** modifies a whole sentence or clause. It contains a noun and a participle and is separated from the rest of the sentence by a comma:

All things considered, the recital was a success.

positive degree   See **degree.**

possessive case   See **case.**

predicate   A word or group of words that expresses action or a state of being in sentences; it consists of one or more verbs plus any complements or modifiers.

A **simple predicate** is the single verb and its auxiliaries, if any:

Iago mercilessly **destroyed** the lives of Othello and Desdemona.

A **complete predicate** is the simple predicate plus any complements or modifiers:

Iago **mercilessly destroyed the lives of Othello and Desdemona.**

predicate adjective   See **complement.**

predicate noun   See **complement.**

preposition A word that establishes a relationship between a noun or pronoun (the object of the preposition) and some other word in the sentence:

After his term **in** office, Jimmy Carter returned **to** Plains, Georgia. [*Term* is linked to *Carter; office* is linked to *term; Plains, Georgia* is linked to *returned.*]

prepositional phrase See **phrase.**

present participle See **verbal.**

present perfect tense See **tense.**

present tense See **tense.**

progressive tense See **tense.**

pronoun A word that substitutes for a noun (its antecedent). A **personal pronoun** refers to people or things: *I, me, you, he, him, she, her, it, we, us, they, them.* A **possessive pronoun** shows ownership. Some possessive pronouns function independently: *mine, yours, his, hers, its, ours, theirs;* some (known as adjective-pronouns) must be used with nouns: *my, your, his, her, our, their.* A **reflexive pronoun** shows that someone or something is acting for itself or on itself: *myself, yourself, himself, herself, itself, ourselves, yourselves, themselves.* An **interrogative pronoun** is used to ask a question: *who, whom, whoever, whomever, what, which, whose.* A **demonstrative pronoun** is used alone: *this, that, these, those.* An **indefinite pronoun** has no particular antecedent but serves as a general subject or object in a sentence: *another, everything, most, somebody,* and others. A **relative pronoun** introduces an adjective or noun clause: *that, what, which, who, whom, whoever, whomever, whose.*

proper adjective An adjective derived from a proper noun: *Belgian lace, Elizabethan sonnet.*

proper noun See **noun.**

quotation See **direct quotation.**

reflexive pronoun Same as intensive pronoun. See **pronoun.**

regular verb See **verb.**

relative pronoun See **pronoun.**

restrictive element   An appositive, phrase, or clause that supplies information necessary to the meaning of a sentence. A restrictive element is not set off by commas:

The dramatic show *Party of Five* was critically successful but only moderately popular. The problems **that five parentless siblings might face** were dealt with honestly.

run-on sentence   See **fused sentence.**

sentence   An independent group of words with a subject and predicate, with a capital at the beginning and with end punctuation. It expresses a grammatically complete thought. For most purposes, sentences are classified by their structure.

A **simple sentence** contains one independent clause and expresses one relationship between a subject and predicate:

The test flight was a success.

A **compound sentence** contains two or more independent clauses joined by a comma and a coordinating conjunction or by a semicolon:

The test flight was a success**, and** we began production on the jet.

A **complex sentence** contains one independent clause and one or more subordinate clauses:

Although there were some problems, the test flight was a success.

A **compound-complex sentence** contains at least two independent clauses and one or more subordinate clauses:

Although there were some problems, the test flight was a success, and we began production on the jet.

In addition, a sentence can be classified by the arrangement of its ideas. A **loose sentence** presents major ideas first and then adds clarifications:

The bus was crowded with students, shoppers, and commuters.

A **periodic sentence** places the major idea or some part of it at the end:

Although we wanted a car with power steering, power brakes, power windows, automatic transmission, air conditioning, and quadraphonic sound, we couldn't afford one.

A **balanced sentence** contains parallel words, phrases, or clauses:

Lawrence was irresponsible, undisciplined, and rowdy, but his brother Jerod was responsible, disciplined, and reserved.

sentence fragment   See **fragment.**

simple predicate   See **predicate.**

simple sentence   See **sentence.**

simple subject   See **subject.**

simple tenses   See **tense.**

subject   The people, places, things, ideas, qualities, or conditions that act or are described in an active sentence or that are acted upon in a passive sentence.

A **simple subject** is the single word or essential group of words that controls the focus of the sentence:

Oppenheimer and Teller, participants in the Manhattan Project, disagreed about the development of the hydrogen bomb.

A **complete subject** is the simple subject plus all related modifiers, phrases, and clauses:

Oppenheimer and Teller, participants in the Manhattan Project, disagreed about the development of the hydrogen bomb.

subjective case   Same as nominative case. See **case.**

subjunctive mood   See **mood.**

subordinate clause   See **clause.**

subordinating conjunction   See **conjunction.**

superlative degree   See **degree.**

tense   The modification of main verbs to indicate when an action occurred or when a state of being existed. **Simple tenses** include the **present** (*he plans, they plan*), **past** (*he planned, they planned*), and **future** (*he will plan, they will plan*). **Perfect tenses** include the **present perfect** (*he has planned, they have planned*), **past perfect** (*he had planned, they had planned*), and **future perfect** (*he will have planned, they will have planned*). The **progressive tenses** indicate habitual or future action (*he is planning, he was planning, he will be planning, he had been planning, they are planning, they were planning, they had been planning, they will have been planning*).

See **verb.**

A word or group of words that expresses action or a state of being. For most purposes, verbs are classified by their function. An **action verb** expresses physical or mental action:

The cat **pounced** on the mouse. I **thought** it was cruel.

A **linking verb** expresses a state of being or condition and joins the subject with a complement:

The cat **seemed** indifferent to my reaction.

Cats **are** skillful predators.

An **auxiliary verb** is used with a main verb to form a verb phrase, commonly used to clarify time references, explain states of being, or ask questions:

We **will** stay on schedule.

Things **could** be worse.

Can you play the harpsichord?

All verbs are classified by the way they form basic verb parts. A **regular verb** forms the past tense by adding *-ed* or *-d* and maintains that form for the past participle: *talk, talked, had talked; close, closed, has closed.* An **irregular verb** follows varied patterns and may change for each form: *go, went, has gone; sing, sang, had sung.*

A verb form used as a noun, adjective, or adverb. A **gerund** is an *-ing* verb form that functions as a noun; the form of a gerund is the same as the present participle:

Hiking is my favorite sport.

An **infinitive** is a verb form that uses *to;* it functions as a noun or adverb:

To open his own shop is Gerhardt's dream. [noun]

Gerhardt is too committed **to give up.** [adverb]

A **participle** is a verb form that uses *-ing, -ed, -d, -n,* or *-t;* it functions as an adjective or adverb. A **present participle** ends in *ing:*

Beaming, Clancey accepted the first-place trophy.

A **past participle** ends in *-ed, -d, -n,* or *-t;* a past participle can also help form a verb phrase:

The window pane, **broken** by a baseball, must be replaced. [adjective]

We have **broken** that window many times. [part of main verb]

See also **phrase.**

verb phrase　See **phrase.**

voice　The form of a transitive verb that illustrates whether the subject *does* something or has something *done to it.*
Active voice indicates that the subject acts:

Roy Hobbs **wrote** the feature article.

Passive voice indicates that the subject completes no action but is instead acted upon:

The feature article **was written** by Roy Hobbs.

Science, Mathematics, and Technology

Timeline of Science, Mathematics, and Technology

c. 300 BC   Theoretical principles of Geometry: Euclid (Egypt).

1527   Use of chemicals to treat diseases: Phillipus Paracelsus (Germany).

1543   Theory of a sun-centered universe: Nicholaus Copernicus (Poland).

1546   Theory of infectious (transmittable) diseases: Girolamo Fracastoro (Italy).

1583   System for classifying plants: Andrea Cesalpino (Italy).

1609   Theory of planetary motion: Johannes Kepler (Germany).

1628   Theory of blood circulation: William Harvey (England).

1637   Theoretical principles of analytic geometry: René Descartes (France).

1662   Boyle's Law (correlation of pressure and volume in gases): Robert Boyle (Ireland).

1665   Theory of gravity: Isaac Newton (England); discovery of light spectrum: Isaac Newton (England).

1669   Theoretical principles of calculus: Isaac Newton (England).

1678   Theory of light waves: Christian Huygens (Netherlands).

1683   Isolation of bacteria: Anton van Leeuwenhoek (Netherlands).

1687   Laws of motion: Isaac Newton (England).

1705   Discovery of Halley's Comet: Edmund Halley (England).

1752   Theory of electricity: Benjamin Franklin (US); theoretical principles of combustion: Antoine Lavoisier (France).

1753   Classification of plants and animals by genus and species: Carolus Linnaeus (Sweden).

1773   Isolation of oxygen: Carl Scheele (Sweden).

1781   Discovery of Uranus (first planet discovered since prehistoric times): William Herschel (England).

1791   Development of the metric system: the Revolutionary Government of France.

1796   Development of the smallpox vaccine: Edward Jenner (England).

1811   Avogadro's Law (correlation of pressure and volume of gases to molecule number): Amedeo Avogadro (Italy).

1825   Invention of the electromagnet: William Sturgeon (England).

1839   Theory of cells in organisms: Theodor Schwann and Matthias Schleiden (Germany).

1840   Discovery of ozone: Christian Schöonbein (Germany); theory of the Ice Age: Louis Agassiz (Switzerland).

1842   First use of anesthetic (ether): Crawford Long (US).

1854   Development of symbolic logic: George Boole (England).

1858   Theory of continental drift: Antonio Snider-Pellegrini (France).

1859   Theory of evolution by natural selection: Charles Darwin (England).

1862 Theory of germs: Louis Pasteur (France).

1865 Theory of heredity: Gregor Mendel (Austria).

1867 First use of antiseptics in surgery: Joseph Lister (England).

1869 Discovery of DNA: Johann Friedrich Meischer (Switzerland).

1871 Development of the periodic table: Dmitry Mendeleev (Russia).

1880 Development of the seismograph: John Milne (England).

1882 Isolation of tuberculosis bacterium: Robert Koch (Germany).

1883 Development of synthetic fibers: Joseph Swann (England).

1885 Development of rabies immunization: Louis Pasteur (France).

1887 Demonstration of antibiotics: Louis Pasteur and Jules-François Joubert (France).

1895 Development of x-rays: Wilhelm Roentgen (Germany).

1897 Identification of the electron: Joseph Thompson (England).

1898 Identification of radioactive elements: Marie Curie and Pierre Curie (France).

1900 Discovery of quanta: Max Planck (Germany).

1904 Theory of psychoanalysis: Sigmund Freud (Austria).

1905 Theory of intelligence testing (IQ): Alfred Binet and Theodore Simon (France); theory of relativity: Albert Einstein (Switzerland).

1907 $E = mc^2$ (theory of mass and energy): Albert Einstein (Switzerland).

1911 First nuclear model of the atom: Ernest Rutherford (England).

1913 Development of quantum theory: Niels Bohr (Denmark).

1919 Discovery of the proton: Ernest Rutherford (England).

1921 Development of insulin: Frederick Banting and J. J. MacLeod (Canada).

1925 Development of theory of quantum mechanics: Werner Heisenberg and Erwin Schrödinger (Germany).

1927 Development of the expanding universe theory: Georges Lemaître (Belgium).

1929 Development of the big bang theory: Edwin Hubble (US).

1932 Identification of the neutron: James Chadwick (England).

1935 Development of the Richter scale (to measure earthquakes): Charles Richter (US).

1938 Development of nuclear fission: Otto Hahn and Fritz Strassmann (Germany).

1942 Development of the first nuclear reactor: Enrico Fermi (US).

1947 Development of the transistor: John Bardeen, William Shockley, Walter Brattain (US); development of carbon-14 dating: Willard Libby (US).

1951 Development of the oral contraceptive: Gregory Pincus, Min Chuch Chang, John Rock, Carl Djerassi (US).

1954 Development of polio vaccine: Jonas Salk (US).

1963 Identification of quasars: Maarten Schmidt (US).

1967   Identification of quarks: Jerome Friedman, Henry Kendall, and Richard Taylor (US).

1968   Discovery of pulsars: Antony Hewish and Jocelyn Bell (England).

1970   Development of liquid crystal displays (LCD) using the twisted nematic effect: Hoffmann-LaRoche (Switzerland).

1982   Invention of the artificial heart: Robert Jarvik (US).

1987   Ceramic superconductor: Paul Chu (US); meningitis vaccine: Connaught Labs (US).

1997   Mammal cloning: Ian Wilmut (Scotland).

Timeline of Air and Space Exploration

1783   Jean-François Pilâtre de Rozier and the Marquis d'Arlandes flew a hot-air balloon in Paris; Jacques-Alexandre-César Charles and Nicolas Robert flew the first hydrogen balloon.

1804   George Cayley constructed and flew a model fixed-wing airplane.

1876   Nikolaus Otto invented the four-stroke engine.

1901   The Wright brothers flew their Number 2 glider at Kitty Hawk.

1903   The Wright brothers flew the first four flights with a powered, controlled airplane.

1908   Henri Farman flew sixteen and a half miles, the first "cross country" flight.

1912   British Avro introduced the first enclosed-cabin airplane.

1913   The first multi-engine airplane was built in Russia.

1915   The first all-metal airplane was produced.

1919   A US Navy airplane completed the first transatlantic flight.

1924   US Army Air Service flyers completed the first around-the-world and transpacific flights.

1926   Robert Goddard demonstrated the first successful rocket in Auburn, MA.

1927   Charles Lindbergh made the first solo, nonstop crossing of the Atlantic.

1930   Frank Whittle patented the turbojet engine.

1936   The first practical helicopter was introduced.

1938   The first commercial airplane with a pressurized cabin was introduced.

1939   Erich Warsitz completed the first jet flight.

1942   Germany successfully launched a liquid-fuel, rocket-propelled ballistic missile.

1947   Charles Yeager flew a rocket-propelled research airplane faster than the speed of sound (Mach 1) over Muroc Dry Lake, CA.

1953   Scott Crossfield flew twice the speed of sound (Mach 2) over Edwards Airforce Base, CA.

1956 Milburn Apt flew three times the speed of sound (Mach 3) over the Mojave Desert, CA.

1957 The Soviet Union launched *Sputnik,* the first man-made satellite; the Soviet Union also launched *Sputnik 2,* carrying a dog into orbit.

1958 The US launched *Explorer 1,* the first US satellite.

1960 The US launched *Tiros I,* the first weather satellite.

1961 Yuri Gagarin became the first man in space, completing one orbit of the earth in the Soviet craft *Vostok 1;* Alan Shepard (US) made a suborbital flight.

1962 John Glenn became the first American in space, in the Mercury spaceship *Friendship 7; Telstar I,* a communications satellite, provided transatlantic television relay.

1963 Valentina Tereshkova became the first woman in space.

1966 The Soviet Union's *Luna 9* made a soft landing on the moon; the US's *Surveyor 1* also landed on the moon; the US's *Lunar Orbiter 1* took high-resolution photographs of the moon.

1968 *Apollo 8*—with Frank Borman, James Lovell, and William Anders—orbited the moon.

1969 *Apollo 11* landed on the moon; Neil Armstrong and Edwin Aldrin were first humans to step on the moon.

1971 *Mariner 9* surveyed Mars from orbit.

1972 *Pioneer 10,* intended to visit the outer planets, was launched from Cape Kennedy.

1973 Charles Conrad, Paul Weitz, and Joseph Kerwin rendezvoused with *Skylab 1,* an orbital space station.

1976 *Viking I* and *Viking II* completed soft landings on Mars; transcontinental service began on the Concorde, the first supersonic commercial airline.

1977 Soviet space laboratory *Salyut 6* was launched and visited by sixteen different crews.

1981 The first US space shuttle—*Columbia*—was launched.

1983 Sally Ride became the first US woman in space.

1986 The shuttle *Challenger* exploded during its launch, killing all seven crew members; the Soviet Union launched the *Mir* space station; Jeana Yeager and Dick Rutan completed the first nonstop, around-the-world airplane flight without refueling.

1990 The Hubble Space Telescope was launched from the shuttle *Discovery*.

1993 The shuttle *Endeavor* carried the first commercial payload into space.

1995 The shuttle *Atlantis* docked with the Soviet space station *Mir.*

Planets of Our Solar System

Mercury

36 million miles from the sun
88 day revolution of the sun
3,032 miles in diameter
0 satellites
0 rings

Venus

67.24 million miles from the sun
225 day revolution
7,519 miles in diameter
0 satellites
0 rings

Earth

92.9 million miles from the sun
365 day revolution
7,926 miles in diameter
1 satellite
0 rings

Mars

141.71 million miles from the sun
687 day revolution
4,194 miles in diameter
2 satellites
0 rings

Jupiter

483.88 million miles from the sun
11.86 year revolution
88,736 miles in diameter
16 satellites
1 ring

Saturn

887.14 million miles from the sun
29.46 year revolution
74,978 miles in diameter
20 satellites
1,000 rings (estimated)

Uranus

1,783.98 million miles from the
   sun
84 year revolution
32,193 miles in diameter
15 satellites
11 rings

Neptune

2,796.46 million miles from the
   sun
165 year revolution
30,775 miles in diameter
8 satellites
4 rings

Pluto

(Classification as a planet now in
   question.)
3,666 million miles from the sun
248 year revolution
1,441 miles in diameter (estimated)
1 satellite
uncertain number of rings

Inventions

c. 90 C.E.   Calculating machine (China)

c. 100   Paper (China)

c. 700   Block printing (Japan) Gunpowder (China)

c. 1400   Movable-type printing (Korea)

c. 1475   Muzzle-loaded rifle (Italy, Germany)

1593   Thermometer: Galileo Galilei (Italy)

1639   Steam Engine: Thomas Savery (England)

1709   Piano: Bartolommeo Cristofori (Italy)

1718   Machine gun: James Puckle (England)

1752   Lightning rod: Benjamin Franklin (US)

c. 1760   Bifocal lens: Benjamin Franklin (US)

1793   Cotton gin: Eli Whitney (US)

1796   Lithography: Alois Senefelder (US)

1801   Electric lamp (arc): Humphrey Davy (England)

1804   Steam locomotive: Richard Trevithick (England)

1816   Bicycle: Karl von Sauerbronn (Germany) Phosphorus match: François Derosne (France)

1819   Stethoscope: R. T. Laënnec (France)

1822   Electric motor: Michael Faraday (England)

1827   Microphone: Charles Wheatstone (England)

1829   Braille: Louis Braille (France)

1832   Electric generator: Michael Faraday (England)

1834   Reaper: Cyrus McCormick (US)

1835   Revolver: Samuel Colt (US)

1837   Telegraph: F. B. Morse (US)

1839   Vulcanized Rubber: Charles Goodyear (US)

1846   Sewing machine: Elias Howe (US)

1850   Refrigerator: Alexander Twining (US), James Harrison (Australia)

1851   Cylinder lock: Linus Yale (US)

1852   Passenger elevator: Elisha Otis (US)

1855   Plastic: Alexander Parkes (England)

1867   Dynamite: Alfred Nobel (Sweden) Fluorescent lamp: A. E. Becquerel (France) Typewriter: Christopher Sholes, Carlos Glidden (US)

1868   Air brake: George Westinghouse (US)

c. 1870   Incandescent lamp: Joseph Swann (England), Thomas Edison (US)

1876   Telephone: Alexander Bell (US)

1877   Phonograph: Thomas Edison (US)

1882   Electric fan: Schuyler (US)

1884   Fountain pen: Lewis Waterman (US); Motorcycle: Edward Butler (England)

1885   Automobile: Karl Benz (Germany)

1886   Coca-Cola: John Pemberton (US)

1888   Camera (hand held): George Eastman (US)

1889   Automatic rifle: John Browning (US)

1891   Zipper: W. L. Judson (US)

1893   Motion picture: Thomas Edison (US)

1895   Wireless telegraphy: Guglielmo Marconi (Italy); X-rays: Wilhelm Roentgen (Germany)

1899   Tape recorder: Valdemar Poulsen (Denmark)

1900   Tractor: Benjamin Holt (US)

1904   Principles of radar: Christian Hulsmeyer (Germany)

1906   Washing Machine: Alva Fisher (US)

1911   Air conditioning: Willis Carrier (US)

1913   Geiger counter: Hans Geiger (Germany)

1923   Television (iconoscope): Vladimir Zworkin (US)

1924   Frozen food: Clarence Birdseye (US)

1929   "Scotch" tape: Richard Drew (US)

1936   Helicopter: Heinrich Focke (Germany)

1938   Xerography (photocopying): Chester Carlson (US) Fiberglass: Corning (US)

1944   Ballpoint pen: Lazio Biro (Argentina)

1946   Computer (electric): Presper Eckert, John Mauchly (US)

1947   Microwave oven: Percy Spenser (US)

1948   Transistor: John Barden, William Shockley, Walter Brattain (US) Velcro: George de Mestral (Sweden)

1951   Oral Contraceptive: Gregory Pincus, Min Chang, John Rock, Carl Djerassi (US)

1955   Fiber optics: Narinder Kapany (England)

1957   Pacemaker: Clarence Lillehie, Earl Bakk (US)

1960   Laser: T. H. Maiman (US)

1964   Synthesizer: Robert Moog (US)

1970   Bar codes: Monarch Marking (US) LCD (liquid crystal display): Hoffmann-La Roche (Switzerland)

1972   Compact disk: RCA (US) Video disk: Philips (Netherlands)

1973   The Internet: Department of Defense (US) CAT (CT) Scan: Godfrey Hounsfield (England)

1974   Airbag: General Motors (US)

1975   VCR (VHS): Matsushita (Japan)

1995   V-Chip: Tom Collings (Canada)

Customary US Measurements

Length

US Unit	Amount	Metric Equivalent
inch	0.083 foot	2.540 centimeters
foot	12 inches (1/3 yard)	0.305 meter
yard	3 feet (36 inches)	0.914 meter
rod	5.5 yards	5.029 meters
mile (land)	1,760 yards (5,280 feet)	1.609 kilometers
mile (nautical)	1.151 miles	1.852 kilometers

Liquid Capacity

US Unit	Amount	Metric Equivalent
fluid ounce	8 drams	29.573 milliliters
pint	16 fluid ounces	0.473 liter
quart	2 pints	0.946 liter
gallon	4 quarts	3.785 liters
barrel	31–42 gallons	no equivalent

Weight

US Unit	Amount		Metric Equivalent
grain	0.036 dram	0.002285 ounce	64.798 milligrams
dram	27.344 grains	0.0625 ounce	1.772 grams
ounce	16 drams	437.5 grains	28.350 grams
pound	16 ounces	7,000 grains	453.592 grams
short ton	2,000 pounds	1,000 kilograms	0.907 metric ton
long ton	1.12 short tons	2,240 pounds	1.016 metric tons

Metric Measurements

Length

Metric Unit	Number of Meters	US Equivalent
millimeter	0.001	0.039 inch
centimeter	0.01	0.394 inch
decimeter	0.1	3.937 inches
meter	1	39.370 inches
decameter	10	32.808 feet
hectometer	100	109.361 yards
kilometer	1,000	0.621 mile
myriameter	10,000	6.214 miles

Liquid Capacity

Metric Unit	Number of Liters	US Equivalent
milliliter	0.001	0.271 fluid dram
centiliter	0.01	0.338 fluid ounce
deciliter	0.10	0.211 pint
liter	1	1.057 quarts
decaliter	10	2.642 gallons
hectoliter	100	no equivalent
kiloliter	1,000	no equivalent

Weight

Metric Unit	Number of Grams	US Equivalent
milligram	0.001	0.015 grain
centigram	0.01	0.154 grain
decigram	0.10	1.543 grains
gram	1	0.035 ounce
decagram	10	0.353 ounce
hectogram	100	3.527 ounces
kilogram	1,000	2.205 pounds
quintal	100,000	220.462 pounds
metric ton	1,000,000	1.102 tons

Computer Terminology

ASCII   (American Standard Code for Information Interchange). An unformatted, universally readable version of a document.

Bit   (Binary Digit). The smallest unit of computer data, represented in *0*s or *1*s.

Bookmark   An electronic selection or listing of a URL so that it can be automatically recalled at a later time.

Boolean Search   A process that allows for combinations of search terms using *and*, *or*, or *not*.

Browser   A software system that allows users to gain access to the Internet. Examples: Microsoft Internet Explorer and Netscape Navigator.

Bug   A recurring problem caused by an error in computer code or logic.

Byte   (Binary Term). A combination of eight or sixteen bits of data that represent a character.

CD-ROM   (Compact Disc—Read Only Memory). A compact disc that stores encoded files to be read (but not added to or modified) using laser optics.

Periodic Table of the Elements

Legend:
- Alkali metals
- Alkaline earth metals
- Transition metals
- Lanthanide series
- Actinide series
- Other metals
- Nonmetals
- Noble gases

Atomic Number — **2**

Symbol — **He** Helium

Atomic Weight (or Mass Number of most stable isotope if in parentheses) — 4.00260

(Names of elements 104–109 subject to approval by International Union of Pure & Applied Chemistry.)

1a	2a	3b	4b	5b	6b	7b		8		1b	2b	3a	4a	5a	6a	7a	0
1 **H** Hydrogen 1.00797																	2 **He** Helium 4.00260
3 **Li** Lithium 6.941	4 **Be** Beryllium 9.0128											5 **B** Boron 10.811	6 **C** Carbon 12.01115	7 **N** Nitrogen 14.0067	8 **O** Oxygen 15.9994	9 **F** Fluorine 18.9984	10 **Ne** Neon 20.179
11 **Na** Sodium 22.9898	12 **Mg** Magnesium 24.305											13 **Al** Aluminum 26.9815	14 **Si** Silicon 28.0855	15 **P** Phosphorus 30.9738	16 **S** Sulfur 32.064	17 **Cl** Chlorine 35.453	18 **Ar** Argon 39.948
19 **K** Potassium 39.0983	20 **Ca** Calcium 40.08	21 **Sc** Scandium 44.9559	22 **Ti** Titanium 47.88	23 **V** Vanadium 50.94	24 **Cr** Chromium 51.996	25 **Mn** Manganese 54.9380	26 **Fe** Iron 55.847	27 **Co** Cobalt 58.9332	28 **Ni** Nickel 58.69	29 **Cu** Copper 63.546	30 **Zn** Zinc 65.39	31 **Ga** Gallium 69.72	32 **Ge** Germanium 72.59	33 **As** Arsenic 74.9216	34 **Se** Selenium 78.96	35 **Br** Bromine 79.904	36 **Kr** Krypton 83.80
37 **Rb** Rubidium 85.4678	38 **Sr** Strontium 87.62	39 **Y** Yttrium 88.905	40 **Zr** Zirconium 91.224	41 **Nb** Niobium 92.906	42 **Mo** Molybdenum 95.94	43 **Tc** Technetium (98)	44 **Ru** Ruthenium 101.07	45 **Rh** Rhodium 102.906	46 **Pd** Palladium 106.42	47 **Ag** Silver 107.868	48 **Cd** Cadmium 112.41	49 **In** Indium 114.82	50 **Sn** Tin 118.71	51 **Sb** Antimony 121.75	52 **Te** Tellurium 127.60	53 **I** Iodine 126.905	54 **Xe** Xenon 131.29
55 **Cs** Cesium 132.905	56 **Ba** Barium 137.33	57–71* Lanthanides	72 **Hf** Hafnium 178.49	73 **Ta** Tantalum 180.948	74 **W** Tungsten 183.85	75 **Re** Rhenium 186.207	76 **Os** Osmium 190.2	77 **Ir** Iridium 192.22	78 **Pt** Platinum 195.08	79 **Au** Gold 196.967	80 **Hg** Mercury 200.59	81 **Tl** Thallium 204.383	82 **Pb** Lead 207.19	83 **Bi** Bismuth 208.980	84 **Po** Polonium (209)	85 **At** Astatine (210)	86 **Rn** Radon (222)
87 **Fr** Francium (223)	88 **Ra** Radium 226.025	89–103** Actinides (227)	104 **Db** Dubnium (261)	105 **Jl** Joliotium (262)	106 **Rf** Rutherfordium (263)	107 **Bh** Bohrium (262)	108 **Hn** Hahnium (265)	109 **Mt** Meitnerium (266)	110 (269)	111 (272)							

*Lanthanides	57 **La** Lanthanium 138.906	58 **Ce** Cerium 140.12	59 **Pr** Praseodymium 140.908	60 **Nd** Neodymium 144.24	61 **Pm** Promethium (145)	62 **Sm** Samarium 150.36	63 **Eu** Europium 151.96	64 **Gd** Gadolinium 157.25	65 **Tb** Terbium 158.925	66 **Dy** Dysprosium 162.50	67 **Ho** Holmium 164.930	68 **Er** Erbium 167.26	69 **Tm** Thulium 168.934	70 **Yb** Ytterbium 173.04	71 **Lu** Lutetium 174.967
**Actinides	89 **Ac** Actinium 227.028	90 **Th** Thorium 232.038	91 **Pa** Protactinium 231.036	92 **U** Uranium 238.029	93 **Np** Neptunium 237.048	94 **Pu** Plutonium (244)	95 **Am** Americium (243)	96 **Cm** Curium (247)	97 **Bk** Berkelium (247)	98 **Cf** Californium (251)	99 **Es** Einsteinium (252)	100 **Fm** Fermium (257)	101 **Md** Mendelevium (258)	102 **No** Nobelium (259)	103 **Lr** Lawrencium (260)

Chip   An integrated circuit produced on a small piece of semiconducting material.

CPU   (Central Processing Unit). The central system of a computer that controls its functions.

Database   A file containing data records that can be configured and interpreted in a variety of ways.

Desktop Publishing   The use of computer software that combines text and graphics (usually printed on laser printers) to reproduce the look of typeset materials.

Disk   A magnetized round plastic (floppy) or metal (hard) device that stores binary information in the form of files.

Domain   Words or abbreviations that, as part of an Internet address, describe the kind of source. Examples: *com* for "commercial" site, *edu* for "educational" site, or *gov* for "government" site.

DOS   (Disk Operating System). A disk-based system that controls a computer's functions.

Download   To copy a file from a remote computer or Web site via the Internet.

E-mail   (Electronic Mail). Electronic correspondence and materials sent via the Internet.

Encryption   Encoding information so that unauthorized users cannot gain access to it.

FAQ   (Frequently Asked Questions). A document providing answers to often-asked questions about a topic or Internet site.

File   A document that contains stored information. Examples: A computer program, a graphic element, or a personally created document.

Flame   An insulting or derogatory message, often on listservs or news groups.

FTP   (File Transfer Protocol). A method for transferring files via the Internet.

Gigabyte   (GB). 1024 megabytes. (See megabytes.)

Graphic User Interface   (GUI). A graphically oriented operating system that uses icons and menus that users select with a clickable mouse. Example: Microsoft Windows.

Hard copy   A printed copy of a document or file.

Hardware   The mechanical equipment of a computer system. Examples: computer, monitor, disk drive, printer, modem, scanner.

Home Page   The initial page of a site on the Internet, providing additional links to additional material within the site, as well as possible links to other sites.

HTML (Hypertext Markup Language). A markup language used to structure text and multimedia documents and to set up hyperlinks between documents.

HTTP (Hypertext Transport Protocol). The primary protocol that allows users to connect with Web sites on the Internet.

Hypertext A complex system (using nonsequential connections) for creating links among elements (pages, features within pages, images, videos, other sites, and so on) on the Internet.

Icon A small, symbolic image used in graphic interfaces to represent a function or feature. Example: A magnifying glass to represent the "enlarge image" function.

Internet A complex, high-speed network of computers that allows users to send and collect electronic information (in its many forms) around the world.

JPEG (Joint Photographic Experts Group). A file format for encoding graphics, usually on the Internet.

Keyword Search A process (using a search engine) for locating information using key words.

Kilobytes (K). 1,024 bytes.

Link A connection among elements of a Web site and among different Web sites.

Megabyte (MB). 1,048,576 bytes.

Menu A list of options from which to choose a function, select a format, or designate a file.

Modem (Modulator-Demodulator). A device that allows computers to send and receive electronic information over telephone lines.

Network A connected group of computers that share resources.

Peripheral A supplemental device—printer, modem, joystick, speakers—linked to and controlled by a computer.

Protocol A code that allows computers to connect with appropriate sources. Example: HTTP, FTP. (See URL.)

Search Engine An Internet program that locates sites using keyword searching. Examples: HotBot, Alta Vista, Yahoo, Lycos.

Server A computer that runs programs (within networks) or allows information to be transferred (on the Internet).

Software The computer programs that make computers (hardware) operate.

Upload To send a file to a remote computer or Web site via the Internet.

URL (Uniform Resource Locator). An Internet address, composed of sequenced elements (protocol//domain name.directory path.file name.domain). Example: <http://www.whitehouse.gov>.

Usenet A network of worldwide discussion groups.
Virus An invasive program that "infects" computer files, thereby making them inoperable.
Web site A set of interconnected Web pages, generally located on the same server, maintained as a collection of information by a person, group, or organization.
World Wide Web (WWW). The interlinked, hypertext-based network of electronic materials that is accessible with a browser.

Language, Literature, and the Arts

Timeline of British Literature

Old English Period (c. 449–1100)

c. 675 Caedmon (earliest English poet)
c. 700 *Beowulf*
1066 Norman Conquest
1086 *Domesday Book* (census)

Anglo-Norman Period (1100–1350)

c. 1139 Geoffrey of Monmouth, *History of the Kings of Britain*
1348 Beginning of the Black Death in England

Middle English Period (1350–1500)

c. 1380 English translation of the Bible by John Wycliffe
c. 1387 Geoffrey Chaucer, *Canterbury Tales*
c. 1450 Johann Gutenberg: development of the printing press
1476 William Caxton introduces printing press in England
1485 Thomas Malory, *Le Morte d'Arthur*

The Renaissance: Early Tudor Age (1500–1557)

1516 Thomas More, *Utopia*
1535 King Henry VIII makes the protestant Anglican Church England's official religion

The Renaissance: Elizabethan Age (1558–1603)

1577 Raphael Holinshed, *Chronicle of England, Scotland, and Ireland*
1588 Christopher Marlowe, *Doctor Faustus*
1590 Edmund Spenser, *The Faerie Queene*
1594 William Shakespeare, *Romeo and Juliet*
1600 William Shakespeare, *Hamlet*

The Renaissance: Jacobean Age (1603–1625)

1605   William Shakespeare, *Macbeth* and *King Lear*
1606   Ben Jonson, *Volpone*
1609   William Shakespeare, sonnets
1611   King James version of the Bible

Caroline Period (1625–1649)

1638   John Milton, *Lycidas*
1642   English Civil War

Neoclassical Period: Restoration Age (1660–1798)

1667   John Milton, *Paradise Lost*
1676   George Etherege, *The Man of Mode*
1678   John Bunyan, *Pilgrim's Progress*

Neoclassical Period: Augustan Age (1700–1750)

1712   Alexander Pope, *The Rape of the Lock*
1719   Daniel Defoe, *Robinson Crusoe*
1726   Jonathan Swift, *Gulliver's Travels*
1749   Henry Fielding, *Tom Jones*

Neoclassical Period: Age of Johnson (1750–1798)

1755   Samuel Johnson, *Dictionary of the English Language*
1773   Oliver Goldsmith, *She Stoops to Conquer*
1777   Richard Brinsley Sheridan, *The School for Scandal*
1789   William Blake, *Songs of Innocence*
1792   Mary Wollstonecraft, *The Rights of Woman*

Romantic Period: Romantic Age (1798–1832)

1798   William Wordsworth and Samuel Coleridge, *Lyrical Ballads*
1813   Jane Austen, *Pride and Prejudice*
　　　　Percy Bysshe Shelley, *Queen Mab*
1818   Mary Shelley, *Frankenstein*
1819   Lord Byron, *Don Juan*
1820   John Keats, *The Eve of St. Agnes, and Other Poems*

Romantic Period: Victorian Age (1832–1870)

1842   Robert Browning, *Dramatic Lyrics*
　　　　Alfred Lord Tennyson, *Poems*
1847   Emily Brontë, *Wuthering Heights*
　　　　William Makepeace Thackeray, *Vanity Fair*

1853	Charles Dickens, *Bleak House*
1865	Lewis Carroll, *Alice in Wonderland*

Realistic Period: Late Victorian Age (1870–1901)

1872	George Eliot, *Middlemarch*
1878	Thomas Hardy, *The Return of the Native*
1895	Oscar Wilde, *The Importance of Being Earnest*
1896	A. E. Housman, *A Shropshire Lad*
1898	H. G. Welles, *The War of the Worlds*
1900	Joseph Conrad, *Lord Jim*

Realistic Period: Edwardian Age (1901–1914)

1903	Samuel Butler, *The Way of All Flesh*
1913	D. H. Lawrence, *Sons and Lovers*

Modernist Period: Georgian Age (1914–1940)

1916	James Joyce, *Portrait of an Artist as a Young Man*
1920	D. H. Lawrence, *Women in Love*
1922	James Joyce, *Ulysses*
1923	George Bernard Shaw, *Saint Joan*
1924	E. M. Forster, *A Passage to India*
1925	Virginia Woolf, *Mrs. Dalloway*
1928	*Oxford English Dictionary*
1932	Aldous Huxley, *Brave New World*
1933	William Butler Yeats, *Collected Poems*

Modernist Period: Diminishing Age (1940–1965)

1945	Evelyn Waugh, *Brideshead Revisited*
1949	George Orwell, *Nineteen Eighty-Four*
1952	Samuel Beckett, *Waiting for Godot*

Post-Modernist Period (1965–   )

1965	Harold Pinter, *The Homecoming*
1967	Tom Stoppard, *Rosencrantz and Guildenstern Are Dead*
1968	Iris Murdoch, *Nice and the Good*
1973	Peter Shaffer, *Equus*
1976	Ted Hughes, *A Season of Songs*
1983	William Trevor, *Fools of Fortune*
1988	Salman Rushdie, *Satanic Verses*
1996	Beryl Bainbridge, *Every Man for Himself*
1998	Justin Cartwright, *Leading the Cheers*

Timeline of American Literature

Colonial Period (1607–1765)

1640 *Bay Psalm Book,* first book published in the American colonies.
1650 Anne Bradstreet, *Tenth Muse, Lately Sprung Up in America*
1710 Cotton Mather, *Essays to Do Good*
1732 Benjamin Franklin, *Poor Richard's Almanac*
1741 Jonathan Edwards, *Sinners in the Hands of an Angry God*

Nationalist Period: Revolutionary Age (1765–1790)

1776 Thomas Paine, *Common Sense*
1786 Philip Freneau, *Poems*

Nationalist Period: Federalist Age (1790–1830)

1791 Thomas Paine, *The Rights of Man*
1806 Noah Webster, *Compendious Dictionary*
1819 Washington Irving, *The Sketch Book of Geoffrey Crayon, Gent.*
1826 James Fenimore Cooper, *The Last of the Mohicans*

Romantic Period (1830–1865)

1837 Ralph Waldo Emerson, *The American Scholar*
1840 Edgar Allan Poe, *Tales of the Grotesque and the Arabesque*
1841 Henry Wadsworth Longfellow, *Ballads and Other Poems*
1850 Nathaniel Hawthorne, *The Scarlet Letter*
1851 Herman Melville, *Moby Dick*
1852 Harriet Beecher Stowe, *Uncle Tom's Cabin*
1854 Henry David Thoreau, *Walden*
1855 Walt Whitman, *Leaves of Grass*
1863 Abraham Lincoln, Gettysburg Address

Realistic Period (1865–1900)

1868 Louisa May Alcott, *Little Women*
1876 Mark Twain, *Tom Sawyer*
1884 Mark Twain, *The Adventures of Huckleberry Finn*
1892 Anna Julia Cooper, *A Voice from the South*
1895 Stephen Crane, *The Red Badge of Courage*
1896 Sarah Orne Jewett, *The Country of the Pointed Furs*
1899 Kate Chopin, *The Awakening*

Naturalistic Period (1900–1930)

1900 Theodore Dreiser, *Sister Carrie*
1901 Booker T. Washington, *Up from Slavery*

1903 Henry James, *The Ambassadors*
   W. E. B. DuBois, *The Souls of Black Folk*
1905 Edith Wharton, *The House of Mirth*
1906 Upton Sinclair, *The Jungle*
1914 Robert Frost, *North of Boston*
1916 Susan Gaspell, *Trifles*
1917 T. S. Eliot, *The Love Song of J. Alfred Prufrock*
1918 Willa Cather, *My Antonia*
1921 Eugene O'Neill, *Anna Christie*
1923 William Carlos Williams, *Spring and All*
   Jean Toomer, *Cane*
1925 F. Scott Fitzgerald, *The Great Gatsby*
   Countee Cullen, *Color*
1926 Ernest Hemingway, *The Sun Also Rises*
1928 Claude McKay, *Home to Harlem*
1929 William Faulkner, *The Sound and the Fury*

Period of Conformity and Criticism (1930–1960)

1937 Zora Neale Hurston, *Their Eyes Were Watching God*
1938 Thornton Wilder, *Our Town*
1939 John Steinbeck, *The Grapes of Wrath*
   Pietro Di Donato, *Christ in Concrete*
1940 Ernest Hemingway, *For Whom the Bell Tolls*
   Thomas Wolfe, *You Can't Go Home Again*
   Richard Wright, *Native Son*
   Katherine Anne Porter, *Flowering Judas and Other Stories*
1946 Robert Penn Warren, *All the King's Men*
1947 Tennessee Williams, *A Streetcar Named Desire*
1949 Arthur Miller, *The Death of a Salesman*
1951 J. D. Salinger, *The Catcher in the Rye*
   Langston Hughes, *Montage of a Dream Deferred*
1952 Ralph Ellison, *The Invisible Man*
1953 James Baldwin, *Go Tell It on the Mountain*
1956 Eugene O'Neill, *A Long Day's Journey into Night*
   Allen Ginsberg, *Howl and Other Poems*
1959 Lorraine Hansberry, *A Raisin in the Sun*

Period of the Confessional Self (1960–   )

1961 Gwendolyn Brooks, *Selected Poems*
1962 Edward Albee, *Who's Afraid of Virginia Woolf?*
1963 Martin Luther King, Jr., "I Have a Dream"
1964 LeRoi Jones, (Amira Baraka) *Dutchman*
   Malcolm X, *The Autobiography of Malcolm X*

1965   Flannery O'Connor, *Everything That Rises Must Converge*
1968   N. Scott Momaday, *House Made of Dawn*
1972   Ishmael Reed, *Mumbo Jumbo*
   Eudora Welty, *The Optimist's Daughter*
1973   Thomas Pynchon, *Gravity's Rainbow*
1975   Saul Bellow, *Humboldt's Gift*
   Maxine Hong Kingston, *The Woman Warrior*
1977   Leslie Marmon Silko, *Ceremony*
1979   John Cheever, *The Stories of John Cheever*
1978   Toni Morrison, *Song of Solomon*
1981   Sylvia Plath, *Collected Poems*
   Richard Rodriguez, *Hunger of Memory*
1983   Alice Walker, *The Color Purple*
1984   Sandra Cisneros, *The House on Mango Street*
1987   August Wilson, *Fences*
1991   Gish Jen, *Imagining America: Stories from the Promised Land*
1997   Philip Roth, *American Pastoral*

Significant Works of World Literature

c. 800 BCE   Homer, *The Iliad* and *The Odyssey* (Greece)
458 BCE   Aeschylus, *Agamemnon* (Greece)
431 BCE   Sophocles, *Oedipus the King* (Greece)
431 BCE   Euripides, *Medea* (Greece)
411 BCE   Aristophanes, *Lysistrata* (Greece)
c. 368 BCE   Plato, *Republic* (Greece)
c. 350 BCE   Aristotle, *Poetics* (Greece)
65 BCE   Seneca, *Phaedra* (Italy)
19 BCE   Virgil, *Aeneid* (Italy)
8 CE   Ovid, *Metamorphoses* (Italy)
c. 633   *The Qur'an*
c. 1000   Murasaki Shikibu, *The Tale of Genji* (Japan)
c. 1100   *Chanson de Roland* (France)
c. 1308   Dante Alighieri, *Divine Comedy* (Italy)
c. 1350   Giovanni Boccaccio, *Decameron* (Italy)
1362   Francesco Petrarch, *The Triumphs* (Italy)
1456   The Gutenberg Bible (Germany)
1509   Erasmus, "The Praise of Folly" (Netherlands)
c. 1516   Ludovico Ariosto, *Orlando Furioso* (Italy)
1524   Nicolo Machiavelli, *Mandragola* (Italy)
1528   Baldassare Castiglione, *The Courtier* (Italy)
1532   Nicolo Machiavelli, *The Prince* (Italy)

1580   Montaigne, *Essays* (France)
1592   Wu Ch'eng-en, *Monkey* (China)
1605   Miguel de Cervantes, *Don Quixote* (Spain)
c. 1636   Calderón, *Life Is a Dream* (Spain)
1636   Pierre Corneille, *The Cid* (France)
1664   Molière, *Tartuffe* (France)
1677   Racine, *Phaedra* (France)
1758   Voltaire, *Candide* (France)
1770   Jean Jacques Rousseau, *Confessions* (France)
1783   Beaumarchais, *Marriage of Figaro* (France)
1808   Johann Wolfgang von Goethe, *Faust* (Germany)
1854   George Sand, *The Story of My Life* (France)
1856   Gustave Flaubert, *Madame Bovary* (France)
1857   Charles Baudelaire, *Flowers of Evil* (France)
1862   Ivan Turgenev, *Fathers and Sons* (Russia)
1862   Victor Hugo, *Les Misérables* (France)
1865   Leo Tolstoy, *War and Peace* (Russia)
1866   Fyodor Dostoevsky, *Crime and Punishment* (Russia)
1879   Henrik Ibsen, *A Doll's House* (Norway)
        Georg Büchner, *Woyzeck* (Germany)
1888   August Strindberg, *Miss Julie* (Sweden)
1899   Machado de Assis, *Dom Casmurro* (Brazil)
1900   Sigmund Freud, *Interpretation of Dreams* (Austria)
1904   Anton Chekhov, *The Cherry Orchard* (Russia)
1912   Rabindranath Tagore, *Gitanjali* (India)
1913   Marcel Proust, *Remembrance of Things Past* (France)
1915   Ryonosuke Akutagawa, *Rashomon* (Japan)
1922   Katherine Mansfield, *The Garden Party and Other Stories*
        (New Zealand)
1924   Thomas Mann, *The Magic Mountain* (Germany)
        Pablo Neruda, *Twenty Love Poems and a Song of Despair* (Chile)
1925   Franz Kafka, *The Trial* (Czechoslovakia)
1934   Bruno Schulz, *The Street of Crocodiles* (Poland)
1935   Luigi Pirandello, *Six Characters in Search of an Author* (Italy)
1939   Bertolt Brecht, *Mother Courage and Her Children* (Germany)
1941   Jorge Luis Borges, *The Garden of Forking Paths* (Argentina)
1942   Albert Camus, *The Stranger* (France)
1943   Jean Anouilh, *Antigone* (France)
1944   Jean-Paul Sartre, *No Exit* (France)
1945   Jean Giraudoux, *The Madwoman of Chaillot* (France)
1947   Jean Genet, *The Maids* (France)

1947 Naguib Mahfouz, *Midaq Alley* (Egypt)
1948 Yasunari Kawabata, *Snow Country* (Japan)
1950 Eugene Ionesco, *The Bald Soprano* (France)
1952 Samuel Beckett, *Waiting for Godot* (France)
1954 Camara Laye, *The Radiance of the King* (Guinea)
1955 Patrick White, *The Tree of Man* (Australia)
1958 Chinua Achebe, *Things Fall Apart* (Nigeria)
1959 Günter Grass, *The Tin Drum* (Germany)
1963 Yukio Mishima, *The Sailor Who Fell from Grace with the Sea* (Japan)
1967 Gabriel García Márquez, *One Hundred Years of Solitude* (Colombia)
1979 Nadine Gordimer, *Burger's Daughter* (South Africa)
1981 Wole Soyinka, *Ake: The Years of Childhood* (Nigeria)
1984 Milan Kundera, *The Unbearable Lightness of Being* (Czechoslovakia)
1987 Octavio Paz, *The Collected Poems* (Mexico)
1989 Dario Fo, *The Pope and the Witch* (Italy)
1990 Derek Walcott, *Omeros* (St. Lucia)

Timeline of Western Art

Early Dynastic Period: Egypt (3000 BCE–2500 BCE)
Old Kingdom: Egypt (2500 BCE–2000 BCE)
Middle Kingdom: Egypt (2000 BCE–1500 BCE)
Bronze Age: Greece (1750 BCE–1000 BCE)
Black-figure vase painting (Greece)
New Kingdom: Egypt (1500 BCE–1000 BCE)
Archaic Period: Greece (1000 BCE–650 BCE)
Red-figure vase painting (Greece)
Classical Period: Greece (650 BCE–480 BCE)
Temple of Zeus at Olympia (Greece)
The Parthenon (Greece)
Goddess of Victory (Greece)
Hellenistic Period: Greece (320 BCE–1 CE)
Venus de Milo (Greece)
Laocoön (Greece)
Roman Empire: Italy (1 CE–400)
Pompeian paintings (Italy)
Byzantine Empire: Eastern Europe (400–750)
Mosaics in churches (Eastern Europe)
Carolingian Period: Europe (750–900)
Aachen Cathedral (Germany)

Romanesque Period: Eastern Europe (750–900)
Bronze doors of Hildesheim (Germany)
Bayeux Tapestry (France)
Gothic Period: Europe (1200–1400)
Chartres Cathedral (France)
Notre Dame Cathedral (France)
The Renaissance: Europe (1300–1500)
Doge's Palace (Italy)
Donatello (sculptor: Italy)
Jan Van Eyck (painter: Belgium [Flanders])
Bellini (painter: Italy)
Sandro Botticelli (painter: Italy)
Leonardo da Vinci (painter, scientist, writer: Italy)
Albrecht Dürer (painter, graphic artist: Germany)
Michelangelo Buonarroti (painter, sculptor, architect, writer: Italy)
Raphael (painter, architect: Italy)
Mannerist Period: Europe (1500–1600)
Titian (painter: Italy)
Hans Holbein "The Elder" (painter: Germany)
Andrea Palladio (architect: Italy)
Pieter Brueghel "The Elder" (painter: Belgium)
El Greco (painter, sculptor: Spain)
Baroque Period: Europe (1600–1700)
Peter Paul Rubens (painter: Belgium)
Sir Anthony Van Dyck (painter: Belgium)
Rembrandt van Rijn (painter: Netherlands)
Jan Vermeer (painter: Netherlands)
Versailles Palace (France)
Artemesia Gentileschi (painter: Italy)
Rococo Period: Europe (1700–1750)
François Boucher (painter: France)
Neoclassical Period: Europe and US (1750–1800)
Jacques-Louis David (painter: France)
Sir Joshua Reynolds (painter, writer: England)
Thomas Gainsborough (painter: England)
Romantic Period: Europe and US (1800–1850)
Francisco José Goya (painter: Spain)
William Blake (artist, writer: England)
Joseph Turner (painter: England)
Eugène Delacroix (painter: France)
Pre-Raphaelite Period: Europe (1850–1870)
Dante Rossetti (painter: England)

Impressionistic Period: Europe and US (1860–1880)
Claude Monet (painter: France)
Pierre Renoir (painter: France)
Edgar Degas (painter, sculptor: France)
James Whistler (painter: US)
Edouard Manet (painter: France)
Mary Stevenson Cassatt (painter: US)
Post-Impressionist Period: Europe and US (1880–1905)
Paul Cézanne (painter: France)
Paul Gauguin (painter: France)
Vincent van Gogh (painter: Netherlands)
John Singer Sargent (painter: US)
Auguste Rodin (sculptor: France)
Henri de Toulouse-Lautrec (painter: France)
Fauvist Period: Europe and US (1900–1910)
Henri Matisse (painter, sculptor: France)
Cubist Period: Europe and US (1910–1930)
Pablo Picasso (painter, sculptor, graphic artist: Spain)
Georges Braque (painter: France)
Paul Klee (painter: Switzerland)
Edward Hopper (painter: US)
Abstract Expressionist Period: Europe and US (1930–1960)
Wassily Kandinsky (painter: Russia)
Jackson Pollock (painter: US)
Willem de Kooning (painter: US)
Henry Moore (sculptor: England)
Andrew Wyeth (painter: US)
Georgia O'Keefe (painter: US)
Joan Miró (painter: Spain)
Marc Chagall (painter, graphic artist: Belarus/France)
Salvador Dali (painter: Spain)
Frida Kahlo (painter: Mexico)
Diego Rivera (painter, muralist: Mexico)
Pop Art Period: England and US (1960–1970)
Jasper Johns (painter, sculptor: US)
Robert Rauschenberg (painter: US)
Roy Lichtenstein (painter, sculptor: US)
Andy Warhol (painter: US)
Post-Modern Period: Europe and US (1970–   )
David Hockney (painter: US)
Christo (sculptor: US)

Robert Mapplethorpe (photographer: US)
Jean-Michel Basquiat (painter: US)

Significant Composers: Classical, Jazz, Opera, and Musical Theater

1659–1695   Henry Purcell (England): orchestral works, operas
1678–1741   Antonio Vivaldi (Italy): concertos
1685–1750   Johann Sebastian Bach (Germany): concertos, orchestral works
1685–1759   George Frederick Handel (England): oratorios, orchestral works
1732–1809   Franz Joseph Haydn (Austria): symphonies
1756–1791   Wolfgang Amadeus Mozart (Austria): symphonies, masses, operas, concertos
1770–1827   Ludwig van Beethoven (Germany): symphonies, concertos
1792–1868   Gioachino Rossini (Italy): operas
1797–1828   Franz Schubert (Austria): symphonies
1803–1869   Hector Berlioz (France): symphonies, orchestral works
1809–1847   Felix Mendelssohn (Germany): symphonies, concertos
1810–1849   Frédéric Chopin (Poland): concertos, waltzes
1811–1886   Franz Liszt (Germany): symphonies, concertos
1813–1883   Richard Wagner (Germany): operas, orchestral works
1813–1901   Giuseppe Verdi (Italy): operas
1833–1897   Johannes Brahms (Austria): symphonies, concertos
1836–1911   William Gilbert (England): operettas
1838–1875   Georges Bizet (France): operas, symphonies
1840–1893   Peter Ilyich Tchaikovsky (Russia): concertos, symphonies, ballets
1841–1904   Antonin Dvořák (Czechoslovakia): symphonies, concertos
1842–1900   Arthur Sullivan (England): operettas
1844–1908   Nikolai Rimsky-Korsakov (Russia): orchestral works
1858–1924   Giacomo Puccini (Italy): operas
1860–1911   Gustav Mahler (Czechoslovakia): symphonies
1862–1918   Claude Debussy (France): orchestral music
1864–1949   Richard Strauss (Germany): symphonies, operas
1865–1957   Jean Sibelius (Finland): symphonies
1868–1917   Scott Joplin (US): piano (ragtime), operas
1873–1958   W. C. Handy (US): piano, instrumental works (jazz)
1873–1943   Sergei Rachmaninoff (Russia): concertos
1875–1937   Maurice Ravel (France): orchestral works
1881–1945   Bela Bartók (Hungary): concertos, orchestral works

1882–1971	Igor Stravinsky (Russia): orchestral works
1885–1945	Jerome Kern (US): musicals
1888–1989	Irving Berlin (US): musicals, film music
1889–1974	Duke Ellington (US): instrumental works (jazz)
1891–1964	Cole Porter (US): musicals, film music
1891–1953	Sergei Prokofiev (Russia): ballets, symphonies
1898–1937	George Gershwin (US): orchestral works, concertos, operas
1900–1990	Aaron Copland (US): orchestral works
1902–1979	Richard Rodgers (US): musicals
1904–1988	Frederick Loewe (US): musicals
1904–1944	Glenn Miller (US): instrumental works (swing)
1906–1975	Dmitri Shostakovich (Russia): symphonies
1909–1986	Benny Goodman (US): instrumental works (swing)
1910–1981	Samuel Barber (US): orchestral works
1913–1976	Benjamin Britten (England): orchestral works, operas
1918–1990	Leonard Bernstein (US): instrumental works, operas, musicals
1930–	Stephen Sondheim (US): musicals
1937–	Philip Glass (US): instrumental works, operas

Greek and Roman Gods

Greek Name	*Roman Name*	*Role and Relationship*
Apollo	Apollo	God of beauty, poetry, music; son of Zeus and Leto; twin of Artemis
Aphrodite	Venus	Goddess of love and beauty; daughter of Zeus; wife of Hephaestus
Ares	Mars	God of war; son of Zeus and Hera
Artemis	Diana	Goddess of the moon; huntress; daughter of Zeus and Leto; twin of Apollo
Athena	Minerva	Goddess of wisdom; sprang from Zeus's forehead, in full armor
Hades	Pluto	God of the underworld; brother of Zeus
Hephaestus	Vulcan	God of fire; blacksmith; son of Zeus and Hera; husband of Aphrodite
Hera	Juno	Queen of Heaven; wife of Zeus
Hermes	Mercury	God of physicians and thieves; messenger; son of Zeus and Maia
Hestia	Vesta	Goddess of the hearth; sister of Zeus
Poseidon	Neptune	God of the sea; brother of Zeus
Zeus	Jupiter	God of the heavens; husband of Hera; brother of Hestia, Hades, and Poseidon

THE INDO-EUROPEAN FAMILY OF LANGUAGES

The Indo-European family of languages, of which English is one member, are all descended from the prehistoric Proto-Indo-European language, which was spoken in an as yet unidentified area between eastern Europe and the Aral Sea around the fifth millennium B.C. This chart displays the genetic relationships among the principal languages of the Indo-European family and loosely suggests their geographic

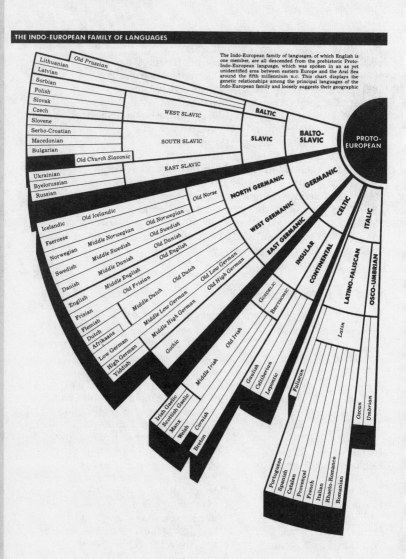

distribution. The European branches are shown in somewhat fuller detail than the Asian ones, and in the Germanic group, to which English belongs, the intermediate historical phases of the languages are also shown. Extinct languages are in italics.

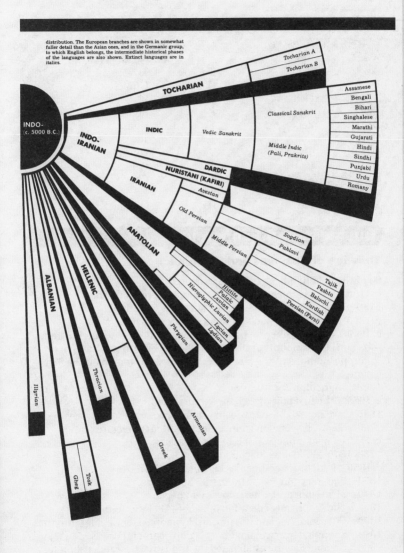

The Greek Alphabet

Letter	Name	Letter	Name
A α	Alpha	N ν	Nu
B β	Beta	Ξ ξ	Xi
Γ γ	Gamma	O o	O(micron)
Δ δ	Delta	Π π	Pi
E ϵ	E(psilon)	P ρ	Rho
Z ζ	Zeta	Σ σ	Sigma
H η	Eta	T τ	Tau
Θ Θ	Theta	Υ υ	U(psilon)
I ι	Iota	Φ ϕ	Phi
K κ	Kappa	X χ	Chi
Λ λ	Lambda	Ψ ψ	Psi
M μ	Mu	Ω ω	Omega

Business and Economics

Timeline of Business and Economics

600 BCE   Standardized coins were created.

c. 1100   The first merchant guilds (unions) were established.

1130   The first records of financial accounts were used.

c. 1300   Commercial banking was introduced in Italy.

c. 1500   Large numbers of people moved to cities; international trade began; large amounts of silver from the New World was brought to Europe; manufacturing increased; property was rented for the first time.

1600s   Agricultural Revolution.

c. 1650   The first bills of exchange were issued.

1656   Sweden established the first state bank.

1700   Steam-powered machinery increased manufacturing.

c. 1750   Paper money went into universal use.

1780–1849   Industrial Revolution.

c. 1850   Joint-stock companies became common.

1850–1900   Second-Phase Industrial Revolution.

1870s   The labor and union movement began.

1886   The American Federation of Labor (AFL) was founded.

1890s   The gold standard was universally adopted for valuing currencies.

1893   Shopping from catalogs began with Sears and Wards.

1900   General Electric established the Industrial Research Laboratory.

1903   The Department of Commerce and Labor was established.

1905   The Supreme Court rejected the maximum work week law; the first nickelodeon (movie theater) opened.

1906   Congress passed the Pure Food and Drug Act.

1908   Harvard University established its business school.

1909   Congress revised copyright laws.

1910   Singer began the manufacture of the electric sewing machine.

1911   The Supreme Court required the dismantling of Standard Oil and the American Tobacco Company.

1913   Ford began assembly-line production of automobiles; the Federal Reserve Act established a central banking system; US adopted the Sixteenth Amendment, which required federal income tax for corporations and individuals.

1914   The Panama Canal opened; the Federal Trade Commission was established; Congress passed the Clayton Antitrust Act.

1916   Germany militarized its economy; the US Tariff Commission was established; the first self-serve grocery store opened.

1920   Commercial radio broadcasting began.

1922   The first shopping center opened in the US; the first paid radio commercial aired.

1923   The A. C. Nielsen Company began media and marketing research; the Supreme Court opposed minimum wage laws.

1924   Congress imposed restrictive immigration laws.

1925   Bell Labs was formed; Sears, Roebuck opened its first retail store.

1926   Mail-order book clubs proliferated; the National Broadcasting Company (NBC) began operation.

1929   Medical insurance was first offered; the US stock market crashed, beginning the Great Depression (followed by others worldwide).

1930   The US banking system failed (followed by others worldwide); vending machines were introduced.

1933   The Tennessee Valley Authority provided major works projects for the unemployed; the US banking system was reorganized.

1934   The Securities Exchange Commission was established; federal credit unions were established.

1935   Congress passed the Social Security Act; the Committee for Industrial Organization (CIO) organized unskilled laborers; France nationalized its banks; Penguin began producing paperback books.

1936   The BBC began television broadcasting.

1938   Congress passed the Fair Labor Standards Act and the Food, Drug, and Cosmetic Act; DuPont introduced nylon.

1939   Television broadcasting began in the US.

1940   Merrill Lynch began small-scale investment services.

1946   Truman ordered the military seizure of US railroads.

1947   The US began the Marshall Plan to rebuild postwar Europe.

1948   Film studios were required to sell their movie theaters.

1952   Hasbro advertised toys on television for the first time; Truman ordered the military seizure of US steel mills.

1953   Congress created the Small Business Administration; the USSR began operation of the first nuclear power plant; McDonalds became a franchised business.

1955   The AFL and CIO merged; Disneyland began operation.

1956   The first enclosed mall opened in the US.

1957   The European Common Market was established.

1958   Congress passed legislation to regulate food additives.

1960   Automation began to replace unskilled laborers in many US factories and plants; OPEC met for the first time.

1963   Congress passed the Equal Pay Act.

1964   Congress passed the Civil Rights Act, with the intention of ending job discrimination.

1965   Medicare and Medicaid coverage began; the first air pollution laws were passed; Congress restricted the use of billboards.

1966   China began the Cultural Revolution.

1968   French workers organized a national strike; the Supreme Court banned housing discrimination; supertankers began shipping oil.

1969   Congress banned the use of DDT.

1970   The Environmental Protection Agency was founded; Congress banned the advertisement of cigarettes and liquor on television and radio; Congress passed laws to ensure workers' health and safety.

1971   Nixon lifted the trade embargo with China; the US had the first trade deficit since 1888; the Supreme Court banned discrimination in hiring.

1972   Congress passed the Consumer Product Safety Act; the pocket calculator was introduced.

1973   The first major oil embargo began.

1976   Apple Computer began operation.

1977   Fiber-optic telephone lines were introduced; the Alaskan Pipeline began operation.

1978   Volkswagen opened the first foreign-owned auto manufacturing plants in the US; Congress passed the Airline Deregulation Act.

1979   Nuclear power was regulated after the Three Mile Island incident; Congress deregulated oil prices; the Supreme Court supported affirmative action programs.

1980 Japan became the world's largest producer of automobiles; Congress deregulated banks and savings and loans; the Cable News Network began broadcasting.

1981 US air traffic controllers went on strike; IBM introduced the personal computer; adjustable-rate mortgages were introduced.

1982 AT&T divided its holdings after losing an antitrust case; *USA Today* began publication.

1983 Compact discs were marketed for the first time.

1985 Cable television offered home shopping for the first time.

1986 The Supreme Court authorized quotas to compensate for past discrimination.

1987 The US stock market crashed.

1990 Congress passed the Americans with Disabilities Act; Poland moved to a market economy; Congress passed the Clean Air Act.

1992 The European market merged.

1994 The North American Free Trade Agreement went into effect.

1999 The Euro was launched, uniting the economies of eleven European nations.

US Businesses with the Greatest Revenues (1997, in millions)

1. General Motors: $178,174
2. Ford Motor: $153,627
3. Exxon: $122,379
4. Wal-Mart: $119,299
5. General Electric: $90,840
6. International Business Machines (IBM): $78,508
7. Chrysler: $61,147
8. Mobil: $59,978
9. Philip Morris: $56,114
10. AT&T: $53,261
11. Boeing: $45,800
12. Texaco: $45,187
13. State Farm: $43,957
14. Hewlett-Packard: $42,895
15. E. I. du Pont: $41,304
16. Sears, Roebuck: $41,296
17. Travelers Group: $37,609
18. Prudential: $37,073
19. Chevron: $36,376
20. Procter & Gamble: $35,764

Largest Gross Domestic Product (1996, in billions)

1. United States $7,661.6
2. China 3,390.0
3. Japan 2,850.0
4. Germany 1,700.0
5. India 1,538.0

6. France 1,220.0
7. United Kingdom 1,190.0
8. Italy 1,122.0
9. Brazil 1,022.0
10. Indonesia 779.7

Basic Consumer Goods Used to Determine the Consumer Price Index

1. Food and beverages
2. Housing
3. Fuel and other utilities
4. Clothing (and upkeep)
5. Private transportation (cars and gasoline)
6. Public transportation (fares)
7. Medical/dental care (and drug prices)
8. Recreation/entertainment
9. Other goods
10. Services

Business and Economics Terminology

Balanced Budget   A budget with receipts that equal its expenditures.

Balance of Payments   An equitable exchange of exports to and imports from a foreign country.

Bear Market   A stock market with falling prices.

Bond   A contractual agreement whereby a borrower and lender determine an interest rate and a payment schedule.

Bull Market   A stock market with rising prices.

Capital Gain or Loss   An increase or decrease in the value of an asset (usually over a fixed period of time).

Consumer Price Index   (CPI). A formula to determine the buying power of consumers (based on changing prices of consumer goods).

Corporate Bond   A bond issued by a company (with a predetermined interest rate and pay-back period).

Deficit   A financial imbalance wherein expenditures exceed receipts.

Deficit Spending   A pattern of governmental budgeting wherein purchases and operating expenses exceed tax revenues.

Deflation   A decrease in the cost (or value) of goods.

Depression   An extended period (usually more than two quarters) of economic decline, usually indicated by failing businesses, low prices, and high unemployment. See *Recession*.

Devaluation   The lowering (officially) of the value of a nation's currency in relation to other currencies.

Discount Rate   The interest rate the Federal Reserve Bank offers to depository institutions (banks and savings and loans).

Disposable Income   The available income after taxes. Alternately, available income after taxes and debt payments.

Diversification   An investment pattern that includes the purchase of varied assets (to avoid vulnerability).

Dividend   A payment (a percentage of profits) paid by a corporation.

Dow Jones Industrial Average   An average of the market prices of leading companies on the New York Stock Exchange.

Federal Deposit Insurance Corporation   (FDIC). A subsidized program to protect accounts from bank failures.

Federal Reserve System   The central bank of the United States (includes twelve Reserve Banks, twenty-four Reserve Branch Banks, all national banks, and other selected financial institutions).

Gross Domestic Product   (GDP). The value of a nation's goods and services (within the nation's borders); used (since 1991) to measure the size of the economy.

Gross National Product   (GNP). The worldwide value of a nation's goods and services (including values outside the nation's borders).

Individual Retirement Account   (IRA). A retirement plan that is separate from federal or job-related plans; enables people to make tax-sheltered investments for use after retirement.

Inflation   An increase in the cost (or value) of goods.

Insider Trading   Investments made with prior knowledge (gained illegally) about a corporation's conditions or plans.

Interest   The charge (identified in percentages) for borrowing money. Alternately, the payment received for investing.

Leading Indicators   Information relating to 11 facets of the economy; used to predict economic change.

Liquid Assets   Assets that can be converted quickly into cash.

Municipal Bond   A bond issued by a governmental unit (state, city, school corporation, for example).

Mutual Fund   A managed investment portfolio that includes a variety of financial assets; cost is determined by the averaged value of all assets.

National Debt   The operating debt of the federal government (*not* the total debt of all people and businesses in the nation).

Option   An agreement to buy or sell at a specific time or price.

Per Capita Income   The average income of a group of people.

Prime Interest Rate   The interest rate lending institutions charge to commercial customers (usually the discount rate plus a small percentage); interest rates for loans to individuals are generally the "prime" plus a percentage.

Producer Price Index   A formula to determine the price of wholesale goods (based on the cost of materials, manufacturing/processing, and marketing).

Public Debt   The operating debt of all sectors of the government (national, state, and local).

Recession   A brief period (usually no more than two quarters) in which prices are low and unemployment is high. See *Depression*.

Savings Association Insurance Fund   (SAIF). A federally subsidized program to protect interest-bearing accounts from savings and loan failures.

Stock (Equity Shares)   Certificates of part ownership of a company.

Surplus   A financial imbalance, wherein receipts exceed expenditures.

Takeover   The purchase of one company by another, or the merger of one company with another; a *takeover* may be "friendly" (agreeable to both companies) or "hostile" (opposed by one company).

United States History and Government

Timeline of United States History

1492   Christopher Columbus's expedition sighted land (the Bahamas).

1497   John Cabot explored the northeastern coast of North America.

1524   Ponce de Léon explored Florida.

1540   Francisco Vásquez de Coronada explored the Southwest.

1565   Pedro Menéndez de Avilés founded St. Augustine, FL.

1607   John Smith founded Jamestown, VA, the first permanent settlement.

1619   The Dutch brought the first black indentured servants to Jamestown.

1620   The Puritans (the *Mayflower*) landed in Plymouth, MA.

1626   Peter Minuit (Dutch) bought Manhattan Island for approximately $24.

1630   John Winthrop helped establish the settlement of Boston, MA.

1636   Roger Williams founded Providence, RI; Harvard College was the first college founded in America; compulsory education was established in Boston.

1640   The *Bay Psalm Book* was the first book printed in the thirteen British colonies.

1664   The English seized New Netherlands and renamed it New York.

1673 Jacques Marquette and Louis Joliet explored the Mississippi River.

1683 William Penn bought the Pennsylvania region from the Delaware Indians.

1692 Witch trials were held in Salem, MA.

1693 College of William and Mary opens as the first state-supported college in the colonies that became the United States.

1699 The French settled the Louisiana and Mississippi areas.

1704 John Campbell published the *Boston News Letter*, the first newspaper in America.

1742 Benjamin Franklin (through his kite experiments) discovered that lightning is electrical.

1754 The French and Indian War began.

1763 The French and Indian War ended.

1765 The British Parliament enacted the Stamp Act.

1766 Parliament repealed the Stamp Act.

1770 British soldiers killed five protesters, which became known as the Boston Massacre.

1773 Protestors threw cargo overboard in what is now known as the Boston Tea Party.

1774 Representatives from the colonies formed the Continental Congress; Rhode Island abolished slavery.

1775 Patrick Henry made his "give me liberty or give me death" speech in Virginia; Paul Revere warned colonists of British invasion; the Continental Congress selected George Washington as commander in chief; colonists won the Battle of Bunker Hill.

1776 The Continental Congress approved the Declaration of Independence; the Revolutionary War began.

1777 The Continental Congress approved the national flag, the Stars and Stripes; France recognized that the colonies were independent.

1781 The Bank of North America was chartered.

1782 The British recognized the independence of the American colonies.

1783 Massachusetts abolished slavery; Washington disbanded the army.

1787 Members of the Constitutional Congress developed the Constitution.

1789 The Constitution went into effect; the colonies became states; George Washington was unanimously selected as president; Congress established the Supreme Court.

1791 The Bill of Rights went into effect.

1792 Congress established the US Mint (Philadelphia); construction began on the White House.

1800 The Federal government moved from Philadelphia, PA, to Washington, DC.

1803 The US made the Louisiana Purchase from France.

1804 Lewis and Clark explored the Northwest.

1808 Congress made it illegal to import slaves (though the practice continued).

1811 The Cumberland Road, a trail through the Appalachian Mountains, opened.

1812 The War of 1812 began.

1814 The British invaded Washington, DC, and burned the Capitol and the White House; Francis Scott Key wrote the "Star Spangled Banner"; the war ended.

1820 The Missouri Compromise limited slavery west of the Mississippi.

1821 Emma Willard founded Troy Female Seminary, the first women's college in the US.

1823 The Monroe Doctrine opposed European military action in the Americas.

1825 The Erie Canal opened the Great Lakes to shipping.

1831 Nat Turner led a slave rebellion in Virginia.

1832 The Black Hawk War pushed many Indian tribes west of the Mississippi.

1833 Oberlin College began coeducational education.

1835 Native American groups in Florida and Georgia were forced to move west of the Mississippi; Texas declared its intention to secede from Mexico.

1836 The Alamo (San Antonio, TX) was attacked; Texas declared its independence.

1838 Cherokee Indians were forced from Georgia to Oklahoma along the "Trail of Tears."

1841 The first wagon train left from Missouri for California.

1844 William Morse sent a telegraph message from Washington, DC, to Baltimore, MD.

1846 The Mexican War began over disputes about Texan territories.

1848 Mexico relinquished claims to Texas and California; Prospectors discovered gold in California, which prompted the "Gold Rush"; Lucretia Mott and Elizabeth Stanton organized the Women's Rights Convention in Seneca Falls, NY.

1853 Matthew Perry negotiated a treaty to open Japan to US commercial interests.

1855 The first bridges spanned the Mississippi River.

1857 The Supreme Court's Dred Scott Decision asserted that slaves could not become citizens, remained slaves even in free states, and allowed slavery in territories.

1858   Lincoln and Douglas debated in Illinois.

1860   Abraham Lincoln was elected president; a Pony Express route opened between St. Joseph, MO, and Sacramento, CA.

1861   Southern states formed the Confederate States of America; Jefferson Davis was named president; the Civil War began; telegraph lines extended across the continent.

1862   Congress approved the Homestead Act (free farmland for settlers) and the Land Grant Act.

1863   Lincoln issued the Emancipation Proclamation; Lincoln delivered the Gettysburg Address; protestors opposed military service in the New York draft riots.

1864   General Sherman completed his "March to the Sea."

1865   General Lee surrendered to General Grant at Appomattox, VA; John Wilkes Booth shot and killed President Lincoln at Ford's Theater in Washington, DC; Congress passed the 13th Amendment, which abolished slavery.

1866   The Ku Klux Klan was formed; Congress organized the Southern Reconstruction.

1867   Russia sold Alaska to the US.

1868   Andrew Johnson was impeached by the House and acquitted by the Senate.

1869   Central Pacific Railroad and Union Pacific Railroad joined in Promontory, UT, completing the transcontinental railroad.

1871   Chicago was destroyed by the "Great Fire."

1872   Congress established Yellowstone, the first national park.

1873   The first nursing school was established at Bellevue Hospital in New York.

1875   Congress passed the Civil Rights Act, which provided blacks with equal accommodations and jury duties.

1876   Reconstruction ended; George Custer and his troops were defeated at the Battle of the Little Big Horn, MT.

1878   Commercial telephone service was established in New Haven, CT.

1879   The first Woolworth's five-and-dime store opened in Utica, NY.

1881   Booker Washington founded Tuskegee Institute.

1883   The Brooklyn Bridge spanned the East River; the Supreme Court struck down the Civil Rights Act of 1875.

1886   Geronimo surrendered; the Statue of Liberty was dedicated; twenty-five smaller unions formed the American Federation of Labor (AFL).

1889   US troops and Indians fought the Battle of Wounded Knee, SD.

1891   Congress passed the Forest Reserve Act, which established national forests and parks.

1892   Immigrant Services opened on Ellis Island, NY.

1894   Thomas Edison showed a motion picture publicly.

1896   The Supreme Court, in *Plessy* v. *Ferguson*, established the "separate but equal" doctrine, thereby allowing further segregation.

1898   The Spanish allegedly blew up the *Maine*, a US battleship, thereby prompting the Spanish-American War.

1900   The International "Ladies" Garment Workers Union was organized.

1901   Leon Czolgosz shot and killed President McKinley.

1903   The US and Panama signed an agreement to ensure the building of the Panama Canal; Orville and Wilbur Wright flew the first airplane at Kitty Hawk, NC.

1906   A major earthquake destroyed San Francisco.

1908   Henry Ford introduced the Model T.

1909   Robert Peary asserted that he reached the North Pole; the National Association for the Advancement of Colored People (NAACP) was founded.

1910   The Boy Scouts of America was founded.

1911   The Supreme Court split the Standard Oil Company monopoly.

1912   American Girl Guides (later the Girl Scouts) was founded.

1913   Congress approved the Federal Reserve System.

1914   The Panama Canal opened.

1915   Alexander Bell and Thomas Watson completed the first transcontinental telephone call (New York to San Francisco).

1916   Jeannette Rankin (R-MT) was the first woman to be elected to the House of Representatives.

1917   The US declared war on Germany (World War I); Congress passed the law that provided for the draft; Congress also passed the Eighteenth Amendment, establishing Prohibition.

1919   The Versailles Treaty was signed, ending World War I.

1920   Commercial radio broadcasting began; Congress passed the 19th Amendment, enabling women to vote; the League of Women Voters was founded.

1923   A film with sound was presented publicly for the first time.

1924   Congress passed a law making Native Americans citizens; Nellie Ross was the first woman elected governor (WY).

1925   John Scopes was convicted of teaching evolution (TN).

1927   Charles Lindbergh flew *The Spirit of St. Louis* nonstop from New York to Paris.

1929   The Stock Market crashed, beginning the Great Depression.

1931   The Empire State Building was completed.

1932   Charles Lindbergh's son was kidnapped and later found dead; Franklin Roosevelt was elected president.

1933 Roosevelt closed all banks; in 100 days, Congress passed "New Deal" legislation to develop work projects, control banking, control agricultural prices, control wages, compensate the unemployed, and control industrial production; Congress voted to end Prohibition.

1935 Congress passed the Social Security Act; the Committee for Industrial Organization (CIO) was formed.

1940 Congress approved a peacetime draft.

1941 Japan attacked ships at Pearl Harbor; US declared war on Japan, Germany, and Italy and entered World War II.

1942 The US government placed Japanese-Americans who lived in western states in detention camps; US military forces were engaged in the Pacific, north Africa, and Europe.

1943 The US government began withholding taxes.

1944 US Allied forces landed at Normandy, beginning the invasion of northern Europe; Congress passed the G.I. Bill of Rights.

1945 Roosevelt, Churchill, and Stalin met at Yalta; Roosevelt died, and Truman became president; Germany surrendered; the atomic bomb was tested at Los Alamos, NM; atomic bombs were dropped on Hiroshima and Nagasaki; Japan surrendered, officially ending World War II; US, Britain, and USSR divided Germany and other territories; US troops were sent to Korea.

1946 US government granted the Philippines independence.

1947 Congress passed the Taft-Hartley Act (to control union strikes), Truman vetoed it, and Congress overrode the veto; the Marshall Plan provided financial assistance for rebuilding Europe.

1948 USSR closed the East German border; US and British troops air-lifted supplies and aid to West Berlin.

1949 US troops left Korea; NATO was formed by US, Canada, and ten countries in western Europe.

1950 North Korea invaded South Korea; US troops returned; the US sent military advisors to South Vietnam.

1951 Truman removed Douglas MacArthur from Asian command; the first transcontinental television broadcast was made.

1952 Congress passed the Immigration and Naturalization Act; the hydrogen bomb was tested in the Pacific.

1953 The Korean peace agreement was signed.

1954 The McCarthy Hearings began in Congress; the Supreme Court ruled, in *Brown* v. *Board of Education of Topeka*, that racial segregation was illegal.

1955 The US military began providing military training for the South Vietnamese army; Rosa Parks refused to give up her seat on the bus in Montgomery, AL; the AFL and CIO (two major unions) merged.

1956   Congress approved the Highway Act, beginning the interstate highway system; the first transatlantic telephone cable was laid.

1957   Congress passed a civil rights bill to ensure voting rights for blacks; US troops were sent to Little Rock, AK, to ensure that black students could attend the public, all-white high school.

1958   The first US satellite was launched from Cape Canaveral, FL.

1960   Civil rights protests were prevalent in southern states; Congress passed the Voting Rights Act ; Richard Nixon and John Kennedy participated in the first televised presidential debate.

1961   The US broke diplomatic ties with Cuba; the Bay of Pigs invasion failed to overthrow Fidel Castro (Cuba); the Peace Corps was created; Alan Shepard completed the US's first suborbital space flight.

1962   John Glenn completed the first orbital flight; James Meredith was the first black student to enroll at the University of Mississippi; the "Cuban Missile Crisis" ended (after naval blockades) when the Soviets removed military equipment from Cuba.

1963   The Supreme Court ruled that defendants have rights to receive legal counsel and that illegally obtained evidence may not be used in a trial; they also ruled that requiring students to recite Bible verses was illegal in public schools; 200,000 people took part in the "March on Washington"; John Kennedy was assassinated in Dallas, TX, and Lyndon Johnson became president.

1964   Congress established Medicare and Medicaid; Congress passed the Tonkin Gulf Resolution; Congress provided funding for Johnson's "War on Poverty"; the Warren Commission published its report on the Kennedy assassination.

1965   Malcolm X was assassinated in New York City; Martin Luther King, Jr., organized and led the March from Selma to Montgomery, AL; blacks rioted in Watts, CA.

1967   Thurgood Marshall became the first black justice on the Supreme Court.

1968   Martin Luther King, Jr., was assassinated in Memphis, TN; Robert Kennedy was assassinated in Los Angeles, CA.

1969   The US began peace talks with Vietnam; *Apollo 11* landed on the moon; the Woodstock Music Festival was held in Bethel, NY.

1970   The "Chicago 7" were tried for inciting riots; four student protesters were killed at Kent State University (OH).

1971   The 26th Amendment lowered the voting age to eighteen.

1972   Richard Nixon visited China; Nixon visited the USSR; five men were arrested after a break-in at the Watergate (Washington, DC).

1973   The Supreme Court, in *Roe* v. *Wade*, ruled that abortions were legal and that states could not establish separate policies; the Paris

Peace Agreements concluded, and US troops left Vietnam; the military draft was discontinued; the Watergate case resulted in the resignation—and often conviction—of many of Nixon's chief aides.

1974 Congress began Nixon's impeachment hearings; Nixon resigned from office and Gerald Ford became president.

1975 The US evacuated remaining personnel from South Vietnam; North Vietnamese forces invaded.

1976 The US celebrated its bicentennial (200-year anniversary).

1978 The Supreme Court, in *Bakke* v. *University of California*, made it illegal to use racial quotas.

1979 The Three Mile Island (PA) nuclear reactor released radiation after a partial meltdown; Iranian nationalists held sixty-three Americans hostage in Tehran.

1981 American hostages in Iran were released; the space shuttle (*Columbia*) was launched; Sandra Day O'Connor became the first woman appointed to the Supreme Court.

1983 Sally Ride became the first US female astronaut; a bomb killed 241 soldiers in Lebanon; US troops invaded Grenada.

1985 Terrorist activities escalated in eastern Europe and the Middle East.

1986 The shuttle *Challenger* exploded immediately after lift-off; Congress placed economic sanctions on South Africa (to end apartheid).

1987 The Dow Jones average dropped over 500 points.

1988 A new federal policy provided amnesty to illegal aliens in the US.

1989 The *Exxon Valdez* created a large oil spill in Prince William Sound (AK); Congress passed legislation to save the failing savings and loan business.

1990 Congress passed the Americans with Disabilities Act; Iraq invaded Kuwait, beginning the Persian Gulf War.

1991 The Persian Gulf War ended; Clarence Thomas was appointed to the Supreme Court, in spite of the testimony of Anita Hill.

1992 Following the acquittal of the police officers who beat motorist Rodney King, riots broke out in Los Angeles, CA.

1993 Terrorists bombed the World Trade Center in New York City; Janet Reno became the first female attorney general; federal agents surrounded and then burned down the Branch Davidian compound (Waco, TX); flooding devastated the Midwest; Congress passed the "Brady Bill" (gun control).

1994 Congress approved the North American Free Trade Agreement (NAFTA); Kenneth Starr was appointed as independent counsel in the Whitewater Hearings; Paula Jones filed a sexual harassment suit against President Bill Clinton.

1995 A truck bomb destroyed a federal office building in Oklahoma City; O. J. Simpson was found not guilty in criminal court.

1996 Congress passed the Welfare Reform Bill (shifting welfare management to the states).

1997 Madeleine Albright became the first female secretary of state; Timothy McVeigh was convicted in the Oklahoma City bombing.

1998 Bill Clinton was impeached by the US House of Representatives for perjury.

1999 Bill Clinton was acquitted by the US Senate.

United States Presidents

D = Democrat   R = Republican

1. **George Washington** (1732–1799)
   Term: 1789–1797, Federalist
2. **John Adams** (1735–1826)
   Term: 1797–1801, Federalist
3. **Thomas Jefferson** (1743–1826)
   Term: 1801–1809, Democratic-Republican
4. **James Madison** (1751–1836)
   Term: 1809–1817, Democratic-Republican
5. **James Monroe** (1758–1831)
   Term: 1817–1825, Democratic-Republican
6. **John Quincy Adams** (1767–1848)
   Term: 1825–1829, Democratic-Republican
7. **Andrew Jackson** (1767–1845)
   Term: 1829–1837, D
8. **Martin Van Buren** (1782–1864)
   Term: 1837–1841, D
9. **William Henry Harrison** (1773–1841)
   Term: 1841, Whig
10. **John Tyler** (1790–1862)
    Term: 1841–1845, Whig
11. **James K. Polk** (1795–1849)
    Term: 1845–1849, D
12. **Zachary Taylor** (1784–1850)
    Term: 1849–1850, Whig
13. **Millard Fillmore** (1800–1874)
    Term: 1850–1853, Whig
14. **Franklin Pierce** (1804–1869)
    Term: 1853–1857, D
15. **James Buchanan** (1791–1868)
    Term: 1857–1861, D
16. **Abraham Lincoln** (1809–1865)
    Term: 1861–1865, R
17. **Andrew Johnson** (1808–1875)
    Term: 1865–1869, Union
18. **Ulysses S. Grant** (1822–1885)
    Term: 1869–1877, R
19. **Rutherford B. Hayes** (1822–1893)
    Term: 1877–1881, R
20. **James Garfield** (1831–1881)
    Term: 1881, R
21. **Chester A. Arthur** (1830–1886)
    Term: 1881–1885, R
22. **Grover Cleveland** (1837–1908)
    Term: 1885–1889, D
23. **Benjamin Harrison** (1833–1901)
    Term: 1889–1893, R

24. **Grover Cleveland**
    (1837–1908)
    Term: 1893–1897, D
25. **William McKinley**
    (1843–1901)
    Term: 1897–1901, R
26. **Theodore Roosevelt**
    (1858–1919)
    Term: 1901–1909, R
27. **William H. Taft** (1857–1930)
    Term: 1909–1913, R
28. **Woodrow Wilson** (1856–1924)
    Term: 1913–1921, D
29. **Warren G. Harding**
    (1865–1923)
    Term: 1921–1923, R
30. **Calvin Coolidge**
    (1872–1933)
    Term: 1923–1929, R
31. **Herbert Hoover** (1874–1964)
    Term: 1929–1933, R
32. **Franklin D. Roosevelt**
    (1882–1945)
    Term: 1933–1945, D
33. **Harry S. Truman**
    (1884–1972)
    Term: 1945–1953, D
34. **Dwight D. Eisenhower**
    (1890–1969)
    Term: 1953–1961, R
35. **John F. Kennedy**
    (1917–1963)
    Term: 1961–1963, D
36. **Lyndon B. Johnson**
    (1908–1973)
    Term: 1963–1969, D
37. **Richard M. Nixon**
    (1913–1994)
    Term: 1969–1974, R
38. **Gerald R. Ford** (1913–)
    Term: 1974–1977, R
39. **Jimmy Carter** (1924–)
    Term: 1977–1981, D
40. **Ronald Reagan** (1911–)
    Term: 1981–1989, R
41. **George Bush** (1924–)
    Term: 1989–1993, R
42. **William J. Clinton** (1946–)
    Term: 1993–, D

Members of the Supreme Court (1999)

<http://www.uscourts.gov/>
<http://supct.law.cornell.edu/supct/justices/>

William H. Rehnquist, Chief Justice
    Term: 1986–present; Associate
    Justice: 1972–1986; appointed by Ronald Reagan
John Paul Stevens, Associate Justice
    Term: 1975–present; appointed by Gerald Ford
Sandra Day O'Connor, Associate Justice
    Term: 1981–present; appointed by Ronald Reagan
Antonin Scalia, Associate Justice
    Term: 1986–present; appointed by Ronald Reagan

Anthony M. Kennedy, Associate Justice
  Term: 1988–present; appointed by Ronald Reagan
David H. Souter, Associate Justice
  Term: 1990–present; appointed by George Bush
Clarence Thomas, Associate Justice
  Term: 1991–present; appointed by George Bush
Ruth Bader Ginsburg, Associate Justice
  Term: 1993–present; appointed by William Clinton
Stephen G. Breyer, Associate Justice
  Term: 1994–present; appointed by William Clinton

Executive Departments and Agencies

Council of Economic Advisors (CEA): est. 1946

Mission: To analyze and interpret economic trends, review programs, and help develop national economic policy.
<http://www.whitehouse.gov/WH/EOP/CEA/html/CEA.html>

Council on Environmental Quality (CEQ): est. 1969

Mission: To oversee policy implementation, review programs, analyze trends, coordinate national environmental efforts, and develop environmental policy.
<http://www.whitehouse.gov/CEQ/>

National Security Council (NSC): est. 1947

Mission: To advise the president on national security and foreign policy matters, assist in instituting policies, and coordinate local, state, and national agencies.
<http://www.whitehouse.gov/WH/EOP/NSG/html/nschome.html>

Office of Administration: est. 1977

Mission: To provide administrative support services to all units within the Executive Office of the President.
<http://www.whitehouse.gov/WH/EOP/html/other/OA.html>

Office of Management and Budget (OMB): est. 1970

Mission: To analyze and interpret data related to national spending, develop and execute fiscal policies and programs, and monitor legislative spending.
<http://www.whitehouse.gov/OMB/>

Office of Science and Technology Policy (OSTP): est. 1976

Mission: To promote the advancement of science and technology, foster research and development, administer programs, support initiatives, and provide grants.
<http://www.whitehouse.gov/WH/EOP/OSTP/html/OSTP_Home.html>

Office of the United States Trade Representative (OUSTR): est. 1963

Mission: To promote US trade within international markets, negotiate agreements, and gather and analyze information related to world trade.
<http://www.ustr.gov/>

Office of National Drug Control Policy (ONDCP): est. 1989

Mission: To analyze and interpret trends in drug use, review programs, coordinate national drug-control efforts, and develop drug-related policies
<http://www.whitehousedrugpolicy.gov/>

Department of State: est. 1781

Mission: To maintain international relations, defend US interests, address crises, coordinate diplomatic efforts, negotiate agreements, protect US citizens abroad, and support US business.
<http://www.state.gov/>

Department of the Treasury: est. 1789

Mission: To maintain a stable US economy, promote economic stability abroad, manage government finances, and protect financial institutions.
<http://www.ustreas.gov/>

Department of Defense: est. 1947

Mission: To provide military forces to deter war and ensure national security; in times of war, to protect US citizens, property, and interests.
<http://www.defenselink.mil/>

Department of Justice: est. 1870

Mission: To protect civil rights, enforce drug and antitrust laws, monitor immigration, investigate criminal actions, supervise the prison system, and gather information (FBI).
<http://www.usdoj.gov/>

Department of the Interior: est. 1849

Mission: To protect national resources, monitor wildlife, supervise land management, operate national parks, control mining, and respond to the needs of Native Americans.
<http://www.doi.gov/index/html>

Department of Agriculture: est. 1889

Mission: To protect land and national resources, monitor the food supply, support US farming, and expand global markets for US agricultural goods.
<http://www.usda.gov>

Department of Commerce: est. 1903

Mission: To encourage sustainable economic growth, create jobs, manage resources, and increase US competitiveness in a global economy.
<http://www.doc.gov/>

Department of Labor: est. 1913

Mission: To enforce labor laws, protect wages, ensure the safety of workers, assure equal opportunity, provide unemployment compensation, and generate labor statistics.
<http://www.dol.gov/>

Department of Health and Human Services: est. 1953

Mission: To protect the health of US citizens, ensure drug and food safety, conduct and sponsor medical and social research, and administer Medicare and Medicaid.
<http://www.os.dhhs.gov/>

Department of Housing and Urban Development: est. 1965

Mission: To provide suitable housing for US citizens, ensure fairness in housing availability, promote economic development, and coordinate efforts to help the homeless.
<http://www.hud.gov/>

Department of Transportation: est. 1966

Mission: To maintain US highways, promote traffic safety, sponsor research, and encourage suitable aviation, shipping, and ground transportation.
<http://www.dot.gov/>

Department of Energy: est. 1977

Mission: To provide national energy security, maintain environmental quality, and promote research and development of alternative energy sources.
<http://home.doe.gov/>

Department of Education: est. 1979

Mission: To provide equal access and promote excellence in US schools, administer programs, support initiatives, provide grants, and generate educational statistics.
<http://www.ed.gov/>

Department of Veterans' Affairs: est. 1989

Mission: To promote the interests of veterans, address their special needs, and administer specialized support programs.
<http://www.va.gov/>

US Census Bureau: est. 1902

Mission: To collect and provide information about Americans and the US economy for other agencies.
<http://www.census.gov/>

The White House: first occupied in 1800

Mission: To provide a residence for the presidential family, a place for state functions, and office spaces for the president and executive staff.
<http://www.whitehouse.gov>

Independent Agencies

Central Intelligence Agency (CIA): est. 1947

Mission: To gather information related to national security, provide counterintelligence information, and gather data in times of crisis or war.
<http://www.odci.gov/>

Consumer Product Safety Commission (CPSC): est. 1972

Mission: To evaluate products, promote safety research, guide industry standards, recall unsafe products, and reduce risks involved with product use.
<http://www.cpsc.gov/>

Environmental Protection Agency (EPA): est. 1970

Mission: To protect the health of US citizens, promote environmental awareness, and safeguard the nation's air, water, and land.
<http://www.epa.gov/>

Equal Employment Opportunity Commission (EEOC): est. 1965

Mission: To promote equal opportunity, enforce civil rights laws, develop policies, help implement initiatives, and increase awareness of civil rights issues.
<http://www.access.gpo.gov/eeoc/index.html>

Federal Deposit Insurance Corporation (FDIC): est. 1933

Mission: To protect investments in approved financial institutions, monitor economic trends, and administer investment programs.
<http://www.fdic.gov/>

Federal Election Commission (FEC): est. 1974

Mission: To ensure the fairness of elections, monitor voting practices and procedures, encourage registration and voting, and gather and share data on campaign contributions.
<http://www.fec.gov/>

Federal Emergency Management Agency (FEMA): est. 1979

Mission: To aid victims of disasters, coordinate emergency management systems (local, state, and national), and encourage emergency readiness.
<http://www.fema.gov/>

Federal Maritime Commission (FMC): est. 1961

Mission: To enforce shipping laws that regulate foreign trade, regulate tariff rates, and investigate violations.
<http://www.fmc.gov/>

Federal Reserve System (FRS), Board of Governors of: est. 1913

Mission: To ensure a stable but flexible financial system, set monetary policy, regulate banks, control economic risk factors, and provide

information to other agencies.
<http://www.bog.frs.fed.us/>

Federal Trade Commission (FTC): est. 1914

Mission: To ensure fair business competition, enforce antitrust and consumer protection laws, assist other agencies, and educate American consumers.
<http://www.ftc.gov/>

General Accounting Office (GAO): est. 1921

Mission: To audit the financial operations (receipts and disbursements) of government agencies and programs and report to Congress.
<http://www.gao.gov/>

Government Printing Office (GPO): est. 1860

Mission: To print and bind materials (reports, summaries, documents, books, and so on) used by or disseminated by all branches of the government.
<http://www.access.gpo.gov/su_docs/aces/aaces002.html>

Library of Congress (LC): est. 1800

Mission: Initially, to provide resources for only members of Congress; currently, to serve as a national (and international) depository of resource materials.
<http://lcweb.loc.gov/>

National Aeronautics and Space Administration (NASA): est. 1958

Mission: To expand knowledge of the atmosphere and space, sponsor research, and develop aircraft, missiles, and space vehicles.
<http://www.nasa.gov/NASA_homepage.html>

National Endowment for the Arts (NEA): est. 1965

Mission: To promote creativity in the arts, cultivate a sense of community spirit and support, and foster an appreciation of the arts.
<http://arts.endow.gov/>

National Endowment for the Humanities (NEH): est. 1965

Mission: To celebrate cultural and intellectual resources, support education, sponsor research, and promote a knowledge of history, culture, and thought.
<http://www.neh.fed.us>

National Labor Relations Board (NLRB): est. 1935

Mission: To coordinate union and labor policies, supervise voting for possible union start-up, and prosecute violations of labor laws.
<http://epfnet.org/nlrb.htm>

National Science Foundation (NSF): est. 1950

Mission: To promote science and engineering and support

research and educational efforts in the sciences.
<http://www.nsf.gov/>

National Transportation Safety Board (NTSB): est. 1975

Mission: To investigate aviation accidents (as well as those involving other means of transportation), issue safety regulations, and provide a database of accident information.
<http://www.ntsb.gov/>

Nuclear Regulatory Commission (NRC): est. 1975

Mission: To supervise the use of nuclear materials in the US, ensure health and safety, and monitor research and commercial uses of nuclear materials.
<http://www.nrc.gov/>

Office of Personnel Management (OPM): est. 1979

Mission: To control the procedures for federal employment, administer retirement, and manage health care programs.
<http://www.opm.gov/>

Securities and Exchange Commission (SEC): est. 1934

Mission: To administer laws related to stock and bond markets, ensure fair trading practices, and regulate brokerages.
<http://www.sec.gov/>

Selective Service System (SSS): est. 1940

Mission: To provide manpower to the armed forces in times of war or national emergency and, in peacetime, register males for prospective service.
<http://www.sss.gov/>

Small Business Administration (SBA): est. 1953

Mission: To promote small business opportunities and encourage technical advances for small businesses.
<http://www.sbaonline.sba.gov/>

Smithsonian Institution (SI): est. 1846

Mission: To serve as a depository of artifacts and specimens that are of value to our history and culture, promote research, and provide educational programs.
<http://www.si.edu>

Tennessee Valley Authority (TVA): est. 1933

Mission: To produce electricity, promote regional economic development, and sponsor environmental research.
<http://www.tva.gov/>

US International Trade Commission (USITC): est. 1916

Mission: To analyze import-export data, share information with other agencies, and counter unfair trade practices.
<http://www.usitc.gov/>

US Postal Service (USPS): est. 1775

Mission: To provide for the delivery of mail.
<http://www.usps.gov/>

Geography and the Environment

Geologic Time Scale

Eon	Era	Period	Epoch	Millions of years ago	Significant biological and geological events
Phanerozoic	Cenozoic	Quaternary	Holocene	-0.01	End of last ice age
			Pleistocene	2	Beginning of ice ages; earliest humans
		Tertiary	Pliocene	5	
			Miocene	24	
			Oligocene	37	First primates
			Eocene	58	
			Paleocene	65	K-T Event (extinction of dinosaurs)
	Mesozoic	Cretaceous			Formation of Rocky Mountains
					First flowering plants
				144	First placental mammals
		Jurassic			
				208	First birds and mammals
					Pangaea starts breaking up
		Triassic			First dinosaurs
				245	Largest extinction event ("Great Dying")
	Paleozoic	Permian			
					Pangaea forms
				285	
		Carboniferous — Pennsylvanian			Great coal-forming forests
				320	
		Carboniferous — Mississippian		360	First reptiles
		Devonian			First amphibians
				408	
		Silurian			First land plants
				438	Proterozoic supercontinent rifts
		Ordovician			First fish
				505	
		Cambrian		570	Cambrian explosion
Proterozoic					Formation of Proterozoic supercontinent
					First multicelled organisms
				2500	Formation of North American core
Archean					First one-celled organisms
				4000	Oldest rocks
Hadean				4600	Formation of Earth

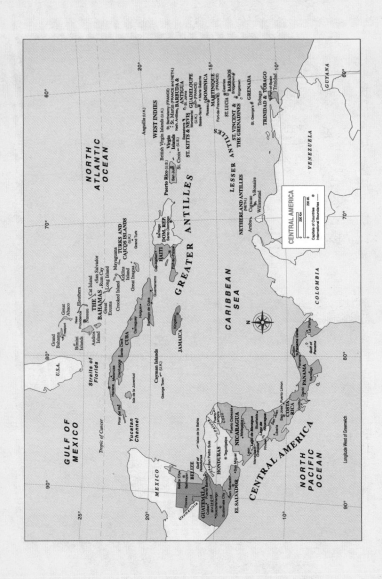

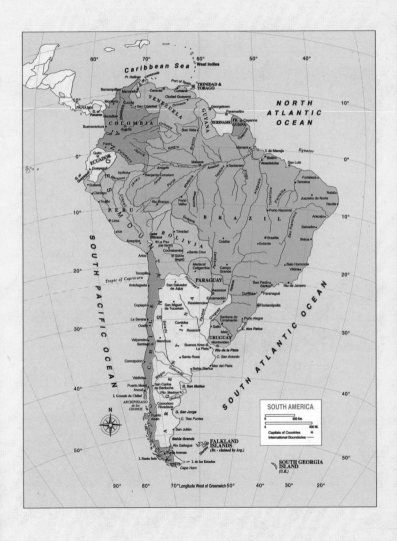

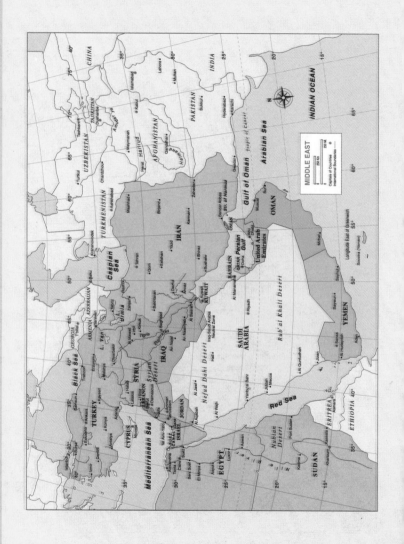

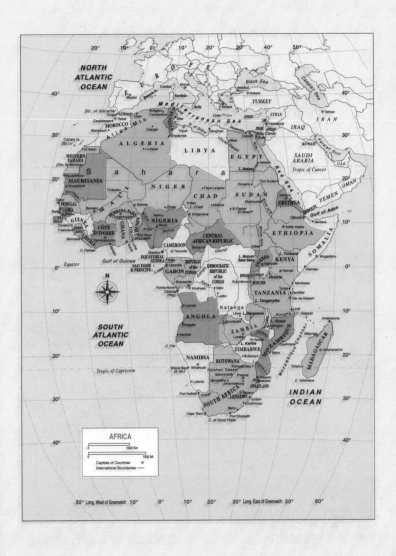

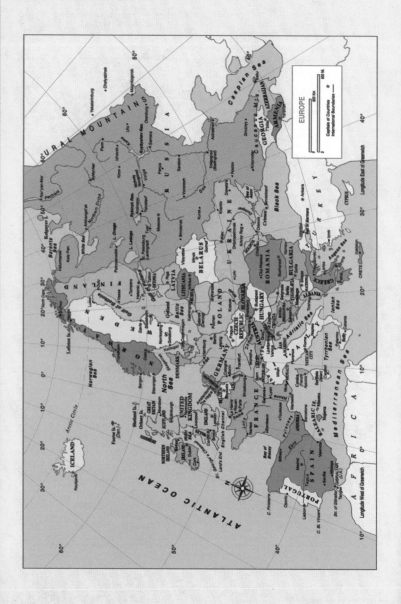

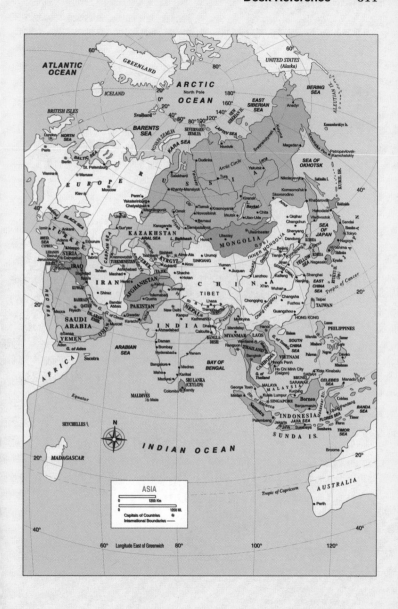

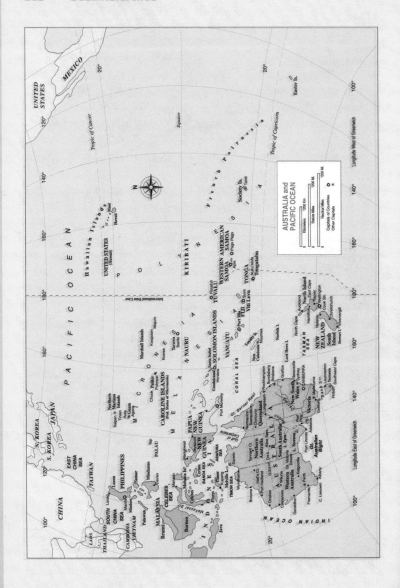

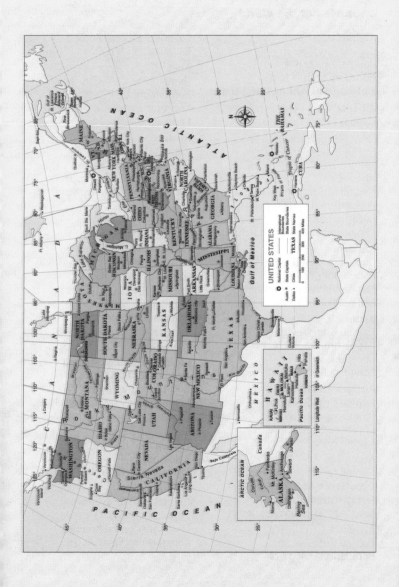

Countries of the World

Afghanistan
Capital City: Kabul
Population: 22,664,136
Location: Middle East
Language(s): Pushtu, Dari Persian

Albania
Capital City: Tiranë
Population: 3,249,136
Location: Eastern Europe
Language(s): Albanian, Greek

Algeria
Capital City: Algiers
Population: 16,948,000
Location: Africa
Language(s): Arabic, French

Andorra
Capital City: Andorra la Vella
Population: 72,766
Location: Western Europe
Language(s): Catalán, French

Angola
Capital City: Luanda
Population: 10,342,899
Location: Africa
Language(s): Bantu, Portuguese

Antigua and Barbuda
Capital City: St. John's
Population: 65,647
Location: Central America
Language(s): English

Argentina
Capital City: Buenos Aires
Population: 34,672,997
Location: South America
Language(s): Spanish, English

Armenia
Capital City: Yerevan
Population: 3,463,574
Location: Eastern Europe
Language(s): Armenian

Australia
Capital City: Canberra
Population: 18,438,824
Location: Pacific Ocean
Language(s): English

Austria
Capital City: Vienna
Population: 8,047,000
Location: Western Europe
Language(s): German, Slovene

Azerbaijan
Capital City: Baku
Population: 7,735,918
Location: Eastern Europe
Language(s): Azerbaijani Turkic

Bahamas
Capital City: Nassau
Population: 262,034
Location: Central America
Language(s): English

Bahrain
Capital City: Al-Manámah
Population: 603,318
Location: Middle East
Language(s): Arabic, English

Bangladesh
Capital City: Dhaka
Population: 125,340,261
Location: Asia
Language(s): Bengali, English

Barbados
Capital City: Bridgetown
Population: 257,731
Location: Central America
Language(s): English

Belarus
Capital City: Minsk
Population: 10,439,916
Location: Eastern Europe
Language(s): Belarussian, Russian

Belgium
Capital City: Brussels
Population: 10,203,683
Location: Western Europe
Language(s): Dutch, French

Belize
Capital City: Belmopan
Population: 224,663
Location: Central America
Language(s): English, Spanish

Benin
Capital City: Porto-Novo
Population: 5,902,178
Location: Africa
Language(s): French, African languages

Bhutan
Capital City: Thimphu
Population: 1,865,191
Location: Asia
Language(s): Dzongkha

Bolivia
Capital City: Sucre
Population: 7,669,868
Location: South America
Language(s): Spanish, Quechua

Bosnia and Herzegovina
Capital City: Sarajevo
Population: 2,607,734
Location: Eastern Europe
Language(s): Bosnian

Botswana
Capital City: Gaborone
Population: 1,500,765

Location: Africa
Language(s): English, Setswana

Brazil
Capital City: Brasilla
Population: 164,511,366
Location: South America
Language(s): Portuguese

Brunei Darussalam
Capital City: Bandar Seri Begawan
Population: 307,616
Location: Asia
Language(s): Malay, Chinese

Bulgaria
Capital City: Sofia
Population: 8,652,745
Location: Eastern Europe
Language(s): Bulgarian

Burkina Faso
Capital City: Ouagadougou
Population: 10,891,159
Location: Africa
Language(s): French, tribal languages

Burma or Myanmar
Capital City: Rangoon
Population: 46,821,943
Location: Asia
Language(s): Burmese, minority languages

Burundi
Capital City: Bujumbura
Population: 6,52,614
Location: Africa
Language(s): Kirundi, French

Cambodia
Capital City: Phnom Penh
Population: 11,163,861
Location: Asia
Language(s): Khmer, French

Cameroon
Capital City: Yaoundé
Population: 14,677,510
Location: Africa
Language(s): French, English

Canada
Capital City: Ottawa, Ontario
Population: 29,123,194
Location: North America
Language(s): English, French

Cape Verde
Capital City: Praia
Population: 393,843
Location: Africa
Language(s): Portuguese, Criuolo

Central African Republic
Capital City: Bangui
Population: 3,342,051
Location: Africa
Language(s): French, Sangho

Chad
Capital City: N'Djamena
Population: 7,166,023
Location: Africa
Language(s): French, Arabic

Chile
Capital City: Santiago
Population: 14,508,168
Location: South America
Language(s): Spanish

China
Capital City: Beijing
Population: 1,221,591,778
Location: Asia
Language(s): Chinese, Mandarin

Colombia
Capital City: Santafé de Bogotá
Population: 37,418,290

Location: South America
Language(s): Spanish

Comoros
Capital City: Moroni
Population: 589,797
Location: Africa
Language(s): Shaafi Islam, Malagasu

Congo
Capital City: Brazzaville
Population: 2,583,198
Location: Africa
Language(s): French, English

Congo, Democratic Republic of
Capital City: Kinshasa
Population: 47,440,362
Location: Africa
Language(s): French, English,
    Bantu dialects

Costa Rica
Capital City: San José
Population: 3,534,174
Location: Central America
Language(s): Spanish

Côte d'Ivoire
Capital City: Yamoussoukro
Population: 14,986,218
Location: Africa
Language(s): French, African lan-
    guages

Croatia
Capital City: Zagreb
Population: 5,026,995
Location: Eastern Europe
Language(s): Croatian

Cuba
Capital City: Havana
Population: 10,999,041
Location: North America
Language(s): Spanish

Cyprus
Capital City: Lefkosia
Population: 752,808
Location: Middle East
Language(s): Greek, Turkish

Northern Cyprus
Capital City: Nicosia North
Population: 175,494
Location: Middle East
Language(s): Turkish

Czech Republic
Capital City: Prague
Population: 10,318,958
Location: Eastern Europe
Language(s): Czech

Denmark
Capital City: Copenhagen
Population: 5,268,775
Location: Western Europe
Language(s): Danish, Faroese

Djibouti
Capital City: Djobouti
Population: 434,116
Location: Africa
Language(s): Arabic, French

Dominica
Capital City: Roseau
Population: 83,226
Location: Central America
Language(s): English, French
 patois

Dominican Republic
Capital City: Santo Domingo
Population: 8,228,151
Location: Central America
Language(s): Spanish, English

Ecuador
Capital City: Quito
Population: 11,690,535
Location: South America
Language(s): Spanish

Egypt
Capital City: Cairo
Population: 64,791,891
Location: Middle East
Language(s): Arabic

El Salvador
Capital City: San Salvador
Population: 5,661,827
Location: Central America
Language(s): Spanish

Equatorial Guinea
Capital City: Malabo
Population: 442,516
Location: Africa
Language(s): Spanish, English

Eritrea
Capital City: Asmara
Population: 3,589,687
Location: Africa
Language(s): Afar, Bilen

Estonia
Capital City: Tallinn
Population: 1,444,721
Location: Eastern Europe
Language(s): Estonian, Russian

Ethiopia
Capital City: Addis Ababa
Population: 58,732,577
Location: Africa
Language(s): Amharic, English

Fiji
Capital City: Suva
Population: 792,441
Location: Pacific Ocean
Language(s): Fijian, Hindustani

Finland
Capital City: Helsinki
Population: 5,109,148
Location: Western Europe
Language(s): Finnish, Swedish

France
Capital City: Paris
Population: 58,470,421
Location: Western Europe
Language(s): French

Gabon
Capital City: Libreville
Population: 1,190,159
Location: Africa
Language(s): French

The Gambia
Capital City: Banjul
Population: 1,248,085
Location: Africa
Language(s): native languages,
   English

Georgia
Capital City: Tbilisi
Population: 5,174,642
Location: Eastern Europe
Language(s): Georgian, Russian

Germany
Capital City: Berlin
Population: 84,068,216
Location: Western Europe
Language(s): German

Ghana
Capital City: Accra
Population: 18,100,703
Location: Africa
Language(s): English, native lan-
   guages

Greece
Capital City: Athens
Population: 10,583,126
Location: Eastern Europe
Language(s): Greek

Grenada
Capital City: St. George's
Population: 95,537
Location: Central America
Language(s): English

Guatemala
Capital City: Guatemala City
Population: 11,558,407
Location: Central America
Language(s): Spanish, native lan-
   guages

Guinea
Capital City: Conakry
Population: 7,405,375
Location: Africa
Language(s): French, native lan-
   guages

Guinea-Bissau
Capital City: Bissau
Population: 1,178,584
Location: Africa
Language(s): Portuguese, Criolo

Guyana
Capital City: Georgetown
Population: 706,116
Location: South America
Language(s): English, Amerindian
   dialects

Haiti
Capital City: Port-au-Prince
Population: 6,611,407
Location: Central America
Language(s): Creole, French

Honduras
Capital City: Tegucigalpa
Population: 5,751,384
Location: Central America
Language(s): Spanish, English

Hungary
Capital City: Budapest
Population: 9,935,774
Location: Eastern Europe
Language(s): Magyar

Iceland
Capital City: Reykjavik
Population: 272,555
Location: Western Europe
Language(s): Icelandic

India
Capital City: New Delhi
Population: 967,612,804
Location: Asia
Language(s): Hindi, English

Indonesia
Capital City: Jakarta
Population: 209,774,138
Location: Asia
Language(s): Bahasa Indonesia,
  Dutch

Iran
Capital City: Teheran
Population: 67,540,002
Location: Middle East
Language(s): Farsi, Azari

Iraq
Capital City: Bagdad
Population: 22,219,289
Location: Middle East
Language(s): Arabic, Kurdish

Ireland
Capital City: Dublin
Population: 3,555,500
Location: Western Europe
Language(s): Irish, English

Israel
Capital City: Jerusalem
Population: 5,534,672
Location: Middle East
Language(s): Hebrew, Arabic

Italy
Capital City: Rome
Population: 57,534,088
Location: Western Europe
Language(s): Italian

Jamaica
Capital City: Kingston
Population: 2,615,582
Location: Central America
Language(s): English, Jamaican
  Creole

Japan
Capital City: Tokyo
Population: 125,716,637
Location: Asia
Language(s): Japanese

Jordan
Capital City: Amman
Population: 4,324,638
Location: Middle East
Language(s): Arabic, English

Kazakhstan
Capital City: Almaty
Population: 16,898,572
Location: Asia
Language(s): Kazakh

Kenya
Capital City: Nairobi
Population: 28,803,085
Location: Africa
Language(s): English, Swahili

Kiribati
Capital City: Tarawa
Population: 82,449
Location: Pacific Ocean
Language(s): English

Korea, North
Capital City: Pyongyang
Population: 24,317,004
Location: Asia
Language(s): Korean

Korea, South
Capital City: Seoul
Population: 45,948,811
Location: Asia
Language(s): Korean

Kuwait
Capital City: Kuwait
Population: 2,076,805
Location: Middle East
Language(s): Arabic, English

Kyrgyzstan
Capital City: Bishkek
Population: 4,540,185
Location: Asia
Language(s): Kyrgyz

Laos
Capital City: Vientiane
Population: 5,116,959
Location: Asia
Language(s): Lao, French

Latvia
Capital City: Riga
Population: 2,437,649
Location: Eastern Europe
Language(s): Latvian

Lebanon
Capital City: Beirut
Population: 3,858,736
Location: Middle East
Language(s): Arabic, French

Lesotho
Capital City: Maseru
Population: 2,007,814
Location: Africa
Language(s): English, Sesotho

Liberia
Capital City: Monrovia
Population: 2,602,068
Location: Africa
Language(s): English, native dialects

Libya
Capital City: Tripoli
Population: 5,648,359
Location: Africa
Language(s): Arabic, Italian

Liechtenstein
Capital City: Vaduz
Population: 31,461
Location: Western Europe
Language(s): German

Lithuania
Capital City: Vilnius
Population: 3,635,932
Location: Eastern Europe
Language(s): Lithuanian

Luxembourg
Capital City: Luxembourg
Population: 422,474
Location: Western Europe
Language(s): Luxembourgish,
  French

Macedonia
Capital City: Skopje
Population: 2,113,866
Location: Eastern Europe
Language(s): Macedonian,
  Albanian

Madagascar
Capital City: Antananarivo
Population: 14,061,627
Location: Africa
Language(s): Malagasy, French

Malawi
Capital City: Lilongwe
Population: 9,609,081

Location: Africa
Language(s): English, Chichewa

Malaysia
Capital City: Kuala Lumpur
Population: 20,376,235
Location: Asia
Language(s): Malay, Chinese

Maldives
Capital City: Malé
Population: 280,391
Location: Asia
Language(s): Dhivehi

Mali
Capital City: Bamako
Population: 9,945,883
Location: Africa
Language(s): French, African
  languages

Malta
Capital City: Valletta
Population: 379,365
Location: Western Europe
Language(s): Maltese, English

Marshall Islands
Capital City: Majuro
Population: 60,652
Location: Pacific Ocean
Language(s): Marshallese, English

Mauritania
Capital City: Nouakchott
Population: 2,411,317
Location: Africa
Language(s): Arabic, French

Mauritius
Capital City: Port Luis
Population: 1,154,272
Location: Africa
Language(s): English, French

Mexico
Capital City: Mexico City
Population: 97,563,374
Location: North America
Language(s): Spanish, Indian
  languages

Micronesia
Capital City: Palikir
Population: 106,000
Location: Pacific Ocean
Language(s): English, native
  languages

Moldova
Capital City: Chisinau
Population: 4,475,232
Location: Eastern Europe
Language(s): Romanian

Monaco
Capital City: Monaco
Population: 31,892
Location: Western Europe
Language(s): French, Monégasque

Mongolia
Capital City: Ulan Bator
Population: 2,538,211
Location: Asia
Language(s): Mongolian, Turkic

Morocco
Capital City: Rabat
Population: 30,391,423
Location: Africa
Language(s): Arabic, French

Mozambique
Capital City: Maputo
Population: 18,165,476
Location: Africa
Language(s): Portuguese, Bantu

Namibia
Capital City: Windhoek
Population: 1,727,183

Location: Africa
Language(s): Afrikaans, German

Nauru
Capital City: Yaren
Population: 10,390
Location: Pacific Ocean
Language(s): Nauruan, English

Nepal
Capital City: Kathmandu
Population: 22,641,061
Location: Asia
Language(s): Nepali, Newari

The Netherlands
Capital City: Amsterdam
Population: 15,653,091
Location: Western Europe
Language(s): Dutch

New Zealand
Capital City: Wellington
Population: 3,587,275
Location: Pacific Ocean
Language(s): English, Maori

Nicaragua
Capital City: Managua
Population: 4,386,399
Location: Central America
Language(s): Spanish

Niger
Capital City: Niamey
Population: 9,388,859
Location: Africa
Language(s): French, Hausa

Nigeria
Capital City: Abuja
Population: 107,129,469
Location: Africa
Language(s): English, Hausa

Norway
Capital City: Oslo
Population: 4,404,456

Location: Western Europe
Language(s): Norwegian

Oman
Capital City: Muscat
Population: 2,264,590
Location: Middle East
Language(s): Arabic, English

Pakistan
Capital City: Islamabad
Population: 134,185,299
Location: Middle East
Language(s): Urdu, English

Palau
Capital City: Koror
Population: 17,240
Location: Pacific Ocean
Language(s): Palauan, English

Panama
Capital City: Panama City
Population: 2,693,417
Location: Central America
Language(s): Spanish, English

Papua New Guinea
Capital City: Port Moresby
Population: 4,496,221
Location: Pacific Ocean
Language(s): English, Melanesian

Paraguay
Capital City: Asunción
Population: 5,651,634
Location: South America
Language(s): Spanish, Guarani

Peru
Capital City: Lima
Population: 24,949,512
Location: South America
Language(s): Spanish, Quéchua

The Philippines
Capital City: Manilla
Population: 76,103,564

Location: Asia
Language(s): Filipino, English

Poland
Capital City: Warsaw
Population: 38,700,291
Location: Eastern Europe
Language(s): Polish

Portugal
Capital City: Lisbon
Population: 9,867,654
Location: Western Europe
Language(s): Portuguese

Qatar
Capital City: Doha
Population: 665,485
Location: Middle East
Language(s): Arabic, English

Romania
Capital City: Bucharest
Population: 21,399,114
Location: Eastern Europe
Language(s): Romanian

Russia
Capital City: Moscow
Population: 147,987,101
Location: Eastern Europe
Language(s): Russian

Rwanda
Capital City: Kigali
Population: 7,737,537
Location: Africa
Language(s): Kinyarwanda, French

St. Kitts and Nevis
Capital City: Basseterre
Population: 41,803
Location: Central America
Language(s): English

St. Lucia
Capital City: Casteries
Population: 159,639

Location: Central America
Language(s): English

St. Vincent and the Grenadines
Capital City: Kingstown
Population: 119,092
Location: Central America
Language(s): English

Samoa
Capital City: Apia
Population: 219,509
Location: Pacific Ocean
Language(s): Samoan, English

San Marino
Capital City: San Marino
Population: 24,714
Location: Western Europe
Language(s): Italian

São Tomé and Príncipe
Capital City: São Tomé
Population: 147,865
Location: Africa
Language(s): Portuguese

Saudi Arabia
Capital City: Riyadh
Population: 20,087,965
Location: Middle East
Language(s): Arabic, English

Senegal
Capital City: Dakar
Population: 9,403,546
Location: Africa
Language(s): French, Wolof

Seychelles
Capital City: Victoria
Population: 78,142
Location: Africa
Language(s): English, French

Sierra Leone
Capital City: Freetown
Population: 4,891,546

Location: Africa
Language(s): English, Mende

Singapore
Capital City: Singapore
Population: 3,461,929
Location: Asia
Language(s): Malay, Chinese

Slovakia
Capital City: Bratislava
Population: 5,393,016
Location: Eastern Europe
Language(s): Slovak, Hungarian

Slovenia
Capital City: Ljubljana
Population: 1,945,998
Location: Eastern Europe
Language(s): Slovenian, Serbo-
  Croatian

Solomon Islands
Capital City: Honiara
Population: 426,855
Location: Pacific Ocean
Language(s): English, Solomon Pijin

Somalia
Capital City: Mogadishu
Population: 9,940,232
Location: Africa
Language(s): Somali, Arabic

South Africa
Capital City: Pretoria, Cape Town
Population: 42,327,458
Location: Africa
Language(s): English, Afrikaans

Spain
Capital City: Madrid
Population: 39,244,195
Location: Western Europe
Language(s): Spanish, Basque

Sri Lanka
Capital City: Sri Jayewardenepura
  Kotte

Population: 18,762,075
Location: Asia
Language(s): Sinhala, Tamil

Sudan
Capital City: Khartoum
Population: 32,594,128
Location: Africa
Language(s): Arabic, English

Suriname
Capital City: Paramaribo
Population: 443,446
Location: South America
Language(s): Dutch, Surinamese

Swaziland
Capital City: Mbabane
Population: 1,031,600
Location: Africa
Language(s): English, Swazi

Sweden
Capital City: Stockholm
Population: 8,946,193
Location: Western Europe
Language(s): Swedish

Switzerland
Capital City: Bern
Population: 7,248,984
Location: Western Europe
Language(s): German, French,
  Italian, Romansch

Syria
Capital City: Damascus
Population: 16,137,899
Location: Middle East
Language(s): Arabic, French

Taiwan
Capital City: Taipei
Population: 21,655,515
Location: Asia
Language(s): Chinese (Mandarin)

Tajikistan
Capital City: Dushanbe
Population: 6,013,855
Location: Asia
Language(s): Tajik

Tanzania
Capital City: Dar es Salaam
Population: 29,460,753
Location: Africa
Language(s): Swahili, English

Thailand
Capital City: Bangkok
Population: 59,450,818
Location: Asia
Language(s): Thai, Chinese

Togo
Capital City: Lomé
Population: 4,735,610
Location: Africa
Language(s): Ewé, Mina

Tonga
Capital City: Nukualofa
Population: 107,335
Location: Pacific Ocean
Language(s): Tongan, English

Trinidad and Tobago
Capital City: Port-of-Spain
Population: 1,273,141
Location: Central America
Language(s): English, Hindi

Tunisia
Capital City: Tunis
Population: 9,183,097
Location: Africa
Language(s): Arabic, French

Turkey
Capital City: Ankara
Population: 63,528,225
Location: Middle East
Language(s): Turkish

Turkmenistan
Capital City: Ashgabat
Population: 4,225,351
Location: Middle East
Language(s): Turkmen, Russian

Tuvalu
Capital City: Funafuti
Population: 10,297
Location: Pacific Ocean
Language(s): Tuvaluan, English

Uganda
Capital City: Kampala
Population: 20,604,874
Location: Africa
Language(s): English, Swahili

Ukraine
Capital City: Kiev
Population: 50,684,635
Location: Eastern Europe
Language(s): Ukrainian

United Arab Emirates
Capital City: Abu Dhabi
Population: 2,262,309
Location: Middle East
Language(s): Arabic, English

United Kingdom
Capital City: London
Population: 58,610,182
Location: Western Europe
Language(s): English, Welsh

United States
Capital City: Washington, DC
Population: 268,103,439
Location: North America
Language(s): English

Uruguay
Capital City: Montevideo
Population: 3,261,707
Location: South America
Language(s): Spanish

Uzbekistan
Capital City: Tashkent
Population: 23,860,452
Location: Asia
Language(s): Uzbek, Russian

Vanuatu
Capital City: Port Vila
Population: 181,358
Location: Pacific Ocean
Language(s): English, French

Vatican City
Population: 1,000
Location: Western Europe
Language(s): Latin, Italian

Venezuela
Capital City: Caracas
Population: 22,396,407
Location: South America
Language(s): Spanish, Indian
   languages

Vietnam
Capital City: Hanoi
Population: 75,123,880
Location: Asia

Language(s): Vietnamese,
   French

Yemen
Capital City: Sanaá
Population: 13,972,477
Location: Middle East
Language(s): Arabic

Yugoslavia
Capital City: Belgrade
Population: 10,611,558
Location: Eastern Europe
Language(s): Serbo-Croatian

Zambia
Capital City: Lusaka
Population: 9,349,975
Location: Africa
Language(s): English, Native
   languages

Zimbabwe
Capital City: Harare
Population: 11,423,175
Location: Africa
Language(s): English, Ndebele
   Shona

Cities

Largest American Cities (1996)

1.	New York, NY	7,380,906
2.	Los Angeles, CA	3,553,638
3.	Chicago, IL	2,721,547
4.	Houston, TX	1,744,058
5.	Philadelphia, PA	1,478,002
6.	San Diego, CA	1,171,121
7.	Phoenix, AZ	1,159,014
8.	San Antonio, TX	1,067,816
9.	Dallas, TX	1,053,292
10.	Detroit, MI	1,000,272

Largest Cities in the World (Metropolitan Areas, 1995)

1.	Toyko, Japan	26,959,000
2.	Mexico City, Mexico	16,562,000
3.	Sao Paulo, Brazil	16,533,000
4.	New York, US	16,332,000
5.	Mumbai (Bombay), India	15,138,000
6.	Shanghai, China	13,584,000
7.	Los Angeles, US	12,410,000
8.	Calcutta, India	11,932,000
9.	Buenos Aires, Argentina	11,802,000
10.	Seoul, South Korea	11,609,000

Selected Environmental Organizations

American Conservation Association (ACA): est. 1958
Mission: Raise awareness of environmental issues.
Publications: none
Contact: 30 Rockefeller Plaza, Rm 5600, New York, NY 10112

Americans for the Environment (AFE): est. 1982
Mission: Educate citizens and encourage political action.
Publications: *Lobbying Strategies, The Power of the Green Vote*
Contact (e-mail): afedc@igc.apc.org

Center for Environmental Information (CEI): est. 1974
Mission: Disseminate information on environmental issues.
Publications: *CEI Sphere, Global Climate Change Digest*
Contact: <http://www.awa.com/nature/cei>

Center for Environmental Study (CES): est. 1969
Mission: Increase awareness of environmental issues through education.
Publications: *Caring for Planet Earth*
Contact: <http://www.cesmi.org>

Center for International Environmental Law (CIEL): est. 1989
Mission: Strengthen environmental laws and improve public policy.
Publications: none
Contact: <http://www.econet.apc.org/ciel/>

Center for Marine Conservation (CMC): est. 1989
Mission: Protect marine wildlife and habitats.
Publications: *Coastal Connection, Marine Conservation News*
Contact: 7125 DeSales St. NW, Ste. 600, Washington, DC 20036

Citizens for a Better Environment (CBE): est. 1971
Mission: Reduce toxic substances in the air, water, and land.

Publications: *Environmental Review*

Contact: <http://www.cbemn.org>

Conservation International (CI): est. 1987

Mission: Unite corporations and individuals in conservation efforts.

Publications: *Orion National Quarterly*

Contact: 2501 M. St. NW, Ste 200, Washington, DC 20037

Environmental Defense Fund (EDF): est. 1967

Mission: Create innovative, realistic solutions to environmental problems.

Publications: *EDF Newsletter, Recycling World*

Contact: <http://www.edf.org>

Friends of the Earth (FOE): est. 1969

Mission: Protect the planet from environmental damage.

Publications: *Friends of the Earth*

Contact: <htttp://www.foe.org>

Greenpeace: est. 1971

Mission: Use direct action and bearing witness to protect the environment.

Publication: *Greenpeace Magazine*

Contact: <http://www.greenpeaceusa.org>

Institute of Environmental Sciences (IES): est. 1959

Mission: Develop technology and scientific procedures in a safe environment.

Publications: *Journal of the Institute of Environmental Sciences*

Contact: <http://intenvsci.org>

Renew America (RA): est. 1986

Mission: Develop a sustainable, safe environment.

Publication: *Environmental Success Index*

Contact: <http://www.crest.org/renew-america>

Student Conservation Association (SCA): est. 1957

Mission: Develop awareness of environmental issues.

Publications: *Earth Work*

Contact: <http://www.sca-inc.org>

Student Environmental Action Coalition (SEAC): est. 1989

Mission: Empower students as they work to protect the environment.

Publications: *Threshold*

Contact: <http://www.seac.org>

Wildlife Conservation Society (WCS): est. 1895

Mission: Maintain habitats and ecosystems to support wildlife.

Publications: *Wildlife Conservation*

Contact: <http://www.wcs.org>

World Wildlife Federation (WWF): est. 1961

Mission: Protect biological resources.

Publications: *WWF Newsletter*

Contact: <http://wwf.org>

General Reference

Roman Numerals

Roman numerals are formed by adding or subtracting from the "base numbers" *V, X, L, C,* and their variations; numbers that precede one of these numbers are subtracted (IX = [10-1 = 9]), while numbers that follow are added (XII [10+2 = 12]).

Arabic Number	Roman Numeral	Arabic Number	Roman Numeral
1	I	50	L
2	II	60	LX
3	III	70	LXX
4	IV	80	LXXX
5	V	90	XC
6	VI	100	C
7	VII	500	D
8	VIII	1,000	M̲
9	IX	5,000	V̲
10	X	10,000	X̲
20	XX	50,000	L̲
30	XXX	100,000	C̲
40	XL		

Selected Professional Organizations

Art

College Art Association (CAA): est. 1911
Web site: <http://www.collegeart.org>
National Association of Schools of Art and Design (NASAD): est. 1944
Web site: <http://www.arts-accredit.org>

Athletic Training

American College of Sports Medicine (ACSM): est. 1954
Web site: <http://www.acsm.org>

National Athletic Trainers' Association (NATA): est. 1950
Web site: <http://www.nata.org>

Business

American Management Association (AMA): est. 1923
Web site: <http://www.amanet.org>
Association for Business Communication (ABC): est. 1935
Web site: none
Decision Sciences Institute (DSI): est. 1969
Web site: <http://dsi.gsu.edu>

National Business Education Association (NBEA): est. 1892
Web site: <http://www.nbea.org/nbea.html>

Chemistry

American Chemical Society (ACS): est. 1876
Web site: <http://www.acs.org>
American Physical Society (APS): est. 1899
Web site: <http://www.aps.org>

Communication

National Communication Association (NCA): est. 1914
Web site: none
Society for Technical Communication (STC): est. 1953
Web site: <http://www.stc-va.org>

Counseling

American College Counseling Association (ACCA): est. 1991
Web site: <http://www.collegecounseling.org>
American Counseling Association (ACA): est. 1952
Web site: <http://www.counseling.org>

Criminology

Academy of Criminal Justice Sciences (ACJS): est. 1963
Web site: <http://www.nku.edu/~acjs/>
American Society of Criminology (ASC): est. 1941
Web site: <http://www.asc41.com/>

Curriculum and Instruction

Association of Supervision and Curriculum Development (ASCD): est. 1943
Web site: <http://www.ascd.org>
Association of Teacher Educators (ATE): est. 1920
Web site: <http://www.siu.edu/departments/coes/ate/>

Economics

American Economic Association (AEA): est. 1885
Web site: <http://www.vanderbilt.edu/AEA>
National Council on Economic Education (NCEE): est. 1949
Web site: <http://www.nationalcouncil.org>

Educational Administration

American Council on Education (ACE): est. 1918
Web site: <http://www.acenet.edu>
University Continuing Education Association (UCEA): est. 1915
Web site: <http://www.nucea.edu>

Electronics and Computer Technology

American Electronics Association (AEA): est. 1943
Web site: <http://www.aeanet.org>
Computing Technology Industry Association (CTIA): est. 1982
Web site: <http://www.comptia.org>

Engineering

American Association of Engineering Societies (AAES): est. 1979
Web site: <http://www.aaes.org>
Engineering Foundation (EF): est. 1914
Web site: <http://www.enfnd. org>

English

Modern Language Association (MLA): est. 1883
Web site: <http://www.mla.org/>
National Council of Teachers of English (NCTE): est. 1911
Web site: <http://www.ncte.org>

Family and Consumer Sciences

American Association of Family and Consumer Sciences (AAFCS): est. 1909
Web site: <http://www.aafcs.org>
Home Economics Educators Association (HEEA): est. 1927
Web site: none

Foreign Languages and Literatures

American Association for Teachers of Spanish and Portuguese (AATSP): est. 1917
Web site: <http://www.aatsp. org>
NOTE: Similar organizations exist for other languages: AATG, AATF, AATR
Modern Language Association (MLA): est. 1883
Web site: <http://www.mla.org/>

Geography, Geology, and Anthropology

Association of American Geographers (AAG): est. 1904
Web site: <http://www.aag.org>
National Council of Geographic Education (NCGE): est. 1915
Web site: <http://www.ncge. com>

Health and Safety

American Public Health Association (APHA): est. 1872
Web site: <http://www.apha. org>
National Safety Council (NSC): est. 1913
Web site: <http://www.nsc.org>

History

National Council of History Educators (NCHE): est. 1990
Web site: <http://www.history. org/nche>
World History Association (WHA): est. 1982
Web site: <http://www.hartford-hwp.com/wha/>

Industrial and Mechanical Technology

Council on Technology Teacher Education (CTTE): est. 1950
Web site: <http://www.teched.vt. edu/cttel>
National Association of Industrial Technology (NAIT): est. 1967
Web site: <http://www.nait.org>

Life Sciences

American Association for the Advancement of Science (AAAS): est. 1848
Web site: <http://www.aaas.org>
National Wildlife Federation (NWF): est. 1936
Web site: <http://www.nwf.org>

Manufacturing

National Association of Industrial Technology (NAIT): est. 1967
Web site: <http://www.nait.org>
Society of Manufacturing Engineers (SME): est. 1932
Web site: <http://www.sme.org>

Mathematics and Computer Science

Mathematical Association of America (MAA): est. 1915
Web site: <http://www.maa.org>
National Council of Teachers of Mathematics (NCTM): est. 1920
Web site: <http://www.nctm.org>

Medicine

American College of Physicians (ACP): est. 1915
Web site: <http://www.acponline.org>
American Medical Association (AMA): est. 1847
Web site: <http://www.ama-assn.org>
American Nurses Association (ANA): est. 1896
Web site: <http://www.nursingworld.org>

National League of Nursing (NLN): est. 1952
Web site: <http://www.nln.org>

Music

Music Education National Conference (MENC): est. 1923
Web site: <http://www.menc.org>
National Association of Schools of Music (NASM): est. 1924
Web site: <http://www.arts-accredit.org>

Philosophy

American Catholic Philosophy Association (ACPA): est. 1926
Web site: <http://www.cua.edu/www/org/acpa>
American Philosophical Association (APA): est. 1900
Web site: <http://www.udel.edu/apa>

Physical Education

American Alliance for Health, Physical Education, Recreation, and Dance (AAHPERD): est. 1885
Web site: <http://www.aahperd.org>
American College of Sports Medicine (ACSM): est. 1954
Web site: <http://www.acsm.org>

Physics

American Association of Physics Teachers (AAPT): est. 1930
Web site: <http://www.aapt.org>

Institute of Physics (IOP): est. 1914
Web site: <http://www.iop.org>

Political Science

Academy of Political Science (APS): est. 1880
Web site: <http://www.epn.org/psq.html>

American Political Science Association (APSA): est. 1903
Web site: <http://www.apsanet.org>

Psychology

American Psychological Association (APA): est. 1892
Web site: <http://www.apa.org>

Psychological Society (PS): est. 1960
Web site: none

Recreation and Sport Management

North American Society for Sport Management (NASSM): est. 1985

Web site: <http://www.unb.ca/web/sportmanagement/index.html>

Resort and Commercial Recreation Association (RCRA): est. 1981
Web site: none

Social Work

Council of Social Work Education (CSWE): est. 1952
Web site: <http://www.cswe.org>

National Association of Social Workers (NASW): est. 1955
Web site: <http://www.naswdc.org>

Sociology

American Sociological Association (ASA): est. 1905
Web site: none

Society of Applied Sociology (SAS): est. 1984
Web site: <http://www.appliedsoc.org>

Wonders of the World

Seven Wonders of the Ancient World

1. Pyramids of Giza: the three pyramid tombs of the pharaohs
2. Hanging Gardens of Babylon: an extensive series of terraced gardens
3. Statue of Zeus at Olympia: a large statue of the seated god
4. Temple of Artemis: an enormous, highly decorated temple
5. Mausoleum of Halicarnassus: a massive and elaborate tomb
6. Colossus of Rhodes: a large statue built at the harbor of Rhodes
7. Lighthouse at Alexandria: an enormous lighthouse on the Egyptian coast

Seven Wonders of the Natural World

1. Mount Everest (Nepal): the world's tallest mountain
2. Victoria Falls (Zimbabwe): a massive (in both height and width) waterfall
3. Grand Canyon (US): a spectacular network of eroded canyons
4. Great Barrier Reef (Australia): the largest and most varied reef in the world
5. Northern Lights: atmospheric lights above the northern hemisphere
6. Parícutin (Mexico): a powerful, active volcano
7. Harbor of Rio de Janeiro (Brazil): a geologically unique harbor

INDEX

Revision Checklists

Content

❏ Are the title and the introductory strategy interesting, clear, and appropriate in tone?

❏ Does the thesis statement clearly present the topic and your opinion about it?

❏ Do the topics of the paragraphs support the thesis statement? Are they clearly stated?

❏ Are the topics presented in a clear, emphatic order?

❏ Are the paragraphs adequately developed? Is there enough detail? Are there enough examples? Does information in each paragraph relate to the thesis statement?

❏ Are the summary and concluding strategy effective?

Style

❏ Do the lengths and types of sentences vary?

❏ Do sentences clearly and concisely express their meaning?

❏ Are word choices vivid, accurate, and appropriate?

❏ Do most sentences use the active voice?

❏ Do transitions adequately relate ideas?

Technical Errors and Inconsistencies

❏ Are all words correctly spelled? (When in doubt, always look up the correct spelling in your dictionary or use a spell checker.)

❏ Are any necessary words omitted? Are any words unnecessarily repeated?

❏ Is punctuation accurate? (See "Punctuation," starting on page 265.)

❏ Are elements of mechanics properly used? (See "Mechanics," starting on page 313.)

❏ Are all sentences complete?

❏ Do nouns and pronouns and subjects and verbs agree in number and gender as appropriate?

❏ Are all pronoun antecedents clear?

❏ Are all modifiers logically positioned?